An Introduction to
EU COMPETITION LAW

Succinct and concise, this textbook covers all the procedural and substantive aspects of EU competition law. It explores primary and secondary law through the prism of ECJ case law. Abuse of a dominant position and merger control are discussed and a separate chapter on cartels ensures the student receives the broadest possible perspective on the subject. In addition, the book's consistent structure aids understanding: section summaries underline key principles, questions reinforce learning and essay discussion topics encourage further exploration. By setting out the economic principles which underpin the subject, the author allows the student to engage with the complexity of competition law with confidence. Integrated examples and an uncluttered writing style make this required reading for all students of the subject.

Moritz Lorenz is a practitioner at Freshfields Bruckhaus Deringer. Specialising in EU competition law, he advises on all major areas including cartels, merger control, dominance, supply agreements, licences and cooperation agreements. He also teaches competition law at Halle University.

An Introduction to
EU COMPETITION
LAW

Moritz Lorenz

Section on the Economic Foundations of EU
Competition Law contributed by

Julia Dietrich

CAMBRIDGE
UNIVERSITY PRESS

CAMBRIDGE UNIVERSITY PRESS
Cambridge, New York, Melbourne, Madrid, Cape Town,
Singapore, São Paulo, Delhi, Mexico City

Cambridge University Press
The Edinburgh Building, Cambridge CB2 8RU, UK

Published in the United States of America by Cambridge University Press, New York

www.cambridge.org
Information on this title: www.cambridge.org/9781107018174

First published 2013

Printed and bound by CPI Group (UK) Ltd, Croydon CR0 4YY

A catalogue record for this publication is available from the British Library

Library of Congress Cataloguing in Publication Data
Lorenz, Moritz, 1974–
An introduction to EU competition law / Moritz Lorenz.
    p.   cm.
"Section on the Economic Foundations of EU competition law contributed by Julia Dietrich."
ISBN 978-1-107-01817-4
1. Antitrust law – European Union countries.   2. Restraint of trade – European Union countries.   I. Title.   II. Title:
Introduction to European Union competition law.
KJE6456.L67   2013
343.2407′21–dc23   2012039598

ISBN 978-1-107-01817-4 Hardback
ISBN 978-1-107-67261-1 Paperback

CONTENTS

TABLE OF CASES

TABLE OF STATUTES

PREFACE

This short textbook on EU competition law reflects my teaching experiences as a guest lecturer at Martin Luther University Halle-Wittenberg. The author is most grateful to Professor Christian Tietje for giving him the opportunity to teach competition law in one of the master programmes of the university without which this book would not have been written.

Huge thanks also have to be extended to Professor Thomas Lübbig of Freshfields Bruckhaus Deringer who allowed me to gather the practical experience with EU competition law that is also incorporated in this book.

The author is indebted to Julia Dietrich of Frontier Economics for kindly agreeing to write the section on the economic foundations of EU competition law for this book. Valuable contributions have also been made by Mariusz Motyka-Mojkowski, Uwe Salaschek and Sebastian Zachow.

The views and errors expressed in this book are entirely my own.

1 Economic and legal foundations of EU competition law

A. The idea of competition

1. THE BENEFITS OF COMPETITION

There is a general belief among societies that have adopted the market economy as their economic model that competition brings various benefits. Competition is believed to ensure low prices and a broad range of choices for consumers as well as overall efficiency and innovation. This is also reflected in statements of the Directorate General for Competition (DG COMP) of the European Commission (hereinafter: the Commission):

Competition is a basic mechanism of the market economy which encourages companies to offer consumers goods and services at the most favourable terms. It encourages efficiency and innovation and reduces prices. In order to be effective, competition requires companies to act independently of each other, but subject to the competitive pressure exerted by the others.[1]

The last sentence of the above statement indicates what lies at the core of the concept of competition: the view that consumers and suppliers should interact freely and according to their own incentives, without any coordination between market players. In such a setting, competition will act as a self-regulating mechanism, an 'invisible hand', that drives prices down to their socially optimal level and ensures maximum welfare for society as a whole.

The term 'invisible hand' was phrased by Adam Smith in his book *The Wealth of Nations* in the eighteenth century.[2] Smith used the term 'invisible hand' in a specific context, namely a discussion of domestic versus foreign trade. However, the concept has since been generalised to the functioning of the market in general. Indeed, Smith stated that the invisible hand worked in the case of domestic versus foreign trade

---

Section A has been contributed by Julia Dietrich.

[1] DG COMP website at http://ec.europa.eu/competition/antitrust/overview_en.html.

[2] Smith, *The Wealth of Nations* (1776), Book 4, Chapter 2: Of restraints upon importation from foreign countries of such goods as can be produced at home.

'as in many other cases', already indicating the potential wider application of the concept himself. Smith also clearly recognised that the invisible hand would be steered by each market player striving for its own goals: 'It is not from the benevolence of the butcher, the brewer, or the baker that we expect our dinner, but from their regard to their own interest.'[3]

Although Smith believed in the self-regulating forces of the market, he also realised that, if completely left on their own, suppliers would have an incentive to reduce the competitive pressures exerted upon them by other market players:

People of the same trade seldom meet together, even for merriment and diversion, but the conversation ends in a conspiracy against the public or in some contrivance to raise prices. It is impossible indeed to prevent such meetings, by any law which could be executed, or would be consistent with liberty and justice. But though the law cannot hinder people of the same trade from sometimes assembling together, it ought to do nothing to facilitate such assemblies, much less to render them necessary.[4]

Smith had a rather negative view of the ability of government to prevent meetings between suppliers that would restrict competition. He merely requested that government should not do anything to promote such developments. In contrast to this, current competition law takes a much more positive view. In fact, EU competition law does not only prohibit agreements between undertakings that could reduce competition, but also seeks to prevent other forms of potential distortion of competition, such as a dominant firm abusing its market power (for example by employing pricing strategies that aim at excluding competitors from the market), a merger leading to a change in market structure that would result in a significant impediment of competition or State aid granted by governments that would create distortions in the market.[5]

Competition law seeks to protect competition for the benefit of society as a whole, but this does not necessarily mean protecting individual competitors. This view is clearly mirrored in statements of the Commission:

The emphasis of the Commission's enforcement activity in relation to [the prevention of] exclusionary conduct is on safeguarding the competitive process in the internal market and ensuring that undertakings which hold a dominant position do not exclude their competitors by other means than competing on the merits of the products or services they provide. In doing so the Commission is mindful that what really matters is protecting an effective competitive process and not simply protecting competitors. This may well mean that competitors

---

[3] Ibid., Book 1, Chapter 2: Of the principle which gives occasion to the division of labour.

[4] Ibid., Book 1, Chapter 10: Of wages and profit in the different employments of labour and stock, part II.

[5] The relevant legal provisions are set out in Articles 101 (anticompetitive agreements), 102 (abuse of dominance) and 107–109 (State aid) of the Treaty on the Functioning of the European Union (hereinafter: TFEU) and in the EU Merger Regulation.

who deliver less to consumers in terms of price, choice, quality and innovation will leave the market.[6]

By forcing firms to compete with each other, the market mechanism will inevitably lead to winners and losers. Some firms might see a fall in profits or might even be driven out of the market completely if other firms are more successful at providing consumers with what they want or doing so at lower cost. However, this is exactly why competition is considered beneficial: by constantly forcing firms to improve what they offer through lower prices, lower costs, innovative product features or additional services, competition keeps firms 'on their toes', which will benefit consumers and society as a whole.

Summary of Section 1

Competition is believed to lead to lower prices, cost efficiency, more choice for consumers and innovation.

EU competition law aims at ensuring that these benefits will be achieved by (i) prohibiting agreements between firms that restrict competition, (ii) prohibiting the abuse of a dominant position by an undertaking, e.g. by employing pricing strategies that aim at excluding competitors, (iii) preventing mergers that would lead to a significant impediment of effective competition and (iv) prohibiting State subsidies that would lead to distortions in the market.

In doing so, the focus of EU competition policy is the protection of the competitive process, not necessarily of individual competitors.

2. THE ECONOMIC PRINCIPLES OF COMPETITION

Central to the idea of competition is the idea of a market place where sellers and buyers meet.

- Sellers would like the price to be as high as possible to maximise profits. The higher the price, the higher the quantity that sellers wish to sell. As a result, the supply curve in a given market is usually upward sloping, as shown in Figure 1.
- Buyers, on the other hand, usually prefer to buy products at as low a price as possible. The lower the price, the higher the quantity that buyers wish to purchase. This is reflected in a downward sloping demand curve as shown in Figure 1.

The interaction of supply and demand will determine the equilibrium price in a market. At the equilibrium price, which is given by the intersection of the supply

---

[6] Commission, Guidance on the Commission's enforcement priorities in applying Article 82 of the EC Treaty to abusive exclusionary conduct by dominant undertakings, OJ No. C 45 of 24 February 2009, p. 7, para. 6.

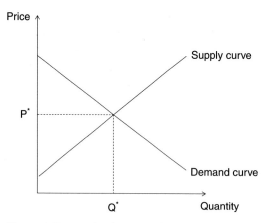

Figure 1 Interaction between demand and supply determines the market-clearing price

and demand curves, sellers will receive the price they want to receive for the quantity they wish to sell and buyers will pay the price they are willing to pay for the given quantity.

In principle, the objectives of sellers and buyers act antagonistically to each other, with sellers preferring prices to be as high as possible and buyers preferring prices to be as low as possible. In such a setting, competition between sellers will lead to additional factors that influence what is produced at what cost and how much buyers have to pay.

- If one seller offers the same product for less than the other sellers, buyers will naturally want to buy the product from him. Where there is competition between sellers, therefore, there is pressure on sellers to lower prices.
- An alternative way for a seller to maximise profits without increasing prices is to reduce the cost of supply. Competition between sellers, therefore, encourages them to constantly review their own business processes and to seek to operate with greater efficiency.
- Finally, sellers can also attract more custom by improving or differentiating their product. Competition between sellers, therefore, encourages producers constantly to review the quality of their products and to seek to improve what they offer through innovation. At the same time, competition ensures that buyers will have a broad range of products to choose from.
  - If a seller offers a product that is generally better than other products but offered at the same price, buyers will seek to purchase the better product.
  - If one seller offers a product that is slightly different from other products and therefore more appealing to a certain buyer group, this will increase custom from this buyer group.

The discussion above illustrates the general mechanism of how competition can lead to lower prices, efficiency, increased choice and innovation. Over the centuries, economists have developed various models that seek to put the principle of competition, or lack thereof, into more technical terms. In the following sections, three different types of model will be discussed. They include the two most extreme forms of market structure, perfect competition and monopoly. The third group describes situations that lie between these two extremes: cases where firms face a limited number of competitors and realise their mutual interdependence. Reflecting the differences in market structure and competitive conditions, each of the different models leads to different conclusions regarding social welfare.

Summary of Section 2

The idea of a market place where buyers and sellers meet is central to the idea of competition.

The objectives of sellers and buyers act antagonistically to each other, with sellers preferring prices to be as high as possible and buyers preferring prices to be as low as possible.

In such a setting, competition between sellers will lead to lower prices, efficiency, increased choice and innovation.

3. THE BENCHMARK OF PERFECT COMPETITION

The economic model of perfect competition illustrates a world in which the benefits from competition are fully maximised. It should be noted upfront that the model assumes a highly idealised situation that is rarely seen in practice. Nevertheless, it provides a useful benchmark against which other, potentially more realistic, models of competition can be compared.

The model of perfect competition is based on several important assumptions regarding the features of the market:[7]

- Products are assumed to be homogeneous, i.e. all producers offer exactly the same product.
- There are a large number of firms supplying the product, which implies that the behaviour of each individual firm does not have any influence on the market price – firms are assumed to be price takers.

[7] For an introductory discussion of the model of perfect competition, see for example Frank, *Microeconomics and Behaviour*, International Edition, 8th edn (McGraw-Hill, 2010), chapter 11. A more technical discussion is provided in Martin, *Industrial Economics: Economic Analysis and Public Policy*, 2nd edn (Prentice-Hall, 1994), pp. 14–22.

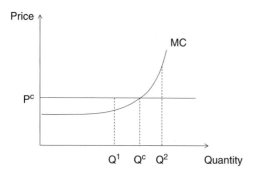

Figure 2 Output decision of a firm under perfect competition

- There are no barriers to entry and exit, i.e. firms can easily enter into and exit from the market without incurring any costs.
- There is perfect information for all firms and all buyers in the market.

In the setting described above, each firm will realise that its own output decision will not affect the market price. Instead, each firm will take the market price as given and adjust its own output so as to maximise profits. In equilibrium, each firm will set its own output so that its marginal cost of production, which reflects the cost of supplying one additional unit of output, equals the market price.

The rationale behind this output-setting decision is illustrated in Figure 2, which shows the marginal cost curve (MC) of an individual firm.[8] The horizontal line reflects the demand curve faced by the individual firm: since the firm is a price taker, it will not be able to sell anything at a price other than P^c. However, at P^c, the firm will be able to sell as much output as it wishes.

To see why setting output so that marginal cost equals the market price is profit-maximising for the firm, let us assume that the firm initially decided to set output at level Q^1, which is below the profit-maximising output level Q^c. At this point, the marginal cost of increasing output by one unit would be lower than the gain from doing so, as reflected by the market price. The firm could increase profits by supplying one more unit of output; it would consequently have an incentive to *increase* output.

Contrary, at output level Q^2, which lies above the optimal output level, the marginal cost of production would be higher than the market price. At this point, the firm would actually gain from reducing output: for each unit it supplied less, it would lose the market price, but it would also save the respective marginal cost, which is higher than the market price. As a consequence, at Q^2 the firm would have an incentive to *reduce* output.

[8] In this example, marginal costs are upward sloping, i.e. the additional cost of supplying one more unit of output increases the higher the existing output. This reflects what economists call 'diminishing marginal productivity': the more output a firm already produces with a given stock of fixed capital, the more costly it will be to produce an additional unit of output. See e.g. Martin, *Industrial Economics*, pp. 18–19.

It is only at output level Q^c, where the market price equals the firm's marginal cost, that the firm would neither have an incentive to increase nor to decrease output. This point therefore reflects the profit-maximising output decision for this firm. All other firms will face the same output decision-making process and will also set their output so that their marginal cost is equal to the market price. In equilibrium, all firms will therefore supply at the same marginal cost, which will be the same as the market price.

Another implication of perfect competition is that firms will not earn any positive profits in the long run. To see this, recall that perfect competition assumes that free entry into and exit from the market is possible.

- As a consequence, if firms were earning positive profits in the short run, this would induce entry of new firms into the market. Additional firms entering the market would lead to an increase in overall supply, an erosion of the market price and hence a reduction in profits that were previously available. Entry would persist until the market price had fallen down to the average cost of production. At this point, all firms would earn zero economic profit and there would be no incentive for further entry.[9]
- Analogous to the process of entry eroding positive profits, firms would have an incentive to exit the market if the short-run equilibrium was such that firms would make a loss, i.e. if the market price was below average cost. In this case, market exit would cause total market supply to fall and hence the market price to rise. Firms would leave the market until the market price was high enough to equal the average cost of production. Again, firms would earn zero economic profits in equilibrium.

In the long run, the condition that all firms will set output so that the market price equals their marginal cost of production will still hold. Each individual firm will continue to set its own output so that this condition is satisfied. Combined with the condition that firms will not be able to earn any profits, this implies that under perfect competition in the long run marginal cost will equal average cost, which will both equal the market price.

As mentioned at the beginning of this section, perfect competition is the economic model in which the benefits from competition are highest and social welfare is

---

[9] Economic profit is different from accounting profit, which is usually defined as the difference between total revenues and all explicit costs associated with generating a certain output. In contrast, economic profit also reflects implicit costs such as the opportunity cost of land, capital and other production factors. Opportunity cost is the value a producer would receive for his assets if they were put to an alternative use. For example, let us assume that a firm owns a machine that it uses to produce a certain good and that instead of using the machine itself, the firm could rent it out to another firm for 100 euros. In this case, the opportunity cost of using the machine for the production of the good is 100 euros. Economic profit takes such implicit costs into account. The opportunity costs of the entrepreneur are also referred to as *normal* profit, i.e. the profit required to make the entrepreneur indifferent between being in the market or not. Accounting profit usually consists of normal profit and potential super-normal or economic profits. Under perfect competition, economic profit will be zero in the long run, i.e. firms will only earn the normal profit required to cover their opportunity cost. However, firms' accounting profits may still be above zero.

maximised. In particular, perfect competition leads to what economists refer to as 'allocative efficiency' and 'productive efficiency'.[10]

- Allocative efficiency refers to a situation where resources are allocated to the production of goods and services that society values most. In such a scenario, all possible gains from an exchange are realised. This is the case under perfect competition: producers supply the good at the profit-maximising level so that the market price, which reflects the value consumers attach to the good in question, equals the marginal and average cost of production. In the perfectly competitive equilibrium, neither producers nor consumers could be made better off by increasing or decreasing production.
- Productive efficiency refers to a situation where goods are produced at the lowest possible cost. As described above, under perfect competition firms will in equilibrium not earn any economic profits. This implies that the respective goods will be produced at the lowest possible cost: if a firm had higher costs than its competitors, it would actually make a loss and need to leave the market. The desire to maximise profits will provide an incentive for all firms to operate as efficiently as possible.[11]

The welfare implications of perfect competition can also be illustrated graphically. Figure 3 shows the long-run market outcome under perfect competition. Suppliers provide a total quantity of Q^c at the market price P^c, which is equal to marginal cost (MC) and average cost (AC) of production.

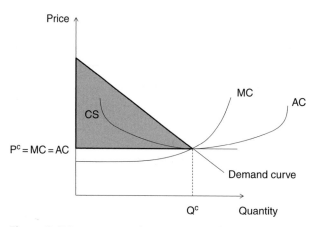

Figure 3 Price, output and consumer surplus under perfect competition

---

[10] See, for example, Bishop and Walker, *The Economics of EC Competition Law: Concepts, Application and Measurement*, 3rd edn (Sweet & Maxwell, 2010), p. 25.
[11] In fact, what will ensure productive efficiency under perfect competition in the long run is the requirement that the market price will be equal to marginal and average cost of production at the same time. According to economic theory, unless marginal costs are constant, the marginal and average cost curves will intersect, i.e. be identical, at the minimum point of the average cost curve.

- In equilibrium, output is maximised at Q^c, given the cost of supply. This reflects allocative efficiency.
- At the same time, the market price is equal to the lowest point on the average cost curve, which reflects productive efficiency. Producers do not make any economic profits.
- Consumers are able to purchase the good at the competitive price P^c. The triangle between the cost of supply and the demand curve is what economists refer to as 'consumer surplus' (CS). It reflects the difference between the value that consumers place on the good in question and the price they have to pay for it. Under perfect competition, consumers purchase Q^c at price P^c. However, for a volume smaller than Q^c, consumers would have been willing to pay a price above P^c. The difference between the willingness to pay (reflected by the demand curve) and the market price is welfare accruing to consumers. Under perfect competition, consumer surplus is maximised.

As mentioned at the beginning of this section, in real life only very few, if any, industries are characterised by the features underlying the model of perfect competition. For example, there are often only a limited number of suppliers active in a market and products tend to be differentiated to some extent in the real world. In addition, entry to and exit from a market is often not costless, but requires some investment. As such, perfect competition remains an idealistic benchmark for the level of efficiency that could be obtained from competition in theory.

Summary of Section 3

The model of perfect competition assumes that products are homogeneous, there are a large number of firms in the market that all act as price takers, there are no barriers to entry and exit and all sellers and buyers in the market have perfect information.

Under perfect competition, prices will be as low as possible given the cost structure of suppliers and output will be maximised. As a consequence, social welfare will be maximised and both allocative and productive efficiency will be achieved.

While the assumptions underlying perfect competition are rarely fulfilled in practice, the model still provides a useful benchmark of the potential benefits resulting from competition.

4. MONOPOLY – THE OTHER EXTREME

Perfect competition assumes a large number of producers that all act as price takers. At the other end of the spectrum lies the economic model of monopoly.[12] In complete

[12] For an introductory and a more technical discussion of monopoly see Frank, *Microeconomics and Behaviour*, chapter 12, and Martin, *Industrial Economics*, pp. 23–31 respectively.

contrast to perfect competition, under monopoly there is only one producer offering the good in question. This producer does not face any competition, neither actual nor potential. Entry into the market is assumed to be blocked (or the costs of market entry are assumed to be prohibitively high).

Economists usually consider four potential sources of monopoly:

(i)   exclusive control over important inputs,
(ii) patents,
(iii) government licences or franchises, and
(iv) economies of scale.[13]

Contrary to suppliers under perfect competition, the monopolist's output decision will directly affect the market price, since it is the only seller of the good. As such, the monopolist is a price setter instead of a price taker. The only restriction it faces in its price-setting is the reaction of consumer demand. To see this, recall that demand for a product is usually lower the higher the price. The higher the price the monopolist sets, the lower the quantity consumers will be willing to purchase. The monopolist therefore faces a trade-off between higher prices and lower volumes being sold. Contrary to the situation of a firm under perfect competition, whose individual demand curve will be horizontal, the monopolist faces a downward sloping demand curve.

For the monopolist, the relevant price variable to consider when setting its output is marginal revenue, the change in revenue the monopolist would gain from a change in output. Marginal revenue will always be lower than the market price because, in order to induce consumers to buy more (i.e. to 'force' consumers to move down the demand curve), the monopolist will need to reduce the price for all units of output.

In equilibrium, the monopolist will set its output so that its marginal cost of supply will equal marginal revenue. At this point, the monopolist will maximise its profit. If marginal revenue was higher than marginal cost, the monopolist could increase its profits by expanding output further. If marginal revenue was lower than marginal cost, the monopolist would be better off reducing output again, saving on marginal costs and reaching a higher market-clearing price.[14]

The market outcome is shown graphically in Figure 4. The monopolist sets output at Q^m, where marginal cost (MC) and marginal revenue (MR) intersect. Consumers are willing to pay P^m for this level of output, i.e. P^m becomes the market price. Since P^m is

---

[13] Frank, *Microeconomics and Behaviour*, pp. 373–7. Economies of scale mean that the cost of production is lower the more is produced, i.e. that the average cost curve is downward sloping. In such a case, which is also referred to as a natural monopoly, a monopolist will be the least costly way of serving the market (see Bannock and Baxter, *The Penguin Dictionary of Economics*, 8th edn (Penguin, 2011), p. 263).

[14] Although they might appear different, the output decision of a monopolist follows in fact the same logic as the output decision of a firm under perfect competition: setting output so that the change in revenue is equal to margin cost. The difference is that for firms under perfect competition the market price is equal to marginal revenue because the firm's own output decision does not affect the market price. Under monopoly, the output decision of the firm affects the market price and, as a result, marginal revenue is lower than the market price.

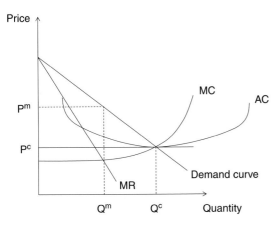

Figure 4 Output decision of a monopolist

higher than the cost of supplying output at Q^m, the monopolist will earn a profit on each unit. Compared to the equilibrium under perfect competition (shown as P^c and Q^c in the chart), prices under monopoly will be higher and overall output lower.

Overall, the monopoly outcome shown in Figure 4 leads to lower efficiency than the outcome under perfect competition:

- Allocative efficiency is no longer ensured – the reduction in output compared to the perfectly competitive equilibrium leads to an inefficient reallocation of resources to other markets. In addition, consumers must pay a price that exceeds the cost of production.
- Productive efficiency is also no longer guaranteed. The monopolist will earn a positive economic profit on each unit sold. Since market entry is not possible, this profit will not be eroded and, as a consequence, the monopolist will not be forced to adjust output so that the market price equals the lowest average cost of production. As shown in Figure 4, for the monopolistic level of output, average cost will in most cases be higher than at its lowest level.[15]

The welfare implications of a monopoly are shown graphically in Figure 5 (for simplicity marginal costs are assumed to be constant in the chart).

- Compared to the market outcome under perfect competition, consumer surplus (CS) is significantly lower, given the lower output and higher prices.
- Some of the consumer surplus that would be realised under perfect competition is transferred from consumers to the monopolist as profits. Whether or not this reallocation is perceived as problematic will depend on the welfare standard applied

---

[15] The loss of productive efficiency will not be an issue in case of a natural monopoly, i.e. a scenario where economies of scale are the source of monopoly and the average cost curve is downward sloping. In such a scenario, concentrating all supplies in the hand of one producer will ensure that production occurs at the lowest possible cost that can be achieved given total demand for the product in question.

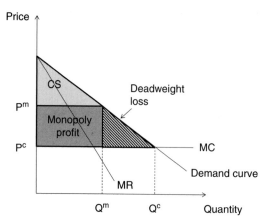

Figure 5 Welfare implications of a monopoly

in a society: if maximisation of consumer welfare is seen as the relevant standard, the transfer from consumers to the producer should be considered as a welfare loss. If maximisation of total welfare, i.e. consumer surplus plus firm's profits, is considered the relevant standard, the conversion of consumer surplus into monopolist profits should not cause any concern. The key objective of EU competition law is the protection of consumer welfare, which means that under EU competition law the transfer of consumer surplus to producers would be seen as critical.[16]

- Finally, some part of the consumer surplus that would exist under perfect competition is completely lost under a monopoly. Economists refer to this as the 'deadweight loss', which reflects the inefficiency related to monopoly. Irrespective of how the transfer of some of the consumer surplus to producers is perceived, total welfare will therefore always be lower under monopoly than under perfect competition.

The discussion above focused on the short-term loss of efficiency due to monopoly. In addition, monopolistic market structures carry the risk of a loss of dynamic efficiency. Due to the absence of competitive constraints, the monopolist may not strive to produce as efficiently as possible. This is also referred to as the risk of X-inefficiency.[17] Since the monopolist does not face any threat of competitive entry,

---

[16] The consumer welfare standard of EU competition law can, for example, be seen in statements made by the Commissioner for Competition, Joaquín Almunia, in his speech at the European Competition Day 2010 in Madrid: 'All of us here today know very well what our ultimate objective is: competition policy is a tool at the service of consumers. Consumer welfare is at the heart of our policy and its achievement drives our priorities and guides our decisions' (European Commission, SPEECH/10/233, delivered 12 May 2010).

[17] The concept of X-inefficiency was originally developed by Harvey Leibenstein, see Leibenstein, 'Allocative Efficiency vs. "X-Efficiency"', *American Economic Review*, **56** (1966), 392. The concept of X-inefficiency is based on the realisation that in practice firms do not always operate at the lowest possible cost. This represents a deviation from the usual assumption in economics that firms will seek to reduce costs as much as possible in order to maximise profits.

it may also have less of an incentive to invest in innovation, jeopardising the dynamic benefits associated with competition.[18]

Summary of Section 4

Under monopoly, there is only one supplier, which will realise that its output decision will have an effect on the market price. In other words, the monopolist will act as a price setter instead of as a price taker.

The level of output under monopoly will be lower and prices will be higher than under perfect competition. Allocative and productive efficiency will not be achieved.

Compared to perfect competition, some of the consumer welfare will be transferred to the monopolist as profit. In addition, monopoly leads to a deadweight loss, i.e. a net reduction in social welfare compared to the outcome under perfect competition.

5. OLIGOPOLISTIC COMPETITION

The models of perfect competition and monopoly reflect the two most extreme forms of market outcomes. They are useful to illustrate the benefits of competition and the welfare losses associated with market power. However, in real life markets are rarely characterised by the extreme assumptions underlying these two models. Many of the markets we observe in reality are not characterised by a huge number of firms all acting as price takers or a single firm that can set prices without considering any competitive response. Instead, markets are often characterised by a limited number of firms that are aware of each other's existence and their mutual interdependence. In economics, oligopoly models have been developed to describe and analyse such markets.

Oligopoly models allow for interaction between firms in a given market. With a limited number of firms, suppliers will realise that their behaviour, e.g. in relation to output- and price-setting, will affect the behaviour of others. They will therefore factor this into their own decision-making. There are various oligopoly models. The two best known were developed by the Frenchmen Augustin Cournot and Joseph Bertrand in the nineteenth century.

- Cournot competition assumes that firms compete on quantity. Suppliers will make their output decisions and prices will then form to clear the market. Cournot competition reflects industries where capacity decisions are sunk, i.e. capacity cannot easily be taken out of the market once installed, and where production is

---

[18] However, the prospect of holding monopoly power, at least for a certain period of time, may also promote innovation. This is what underlies the idea of patents: patents reward firms for their investment in innovation, e.g. pharmaceutical research, with a legal monopoly for a certain, limited period of time.

inert and cannot easily be adjusted once the initial output decision has been made. Examples of this type of industry are the mining industry or the production of chemicals.

- Bertrand competition assumes that firms compete on prices. Suppliers will determine the price they want to charge and will then supply as much as is demanded in the market at this price. The model of Bertrand competition is suited for industries where changes in output can easily be made and there are no significant capacity restrictions. An example of this type of competition is the insurance industry.

The following sections describe these two models of oligopoly and their implications for social welfare in more detail.

5.1 Cournot competition

The simplest form of the Cournot model of competition assumes that there are only two suppliers in the market that sell a standardised product and face the same cost of supply. Each firm will need to decide how much output to put on the market. It is assumed that firms need to make their output decisions simultaneously. In addition, each firm assumes that the other firm will hold its output constant, i.e. will not respond dynamically to its own behaviour.[19]

In the setting described above, each firm will optimise its own profits by following the same rationale as the firms under perfect competition and as a monopolist: by equating its marginal cost to the marginal revenue of supply.[20] However, contrary to a firm's behaviour under perfect competition and monopoly, the best response of a Cournot oligopolist in terms of its own output decision will depend on how much is supplied by its rival.

- If its competitor did not supply anything, the oligopolist's best, i.e. profit-maximising, response would be to choose the output level that a monopolist would choose.
- If its competitor supplied the same output as would emerge under perfect competition, i.e. to maximise output given the cost of supply, the best response of the oligopolist's firm would be not to supply anything at all.
- Assuming its competitor supplied an output level between these two extremes, the firm's best response would lie between supplying nothing and supplying the monopoly level of output, depending on the output level of the second firm.

The set of best responses can be derived mathematically and summarised in a so-called 'reaction curve'. Figure 6 shows the reaction curve for Firm 1 as described above.

---

[19] Frank, *Microeconomics and Behaviour*, pp. 429–34 and Martin, *Industrial Economics*, pp. 118–30.
[20] Recall that under perfect competition, marginal revenue is the same as the market price.

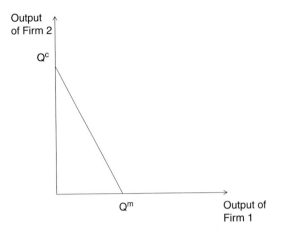

Figure 6 Firm 1's reaction curve – optimal output given output decision of Firm 2

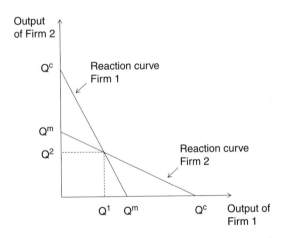

Figure 7 Equilibrium output decision in Cournot duopoly

In a symmetric oligopoly, both competitors will face the same set of best responses, i.e. the same reaction curves. In addition, they will both anticipate the best response of each other. In equilibrium, both firms will therefore set their output at the point where the two reaction curves intersect. This is shown in Figure 7. Firm 1 will supply Q^1 and Firm 2 will supply Q^2. The market price, which is not shown in the chart, will form to clear the market, given total supply of Q^1+Q^2.

What are the welfare implications of Cournot competition? To answer this question, we can compare the outcome under Cournot competition to the outcome we would expect under perfect competition and monopoly. Figure 8 replicates Figure 7 with two lines being added.

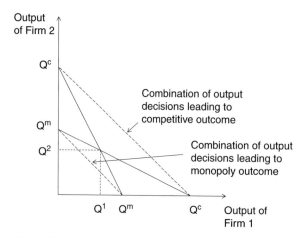

Figure 8 Comparison of Cournot outcome to outcomes under perfect competition and monopoly

- The first line to the right of the Cournot equilibrium outcome shows all combinations of output of Firms 1 and 2 that would result in the same total output (and therefore the same market price) as under perfect competition.
- The line to the left of the Cournot equilibrium shows all combinations of output that would result in the same output (and hence market price) as under monopoly.

It can be seen that Cournot competition leads to a market outcome that lies between that under perfect competition and that under monopoly. With Cournot competition, total output will be higher than under monopoly, but lower than under perfect competition. This implies that the market price will, in equilibrium, be higher than under perfect competition but lower than under monopoly. As a consequence, total welfare will be lower than under perfect competition but higher than under monopoly.

The example set out above assumed that there were only two firms in the market. What would be the prediction of the model if there were more firms in the market? In fact, the Cournot model of competition predicts that as more firms are added to the market, the equilibrium outcome moves closer and closer to the competitive outcome. In other words: the more firms there are in the market, the closer total output and the resulting market price will be to the outcome under perfect competition and the lower the welfare losses associated with oligopoly will be.

The original Cournot model treats the number of firms in the market as exogenous, i.e. as given. However, assuming that entry into and exit from the market is possible, we can make some predictions about the number of firms the market can sustain. As set out above, under Cournot competition the market price will be above the price in perfect competition and therefore above marginal cost. In such a setting, the number of firms that can be sustained in the market will depend on how large fixed costs are relative to the profit that firms earn at the equilibrium level of output. The lower fixed costs are, the smaller the profit a firm needs to earn to be able to cover these costs and the lower the market price can be, which means that a larger number of firms can be sustained in the market. On the other hand, if fixed costs are high, firms will need to earn higher profits to cover these costs, which means that the market price will need to be higher to be sustainable, thus supporting only a smaller number of firms in the market.[21]

5.2 Bertrand competition

The Cournot model of competition assumes that firms compete on quantities and that the price then forms to clear the market, given the output decisions of all suppliers. In contrast, Bertrand competition assumes that firms compete on price. As under Cournot competition, it is assumed that firms need to make their pricing decisions simultaneously and each firm will expect its competitors to hold their price constant given its own pricing decision.[22]

Under Bertrand competition, the market outcome crucially depends on the level of product differentiation that is assumed. Let us start with the simplest case, assuming that all firms offer exactly the same product, i.e. that products are homogeneous, and that marginal costs are identical across the two firms. These are the same assumptions as under perfect competition and, as will be shown below, in this case Bertrand competition will indeed lead to the same outcome as perfect competition.

Assume that there are only two firms in the market. Each firm will need to determine the price it will charge for its product, anticipating the pricing decision of its rival. In such a setting, both firms will in equilibrium set their price equal to marginal cost. To see this, let us assume that Firm 1 wanted to charge a price above marginal cost. Since products are assumed to be completely homogeneous, this implies that Firm 2 could maximise its own profits by undercutting Firm 1's price by a tiny amount, thus stealing all sales from Firm 1 and supplying the whole market. In turn, Firm 1 could undercut Firm 2 by offering a price slightly below the price of Firm 2 to reverse the outcome. Such undercutting would continue until prices are driven down to marginal cost. Only at this level would the pricing decisions of the two firms be stable: none of the firms would have an incentive to reduce its price further. As a result, in equilibrium, prices under Bertrand competition with

---

[21] Bishop and Walker, *The Economics of EC Competition Law*, pp. 336–7.
[22] Frank, *Microeconomics and Behaviour*, pp. 434–5 and Martin, *Industrial Economics*, pp. 132–8.

homogeneous products will equal marginal cost. Prices and total output will be the same as under perfect competition, implying that social welfare will be maximised.

The conclusion that competition between just a few firms can lead to exactly the same result as competition between a large number of firms appears surprising. However, the market outcome described above is crucially driven by the assumption that products are completely homogeneous.[23] If this assumption, which is often not fulfilled in real life, is relaxed, the predicted outcome under Bertrand competition does differ from that under perfect competition. The resulting economic model is referred to as Bertrand competition with differentiated goods or as monopolistic competition.[24]

With differentiated products, each firm will face a downward sloping demand curve similar to a monopolist: since products are not assumed to be standardised anymore, there will be some consumers that prefer each of the products over the other one. As a result, each firm will face a trade-off between setting higher prices and reducing demand for its own product, implying that each producer faces a downward sloping demand curve for its good.[25]

In such a setting, analogous to the pricing decision of a monopolist, each firm will set its price so that, for the chosen level of output, marginal revenue equals marginal cost. The market outcome under monopolist competition will be similar to the monopolistic outcome in that prices will be above marginal cost and allocative efficiency will not be ensured. Indeed, it can be shown that the market outcome under monopolistic competition will deviate more from the perfectly competitive outcome the more differentiated the products are, i.e. the more market power each individual firm holds. In the extreme, if products are extremely differentiated, each firm might become a de facto monopolist for its own product and the market outcome (and hence the loss of welfare) will be the same as under a true monopoly.

Although the market outcome under Bertrand competition is closer to monopoly when products are differentiated, this does not necessarily imply that firms will earn positive profits as in a monopoly. If there are no barriers to entry, positive profits will

---

[23] As Bishop and Walker point out, the market outcome is also driven by the (often implausible) assumption that the two firms would not be capacity constrained, i.e. that each firm could supply the whole market when undercutting its rival (Bishop and Walker, *The Economics of EC Competition Law*, p. 39).

[24] Ibid., pp. 40–1.

[25] The steepness of the demand curve (or, in economic terms, the elasticity of demand) that each firm faces will depend on the degree of product differentiation. If products are only slightly differentiated, each product will still be quite a strong substitute for the other product. In this case, demand for product A would be expected to react quite strongly to an increase in the price of product A since there would still be many consumers that would perceive product B as a substitute and switch to that product instead. On the other hand, if products are highly differentiated, the elasticity of demand for product A would be lower: since consumers would perceive product B only as a weak substitute, fewer customers would switch from product A to product B if the price for product A increased.

induce entry of additional firms into the market, reducing the demand faced by each individual firm and hence reducing the profits it can earn.[26] As a result, monopolistic competition may still lead to products being supplied at the lowest possible cost and productive efficiency being achieved. However, unless products are completely homogeneous, Bertrand competition will usually lead to a lower level of output and higher prices than perfect competition, meaning that allocative efficiency will not be ensured.

5.3 Oligopolistic competition vs cartel behaviour

It is important to remember that oligopolistic behaviour does not mean that firms are engaging in a cartel or some other form of illegal conduct. Although Cournot and Bertrand competition assumes that firms will be aware of their mutual inter-dependence and will take each other's behaviour into account for their own decision making, this does not mean that they will implicitly or explicitly coordinate their behaviour. All effects described in the previous sections follow solely from each firm's pursuit of its own individual profit-maximising objectives. Although the models of oligopolistic competition described above may result in prices remaining above marginal costs, this does not mean that firms do not compete intensely with each other and that competition is not effective, given the underlying structure of the market.[27]

Nevertheless, as already recognised by Adam Smith in the eighteenth century, firms may of course try to engage in conscious anticompetitive behaviour, e.g. by setting up a cartel that fixes prices, output levels or market shares. In economic terms, such a case would be equivalent to firms trying to coordinate their prices and/or output decisions to move closer to the monopoly market outcome. For example, in case of two Cournot duopolists seeking to engage in a cartel, it would involve their agreeing to move from the competitive equilibrium (marked as A in Figure 9) to a situation closer to the monopoly outcome, such as point B.

Although both firms would be better off at point B than at point A (because they jointly enjoy higher profits), the situation represents a deviation from each firm's profit-maximising strategy.

- Assuming Firm 2 supplied Q^{cartel}, Firm 1's profit-maximising strategy, as reflected in its reaction curve, would not be to supply Q^{cartel}, but to supply Q^*.
- The same holds for Firm 2: if it assumed that Firm 1 would adhere to the cartel agreement and supply Q^{cartel}, its profit-maximising output decision would be to supply Q^{**} instead of Q^{cartel}.

[26] Recall that in a true monopoly, entry into and exit from the market are assumed to be blocked.
[27] See Bishop and Walker, *The Economics of EC Competition Law*, p. 44.

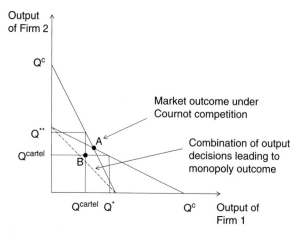

Figure 9 Possible cartel outcome of two Cournot duopolists

This reveals an important fact: although cartel agreements in principle benefit all players, they are often unstable because, individually, each firm has an incentive to deviate from the agreed outcome in the short run and 'cheat' on the other cartel members. In order to remain stable, cartels therefore require some mechanism that allows the cartel members to punish deviations from the agreed outcome, e.g. by increasing output above the individually profit-maximising level in response to cheating. This would lead to a price reduction and thereby punish the deviator. The requirement of a punishment mechanism is also reflected in the European case law on cartels, e.g. the *Airtours* judgment.[28]

Summary of Section 5

Most real-world markets are best characterised by economic models of oligopolistic competition. In an oligopoly, there will be a limited number of firms who will recognise the mutual interdependence of their decisions.

Oligopoly models can be based on quantity- or price-setting. In equilibrium, output will usually be lower than under perfect competition but higher than under monopoly. Likewise, prices will be higher than under perfect competition but higher than under monopoly. As a consequence, social welfare under oligopolistic competition will lie between the level of social welfare achieved under perfect competition and monopoly. The exact outcome will depend on the features of the market at hand, including the cost structure of supply and the degree of product differentiation.

Oligopolistic competition should not be confused with cartel behaviour: even though equilibrium prices may be above costs under oligopoly, this does not mean that firms do not compete intensely with each other.

---

[28] See Chapter 4 for a discussion of the *Airtours* case.

6. THE COMPETITIVE BENCHMARK UNDERLYING EU COMPETITION LAW AND THE CONCEPT OF EFFECTIVE COMPETITION

The previous sections have presented several economic models of competition. It has become clear that market power, in its most extreme form represented by a monopoly, leads to significant welfare losses for society and particularly consumers. On the other hand, perfect competition, while ideal from a social welfare perspective, is unlikely to be found often in real life. While the model helps to understand the benefits arising from competition, the assumptions underlying the perfectly competitive outcome (completely homogeneous products, a large number of suppliers, no barriers to entry and exit and perfect information for all market participants) are strong and rarely fulfilled in practice.

Models of oligopolistic competition are in many ways the most realistic models of competition and therefore most useful to describe and analyse real-world cases. As shown in the previous section, depending on the features of the market the competitive outcome in oligopolistic markets can range from close to perfect competition to close to the monopoly outcome. As a consequence, the implications for social welfare will differ too.

The objective of EU competition law is the protection and promotion of 'effective competition'. For example, the EU Merger Regulation (EUMR) states that '[a] concentration which would significantly impede effective competition, in the common market or in a substantial part of it, in particular as a result of the creation or strengthening of a dominant position, shall be declared incompatible with the common market'.[29]

However, surprisingly neither law nor economics provides a clear definition of what 'effective competition' means.[30] From an economic perspective, the discussion above has made it clear that effective competition cannot be equated with perfect competition in every market. Given that the assumptions underlying the economic model of perfect competition are often not fulfilled in real life, it would not be possible to achieve a perfectly competitive market outcome in every industry.

At the same time, effective competition can also not reasonably be equated with the absence of any market power, i.e. the ability of firms to influence market prices and set prices at a level above costs. As shown earlier, even oligopolistic market outcomes, in which prices often remain above marginal and average costs, can reflect the result of fierce competition between firms. This has also been acknowledged in EC

---

[29] Council Regulation (EC) No. 139/2004 of 20 January 2004 on the control of concentrations between undertakings, OJ No. L 24 of 29 January 2004, p. 1, Art. 2, para. 3 (hereinafter: EUMR).

[30] An excellent discussion of various possible definitions of effective competition, which also covers the economic models described above, can be found in Bishop and Walker, *The Economics of EC Competition Law*, pp. 16–21.

competition law. For example, the EUMR states that '[m]any oligopolistic markets exhibit a healthy degree of competition'.[31]

Although no universal legal or economic definition exists, the concept of effective competition can be traced back to the idea of 'workable competition', which was first formulated by John Maurice Clark in 1940.[32] Clark was one of the first economists to argue that perfect competition was not an appropriate benchmark for competition policy because '"perfect competition" does not and cannot exist and has presumably never existed'.[33] Instead, Clark proposed several criteria to assess what degree of competition could be achieved in a given market. The criteria included, *inter alia*, the level of product differentiation, the number and size-distribution of firms, the method of price-setting, the character and means of market information, the cost structure and the degree of flexibility of capacity. Clark's paper sparked lots of discussion among economists and even today there is no consensus on what workable or effective competition really means. However, there is general agreement that the factors Clark listed in his original paper can be informative of the degree of competition that can reasonably be expected in a given market.

Since publication of Clark's article, economic theory and in particular the branch of industrial organisation have developed a wealth of models that can describe the behaviour of firms and the likely market outcome based on the features of an industry. In this sense, economics can provide the necessary tools to assess the likely welfare implications of certain firm behaviour (e.g. certain pricing strategies like tying and bundling or certain types of rebates employed by a dominant undertaking). Economics can also help to assess whether the change in market structure due to a planned merger or State aid measures is likely to lead to anticompetitive effects.

Summary of Section 6

The objective of EC competition policy is to protect 'effective competition'. While no universal definition of effective competition exists, it can be traced back to the concept of 'workable competition' first developed by J. M. Clark in 1940. Based on this concept, the degree of competition that can realistically be achieved in a given market will depend on the features of the industry at hand. Relevant criteria include the level of product differentiation, the number and size-distribution of firms, the character and means of market information, the underlying cost structure and the degree of flexibility of capacity, i.e. the significance of barriers to entry.

Economic theory provides a broad range of tools and models to describe various forms of firm behaviour and the likely effect of mergers and State aid measures. In this sense, economic theory can help to assess the likely implications of certain conduct or changes in market structure, including the likely effect on social welfare.

---

[31] EUMR Art. 2, para. 25.
[32] Clark, 'Toward a Concept of Workable Competition', *American Economic Review*, 30 (1940), 241.   [33] Ibid.

7. THE LIMITATIONS OF THE MARKET MECHANISM

The objective of competition policy is to ensure that the market mechanism is allowed to function smoothly so that the benefits of competition can be reaped. However, in real life, competition policy cannot be considered in isolation. In practice, competition policy is usually complemented by social, regional, employment, environmental or other policies which may in some cases restrict the scope of competition policy. In certain industries, such as the provision of healthcare or defence, governments may also consider that pure competition would not be the most effective model to provide these services. In these cases, the relevant markets may be shielded from competition, either completely or to a certain extent. Sometimes, the State may even decide to organise the provision of these goods itself rather than leave this to private firms.

The notion underlying all of the above is that while the market mechanism is generally believed to deliver certain benefits, there is also the possibility of 'market failure'. Market failure occurs when the market mechanism leads to an outcome that is not in fact efficient and optimal from a social perspective, but where overall welfare could be improved by some form of intervention.

One reason for market failure can be non-competitive pricing, i.e. situations where firms hold market power and allocative and productive efficiency cannot be achieved. Competition policy seeks to remedy or prevent such situations. However, there are other factors that can lead to market failure even when prices are set competitively. Three of the best-known factors are the existence of externalities, asymmetric information and public goods.

7.1 Externalities

The *Dictionary of Economics* defines externalities, or external effects, as 'consequences for welfare or opportunity costs not fully accounted for in the price and market system'.[34] In other words, externalities arise when the behaviour of an economic agent has implications for other agents that are not reflected in the market system.

A classic example of an externality is a situation where the production process of a firm creates negative effects on the environment, e.g. by releasing toxins in the air. If the firm does not have to compensate society for this negative external effect of its behaviour, it will not take the environmental effect of its output decision into account. In equilibrium, the firm may therefore produce at a level that is profit-maximising from its own private perspective, but that is too high from the perspective

---

[34] Bannock, Baxter and Davis, *Dictionary of Economics*, p. 147.

of society as a whole. In this case, allocative efficiency would not be achieved because social welfare could be increased by forcing the firm to reduce production. This could for example be done by levying a tax on the firm that reflects the external effect of its output decision on the environment. In this way, the externality would be accounted for in the price and market system: it would be internalised by the firm. After this adjustment, the market could be left on its own again to produce the welfare-maximising outcome.

The example described above focused on a negative externality that could distort the efficient functioning of the market. However, externalities can also be positive. One example is network effects. Network effects arise when the value of a product to an individual user increases the more people use the product. For example, the value of owning a fax machine is higher the more people have a fax machine because this will increase the number of people that fax machine owners can communicate with. Similarly, social networks such as Facebook are more valuable to their users the more of the users' friends are also part of the network. In the presence of network effects, the decision of an individual consumer to use a certain good will have positive external effects on others (since an additional user will increase the value that others will derive from the good). However, each individual will most likely not take this positive externality into account in its private decision making. As a consequence, utilisation of certain goods might actually be lower than desired from a social point of view. Assuming that government wanted to remedy such a situation, it could provide additional incentives to individuals, e.g. in the form of a subsidy, to join a certain network.

7.2 Asymmetric information

In addition to externalities, asymmetric information can also be a cause of market failure. You might recall that one of the underlying assumptions of the model of perfect competition is that there is perfect information for all market players, including sellers and buyers. Only if all market players know about the prevailing prices and the features of the relevant products will the market mechanism be able to lead to allocative and productive efficiency. If the required information is not available to everyone in the market, economic agents will base their supply or purchase decisions on an incomplete set of information and the market mechanism will not be able to function effectively.

One of the best-known economic models to illustrate the problems that can be caused by asymmetric information is the 'lemons model', which was developed by George Akerlof.[35] Akerlof used the market for used cars as an example to illustrate

---

[35] Akerlof, *The Market for Lemons: Quality Uncertainty and the Market Mechanism, Quarterly Journal of Economics*, **84** (1970), 485. In 2001, Akerlof was awarded the Nobel Prize in Economics for this paper.

the problems associated with asymmetric information. His model assumed that sellers of used cars accurately know the value and quality of the car they are trying to sell while buyers cannot assess this before they have bought a car and own it. Assuming that there are both high-quality and low-quality cars brought to the market, the price that buyers will be willing to pay will be based on the expected average level of quality in the market. However, at this price owners of high-quality cars will not be willing to sell their cars since they would receive too low a price, given the high quality of their cars. Since owners of high-quality cars will not be able to convince buyers of the better quality of their goods that would justify a higher price, in equilibrium only low-quality cars will be traded (economists refer to this effect as 'adverse selection').

Clearly, this market outcome will not be optimal. On the one hand, buyers will be dissatisfied because the quality of the cars they purchase (which will all be of low quality) will be low. In addition, some transactions that would occur under perfect information will not occur under asymmetric information. In particular, buyers who would be willing to pay a higher price for a high-quality car will not be able to do so because sellers will not be able to convince buyers of the higher quality of their product. As a consequence, the market outcome, although based on the market mechanism, will not lead to allocative efficiency and maximum social welfare. In Akerlof's model, the situation might even get worse over time: as buyers realise the low quality of cars available in the market, they will be willing to pay even less, preventing even more socially optimal transactions (for higher-quality cars at higher prices) from being realised.

Asymmetric information is a key factor present in most insurance markets. Insurance applicants usually have much better information about themselves (e.g. their health or their qualities as a car driver) than is available to the insurance company. The issue is often intensified by the risk of moral hazard, i.e. insurance takers having less of an incentive to behave carefully once they have signed the insurance contract. Government intervention in insurance markets, e.g. through the set-up of mandatory collective health insurance for all citizens, often reflects the desire to ensure adequate insurance coverage for all in the presence of asymmetric information.

7.3 Public goods

Finally, market failure can also be brought about by the existence of public goods. Public goods are goods that, in contrast to private goods, are non-exclusive and sometimes also non-rival.[36]

---

[36] For a more technical discussion of the features and implications of public goods, see Nicholson and Snyder, *Microeconomic Theory – Basic Principles and Extensions*, 11th edn (Thomson, 2012), pp. 28–47.

- Non-exclusivity refers to a situation where once a good is produced, no one can be excluded from benefiting from its availability. For example, once a country has set up a national defence programme, all citizens benefit from it and it would be impossible to exclude individuals from doing so. This feature of public goods is in contrast to pure private goods, which individuals can be excluded from benefiting from. For example, individuals can be excluded from consuming a loaf of bread without paying for it.
- Non-rivalry refers to a situation where the consumption of one additional unit of a good does not involve any additional social marginal costs of production and does not reduce the availability of the good for consumption by others. Again, this can be illustrated using the example of a national defence programme: once the programme is implemented, having one more citizen use the service will not lead to any additional costs for society. Similarly, once a bridge is built, having one additional car drive over it will not involve any additional social costs. Contrarily, if one additional loaf of bread is to be consumed, this will require additional resources to be allocated to the production of bread.

It is especially the non-exclusive nature of public goods that can give rise to market failure. Since no one can be excluded from benefiting from a pure public good, the self-regulating market mechanism based on each individual pursuing his own self-interest will lead to a situation in which less of a public good is produced than would be socially optimal. This is because each individual will have an incentive to free-ride on the public good being available, i.e. contributing less to its production than what he consumes. Since no one can be excluded from consuming a public good, this is a strategy perfectly in line with each individual's self-interest. However, overall, it will leave society worse off. In other words: for public goods, Smith's invisible hand will not lead to the desired outcome.

Given the problems described above, public goods are often provided (or at least organised) by the government rather than the private sector. Examples include national defence, police services, the cleaning of streets and public parks or law enforcement, including competition policy.

Summary of Section 7

Although the market mechanism can deliver overall efficiency and maximise social welfare, it will only be able to do so if there are no distortions arising from externalities, asymmetric information or the existence of public goods.

If the latter are present, additional policies – e.g. social, cultural and environmental – may be required to correct for this and allow the market to function effectively.

As a consequence, competition policy cannot be considered in isolation but must be seen in the context of the overall objectives of a society.

Economic and legal foundations of EU competition law

1

B. The legal foundations of EU competition law

1. THE GOAL OF COMPETITIVE MARKETS

The EU has a number of aspirational objectives, but economic integration has been at the root since the very conception of the EU. Competition is considered to be fundamental to this despite the fact that the reference to 'a high degree of competitiveness' contained in Article 2 of the EC Treaty[37] has been replaced by the objective of a 'highly competitive social market economy aiming at full employment and social progress' as stipulated in Article 3 TEU[38]. The goal of competitiveness is still assumed to be part of the EU's main objectives since it is indispensable for the creation of the internal market under Article 26(2) TFEU.[39] Furthermore, Articles 119 and 120 TFEU oblige the Member States and the Union to act in accordance with the principle of an open economy with free competition.

Although the protection of free competition has been deleted from the catalogue of the EU's objective policies laid down in Article 3 TEU it still remains one of the main points of the EU's economic agenda. This is confirmed by Protocol No. 27 on the Internal Market and Competition which is attached to the Treaties and which constitutes an integral part of the EU's legal order according to Article 51 TEU:

THE HIGH CONTRACTING PARTIES,

CONSIDERING that the internal market as set out in Article 3 of the Treaty on European Union includes a system ensuring that competition is not distorted,

HAVE AGREED that: To this end, the Union shall, if necessary, take action under the provisions of the Treaties, including under Article 352 of the Treaty on the Functioning of the European Union.

---

[37] Treaty establishing the European Community (consolidated version), OJ No. C 321E of 29 December 2006, p. 37.
[38] Treaty on European Union (consolidated version), OJ No. C 115 of 9 May 2008, p. 13 (hereinafter: TEU).
[39] Treaty on the Functioning of the European Union (consolidated version), OJ No. C 115 of 9 May 2008, p. 47.

The various stipulations show that the creation of an internal market with undistorted competition is one of the key policy objectives of the EU.

Summary of Section 1

The EU has many objectives. One of them is the creation of a competitive market economy. Member States have commited to create an internal market that is characterised by undistorted competition.

2. THE GOAL OF MARKET INTEGRATION

Article 3(3) TEU refers to the 'internal market'. The concept of internal market is defined in Article 26(2) TFEU, which states:

The internal market shall comprise an area without internal frontiers in which the free movement of goods, persons, services and capital is ensured in accordance with the provisions of this Treaty.

Accordingly, the internal market is an area in which the fundamental freedoms as stipulated in the TFEU are implemented. The fundamental freedoms contribute to the goal of undistorted competition within the entire EU by ensuring that the Member States do not enact any measures that aim at shielding off their domestic markets from cross-border influxes.

The internal market is a market that shows a higher degree of integration than the common market referred to in earlier European treaties. The creation of an internal or single market has always been an objective of European integration.[40]

In 1976 the European Court of Justice held in *Metro v Commission*[41] that the objectives of the EEC Treaty[42] included the creation of a 'single market' achieving conditions similar to those of a domestic market. In this case the ECJ stated:

The requirement contained in Articles 3 and 85 of the EEC Treaty that competition shall not be distorted implies the existence on the market of workable competition, that is to say the degree of competition necessary to ensure the observance of the basic requirements and the attainment of the objectives of the Treaty, in particular the creation of a single market achieving conditions similar to those of a domestic market. In accordance with this requirement the nature and intensiveness of competition may vary to an extent dictated by the products or services in question and the economic structure of the relevant market sectors.[43]

---

[40] On the current status of EU integration in general see Craig, 'The Treaty of Lisbon: Process, Architecture and Substance', *European Law Review*, 33 (2008), 137.

[41] European Court of Justice (hereinafter: ECJ) (25 October 1977), Case 26/76 – *Metro v Commission (No. 1)* [1977] ECR 1875, para. 20.

[42] One of the predecessor treaties of the TFEU.

[43] ECJ (25 October 1977), Case 26/76 – *Metro v Commission (No. 1)* [1977] ECR 1875 para. 20.

Accordingly, competition and the creation of an internal market are closely interrelated. The enforcement practice of EU competition law shows that it is particularly sensitive to practices which run counter to the goal of market integration. The goal of market integration is less of an issue in national competition laws such as, for instance, those of the Member States or of the US.

The importance of the internal market in the sense of Article 26 TFEU was emphasised by the ECJ in the *Eco Swiss* case. In this judgment it was stated that:

according to Article 3(g) of the Treaty, Article 85 of the Treaty [Article 101 TFEU] constitutes a fundamental provision which is essential for the accomplishment of the tasks entrusted to the Community and, in particular, for the functioning of the internal market.[44]

Alongside the fundamental freedoms the competition rules are therefore crucial to create an internal market. While the fundamental freedoms aim at preventing Member States from interfering with the market mechanism, the competition rules also contain provisions for private undertakings.

Summary of Section 2

The creation of an internal market is a major policy objective of the EU. The internal market is an area without internal frontiers. From this policy objective the goal of market integration can be derived. EU competition law is one of the instruments used by the EU institutions to achieve that goal. EU competition law is very sensitive to any actions by undertakings that contravene the goal of market integration but seek to partition the market or to keep upright national markets.

3. SOURCES OF EU COMPETITION LAW

3.1 Primary legislation

The provisions of primary EU legislation relating to competition law are set out in Title VII, Chapter 1 TFEU.

- Section 1 (comprising Articles 101–106 TFEU) deals with competition rules that apply to undertakings.
- Section 2 (comprising Articles 107–109 TFEU) governs the measures necessary to prevent anticompetitive State aid. These provisions are addressed to States and aim at preventing distortions of competition through the granting of economic benefits to selected undertakings from State resources. This section of the TFEU

---

[44] ECJ (1 July 1999), Case C-126/97 – *Eco Swiss China Time Ltd v Benetton International NV* [1999] ECR I-3055, para. 36.

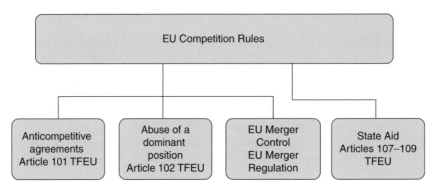

Figure 10 The areas of EU competition law

complements the fundamental freedoms which aim at shielding off national markets from competition from other Member States. State aid has not the effect of shielding off competition from other Member States but improves the competitive position of individual undertakings. This area of law is not included in the term 'competition law' as used in this book.

The areas of EU competition law can be seen in Figure 10.

Article 101(1) TFEU prohibits all agreements between undertakings, decisions by associations of undertakings and concerted practices which may affect trade between Member States and which have as their object or effect the prevention, restriction or distortion of competition within the internal market.

The Article itself provides a non-exhaustive list of examples of agreements which fall within this provision. These include:

(i)   price fixing;
(ii) limiting or controlling production, markets, technical development, or investment;
(iii) sharing markets or sources of supply;
(iv) applying dissimilar conditions to equivalent transactions with other trading parties; and
(v)   making the conclusion of contracts subject to acceptance by the other parties of supplementary and unconnected obligations.

Article 101(2) TFEU provides that any agreement or decision in breach of Article 101(1) TFEU shall be automatically void.

Under Article 101(3) TFEU, Article 101(1) TFEU may be declared inapplicable when the agreements concerned fulfil a number of specified requirements. This is designed to allow those agreements which are *prima facie* anticompetitive, but which on balance benefit consumer welfare when the restrictions of competition and the efficiencies created by the agreement are weighed against each other.

Article 102 TFEU prohibits an undertaking which holds a dominant position in the internal market, or in a substantial part of it, from abusing that position insofar as it may affect trade between the Member States.

This Article also provides a non-exhaustive list of examples of behaviour that would constitute abuse. These include:

(i)   imposing unfair prices or other unfair trading conditions;
(ii) limiting production, markets or technical development to the prejudice of consumers;
(iii) applying dissimilar conditions to equivalent transactions; and
(iv) making the conclusion of contracts subject to acceptance by the other parties of supplementary and unconnected obligations.

Article 101 TFEU, Article 102 TFEU and merger control are often referred to as the 'three pillars' of EU competition law. However, EU merger control is not governed by EU primary law but by a regulation that forms part of EU secondary law. Merger control was introduced at EU level only in 1992, i.e. about three decades after Articles 101 and 102 TFEU entered into force.

As a means to give effect to the principles of Articles 101 and 102 TFEU, there also exists a volume of secondary legislation.

3.2 Secondary legislation

There are a number of different types of secondary legislation in operation within the EU. The various types of secondary legislation are set out in Article 288 TFEU. They include regulations, directives, decisions, recommendations and opinions.

Regulations are binding and directly applicable. They do not require any act of transformation into national law but individuals and undertakings can directly rely upon them. There are a number of regulations relevant in the area of competition law.[45]

The EUMR[46] governs merger control at EU level. The regulation requires compulsory notification to the Commission by the parties of concentrations which exceed certain turnover thresholds.

The Commission has enacted a number of so-called 'block exemption regulations'[47] which set out criteria for the assessment of potentially anticompetitive

---

[45] These regulations are either Council regulations or Commission regulations. Article 103(1) TFEU empowers the Council to adopt regulations in the area of competition law on a proposal from the Commission and after consulting the European Parliament. Council regulations govern in particular the procedure in competition cases, the sanctions to be imposed for violations of the competition rules and the relationship between EU and national competition law. Article 105(3) TFEU is the legal basis for regulations adopted by the Commission. These regulations define categories of agreements that benefit from an exemption from the prohibition laid down in Article 101(1) TFEU under Article 101(3) TFEU (so-called 'block exemption regulations').

[46] Council Regulation (EC) No. 139/2004 of 20 January 2004 on the control of concentrations between undertakings, OJ No. L 24 of 29 January 2004, p. 1

[47] Commission Regulation (EU) No. 330/2010 of 20 April 2010 on the application of Article 101(3) TFEU to categories of vertical agreements and concerted practices, OJ No. L 102 of 23 April 2010, p. 1; Commission Regulation (EU) No. 1217/2010 of 14 December 2010 on the application of Art. 101(3) TFEU to certain categories of research and development agreements, OJ No. L 335 of 18 December 2010, p. 36; Commission

agreements under Article 101(3) TFEU. Agreements that meet the criteria stipulated in a block exemption in general qualify for an exemption from the cartel prohibition of Article 101(1) TFEU. This type of regulation contributes to increasing legal certainty with regard to the availability of an exemption under Article 101(3) TFEU.

The procedural rules applicable to the enforcement of EU competition law are also laid down in a regulation.[48] They are accompanied by an implementing regulation addressing certain procedural issues in greater detail.[49] The Commission has also adopted a regulation on settlement procedures in cartel cases.[50]

Directives are not addressed to individuals or undertakings but to Member States. They require the Member States to enact national legislation to achieve a result defined in the directive. They are binding on the Member State with regard to the result to be achieved but leave the national legislator the choice of form and methods. If a Member State fails to implement a directive within the timeframe stipulated therein individuals and undertakings may rely on the directive under certain conditions. However, in the area of competition law no secondary legislation in the form of a directive has been adopted so far. However, there are a number of directives in the area of State aid and unfair competition law.

Decisions are binding acts in individual cases. A decision typically specifies the persons to whom it is addressed and is binding only on them. There are numerous decisions of the Commission based on competition law provisions. Decisions are the typical instrument used by the Commission to enforce the EU competition rules. A decision will declare a certain behaviour of an undertaking incompatible with the competition rules and impose a fine or it will order the addressee to stop such behaviour. In merger cases the Commission may adopt a decision on the compatibility of the notified transaction with the internal market.

Recommendations and Opinions have no binding force. These acts of soft law rather set out the approach of European institutions to certain legal issues and thus increase legal certainty. In the area of competition law the Commission has used a number of other forms of soft law to communicate its approach to certain issues. In this sense, there is no *numerus clausus* of the types of soft law adopted by the Commission.[51]

Regulation (EU) No. 1218/2010 of 14 December 2010 on the application of Art. 101(3) TFEU to certain categories of specialisation agreements, OJ No. L 335 of 18 December 2010, p. 43; Commission Regulation (EU) No. 461/2010 of 27 May 2010 on the application of Art. 101(3) TFEU to categories of vertical agreements and concerted practices in the motor vehicle sector, OJ No. L 129 of 28 May 2010, p. 52; Commission Regulation (EC) No. 772/2004 of 27 April 2004 on the application of Article 81(3) of the Treaty to categories of technology transfer agreements, OJ No. L 123 of 27 April 2004, p. 11.

[48] Council Regulation (EC) No. 1/2003 of 16 December 2002 on the implementation of the rules on competition laid down in Articles 81 and 82 of the Treaty, OJ No. L 1 of 4 January 2003, p. 1.

[49] Commission Regulation (EC) No. 773/2004 of 7 April 2004 relating to the conduct of proceedings by the Commission pursuant to Articles 81 and 82 of the EC Treaty, OJ No. L 123 of 27 April 2004, p. 18.

[50] Commission Regulation (EC) No. 622/2008 of 30 June 2008 amending Regulation (EC) No. 773/2004, as regards the conduct of settlement procedures in cartel cases, OJ No. L 171 of 1 July 2008, p. 3.

[51] For an analysis of administrative rule-making in the competition law area see Hofmann, 'Negotiated and Non-negotiated Administrative Rule-Making: The Example of EC Competition Policy', *Common Market Law Review*, 43 (2006), 153.

The Commission has issued numerous notices on various aspects of EU competition law such as the Leniency Notice[52] setting out the conditions for immunity from fines or for the reduction of fines in cartel cases. Other notices include the Consolidated Jurisdictional Notice[53] clarifying several concepts under the EUMR and a notice on the definition of the relevant market for purposes of EU competition law.[54]

There are also guidelines issued by the Commission setting out its approach to legal issues surrounding the block exemption regulations.[55] These guidelines have a double function: they comment on the concepts employed by the block exemption regulations and thus provide guidance on their interpretation but they also discuss cases which are not covered by the block exemption regulations.[56]

In 2008 the Commission released a guidance paper on its enforcement priorities in the area of dominance (Article 102 TFEU).[57] In this document the Commission describes the types of abuse of a dominant position that it finds to have the most restrictive effects on competition and the concepts it will apply to assess such abusive conduct.

The Commission also provides informal guidance on practical aspects of competition law procedures. For example, the Commission's Directorate General for Competition in March 2012 issued an 'informal guidance paper on confidentiality claims'[58] giving practical advice on how to identify confidential information in documents submitted to the Commission.

Although Article 288(5) TFEU states that soft law does not have any binding force, it still may have an effect on the application of the EU competition rules by national competition authorities and courts. When national competition authorities or courts apply EU competition law they will have to observe communications of EU institutions on its interpretation. With regard to soft law in the area of social policy the binding effect of a recommendation of the Commission on the courts of the Member States has been confirmed by the ECJ in the *Grimaldi* case.[59] The court held that although recommendations formally are not binding according to Article 288(5) TFEU they still have to be taken into consideration by national courts when interpreting national law

---

[52] Commission Notice on Immunity from fines and reduction of fines in cartel cases, OJ No. C 298 of 8 December 2006, p. 17 (hereinafter: Leniency Notice).

[53] Commission Consolidated Jurisdictional Notice under Council Regulation (EC) No. 139/2004 on the control of concentrations between undertakings, OJ No. C 95 of 16 April 2008, p. 1.

[54] Commission Notice on the definition of the relevant market for purposes of Community competition law, OJ No. C 372 of 9 December 1997, p. 5.

[55] Commission Guidelines on Vertical Restraints, OJ No. C 130 of 19 May 2010, p. 1; Commission Guidelines on the applicability of Article 101 of the Treaty on the Functioning of the European Union to horizontal co-operation agreements, OJ No. C 11 of 14 January 2011, p. 1; Commission Guidelines on the application of Article 81 of the EC Treaty to technology transfer agreements, OJ No. C 101 of 27 April 2004, p. 2.

[56] On the legal nature and function of Commission guidelines see Hofmann, 'Negotiated and Non-negotiated Administrative Rule-Making', 159.

[57] Commission, Guidance on the Commission's enforcement priorities in applying Article 82 of the EC Treaty to abusive exclusionary conduct by dominant undertakings, OJ No. C 45 of 24 February 2009, p. 7.

[58] Available at http://ec.europa.eu/competition/antitrust/guidance_en.pdf.

[59] ECJ (13 December 1989), Case C-322/88, – *Salvatore Grimaldi v Fonds des maladies professionelles* [1989] ECR 4407.

adopted in implementation of Union law.[60] This reasoning is valid *a fortiori* also in the area of competition law where national competition authorities and courts have not just to interpret national law adopted in implementation of Union law but Union law itself.

Summary of Section 3

The key provisions of EU competition law can be found in Articles 101–106 TFEU. Article 101 TFEU prohibits bi- or multilateral restrictions of competition such as anti-competitive agreements. Article 102 TFEU governs unilateral restrictions of competition in the form of the abuse of a dominant position. The legal basis of EU merger control is the EU Merger Regulation. These three areas are commonly referred to as the 'three pillars' of competition law. The key provisions mentioned above are complemented by a number of implementing regulations and soft law providing guidance for their application. Furthermore there is a regulation covering procedure in competition cases.

In individual cases the Commission will act in the form of decisions.

4. THE CHARTER OF FUNDAMENTAL RIGHTS OF THE EUROPEAN UNION AND THE EUROPEAN CONVENTION FOR THE PROTECTION OF HUMAN RIGHTS AND FUNDAMENTAL FREEDOMS

The Charter of Fundamental Rights of the European Union (hereinafter: the Charter)[61] and the European Convention for the Protection of Human Rights and Fundamental Freedoms (hereinafter: the ECHR)[62] are two further sources of law relevant in particular for the procedural aspects of the enforcement of EU competition law.

According to Article 6(1) TEU the Union recognises the rights, freedoms and principles set out in the Charter and attributes to them the same legal value as to the treaties.[63] The Charter comprises in Chapters V and VI a set of rules on citizen's rights and justice. Citizen's rights include the right to good administration (Article 41 of the Charter) which encompasses the right to be heard before any adversely affecting individual measure is taken, the right to have access to file and the obligation of the administration to give reasons for its decisions. The right to good administration also includes that affairs are handled by the EU institutions within a reasonable timeframe.

The chapter on justice provides for a right to an effective remedy and to a fair trial in Article 47. The presumption of innocence and the right of defence are laid down in Article 48 of the Charter.[64]

---

[60]   Ibid., para. 18.
[61]   Charter of Fundamental Rights of the European Union, OJ No. C 364 of 18 December 2000, p. 1.
[62]   Available at http://conventions.coe.int/
[63]   On the status of the Charter in EU law see Craig, 'The Treaty of Lisbon', 161.
[64]   For an analysis of the impact of the Charter on procedures under Regulation 1/2003 see Weiss, 'Human Rights and EU Antitrust Enforcement: News from Lisbon', *European Competition Law Review*, 32 (2011), 186.

Procedures of the Commission and the European courts in the area of competition law have to meet the standards stipulated in the Charter.

Moreover, Article 6(2) TEU requires the EU to become a party to the ECHR.[65] The ECHR offers protection of fundamental civil and political rights and provides for an enforcement mechanism through the European Court of Human Rights (hereinafter: ECtHR), which is an organ of the Council of Europe and based in Strasbourg. Natural and legal persons who deem their rights have been violated in one country can bring their case to the Strasbourg court after exhaustion of domestic remedies.

Whereas all EU Member States are also parties to the ECHR, the EU itself is currently not. Even though the EU is founded on the respect for fundamental rights, the observance of which is ensured by the ECJ, the ECHR and its judicial mechanism do not formally apply to EU acts. On the other hand, all Member States of the EU, as parties to the ECHR, have an obligation to respect the ECHR even when they are applying or implementing EU law. This divergence may be rectified by the EU, as such, becoming a party to the ECHR.

The ECHR provides in Article 6(1) for a right to a fair trial which has to be observed by EU institutions with regard to the enforcement of EU competition law. The accession of the EU to the ECHR has far-reaching consequences for judicial review of Commission decisions enforcing the EU competition rules. Under Article 34 ECHR, natural and legal persons may bring an action to the ECtHR claiming that a competition law procedure under the TFEU infringes the ECHR. Final judgments of the ECJ might be subject to review by the ECtHR.

In reviewing EU law and the legal acts of EU institutions within the ECHR a distinction can be drawn between direct actions and indirect actions, namely, on the one hand, individual applications directed against measures adopted by EU institutions subsequent to the accession of the EU to the ECHR and, on the other, applications against acts adopted by the authorities of the Member States of the EU for the application or implementation of EU law. In the first case, the condition relating to exhaustion of domestic remedies, imposed under Article 35(1) ECHR, will oblige applicants wishing to apply to the ECtHR to refer the matter first to the EU courts, in accordance with the conditions laid down by EU law. Accordingly, it is guaranteed that the review exercised by the ECtHR will be preceded by the internal review carried out by the ECJ.

By contrast, in the second case, the situation is more complex. The applicant will have, first, to refer the matter to the courts of the Member State concerned, which, in accordance with Article 267 TFEU, may or, in certain cases, must refer a question to the ECJ for a preliminary ruling on the interpretation or validity of the provisions of EU law at issue. However, if, for whatever reason, such a reference for a preliminary ruling is not made, the ECtHR will be required to adjudicate on an application calling into question provisions of EU law without the ECJ having the opportunity to review that law.

---

[65] On the implications of the incorporation of the Charter into the TEU and the accession to the ECHR see ibid.

In all probability, that situation should not arise often. The fact remains, however, that it is foreseeable that such a situation might arise because the preliminary ruling procedure may be launched only by national courts and tribunals, to the exclusion of the parties, who are admittedly in a position to suggest a reference for a preliminary ruling, but do not have the power to require it. That means that the reference for a preliminary ruling is normally not a legal remedy to be exhausted by the applicant before referring the matter to the ECtHR.

Delegations of the EU and the ECtHR are currently negotiating a mechanism which would ensure that the ECJ may carry out an internal review before the ECtHR carries out external review.[66]

Summary of Section 4

EU institutions have to observe the Charter of Fundamental Rights of the European Union when applying the EU competition law. This is of relevance in particular for procedural aspects since the Charter includes a right of good administration.

Moreover, the EU has committed itself to become a party of the European Convention for the Protection of Human Rights and Fundamental Freedoms. The Convention provides for a right to a fair trial which will have to be observed by EU institutions with regard to the enforcement of EU competition law. Acts of EU institutions will become reviewable under the Convention. There are currently mechanisms being worked out to align jurisdiction of the EU courts and the European Court of Human Rights which is competent to hear cases in which a violation of the Convention is claimed.

5. SCOPE OF APPLICATION OF EU COMPETITION LAW

5.1 Possible conflicts between the aim of competition and other objectives of the EU

As discussed above, competition policy is just one of a number of policies of the EU, as it promotes various objectives set out in Article 3 TEU. The activities mentioned in Article 3 are numerous and coequal:

Article 3

2. The Union shall offer its citizens an area of freedom, security and justice without internal frontiers, in which the free movement of persons is ensured in conjunction with appropriate measures with respect to external border controls, asylum, immigration and the prevention and combating of crime.

---

[66] On the negotiation process see Joint communication from Presidents Costa and Skouris of 27 January 2011, available at www.echr.coe.int.

3. The Union shall establish an internal market. It shall work for the sustainable development of Europe based on balanced economic growth and price stability, a highly competitive social market economy, aiming at full employment and social progress, and a high level of protection and improvement of the quality of the environment. It shall promote scientific and technological advance. It shall combat social exclusion and discrimination, and shall promote social justice and protection, equality between women and men, solidarity between generations and protection of the rights of the child. It shall promote economic, social and territorial cohesion, and solidarity among Member States. It shall respect its rich cultural and linguistic diversity, and shall ensure that Europe's cultural heritage is safeguarded and enhanced.

4. The Union shall establish an economic and monetary union whose currency is the euro.

The plurality of goals of the EU may potentially lead to conflicts between these various coequal activities. The question arises how to resolve such conflicts and how to reconcile competition policy with other EU policies.

There are essentially two different mechanisms to deal with this problem:

5.2 Exclusion from the scope of competition law

Some matters are excluded from the scope of competition law either by legislation or by jurisprudence.

5.2.1 Exclusion by legislation

Certain issues, which were foreseen to lead to conflicts between competition policy and other EU policies, are addressed by primary EU law itself. Other potential conflicts are resolved by secondary EU legislation. The potential conflicts addressed by EU law include:

a) Agriculture

Article 42 TFEU stipulates that 'the provisions of the Chapter relating to rules on competition shall apply to production of and trade in agricultural products only to the extent determined by the European Parliament and the Council within the framework of Article 43(2)'.

In addition the provision confirms that the objectives of the common agriculture policy, as set out in Article 39 TFEU, should also be taken into account.

b) Defence industry

The EU acknowledges that the individual defence policies of each Member State are also an exceptional area and that EU legislation will be inappropriate in certain aspects. Article 346(1)(b) TFEU states that Member States' production of military equipment will not be affected by EU competition law:

any Member State may take such measures as it considers necessary for the protection of the essential interests of its security which are connected with the production of or trade in arms, munitions and war material; such measures shall not adversely affect the conditions of competition in the common market regarding products which are not intended for specifically military purposes.

c) Certain elements of the traffic sector

Another area in which the EU has acknowledged there may occur conflicts with competition policy is that of transport. In this area there have been a number of regulations passed in order to resolve some of these conflicts by exempting certain activities. A prominent example is Regulation 1017/68[67] as amended by Regulation 169/2009[68] which exempts certain activities in the traffic sector from the competition rules. It has to be noted, however, that the traffic sector has been increasingly opened up to competition in recent decades.

5.2.2 Exclusion by jurisprudence

Some areas of conflict are not covered by legislation, but have instead been dealt with in the case law of the European courts.

Collective bargaining agreements between employers and employees are exempted from EU competition law since the ECJ's ruling in the *Albany* case.[69] EU social policy is overriding here the principles of competition policy. Social policy also prevails in cases involving national health insurance schemes. This can be derived from the ECJ's *FENIN* judgment[70] which exempted the purchasing activities of the Spanish health insurance scheme from the competition rules referring to their close connection to a social activity.

5.3 Influence of other considerations on assessment under the competition rules

In some circumstances it may not be appropriate to entirely exclude a matter from the scope of EU competition law. There may, however, be other considerations that need to be borne in mind when applying the competition rules. In some cases the ECJ has

---

[67] Council Regulation (EEC) No. 1017/68 of 19 July 1968 applying rules of competition to transport by rail, road and inland waterway, OJ No. L 175 of 23 July 1968, p. 1.

[68] Council Regulation (EC) No. 169/2009 of 26 February 2009 applying rules of competition to transport by rail, road and inland waterway, OJ No. L 61 of 5 March 2009, p. 1.

[69] ECJ (21 September 1999), Case C-67/96 – *Albany International BV v Stichting Bedrijfspensioenfonds Textielindustrie* [1999] ECR I-5751, paras. 218 and 224.

[70] ECJ (11 July 2006), Case C-205/03 P – *Federación Española de Empresas de Tecnología Sanitaria (FENIN) v Commission* [2006] ECR I-6295.

exempted certain practices from the scope of EU competition law for reasons of public policy.

In the *Wouters* case,[71] for example, the ECJ held that the Dutch Bar Association's rule which prevented lawyers from entering partnerships with other professionals, such as accountants, could be a breach of Article 101(1) TFEU. It also held, however, that this would only constitute a breach if the rule:

went beyond what was necessary in order to ensure the proper practice of the legal profession.[72]

Accordingly, the ECJ applies a balancing exercise in cases where public policy considerations require certain restrictions of competition. However, there is no general rule exempting restrictions of competition necessary for public policy considerations from the competition rules but just an exemption on a case-by-case basis.

Summary of Section 5

The scope of application of the EU competition rules is limited in various ways. EU primary law gives other policy considerations priority over competition laws in some areas such as agriculture, defence and traffic. In these areas the competition rules apply only to a certain extent.

Furthermore the EU courts have limited the scope of EU competition law in their jurisprudence. They have recognised that other policies take priority over competition law in some areas. For example, collective bargaining agreements can be exempted from the competition rules due to social policy considerations.

Finally, in some cases competition law is applied but in the balancing exercise required under the respective provision other policy considerations outweigh competition concerns.

6. INTERNATIONAL APPLICABILITY

EU competition law is applicable to all restraints of competition which have an effect within the EU, such as, for example, anticompetitive agreements concluded in a third country but relating to competition in the EU market. This principle is usually referred to as 'effects doctrine' and is accepted in many competition laws around the world.

In the *Woodpulp* case[73] the ECJ had to assess whether a concerted practice engaged in by undertakings having their registered offices and production facilities

---

[71] ECJ (19 February 2002), Case C-309/99 – *Wouters and Others* [2002] ECR I-1577.   [72] Ibid., para. 109.

[73] ECJ (27 September 1988), Joined Cases C-89/85, C-104/85, C-114/85, C-116/85, C-117/85, C-125/85, C-126/85 to C-129/85 – *Ahlström Osakeyhtiö and Others v Commission (Woodpulp)* [1988] ECR 5193.

outside the EU falls into the ambit of Article 101(1) TFEU. The ECJ held that EU competition law prohibits all agreements between undertakings and concerted practices which may affect trade between Member States and which have as their object or effect the restriction of competition in the internal market. More specifically the court ruled:

It follows that where those producers concert on the prices to be charged to their customers in the Community [Union] and put that concertation into effect by selling at prices which are actually coordinated, they are taking part in concertation which has the object and effect of restricting competition within the common market within the meaning of Article 85 of the Treaty [Article 101 TFEU].[74]

The ECJ observed that if the applicability of prohibitions laid down under competition law were made to depend on the place where the agreement or practice was formed this would give undertakings an easy means of evading those prohibitions.[75]

Similar considerations apply to the jurisdiction of the Commission in merger control cases. Concentrations between undertakings which have their registered offices and production facilities outside the EU may still be subject to EU merger control if the turnover thresholds stipulated in the EUMR are exceeded. This was disputed in a case where a company established in South Africa notified to the Commission a number of transactions involving other South African entities held by a company incorporated under English law.[76] The Commission concluded that the proposed transactions would have created a dominant duopoly in the platinum group metal industry in the medium term and prohibited the transactions. None of the production sites of the companies involved were located in the EU, which led them to argue in the appeal procedure that the proposed transactions had no effect on competition in the EU and thus would not fall into the Commission's jurisdiction. The court clarified that for the EUMR to apply it is not required that the undertakings in question must be established in the EU or that the production activities covered by the concentration must be carried out within the EU territory.[77] The court held that the EUMR by setting quantitative thresholds based on the worldwide and EU turnover of the undertakings concerned rather ascribes greater importance to sales operations within the internal market as a factor linking the concentration to the EU.[78] If these turnover thresholds are exceeded it is assumed that the proposed transaction will have an effect on competition in the internal market and thus it will fall into the ambit of EU competition law including merger control by the Commission.

---

[74] Ibid., para. 13.   [75] Ibid., para. 16.
[76] General Court (hereinafter: GC) (25 March 1999), Case T-102/96 – *Gencor v Commission* [1999] ECR II-759.
[77] Ibid., para. 79.   [78] Ibid., para. 85.

The court also discussed the compatibility of this interpretation of the effects doctrine with public international law. Application of EU merger control law is justified under public international law when it is foreseeable that a proposed concentration will have an immediate and substantial effect in the EU.[79] A concentration that will lead to a dominant duopoly in the medium term has immediate effect if the creation of such position is not dependent on the future conduct of the undertakings arising from the concentration but from the characteristics of the market and the alteration of its structure. It is not required that a dominant duopoly position is abused to find an immediate effect on competition in the EU.[80] A substantial effect on competition was established in an appraisal of the market shares of the parties to the proposed transactions in the EU market. The market share enjoyed by the dominant duopoly was considered as giving rise to a substantial effect on competition in the EU market.[81] In conclusion, the ECJ did not find any violation of public international law by applying EU merger control law to a foreign-to-foreign transaction.

As a consequence of the effects doctrine, a behaviour relevant for competition in a world market or a number of national markets may be subject to review under several competition laws. The concepts under those competition laws are not harmonised, which may lead to diverging results in different jurisdictions.[82] This is particularly relevant in merger control law where a proposed transaction may obtain approval in some jurisdictions and may be prohibited in others. A prominent example is the GE/Honeywell concentration which was approved in the US but prohibited by the Commission[83] as reinforcing a dominant position in the market for jet engines.[84]

Summary of Section 6

As a general rule, the international applicability of the EU competition rules is determined under the effects doctrine. Under this doctrine any action that has a restrictive effect on competition in the EU falls into the ambit of EU competition law. There is no harmonised international system for competition law enforcement. A

---

[79] Ibid., para. 90.   [80] Ibid., para. 94.   [81] Ibid., para. 97.

[82] Competition authorities tend to cooperate though. Parties in merger cases pending simultaneously at the Commission and the US FTC are usually requested to grant a waiver which allows those authorities to share information about the transaction notified to them. On cooperation of competition authorities within and outside the EU see Canenbley and Rosenthal, 'Co-operation between Antitrust Authorities in- and outside the EU: What does it Mean for Multinational Cooperations?' – Part 1 and Part 2, *European Competition Law Review*, 26 (2005), 106 and 178; Burnside and Crossley, 'Co-operation in Competition: A New Era?' *European Competition Law Review*, 26 (2005), 234.

[83] Commission decision of 3 July 2001, Case COMP/M.2220 – *GE/Honeywell*, available at http://ec.europa.eu/competition/mergers/cases/decisions/m2220_20010703_610_en.pdf.

[84] The decision was upheld on appeal, GC (14 December 2005), Case T-210/01 – *General Electric v Commission* [2005] ECR II-5596.

behaviour that has an effect in several jurisdictions may be subject to review under several competition law regimes.

7. THE RELATIONSHIP BETWEEN EU AND NATIONAL COMPETITION LAW

7.1 General relationship between EU and national law

7.1.1 Direct effect

The relationship of EU law and national law is not explicitly set forth in the EU Treaty. However, there is case law of the European courts clarifying that EU law has a direct effect and can be invoked by individuals before national courts subject to certain conditions.

In the *Van Gend en Loos* case[85] which concerned a conflict between a Dutch customs regulation and a predecessor treaty of the TFEU the ECJ was asked for a preliminary ruling on the question whether nationals of a Member State on the basis of primary EU law can claim individual rights in a national court.

The ECJ ruled that the Treaty's objective is more than simply to set up an international agreement between States; it refers not only to governments, but also to peoples. As the ECJ stated:

the conclusion to be drawn from this is that the community constitutes a new legal order of international law for the benefit of which the states have limited their sovereign rights, albeit within limited fields, and the subjects of which comprise not only member states but also their nationals. Independently of the legislation of member states, community law therefore not only imposes obligations on individuals but is also intended to confer upon them rights which become part of their legal heritage.[86]

The judgment set out criteria for the direct effect of primary EU law, namely that the provision had to:

- be sufficiently clear and precisely stated;
- be non-conditional and not subject to further implementation; and
- confer a specific right on the citizen on which to base his claim.

As a consequence individuals are entitled to rely upon rights that they derive from Union measures if such Union measure is capable of having a direct effect.

---

[85] ECJ (5 February 1962), Case 26/62 – *NV Algemene Transport-en Expeditie van Gend en Loos v Nederlandse Belastingadministratie* [1963] ECR 3.
[86] Ibid., p. 12.

7.1.2 Supremacy (priority of application)

The decision in *Van Gend en Loos* requires Member States to give Union law as much effect as possible in national courts. A logical continuation of the doctrine of direct effect was the development of the doctrine of supremacy of Union law over national law in the event of a conflict.

An indication of this doctrine was given in *Van Gend en Loos*, but the court laid it down more clearly in the *Costa v ENEL* case:[87]

By creating a community of unlimited duration, having its own institutions, its own personality, its own legal capacity and capacity of representation on the international plane and, more particularly, real powers stemming from a limitation of sovereignty or a transfer of powers from the states to the community, the Member States have limited their sovereign rights and have thus created a body of law which binds both their nationals and themselves.[88]

The effect of this judgment is that, in the case of a conflict, Union law takes precedence over national law. The ECJ regarded such primacy as necessary in order to ensure the full effectiveness of EU law. The primacy of EU law is affirmed in a declaration attached to the Treaty:[89]

The Conference recalls that, in accordance with well settled case law of the Court of Justice of the European Union, the Treaties and the law adopted by the Union on the basis of the Treaties have primacy over the law of Member States, under the conditions laid down by the said case law.

7.2 Relationship between EU and national competition law

Following its decision in *Costa v ENEL* the ECJ further addressed the issue of the relationship between EU and national competition law in *Walt Wilhelm v Bundeskartellamt*.[90] In this case it was clarified that, in the event of a conflict, EU competition law would take precedence over national competition law.

Further steps have since been taken to clarify the relationship between EU and national competition law by the implementation of secondary legislation. Chapter I of Regulation 1/2003 specifically addresses the relationship between EU and national competition law.

Article 3(2) of Regulation 1/2003 stipulates the following:

The application of national competition law may not lead to the prohibition of agreements, decisions by associations of undertakings or concerted practices which may affect trade between Member States but which do not restrict competition within the meaning of Article 81(1) of

---

[87] ECJ (3 June 1964), Case 6/64 – *Costa v ENEL* [1964] ECR 585.   [88] Ibid., p. 593.
[89] Declaration concerning primacy (Declaration 17), OJ No. C 115 of 9 May 2008, p. 344.
[90] ECJ (13 February 1969), Case 14/68 – *Walt Wilhelm v Bundeskartellamt* [1969] ECR 1.

the Treaty [Article 101(3) TFEU], or which fulfil the conditions of Article 81(3) of the Treaty [Article 101(3) TFEU] or which are covered by a Regulation for the application of Article 81(3) of the Treaty [Article 101(3) TFEU]. Member States shall not under this Regulation be precluded from adopting and applying on their territory stricter national laws which prohibit or sanction unilateral conduct engaged in by undertakings.

This means that, where there is a conflict between national law and EU competition law, EU competition law prevails. Furthermore, the Member States are barred from applying diverging national law to anticompetitive agreements which are capable of having an effect on trade between Member States and are thus subject to EU competition law. This covers both directions: Member States may neither apply stricter nor more lenient rules to bi- or multilateral restrictions of competition if they have a nexus to the internal market. Since the concept of effect on trade between Member States is very broadly interpreted, there is little room for national law applying to agreements with local or regional effect only. In effect, national competition laws tend to be harmonised with EU competition law in the area of bi- or multilateral restrictions of competition and to employ the same concepts as EU competition law with the exception that no effect on inter-state trade is required.

Member States are, however, permitted to impose stricter rules in relation to unilateral restrictions of competition even if they fall into the ambit of EU competition law. Accordingly, if a certain unilateral practice restrictive of competition is not considered abusive under Article 102 TFEU it still has to be assessed whether this conduct may constitute an abuse of a dominant position under the respective national competition law. Also, national competition law may apply a different concept of dominance to that applied under EU competition law. The threshold to find dominance may be lower in Member States than at EU level or relative strength may suffice to make undertakings an addressee of the dominance rules.

Two exceptions are provided for in Article 3(3) Regulation 1/2003:

Without prejudice to general principles and other provisions of Community law, paragraphs 1 and 2 do not apply when the competition authorities and the courts of the Member States apply national merger control laws nor do they preclude the application of provisions of national law that predominantly pursue an objective different from that pursued by Articles 81 and 82 of the Treaty [Articles 101 and 102 TFEU].

Accordingly, national merger control is not prejudiced by EU competition law. National competition authorities may review concentrations that do not fall into the ambit of EU merger control. EU merger control applies to concentrations that exceed certain turnover thresholds. As a general rule, concentrations that do not exceed these thresholds are subject to review by national competition authorities.[91]

---

[91] The referral mechanisms that may apply although the EU notification thresholds are not exceeded are discussed in Chapter 5.

There may also be differences in the concept of concentration. EU merger control law may not cover certain types of transaction that are notifiable under national merger control law.

The second exception aims at national provisions that pursue predominantly an objective different from that of protecting competition on the market. For example, a law prohibiting unfair trading practices may be applied by national authorities and courts, be they unilateral or contractual, even if this leads to the prohibition of conduct that would be permissible under the EU competition rules.

Summary of Section 7

In case of conflict EU competition law takes priority over national competition law. EU competition law provides that the Member States may not apply stricter rules to bi- or multilateral restrictions of competition. However, in the area of unilateral restrictions Member States are free to adopt stricter rules.

8. ENFORCEMENT

8.1 Institutions involved in the enforcement of EU competition law

8.1.1 The Commission

The Commission is ascribed a key role in the enforcement of EU competition law. Article 105(1) TFEU entrusts to the Commission the task of ensuring 'the application of the principles laid down in Articles 101 and 102'. The Commission may investigate any violations of the EU competition rules when it receives a complaint or on its own motion. The Commission comprises a Directorate General (similar to a department) for each of its policy areas.

The Commission's Directorate General for Competition is the EU's 'competition authority' that carries out investigations of anticompetitive conduct, reviews merger notifications, and prepares a final decision after giving the undertakings involved an opportunity to express their views. It has to be noted that formal decisions are not adopted by the Directorate General for Competition but by the Commission as a whole. Article 250(1) TFEU stipulates that the 'Commission shall act by a majority of its Members'. All Commissioners will vote on whether a decision in the area of competition law is adopted. In this sense, there is a political review of the decisions prepared by the competition specialists of the Directorate General for Competition.

The Commission does not grant any approvals for conduct potentially restrictive of competition other than mergers. In the area of anticompetitive agreements undertakings have to assess themselves whether their conduct restricts competition in the sense of Article 101(1) TFEU and whether it qualifies for an exemption under Article 101(3) TFEU. This system of self-assessment is laid down in Article 1 Regulation 1/2003. It applies also to the abuse of a dominant position.

Under Article 10 Regulation 1/2003 the Commission may by decision declare certain conduct as either not restricting competition and therefore not falling into the ambit of Article 101(1) TFEU or as satisfying the criteria for an exemption stipulated in Article 101(3) TFEU. The Commission may also find a certain behaviour violates or does not violate Article 102 TFEU. Such findings of inapplicability on the Commission's own motion are reserved to exceptional needs for clarification and are not a tool for reviewing and approving individual cases for their compatibility with the competition rules. The purpose of such a finding of inapplicability is described in Recital 14 Regulation 1/2003 as 'clarifying the law and ensuring its consistent application', in particular with regard to 'new types of agreements or practices that have not been settled in the existing case-law and administrative practice'.

When undertakings encounter novel or unresolved questions for the application of the EU competition rules they may seek informal guidance from the Commission. According to Recital 38 Regulation 1/2003 the formal acts of the Commission provided for in that Regulation are without prejudice to the ability of the Commission to issue informal guidance to increase legal certainty.

In the application of the EU competition rules economic considerations have constantly gained importance in the last decades. The increasing influence of economic analysis for Commission decisions in the area of competition policy is reflected in the office of the Chief Competition Economist. The Chief Competition Economist is part of the Commission's Directorate General for Competition, and assists in evaluating the economic impact of its actions. The Chief Competition Economist provides independent guidance on methodological issues of economics and econometrics in the application of EU competition rules. He contributes to individual competition cases (in particular ones involving complex economic issues and quantitative analysis), to the development of general policy instruments, as well as assisting with cases pending before the EU courts.

8.1.2 The Advisory Committee on Restrictive Agreements and Dominant Position

Some of the Commission's draft decisions are discussed in the Advisory Committee on Restrictive Agreements and Dominant Position (hereinafter: the Advisory Committee), bringing together competition experts from the Member States. Before taking a decision to order an infringement to be brought to an end, to make binding the commitments offered by undertakings, to find Article 101(1) TFEU inapplicable or to impose a fine or periodic penalty payment on undertakings, the Commission will consult the Advisory Committee at one of its meetings or by written procedure.[92] The Advisory Committee is not consulted in merger cases though.

The Committee is made up of representatives of national competition authorities. It was established when the enforcement of EU competition law was still concentrated at the Commission to integrate the competition authorities of the Member States in the decision-making process.[93] After the transformation of the procedural rules into the current system of decentralised enforcement and self-assessment the Advisory Committee continues to be consulted by the Commission to obtain the views of the competition authorities of the Member States on draft decisions beyond the cooperation in the European Competition Network. The consultation process with the Advisory Committee is governed by Article 14 Regulation 1/2003.

The Advisory Committee delivers a written opinion on the Commission's preliminary draft decision. Reasons are only given for the positions stated in the opinion if one or more members request this. The opinions therefore tend to be short. The Commission 'shall take the utmost account of the opinion delivered by the Advisory Committee' according to Article 14(5) Regulation 1/2003 and inform the Advisory Committee of the manner in which its opinion has been taken into account.

Where the Advisory Committee delivers a written opinion, this opinion is appended to the draft decision. If the Advisory Committee recommends publication of the opinion, the Commission will publish the opinion in the Official Journal.

8.1.3 The Hearing Officer

The office of the Hearing Officer was created to safeguard the procedural rights of the undertakings which are subject to a procedure under the competition rules towards the Commission. The legal basis of the office of the Hearing Officer are the Terms of Reference of the Hearing Officer.[94] The office of the Hearing Officer is intended to be independent of the Commission's Directorate General for Competition. To this end, Hearing Officers are attached directly to the Commission member responsible for competition and not to the Directorate General for Competition. They are appointed by the Commission.

The Hearing Officer's main roles are to organise and conduct the oral hearing in competition cases and to act as an independent arbiter where a dispute on the

---

[92] For an example of a written opinion of the Advisory Committee in a cartel case, see Opinion of the Advisory Committee on restrictive agreements and dominant position given at its meeting of 5 December 2011 regarding a draft decision relating to Case COMP/39.600 – *Refrigeration compressors*, OJ No. C 122 of 27 April 2012, p. 2.

[93] The legal basis for the Advisory Committee in those times was Article 10 of Regulation 17/62, the predecessor procedural regulation of Regulation 1/2003 that expired on 30 April 2004.

[94] Decision of the President of the European Commission of 13 October 2011 on the function and terms of reference of the hearing officer in certain competition proceedings, OJ No. L 275 of 20 October 2011, p. 29, (hereinafter: the Terms of Reference).

effective exercise of procedural rights between parties and the Commission arises in competition proceedings. An undertaking involved in a competition proceeding may complain to the Hearing Officer if it believes that its procedural rights are not respected by the Commission.

Hearing Officers ensure respect of the right to be heard and may admit third parties to the oral hearing of a competition case if such party is sufficiently affected by the conduct which is the subject of the competition proceedings.[95]

The Hearing Officer also deals with specific issues that may arise in the investigative phase of Commission proceedings, including claims for legal professional privilege, the privilege against self-incrimination, deadlines for replying to decisions requiring information and the right of undertakings and associations of undertakings to be informed of their procedural status. For example, if an undertaking in the course of an inspection by the Commission claims that a certain document is covered by legal professional privilege and the Commission disputes such privilege, the undertaking may ask the Hearing Officer to examine the claim under Article 4 Terms of Reference. The Hearing Officer may review the document and any related documents that he considers necessary for his examination. Following the examination the Hearing Officer will formulate a preliminary view without revealing the content of the document and communicate this view to the responsible director at the Commission and to the undertaking and suggest a mutually acceptable resolution. If the undertaking and the Commission cannot agree on the qualification of the document, the Hearing Officer will submit a reasoned submission to the Commissioner responsible for competition who will decide the issue.

Before the Commission adopts a decision it will send out a draft decision to the potential addressees of the decision to give them an opportunity to present their views (so-called 'statement of objections'). The Commission will set a time limit for the response to the statement of objections. If an addressee of a statement of objections considers that the time limit is too short it may seek an extension by means of a reasoned request to the director responsible for the case under Article 9 Terms of Reference. If such a request is not granted or the applicant disagrees with the length of the extension granted, the request will be referred to the Hearing Officer to take a decision in light of the size and complexity of the file and any other objective obstacles which may be faced by the applicant.

Furthermore, the Hearing Officer has the task of protecting the right to access the file and the undertakings' legitimate interests in confidentiality. For example, where a party has reason to believe that the Commission has in its possession documents which have not been disclosed to it when it accessed the file it may submit a reasoned

---

[95] Article 5 Terms of Reference.

request to the Hearing Officer for access to this document under Article 7 Terms of Reference. The Hearing Officer will decide about access to the document and communicate his decision to the applicant.

After conducting a hearing in a competition case the Hearing Officer will submit an interim report to the Commissioner responsible for competition on the effective exercise of the procedural rights. When the Directorate General for Competition sends its draft decision to the Advisory Committee in the case in question, the Hearing Officer prepares a final report in writing on the respect of the effective exercise of the procedural rights at any stage of the proceedings under Article 16 Terms of Reference. The Hearing Officer's final report, together with the draft decision, is presented to the Commission which will publish it in the Official Journal together with the decision once it is adopted.

8.1.4 The European Ombudsman

The European Ombudsman (hereinafter: the Ombudsman) is an institution created to fight maladministration in the activities of the EU institutions and bodies and to make recommendations with a view to putting an end to it. The European courts are exempt from the investigations of the Ombudsman due to their judicial role.

The office of the Ombudsman has its legal foundation in Article 228 TFEU. The Ombudsman is elected by the European Parliament and is intended to be completely independent in the performance of his duties. To this end, the Ombudsman may not, during his term of office, engage in any other occupation, whether gainful or not. The Ombudsman may be dismissed only by the ECJ at the request of the European Parliament if he no longer fulfils the conditions required for the performance of his duties or if he is guilty of serious misconduct.

The Ombudsman is empowered by Article 228 TFEU to receive complaints from any citizen of the EU or any natural or legal person residing or having its registered office in a Member State concerning instances of maladministration. The Ombudsman can conduct inquiries for which he finds grounds, either on his own initiative or on the basis of complaints submitted to him directly or through a Member of the European Parliament, except where the alleged facts are or have been the subject of legal proceedings. To fulfil his duties, the Ombudsman is entitled to request from the EU institutions any information, as well as access to the files concerned. Officials and other servants of the EU institutions must testify at the request of the Ombudsman.[96] The Ombudsman may also request information from the authorities of the Member States that may help to clarify instances of maladministration by EU institutions.

---

[96] The powers of the Ombudsman are laid down in the Statute of the European Ombudsman, Decision of the European Parliament on the regulations and general conditions governing the performance of the Ombudsman's duties, OJ No. L 113 of 4 May 1994, p. 15 as amended.

The Ombudsman will seek a solution with the institution concerned to eliminate the instance of maladministration and to satisfy the complaint. If the Ombudsman considers that such cooperation has been successful, he closes the case with a reasoned decision of which he will inform the complainant and the institution.[97] Where the Ombudsman establishes an instance of maladministration and fails to reach a solution with the institution concerned, he refers the matter to the institution, body, office or agency concerned, which has a period of three months in which to inform him of its views. The Ombudsman will then forward a report to the European Parliament and the institution, body, office or agency concerned. The person lodging the complaint will also be informed of the outcome of such inquiries.

In the area of competition law[98] complaints to the Ombudsman typically relate to access to documents in the Commission's file which the Commission refuses to grant.[99] In the *E.ON* case,[100] for example, a third party had applied for access to a preliminary assessment drafted by the Commission's Directorate General for Competition in the context of a competition law investigation of the German energy supplier E.ON. The Commission expressed in the preliminary assessment concerns that certain practices of E.ON might be incompatible with EU competition law. E.ON submitted commitments to the Commission in order to address those concerns.

The complainant applied for access to the preliminary assessment under Regulation 1049/2001,[101] the so-called Transparency Regulation which governs access of the public to documents in the files of the EU institutions. The application was rejected by the Commission which invoked certain exceptions from the general obligation to give access to documents upon request. The applicant turned to the Ombudsman and claimed that the rejection of his applications amounted to maladministration.

In his decision the Ombudsman reviewed the Commission's rejection in light of the case law of the European courts on the interpretation of the Transparency Regulation. He found the rejection to be justified under the case law and concluded that there was

---

[97] See Article 6.2 of the Implementing Provisions of the European Ombudsman, Decision of the European Ombudsman adopting implementing provisions, adopted on 8 July 2002, as amended. Available at: www.ombudsman.europa.eu/resources/provisions.faces.

[98] For a description of the role of the Ombudsman in competition law procedures see Diamandouros, 'Improving EU Competition Law Procedures by Applying Principles of Good Administration: The Role of the Ombudsman', *Journal of European Competition Law and Practice*, 1 (2010), 379.

[99] On the competences of the Ombudsman when reviewing complaints relating to access to file in competition cases see Amory and Desmedt, 'The European Ombudsman's First Scrutiny of the EC Commission in Antitrust Matters', *European Competition Law Review*, 30 (2009), 205. For an analysis of a decision of the Ombudsman on a complaint relating to another issue than access to file (failure to take notes during a meeting) see Diamandouros, 'Improving EU Competition Law Procedures', 380.

[100] Decision of the European Ombudsman closing his inquiry into complaint 2953/2008/FOR against the European Commission, 27 July 2010, available at www.ombudsman.europa.eu/en/cases/decision.faces.

[101] Regulation (EC) No. 1049/2001 of the European Parliament and of the Council of 30 May 2001 regarding public access to European Parliament, Council and Commission documents, OJ No. L 145 of 31 May 2001, p. 43.

no maladministration of the Commission.[102] The review of decisions of the Commission in light of the relevant jurisprudence gives the procedures conducted by the Ombudsman certain similarities with a judicial review. However, the Ombudsman cannot adopt any decisions setting aside an act of the Commission or clarifying questions that have been open under the case law so far.[103] To distinguish the Ombudsman's inquiry into an alleged case of maladministration from judicial review it is expressly stated in the decision:

It must be recalled that the highest authority on the meaning and interpretation of European Union law is the Court of Justice.[104]

The relationship between an inquiry of the Ombudsman and judicial review is also addressed in the Statute of the Ombudsman. If the complainant brings an action against the institution which he accuses of maladministration before a European court which concerns the same facts as the complaint to the Ombudsman, the Ombudsman is bound under Articles 1(3) and 2(7) Statute of the Ombudsman to terminate his consideration of the complaint. An example of such a case from the competition area is the *Marine Hoses* case.[105] Again, the complainant had sought access to a Commission document which was denied. He turned to the Ombudsman and also appealed the respective Commission decision in court.[106] Since the complaint and the appeal were largely based on the same facts and arguments, the Ombudsman terminated his consideration of the complaint.

8.1.5 The Court of Justice of the European Union

The Court of Justice of the European Union is the court competent to review decisions of the Commission in competition law cases. The court also rules on the interpretation of EU competition law if such interpretation is disputed in an action pending before a national court.

The Court of Justice of the European Union comprises two judicial bodies: the Court of Justice and the General Court.

Decisions of the Commission can be appealed by natural and legal persons at the General Court on points of fact and of law. The competence of the General Court for

---

[102] On the legal nature of decisions of the Ombudsman and their quality of being subject of court actions at the European courts see Tsadiras, 'The Position of the European Ombudsman in the Community System of Judicial Remedies', *European Law Review*, 35 (2007), 607.

[103] Ibid., on the institutional relationship between the Ombudsman and the European courts.

[104] Decision of the European Ombudsman closing his inquiry into complaint 2953/2008/FOR against the European Commission, 27 July 2010, para. 50.

[105] Decision of the European Ombudsman closing his inquiry into complaint 543/2009/VL against the European Commission, 8 February 2010, available at www.ombudsman.europa.eu/en/cases/decision.faces.

[106] On the case law of the European courts on access to documents see Goddin, 'Recent Judgments regarding Transparency and Access to Documents in the Field of Competition Law: Where Does the Court of Justice of the EU Strike the Balance?', *Journal of European Competition Law and Practice*, 3 (2011), 10.

such appeals is provided for in Article 256(1) TFEU. Judgments of the General Court can be appealed on points of law at the Court of Justice.

The procedure to appeal a Commission decision is the action for annulment laid down in Article 263 TFEU. Under Article 263(4) TFEU any natural or legal person may institute proceedings against an act of an EU institution addressed to that person or which is of direct and individual concern to it. In many competition cases the addressees of a Commission decision imposing a fine or declaring a proposed transaction incompatible with the internal market appeal that decision in an action for annulment. In particular, there is an abundance of judgments concerning Commission decisions imposing a fine for cartel conduct.[107]

Courts of the Member States may have to apply EU competition law in a procedure pending before them. If a dispute on the interpretation of EU law arises that is relevant for the outcome of the procedure the national court has to refer the question on the interpretation of EU law to the ECJ for a preliminary ruling under Article 267 TFEU. It has to be noted that the national court must not refer the entire case to the Court of Justice but has to formulate a precise but abstract question on the interpretation of EU law. The ECJ will review such question and provide an abstract answer in the judgment which the national court has to apply to the specific case pending before it. A typical scenario for a preliminary ruling is a dispute between business partners on the validity of a contract. One party may claim that the contract is void because of a violation of EU competition law due to a certain clause included in it. If there is no case law or other binding act of an EU institution on the compatibility of this type of clause with EU competition law the national court may refer to the ECJ the question whether this type of clause is compatible with EU law. The purpose of such preliminary rulings is to ensure a uniform interpretation of EU law by national courts. There is no second instance at EU level in an action for a preliminary ruling since the first (and last) instance is the ECJ.

8.1.6 National competition authorities

Article 5 Regulation 1/2003 empowers the competition authorities of the Member States to apply Articles 101 and 102 TFEU.[108] This decentralised approach is intended to reduce the Commission's workload by including further authorities in the enforcement of the competition rules that can handle more cases.[109] In effect, many more

---

[107] On the success rate of actions for annulment see Tridimas and Gari, 'Winners and Losers in Luxembourg: A Statistical Analysis of Judicial Review before the European Court of Justice and the Court of First Instance (2001–2005)', *European Law Review*, **38** (2010), 131.

[108] On the duty of national competition authorities to apply EU competition law see Gerber and Cassinis, 'The "Modernisation" of European Community Competition Law: Achieving Consistency in Enforcement' – Part I, *European Competition Law Review*, **27** (2006), 10, 12.

[109] On the implications of the system of shared executive competences for the federal structure of the EU see Schütze, 'From Rome to Lisbon: "Executive Federalism" in the (New) European Union', *Common Market Law Review*, **47** (2010), 1385, 1404.

potential violations of the EU competition rules are investigated by the national competition authorities than by the Commission. In 2011, the Commission investigated 26 cases while national competition authorities investigated 137 cases of potential infringement of Articles 101 or 102 TFEU.[110]

Regulation 1/2003 provides for a number of alternative decisions to be taken by a national competition authority to conclude its investigation. A national competition authority may require that an infringement be brought to an end, ordering interim measures or accept commitments. Where on the basis of the information in their possession the conditions for prohibition are not met they may likewise decide that there are no grounds for action on their part.[111]

This determines to a certain extent the procedural powers of national competition authorities since national procedural rules need to provide for the options enumerated in Regulation 1/2003.[112]

A national competition authority may also impose a fine, periodic penalty payment or any other penalty provided for under national law for a violation of the EU competition rules. This may lead to a divergence of sanctions depending on whether the Commission or a national competition authority investigates a certain anticompetitive conduct and ultimately imposes sanctions against the undertakings involved.

8.1.7 National courts

National courts are empowered to apply Articles 101 and 102 TFEU by Article 6 Regulation 1/2003.[113] This may be the case where a decision of a national competition authority applying EU competition law is appealed under national procedural law or in civil litigation relating to an alleged anticompetitive conduct. Civil litigation may arise where the validity of a contract is disputed that potentially infringes Article 101 or 102 TFEU or where damages are sought from a cartel member.

There are numerous judgments from national courts applying the EU competition rules,[114] which brings about a risk of diverging interpretations of EU law. However, national courts are not entitled to interpret EU competition law in the sense that

---

[110] Statistics of the European Competition Network (hereinafter: the ECN), available at http://ec.europa.eu/competition/ecn/statistics.html.

[111] On the right of national competition authorities to act as a defendant in appeal proceedings concerning the legality of its decisions based upon Article 101 or 102 TFEU see Galletti, 'Effectiveness of EU Competition Law vs. National Procedural Autonomy', *European Law Review*, **39** (2011), 119; Rizzuto, 'The Procedural Implications of VEBIC', *European Competition Law Review*, **32** (2011), 285.

[112] On the consideration of non-competition interests by national competition authorities see Lavrijssen, 'What Role for National Competition Authorities in Protecting Non-competition Interests after Lisbon?' *European Law Review*, **38** (2010), 636.

[113] Arbitrators may also have to apply the EU competition rules, see Stylopoulos, 'Powers and Duties of Arbitrators in the Application of Competition Law: An EC approach in the Light of Recent Developments', *European Competition Law Review*, **30** (2009), 118.

[114] For an overview see Commission's national courts cases database http://ec.europa.eu/competition/elojade/antitrust/nationalcourts/.

they may develop it further on points that had been open before or that they may overrule previous case law. National courts may only apply EU competition law if its interpretation is clear in light of the case law of the European courts and other legal acts of the EU institutions. If there are doubts arising with regard to the interpretation of EU competition law in a procedure pending before a national court it has to formulate a question and to refer it to the ECJ for a preliminary ruling under Article 267 TFEU.

8.2 Coordination of enforcement of EU competition law between EU and Member State institutions

8.2.1 Principle of sincere cooperation

The decentralised enforcement of EU competition law under Regulation 1/2003 carries the risk of parallel enforcement actions of the Commission and national competition authorities that may ultimately result in divergent decisions with regard to the same set of facts. Also, there is a risk that national courts rule on a set of facts that is already subject of an investigation or decision by the Commission. Accordingly, enforcement of EU competition law has to be coordinated between the Commission and the national competition authorities and courts. The measures taken to coordinate the enforcement ensure that enforcement action by EU institutions takes priority over national enforcement action by a competition authority or a court. The obligation of national institutions not to frustrate any EU enforcement action has its legal basis in the principle of sincere cooperation under the EU Treaty. The principle of sincere cooperation stems from Article 4 TEU in the context of relations between the EU and Member States.

In substance, this Article states that the Member States must take all appropriate measures to fulfil their obligations arising out of the Treaty and do nothing detrimental to the proper functioning of the EU. Member States have a duty of sincere cooperation with the EU institutions. Accordingly, they are asked to support EU activities and not to hinder their proper functioning.

Before Regulation 1/2003 entered into force on 1 May 2004, the relationship between enforcement by the Commission and national authorities and courts was governed by the principle of sincere cooperation and the case law of the European courts. In the *Masterfoods* case[115] the ECJ had ruled that national enforcement action may never run counter to EU enforcement action.[116] The case concerned a scenario

---

[115] ECJ (14 December 2000), Case C-344/98 – *Masterfoods Ltd v HB Ice Cream Ltd* [2000] ECR I-11369, paras. 45–60.

[116] For a detailed analysis of the judgment see Komninos, 'Effect of Commission Decisions on Private Antitrust Litigation: Setting the Story Straight', *Common Market Law Review*, **44** (2007), 1387.

where an Irish court had found that a certain behaviour by an undertaking did not violate Article 101 and Article 102 TFEU. While an appeal against this judgment was pending the Commission adopted a decision on the same behaviour and found it to violate Articles 101 and 102 TFEU. The decision was appealed in the General Court. The Irish Supreme Court in its request for a preliminary ruling asked the ECJ whether it had an obligation under the principle of sincere cooperation to stay the procedure while a procedure was pending at the EU courts. This was confirmed by the ECJ which held:

It is also clear from the case-law of the Court that the Member States' duty under Article 5 of the EC Treaty [Article 4 TEU] to take all appropriate measures, whether general or particular, to ensure fulfilment of the obligations arising from Community law and to abstain from any measure which could jeopardise the attainment of the objectives of the Treaty is binding on all the authorities of Member States including, for matters within their jurisdiction, the courts.[117]

These principles have been incorporated into Regulation 1/2003.

8.2.2 Regulation 1/2003

a) Cooperation between the Commission and national competition authorities

When competition authorities of the Member States rule on agreements, decisions or practices under Article 101 or Article 102 TFEU which are already the subject of a Commission decision, they are barred by Article 16(2) Regulation 1/2003 from taking decisions which would run counter to the decision adopted by the Commission. However, this provision would not avoid a scenario in which the competition authority of a Member State adopts a decision while an investigation of the Commission into the same set of facts is still pending and no decision has yet been adopted by the Commission. Article 11 Regulation 1/2003 therefore provides for a close cooperation of the Commission and the competition authorities of the Member States.

The cooperation entails that the competition authorities of the Member States inform the Commission in writing before or immediately commencing the first formal investigative measure to enforce Article 101 or 102 TFEU. No later than 30 days before the adoption of a final decision the competition authorities of the Member States have to inform the Commission about their intended decision. To that effect, they provide the Commission with a summary of the case, the envisaged decision or, in the absence thereof, any other document indicating the proposed course of action.

Furthermore, the initiation by the Commission of a proceeding under Regulation 1/2003 relieves the competition authorities of the Member States of their competence to apply Articles 101 and 102 TFEU according to Article 11(6) Regulation 1/2003. If a

---

[117] ECJ (14 December 2000), Case C-344/98 – *Masterfoods Ltd v HB Ice Cream Ltd* [2000] ECR I-11369, para. 49.

competition authority of a Member State is already acting on a case, the Commission can initiate proceedings only after consulting with that national competition authority.[118]

b) Cooperation between the Commission and national courts

With regard to the relationship between the Commission and national courts the same questions arise as between the Commission and national competition authorities. National courts may hand down a judgment on a set of facts that is under investigation by the Commission or a case may be brought before a national court that has been decided upon already by the Commission.[119]

Article 16(1) Regulation 1/2003 provides that national courts cannot take decisions running counter to the decision adopted by the Commission when they apply Article 101 or 102 TFEU. In addition, they must avoid giving decisions which would conflict with a decision contemplated by the Commission in proceedings it has initiated. To this end, the court may have to stay the proceeding until the Commission has adopted a decision and this decision has become final in the sense that either the time limit for an appeal has expired or the European courts have ruled on it.

The duty to cooperate requires that the Commission and national courts exchange information about proceedings pending before them.

To ensure the close cooperation between the Commission and national courts the Commission, acting on its own initiative, may submit written observations to courts of the Member States.[120] With the permission of the court in question, it may also make oral observations. Member States shall forward to the Commission a copy of any written judgment deciding on the application of Articles 101 or 102 TFEU under Article 15 Regulation 1/2003.[121]

c) Coordination between institutions of the Member States

The decentralised application of EU competition law may also create a need for coordination between competition authorities or courts of the Member States to avoid diverging decisions on the same set of facts.

---

[118] If the Commission decides to investigate a case the undertaking subject to the investigation has no right to request that a national competition authority would be better placed to investigate the case, see Schütze, 'From Rome to Lisbon', 1415.

[119] For a detailed discussion of the interaction of public enforcement by the Commission and private enforcement through procedures before national courts in cartel cases see Komninos, 'Effect of Commission Decisions on Private Antitrust Litigation', 1387.

[120] On those written observations see Wright, 'European Commission Interventions as Amicus Curiae in National Competition Cases: The Preliminary Reference in X BV', *European Competition Law Review*, 30 (2009), 309.

[121] On the Commission's procedural tools to promote consistency of the application of EU competition law in detail see Gerber and Cassinis, 'The "Modernisation" of European Community Competition Law', 10, 14.

Article 13 Regulation 1/2003 therefore stipulates rules for the suspension or termination of proceedings. Where competition authorities of two or more Member States have received a complaint or are acting on their own initiative under Article 101 or Article 102 TFEU against the same agreement, decision of an association or practice, the fact that one authority is dealing with the case shall be sufficient grounds for the others to suspend the proceedings before them or to reject the complaint. The Commission may likewise reject a complaint on the ground that a competition authority of a Member State is dealing with the case. Furthermore, where a competition authority of a Member State or the Commission has received a complaint against an agreement, decision of an association or practice which has already been dealt with by another competition authority, it may reject it.

In addition to the mechanisms laid down in Regulation 1/2003, the Commission and the national competition authorities cooperate in the European Competition Network (ECN).[122] The ECN is intended to ensure an efficient division of work and an effective and consistent application of the EU competition rules. The EU Commission and competition authorities from EU Member States cooperate with each other through the ECN by informing each other of new cases and envisaged enforcement decisions, coordinating investigations,[123] where necessary, and exchanging evidence and other information[124] to which they are entitled under Article 12 Regulation 1/2003.[125]

The basic foundations of the functioning of the ECN are laid out in the Commission Notice on cooperation within the Network of Competition Authorities[126] and in the Joint Statement of the Council and the Commission on the Functioning of the Network of Competition Authorities.[127]

Under the principles of case allocation of the ECN a case should be investigated by a competition authority that is 'well placed' for such investigation.[128] A single

---

[122] The cooperation of competition authorities in the EU is discussed in detail by Burnside and Crossley, 'Co-operation in Competition: A New Era?', 234.

[123] The coordination of investigations within the ECN is complemented by an ECN Model Leniency Programme, see Gauer and Jaspers, 'Designing a European Solution for a "One-Stop Leniency Shop"', *European Competition Law Review*, **27** (2006), 685.

[124] On the exchange of information within the ECN in general see Reichelt, 'To what Extent Does the Co-operation within the European Competition Network Protect the Rights of Undertakings?', *Common Market Law Review*, **42** (2005), 745, 751.

[125] For an in-depth analysis of cooperation within the ECN see Cengiz, 'Multi-level Governance in Competition Policy: the European Competition Network', *European Law Review*, **38** (2010), 660.

[126] Commission Notice on cooperation within the Network of Competition Authorities, OJ No. C 101 of 27 April 2004, p. 43. On the case allocation mechanism under this Notice see Brammer, 'Concurrent Jurisdiction under Regulation 1/2003 and the Issue of Case Allocation', *Common Market Law Review*, **42** (2005), 1383.

[127] Joint Statement of the Council and the Commission on the functioning of the network of Competition Authorities, available at http://ec.europa.eu/competition/ecn/joint_statement_en.pdf.

[128] For a detailed discussion of the concept of 'well placed authority' see Brammer, 'Concurrent Jurisdiction under Regulation 1/2003', 1383, 1388.

competition authority is usually well placed to deal with agreements or practices that substantially affect competition mainly within its territory. Single action may also be appropriate where the action of a single competition authority is sufficient to bring the entire infringement to an end although several competition authorities are well placed for an investigation. There are also instances of parallel action of two or three competition authorities where an agreement or practice has substantial effects on competition mainly in their respective territories and the action of only one competition authority would not suffice to bring the entire infringement to an end or to sanction it adequately. This may be the case where a market-sharing cartel allocates one Member State to a first cartel member located in that Member State and another Member State to another cartel member that is located in that second Member State.

The Commission is considered to be well placed if an agreement or practice has effects on competition in more than three Member States. Moreover, the Commission is well placed if the Union interest requires the adoption of a Commission decision to develop EU competition policy when a new competition issue arises or to ensure effective enforcement.[129]

In order to detect multiple procedures and to ensure that cases are dealt with by a well-placed competition authority the members of the network inform each other at an early stage about the cases pending before them.[130] Cases may be reallocated following such information.[131]

The allocation of cases may have far reaching consequences for the undertakings which are the subject of the respective procedure. Regulation 1/2003 does not provide for any harmonisation of the procedural rules applied by national competition authorities beyond the very general provisions for decisions concluding an investigation of an infringement of Article 101 or Article 102 TFEU. The competition authority in one country may enjoy more investigative powers than the competition authority of another country. A behaviour that could not be proved to have violated the EU competition rules in the second country may be sanctioned in the first country. The same considerations apply to the exchange of information within the ECN since there may be different concepts of legal privilege in different Member States. Information that could not be obtained in one Member State due to procedural law could be provided by another Member State which obtained it under different procedural rules. Commentators therefore argue that case allocation and

---

[129] On the case allocation system see Andreangeli, 'The Impact of the Modernisation Regulation on the Guarantees of Due Process in Competition Proceedings', *European Law Review*, 34 (2006), 342, 343.

[130] On potential conflicts of jurisdiction see Brammer, 'Concurrent Jurisdiction under Regulation 1/2003', 1383, 1401.

[131] Commentators have identified problems of due process caused by the 'opacity' of network management within the ECN, see Cengiz, 'Multi-level Governance in Competition Policy', 660.

information exchange[132] within the ECN lead to problems of due process and potentially also an infringement of the right of defence.[133]

Summary of Section 8

EU competition law is enforced both by EU and national institutions. The Commission is the main enforcement body of EU competition law at EU level. The Commission will investigate individual cases and adopt decisions binding on the parties. Before adopting a decision the Commission will consult the Advisory Committee on Restrictive Agreements and Dominant Position in which the Member States are represented through competition experts.

The role of the Hearing Officer is to safeguard the procedural rights of parties to an investigation by the Commission. Before a final decision is adopted by the Commission, the Hearing Officer may hold a hearing to give all stakeholders an opportunity to present their views. The Hearing Officer will then send a report on the effective exercise of the procedural rights to the Commission.

The European Ombudsman reviews complaints about cases of maladministration in the EU institutions. The Ombudsman will seek a solution with the institution concerned to eliminate the instance of maladministration and to satisfy the complaint. If no adequate solution can be found, the European Ombudsman will inform the European Parliament. In the area of competition law most complaints received by the European Ombudsman relate to disputes about access to file.

Decisions of the Commission can be challenged before the ECJ. The ECJ comprises two judicial bodies. The General Court is the lower instance court and will review cases brought by private litigants in first instance on points of fact and of law. An appeal on points of law may be lodged with the ECJ against judgments of the General Court.

National competition authorities are also entitled to apply EU competition law. National courts also have to observe it. This requires a coordination mechanism in order to avoid diverging decisions of EU and national institutions. National competition authorities will inform the Commission before they take any formal investigative measure in relation to an alleged violation of the EU competition rules. If the Commission commences a procedure, national competition authorities automatically lose competence to review the same set of facts under EU competition law. National courts may not hand down a judgment that runs counter to a Commission decision.

---

[132] On the issues of due process arising from the exchange of information and its use in evidence in other Member States see Andreangeli, 'The Impact of the Modernisation Regulation', 342, 346. On the information exchange mechanism within the ECN in general see Brammer, 'Concurrent Jurisdiction under Regulation 1/2003', 1383, 1392.

[133] On the impact of cooperation of the competition authorities within the ECN on the right of defence see Andreangeli, 'The Impact of the Modernisation Regulation', 342, 348; Reichelt, 'To what Extent Does the Co-operation within the European Competition Network Protect the Rights of Undertakings?', 745.

To this end, national courts and the Commission inform each other about pending procedures. A court may have to stay a procedure until the Commission has adopted a decision. The Commission has also the right to submit written observations to the courts of Member States in proceedings under EU competition law.

The plurality of national enforcement bodies also requires coordination between the authorities and courts of Member States. To this end the European Competition Network has been established. Within this network national competition authorities cooperate by informing each other of new cases and envisaged enforcement decisions, coordinating investigations, where necessary, and exchanging evidence and other information. As a general rule, a case will be allocated to the enforcement body that is best placed for the respective investigation. This is usually the authority in the Member State in which the case to be assessed has the strongest impact.

QUESTIONS ON CHAPTER 1

1. What is the benefit of competition? (A.1)
2. Please describe the central idea of competition. (A.2)
3. Please describe the concept of perfect competition. (A.3)
4. What are the detrimental effects of monopoly? (A.4)
5. What are the characteristics of oligopolistic competition? (A.5)
6. Please describe the concept of effective competition. (A.6)
7. In what situations may the market mechanism have to be complemented by further policies? (A.7)
8. Please describe the role of market integration in EU competition law. (B.2)
9. What types of law does EU competition law comprise? (B.3)
10. What is the role of the Charter and the ECHR for EU competition law? (B.4)
11. What are the conditions for international applicability of EU competition law? (B.6)
12. What is the relationship between EU and national competition law? (B.7.2)
13. Please describe the Commission's role in the enforcement of EU competition law. (B.8.1.1)
14. What is the role of the Hearing Officer in competition cases? (B.8.1.3)
15. Please describe the function of the ECJ in EU competition law. (B.8.1.5)
16. Are national competition authorities and national courts also involved in the enforcement of EU competition law? (B.8.1.6–7)
17. What are the principles for cooperation of EU and national institutions in the enforcement of EU competition law under Regulation 1/2003? (B.8.2)

SUGGESTED ESSAY TOPICS

1. The concept of effective competition in EU competition law
2. Limitations of the scope of application of EU competition law
3. The impact of the market integration goal on EU competition law

2 Key concepts of Article 101 TFEU

1. THE SCHEME OF ARTICLE 101 TFEU

Article 101 TFEU is one of the three pillars of EU competition law.[1] It prohibits restrictive agreements between independent market operators acting either at the same level of the economy (horizontal agreements), often as actual or potential competitors, or at different levels (vertical agreements), mostly as producer and distributor.[2] It also precludes decisions by associations of undertakings and concerted practices. These three types of coordinated market behaviour fall into the ambit of EU competition law if they may affect trade between Member States to an appreciable extent and if they have as their object or effect the prevention, restriction or distortion of competition within the internal market.

1.1 The prohibition – Article 101(1) TFEU

Article 101 TFEU consists of three paragraphs the first of which sets out a general prohibition. It precludes any form of collusion between undertakings which may have an adverse effect on undistorted competition within the internal market. The provision contains a list of different prohibited market conduct types. The list is not exhaustive and comprises the following examples:

- direct or indirect fixing of purchase or selling prices or any other trading conditions;
- limiting or controlling production, markets, technical development, or investment;

---

[1] The other ones being Article 102 TFEU (prohibits the abuse of a dominant position) and the EU Merger Regulation.

[2] On the distinction between horizontal and vertical agreements and the differences in the concept of agreement applied to horizontal and vertical relationships, see Lianos, 'Collusion in Vertical Relations under Article 81 EC', *Common Market Law Review*, 45 (2008), 1027, 1030.

- sharing of markets or sources of supply;
- applying dissimilar conditions to equivalent transactions with other trading parties, thereby placing them at a competitive disadvantage;
- making the conclusion of contracts subject to acceptance by the other parties of supplementary obligations which, by their nature or according to commercial usage, have no connection with the subject of such contracts.

These types of anticompetitive behaviour are discussed in detail in Section 5 below.

In general, market conduct is prohibited under Article 101(1) TFEU if the following criteria are met:

- the market conduct occurs between undertakings (or within an association of undertakings);
- the market conduct coordinates the market behaviour of several undertakings (collusion);
- the market conduct has as its object or effect the prevention, restriction or distortion of competition;
- it has an appreciable effect on competition;
- it has an appreciable effect on trade between Member States.

All of these five criteria will be discussed in detail below.

1.2 Nullity – Article 101(2) TFEU

Article 101(2) TFEU governs the legal consequences of a violation of the prohibition contained in the first paragraph of the provision. Any agreement, decision or concerted practice in breach of Article 101(1) TFEU is automatically void. Beyond these automatic civil law consequences, competition authorities can impose fines on undertakings that are involved in anticompetitive practices.

1.3 Legal exemption – Article 101(3) TFEU

Article 101(3) TFEU provides for an exemption from the prohibition of coordinated market behaviour as stipulated in Article 101(1) TFEU. Generally speaking, an agreement or practice is exempted from the cartel prohibition when its beneficial aspects outweigh its distortive effects.

There are individual exemptions and so-called 'block exemptions'. For some types of agreements which are of particular practical relevance the Commission has enacted block exemption regulations. Agreements falling into the scope of a block exemption benefit from Article 101(3) TFEU. If no block exemption is available, agreements may qualify for an individual exemption. Originally, this individual exemption could be granted only by the Commission. However, since the adoption of Regulation 1/2003 which introduced major changes into the procedural rules for the application of EU competition law, undertakings can no longer apply for an individual exemption at the Commission. Under Regulation 1/2003, undertakings have to assess themselves whether the agreement in question justifies an individual exemption. Article 101(3) TFEU is a legal exception that applies automatically if the criteria stipulated therein are satisfied.

1.4 Interpretation

When interpreting Article 101 TFEU, the ECJ does not stick to the exact analysis of individual words and phrases within the Article, but gives greater weight to the aims and objectives pursued by EU competition policy in general. A 'teleological' approach prevails since the ECJ places more importance on the accordance of the particular interpretation with the Treaty's goals and principles.

Consumer welfare is one of the ultimate goals of Article 101 TFEU.[3] The Commission in recent years stressed the role of consumer welfare for EU competition policy in many of its notices and guidance notes.[4] Competition commissioner Joaquín Almunia has followed his predecessors' policy by maintaining that consumer welfare is at the heart of the Commission's policy and that its achievement drives the Commission's priorities and guides its decisions.[5] Similar statements had earlier been made by Neelie Kroes[6] and Mario Monti.[7]

In its Guidelines on the application of Article 101(3) TFEU the Commission states:

The objective of Article [101 TFEU] is to protect competition on the market as a means of enhancing consumer welfare and of ensuring an efficient allocation of resources. Competition and market integration serve these ends since the creation and preservation of an open single market promotes an efficient allocation of resources throughout the Community for the benefit of consumers.[8]

---

[3] For a discussion of whether consumer welfare is a goal of competition policy, see Kalbfleisch, 'Aiming for Alliance: Competition Law and Consumer Welfare', *Journal of European Competition Law and Practice*, 3 (2011), 108.

[4] On the role of competition policy for consumer protection from an economic point of view, see Smith and King, 'Does Competition Law Adequately Protect Consumers?', *European Competition Law Review*, 28 (2007), 412. For a comparative analysis of the role of consumer welfare in EU and UK competition policy, see Marsden and Whelan, '"Consumer Detriment" and its Application in EC and UK Competition Law', *European Competition Law Review*, 27 (2006), 569.

[5] Commission, SPEECH/10/233, delivered 12 May 2010.

[6] See, e.g., Commission, SPEECH/09/486, delivered 21 October 2009; SPEECH/09/420, delivered 29 September 2009; SPEECH/09/408, delivered 24 September 2009.

[7] See, e.g., Commission, Speech delivered 22 October 2004; SPEECH/04/212, delivered 29 April 2004; SPEECH/03/489, delivered 24 October 2003.

[8] Commission Guidelines on the application of Article 81(3) of the Treaty, OJ No. C 101 of 27 April 2004, p. 97, para. 13.

The General Court followed the approach of the Commission and emphasised the role of consumer welfare as a goal of EU competition policy in the *GlaxoSmithKline Services* case. The court held:

[T]he objective assigned to Article [101(1) TFEU], which constitutes a fundamental provision indispensable for the achievement of the missions entrusted to the Community, in particular for the functioning of the internal market [...] is to prevent undertakings, by restricting competition between themselves or with third parties, from reducing the welfare of the final consumer of the products in question ...[9]

Upon appeal, the ECJ, however, rejected the notion of the role of consumer welfare as a dominant goal of EU competition policy and placed it into a line of several other goals of similar importance:

First of all, there is nothing in that provision to indicate that only those agreements which deprive consumers of certain advantages may have an anticompetitive object. Secondly, it must be borne in mind that the Court has held that, like other competition rules laid down in the Treaty, Article [101(1) TFEU] aims to protect not only the interests of competitors or of consumers, but also the structure of the market and, in so doing, competition as such. Consequently, for a finding that an agreement has an anticompetitive object, it is not necessary that final consumers be deprived of the advantages of effective competition in terms of supply or price.[10]

It can be derived from the judgment that the purpose of Article 101 TFEU is to protect not only consumer welfare, but also competitors and the structure of the market.

As discussed in Chapter 1, another important goal of EU competition policy is market integration. This reflects one of the main policy goals of the EU in general. The ECJ in the *GlaxoSmithKline Services* case confirmed the continuing importance of market integration for the interpretation of Article 101 TFEU:

Thus on a number of occasions the Court has held agreements aimed at partitioning national markets according to national borders or making the interpenetration of national markets more difficult, in particular those aimed at preventing or restricting parallel exports, to be agreements whose object is to restrict competition within the meaning of that article of the Treaty.[11]

Agreements that aim at partitioning the internal market by national borders or other geographic criteria are seen by the ECJ as restricting competition.[12] Market integration is a prerequisite for undistorted competition throughout the EU.

---

[9] GC (27 September 2006), Case T-168/01 – *GlaxoSmithKline Services v Commission* [2006] ECR II-2969, para. 118.

[10] ECJ (6 October 2009), Joined Cases C-501/06 P, C-513/06 P, C-515/06 P, C-519/06 P – *GlaxoSmithKline Services and Others v Commission and Others* [2009] ECR I-9291, para. 63.

[11] Ibid., para. 61.

[12] On the role of market integration for the assessment of cases under Article 101 TFEU, see Nazzini, 'Article 81 EC between Time Present and Time Past: A Normative Critique of "Restriction of Competition" in EU Law', *Common Market Law Review*, 43 (2006), 497, 527.

Summary of Section 1

Article 101 TFEU addresses bilateral and multilateral restrictions of competition. They may occur between undertakings at the same economic level (competitors) or at different levels (non-competitors). They require a certain level of coordination of the market behaviour of at least two undertakings. Such horizontal or vertical restrictions of competitition are prohibited under the first paragraph of Article 101 TFEU.

The legal consequences of a coordination of market behaviour are governed by the second paragraph of Article 101 TFEU. Whatever form the cooperation takes it is automatically void.

In its third paragraph Article 101 TFEU offers a possibility for exemption from the general prohibition of restrictions of competition. If the beneficial effects of a restrictive practice outweigh its negative effects on competition, it may be compatible with the EU competition rules. Undertakings have to assess themselves whether they meet the criteria for an exemption. For a number of agreements with particular practical importance the Commission provides guidance on the interpretation of Article 101 (3) TFEU in block exemption regulations. For other practices an individual assessment has to be carried out.

The interpretation of Article 101 TFEU by the Commission and the ECJ is teleological in the sense that it attributes greater weight to the aims and objectives pursued by the provision than to its individual words and phrases. Consumer welfare is playing an increasingly important role in the interpretation of the EU competition rules.

2. UNDERTAKING

The notion of an 'undertaking' within the meaning of Article 101 TFEU has not been defined by any Treaty provision or any piece of secondary legislation. The word 'undertaking' deliberately avoids the terminology utilised in any of the Member States in order to describe a legal entity.[13] Thus, the term is extraordinarily broad and, for this reason, recourse to the comprehensive jurisprudence of the European courts must be had in order to define the exact scope of the concept of an undertaking. This is of utmost importance as the concept defines the categories of subjects to which the competition rules, in particular Article 101 TFEU, apply.

---

[13] Dunne, 'Knowing When to See It: State Activities, Economic Activities, and the Concept of Undertaking', *Columbia Journal of European Law*, 16 (2010), 427, 434.

2.1 Economic activity

2.1.1 General

When specifying the scope of the concept of an undertaking, the ECJ and the Commission have taken a broad view. In its *Höfner* judgment, the ECJ stated that

the concept of an undertaking encompasses every entity engaged in an economic activity, regardless of the legal status of the entity or the way in which it is financed.[14]

The case concerned a dispute, the outcome of which depended on the question whether the German Federal Office for Employment could be deemed an undertaking for the purposes of the EU competition rules. In order to answer this question of the Higher Regional Court of Munich raised in a request for a preliminary ruling, the ECJ analysed to what extent the employment recruitment by a public employment agency may be regarded as an economic activity. The ECJ came to the conclusion that the fact that employment procurement activities are often entrusted to public agencies cannot affect their economic nature. The ECJ gave two reasons for this conclusion: employment procurement has not always been carried out by public institutions and is not necessarily carried out by public institutions.[15]

There are some limitations to the broad concept of undertaking that is generally applied by the ECJ. In the *Wouters* case, the ECJ gave some indications on these limitations:

[T]he Treaty rules on competition do not apply to activity which, by its nature, its aim and the rules to which it is subject does not belong to the sphere of economic activity [. . .] or which is connected with the exercise of the powers of public authority.[16]

Accordingly, non-economic activities such as social activities or the exercise of the powers of public authority by government agencies are not subject to EU competition law.

2.1.2 Functional approach

In principle, the ECJ takes a functional approach when defining the scope of the concept of undertaking. The ECJ does not take the institutional structure of an entity as a departing point for its analysis but the relevant activity. It depends on the particular function performed by the body involved in the case whether the activity in question is of an economic nature or not. Consequently, various activities of an entity must be considered individually. The same entity may qualify as an

[14] ECJ (23 April 1991), Case C-41/90 – *Höfner and Elser v Macroton GmbH* [1991] ECR I-1979, para. 21.
[15] Ibid., para. 22.
[16] ECJ (19 February 2002), Case C-309/99 – *Wouters and Others* [2002] ECR I-1577, para. 57.

undertaking for purposes of EU competition law with regard to one activity and may fall outside the scope of EU competition law with regard to another activity. This point of view has been confirmed by the General Court in the second *Eurocontrol* judgment. In this case the Commission's argument relied on a prior ECJ judgment that the European Organisation for the Safety of Air Navigation (Eurocontrol) is not an undertaking since its activities are connected with the exercise of powers which are typical for public authorities. In its judgment, the General Court did not follow the arguments brought by the Commission and pointed out that

> various activities of an entity must be considered individually and the treatment of some of them as powers of a public authority does not mean that it must be concluded that the other activities are not economic . . .[17]

This interpretation has also been taken up by the Commission.[18]

2.1.3 Scope of application

According to settled case law, the concept of economic activity shall cover all commercial functions consisting in offering goods and services on a given relevant market irrespective of the source of remuneration. In the *Ambulanz Glöckner* case, the ECJ ruled that ambulance services which provided both emergency transport services and routine patient transports were covered by Article 101 TFEU irrespective of the fact that the operator received payments both from public health institutions and private insurance companies.[19] From the Court's perspective it was decisive to establish that comparable services may also be provided on a fully commercial basis. A similar approach has been taken in the above-mentioned *Höfner* and *Eurocontrol* judgments:

> [T]he fact that the services in question are not at the current time offered by private under-takings does not prevent their being described as an economic activity, since it is possible for them to be carried out by private entities.[20]

In the *Eurocontrol* case, the General Court ruled that provision of assistance in public tender procedures to national administrations constituted an economic activity as, firstly, it was separable from other functions related to powers normally entrusted to public authorities (e.g. development of air safety) and, secondly, there was a market for services on which private companies could easily participate. This judgment has

---

[17] GC (12 December 2006), Case T-155/04 – *SELEX Sistemi Integrati v Commission* [2006] ECR II-4797, para. 54; ECJ (26 March 2009), Case C-113/07 P – *SELEX Sistemi Integrati v Commission and Eurocontrol* [2009] ECR I-2207.

[18] Commission, decision not to raise objections, NN 54/2009, C(2009)8120 final, para. 107.

[19] ECJ (25 October 2001), Case C-475/99 – *Ambulanz Glöckner* [2001] ECR I-8089.

[20] GC (12 December 2006), Case T-155/04 – *SELEX Sistemi Integrati v Commission* [2006] ECR II-4797, para. 89.

been dismissed by the ECJ on the grounds that the activity of providing administrative assistance to national authorities played a direct role in the attainment of the
objectives set out by the convention establishing Eurocontrol and therefore may not
be classified as economic activity.[21]

Article 101 TFEU does not require the entity in question to have an economic
purpose. The concept of undertaking does not presuppose a profit-making intention
either. It is sufficient only to show that an organisation is carrying out some
commercial or economic activity notwithstanding the fact that no profit-motives
are pursued. This understanding applies primarily to sports associations that *ex
definitione* are not profit driven although they engage in diverse economic activities
such as selling broadcasting rights, distributing merchandising articles and concluding marketing and sponsoring agreements.[22]

A similar view has also been taken by the ECJ with regard to public law bodies
fulfilling social functions:

[A] non-profit-making organization which manages an old-age insurance scheme intended to
supplement a basic compulsory scheme, established by law as an optional scheme and
operating according to the principle of capitalization in keeping with the rules laid down by
the authorities in particular with regard to conditions for membership, contributions and
benefits, is an undertaking within the meaning of Article [101 et seq. TFEU].[23]

This judgment of the ECJ illustrates the functional approach again, since two different types of activities (compulsory old-age insurance scheme and voluntary supplementary old-age insurance scheme) of the same public body are categorised
differently.

The application of Article 101(1) TFEU does not depend on the legal status or
structure of the entity in question. It covers not only corporations, partnerships and
trade associations but also state-owned corporations that pursue economic activities.
Even public authorities may fall within the scope of Article 101 TFEU insofar as they
are engaged in activities of an economic nature. The same applies to quasi-
governmental bodies carrying on economic activities and individuals as long as
they do not act as employees or consumers.

For the purpose of Article 101 TFEU, members of the liberal professions can also be
undertakings. According to the ECJ, it is irrelevant whether they provide services of a
public law nature, such as for instance customs agents, notaries or lawyers,[24] or are
members of a regulated profession. A similar approach has been taken with regard to

---

[21] ECJ (26 March 2009), Case C-113/07 P – *SELEX Sistemi Integrati v Commission and Eurocontrol* [2009] ECR
I-2207, para. 76.

[22] Commission decision of 19 April 2001, Case 37.576 – *UEFA's Broadcasting Regulations*, OJ No. L 171 of 26
June 2001, p. 12, para. 47.

[23] ECJ (16 November 1995), Case C-244/94 – *FFSA and Others v Ministère de l'Agriculture et de la Pêche*
[1995] ECR I-4013, para. 22.

[24] For the latter see ECJ (19 February 2002), Case C-309/99 – *Wouters and Others* [2002] ECR I-1577.

agricultural workers, public broadcasters who are members of the European Broadcasting Union, sportsmen and performing artists.[25] Individuals can qualify as undertakings for purposes of EU competition law if they exercise an economic activity that goes beyond private consumption.

2.2 Non-economic activities

The scope of Article 101 TFEU does not encompass activities that are not economic in their nature. The economic/non-economic nature of an activity is not always easy to determine. In fact, despite a reasonable number of judgments on the issue, national courts still do not feel confident to decide this important question on their own.[26] Nonetheless, the European courts have delineated three groups of cases in which the distinction between economic and non-economic activities is of great importance. These are:

- activities by entities fulfilling social functions;
- exercise of public power;
- public procurement for a non-economic activity.

2.2.1 Activities by entities fulfilling social functions

According to settled case law the EU competition rules shall apply to entities providing social protection such as pensions, health insurance or health care when two conditions are met:

- the social scheme in question is based upon the principle of solidarity, and
- it is subject to supervision by the State.[27]

In principle the social aim of an insurance scheme is not in itself sufficient to preclude the activity in question from being classified as an economic activity.

a) Application of the principle of solidarity

An entity providing social protection shall not be deemed as an undertaking when it provides its services on the basis of solidarity. In this context solidarity is defined as an 'inherently uncommercial act of involuntary subsidisation of one social group by another'.[28] Although an overall assessment of the social scheme at issue must be made in each case, it is apparent from the jurisprudence of the ECJ that the requirement of solidarity is in principle fulfilled when the system does not make the amount of

---

[25] Commission decision of 26 May 1978, Case IV/29.559 – *RAI/Unitel*, OJ No. L 157 of 15 June 1978, p. 39.
[26] See Dunne, 'Knowing When to See It', 427, 444.
[27] See, e.g., ECJ (22 January 2002), Case C-218/00 – *Cisal* [2002] ECR I-691.
[28] AG Fennelly, opinion of 6 February 1997 in case C-70/95 – *Sodemare and Others v Regione Lombardia* [1997] ECR I-3395, para. 29.

benefits granted dependent on the contributions paid by the respective members. The level of contributions must also not be proportionate to the risks insured.[29]

In the *Kattner Stahlbau* judgment, the ECJ found that a scheme had a sufficient element of solidarity to prevent the respective body from being characterised as an undertaking despite the fact that there was no maximum cap on contributions and the system itself was applied by a group of entities constituting an oligopoly. From the Court's perspective it was decisive that there was no link between the contributions paid and the benefits granted.[30]

b) State supervision

The operation of the social scheme in question must be subject to state control. It is not, however, necessary for the State supervision to be complete and to cover all activities of the entity at issue. They may be given a certain degree of latitude which must be strictly delimited by law.[31] In the case of a health insurance scheme, for example, the contributions and the benefits must be defined by the State. The ECJ held in the *Kattner Stahlbau* case:

The documents before the Court show that – as the Advocate General found in point 54 of his Opinion – that degree of latitude is established and strictly delimited by law, with the SGB VII [the relevant law] laying down, first, the factors that must be taken into account in calculating the contributions payable under the statutory scheme at issue in the main proceedings and, second, an exhaustive list of benefits provided under that scheme, together with the arrangements for the grant of such benefits.

2.2.2 Exercise of public powers

Certain activities fall outside the scope of Article 101 TFEU when they are connected with the exercise of the powers of a public authority. Since there is no general rule as to the distinction between exercise of State function and carrying out of an economic activity, each case must be analysed individually. The statements made by the ECJ in the *Cali & Figli* case are instructive in this regard. The court contrasted the economic activity with other activities that may be classified as a

task in the public interest which forms part of the essential function of the State [...] and is connected by its nature, its aim and the rules to which it is subject with the exercise of powers [...] which are typically those of a public authority[32]

---

[29] ECJ (16 March 2004), Joined Cases C-264/01, C-306/01, C-354/01, C-355/01 – *AOK-Bundesverband and Others* [2004] ECR I-2493, paras. 51–2; for a discussion of this case see Krajewski and Farley, 'Limited Competition in National Health Systems and the Application of Competition Law: The *AOK Bundesverband* Case', *European Law Review*, **29** (2004), 842.

[30] ECJ (5 March 2009), Case C-350/07 – *Kattner Stahlbau* [2009] ECR I-1513, paras. 44–59.

[31] Ibid., para. 62.

[32] ECJ (18 March 1997), Case C-343/95 – *Cali & Figli v Servizi Ecologici Porto di Genova* [1997] ECR I-1547, para. 23.

and came to the conclusion that anti-pollution surveillance carried out by a company owned by a public port authority did not fall within the scope of the EU competition rules, despite the fact that it was financed by duties paid by all port users.

2.2.3 Public procurement

In the *FENIN* case, the ECJ held that purchasing activities of public authorities were not of an economic nature if they were ancillary to activities pursuing non-economic goals.[33] Spanish public bodies purchasing health services and medicines were considered to fall outside the scope of Article 101(1) TFEU because they were providing health care on the basis of solidarity and in this context their behaviour was clearly not economic. The ECJ argued that, in general, the activity of purchasing goods and services should not be separated from its purpose:

The Court of First Instance rightly deduced, in paragraph 36 of the judgment under appeal, that there is no need to dissociate the activity of purchasing goods from the subsequent use to which they are put in order to determine the nature of that purchasing activity, and that the nature of the purchasing activity must be determined according to whether or not the subsequent use of the purchased goods amounts to an economic activity.[34]

In light of the functional approach the ECJ stipulated, it appears debatable whether the different activities of the Spanish public body in question in the *FENIN* case do not indeed have to be separated. One might also argue that the procurement activity clearly is an economic activity (purchasing goods on a market) while providing health care within the framework of a scheme based on solidarity is not and that the body therefore qualifies as an undertaking when it purchases goods or services on the market and is no undertaking when it provides health care on the basis of a solidarity scheme.

2.3 The 'single economic entity' doctrine

Article 101(1) TFEU does not apply to agreements concluded by two or more legal entities forming a single economic unit. For this reason agreements between a parent and subsidiary company do not fall under the cartel prohibition, since the companies involved constitute a single undertaking.

---

[33] ECJ (11 July 2006), Case C-205/03 P – *Federación Española de Empresas de Tecnología Sanitaria (FENIN) v Commission* [2006] ECR I-6295.
[34] Ibid., para. 26.

2.3.1 Presumption of a single undertaking

Companies belonging to the same corporate group may enter into restrictive agreements with one another so long as they form a single economic entity. In this case the corporate group is considered as one undertaking while a violation of Article 101(1) TFEU requires at least two undertakings or an association of undertakings.

Two entities belonging to the same corporate group are not necessarily considered one undertaking for purposes of EU competition law. Whether they are considered one or two undertakings depends on whether they are independent in their decision making. The ECJ held that two companies belonging to the same corporate group are considered one undertaking if they

form an economic unit within which the subsidiary has no real freedom to determine its course of action on the market, and if the agreements or practices are concerned merely with the internal allocation of tasks as between the undertakings.[35]

It is therefore crucial to establish whether the parties to the agreement are independent in their decision making and that neither of them has sufficient control power over the others. In this assessment various factors need to be examined: shareholders' structure, composition of the board of directors, possible influence by the parent company on the subsidiary's policies, binding effect of the instructions issued by the parent company etc. Only if the market behaviour of the two entities is determined by one decision-making body is there no room for independent competitive behaviour and therefore no room for a restriction of competition.

In cases where the subsidiary is fully owned by the parent undertaking or the parent company owns almost all shares of the subsidiary there is a presumption[36] that the subsidiary's affairs are being controlled.[37] This presumption is rebuttable and the burden of proof rests on the party wishing to prove that there is no single economic unit.

2.3.2 Other cases

The doctrine of 'single economic entity' does not apply in cases in which a subsidiary is owned partially by two or more independent companies and neither of them has

---

[35] ECJ (4 May 1988), Case 30/87 – *Corinne Bodson v Pompes funèbres des régions libérées* [1988] ECR 2479, para. 19.

[36] For a general discussion of presumptions in EU competition law, see Bailey, 'Presumptions in EU Competition Law', *European Competition Law Review*, 31 (2010), 362.

[37] GC (12 December 2007), Case T-112/05 – *Akzo Nobel and Others v Commission* [2007] ECR II-5049, paras. 57–85.

the sole control power over the joint venture.[38] This approach was taken in the *Ijsselcentrale* decision, in which the Commission refused to apply the doctrine of 'single economic entity' because the four Dutch electricity generating companies at issue determined their market conduct independently and did not belong to a single person.[39]

2.4 Principal/agent relationship

Under certain conditions, agreements concluded between agents and their principals may be excluded from the EU competition rules, the prerequisite being that the

agent, although having separate legal personality, does not independently determine his own conduct on the market, but carries out the instructions given to him by his principal [. . .] with which he forms an economic unit.[40]

If the agent does not independently determine its market conduct but simply executes the instructions of the principal, there is no competition between the two entities that could be restricted by the agreement.

In the Guidelines on Vertical Restraints the Commission refers to the risk borne by the agent as an indicator of his independence of the principal:

The determining factor in defining an agency agreement for the application of Article 101(1) is the financial or commercial risk borne by the agent in relation to the activities for which it has been appointed as an agent by the principal. In this respect it is not material for the assessment whether the agent acts for one or several principals. Neither is material for this assessment the qualification given to their agreement by the parties or national legislation.[41]

The more risk the agent bears the more likely it is that he acts as an independent undertaking. In this case, agreements between the principal and the agent fall into the ambit of Article 101(1) TFEU.

---

[38] Commission decision of 15 May 1991, Case IV/32186 – *Gosme/Martell-DMP*, OJ No. L 185 of 11 July 1991, p. 23.

[39] Commission decision of 16 January 1991, Case IV/32.732 – *Ijsselcentrale*, OJ No. L 28 of 2 February 1991, p. 32.

[40] GC (15 September 2005), Case T-325/01 – *DaimlerChrysler v Commission* [2005] ECR II-3319, para. 88; for a discussion of this case see Henty, 'Agency Agreements – What are the Risks? The CFI's Judgment in DaimlerChrysler AG v Commission', *European Competition Law Review*, **27** (2006), 102.

[41] Commission Guidelines on Vertical Restraints, OJ No. C 130 of 19 May 2010, p. 1, para. 13.

Summary of Section 2

The EU competition rules apply to undertakings. The concept of an undertaking thus defines the reach of Article 101(1) TFEU: only the coordination of the market behaviour of entities which qualify as undertakings can violate Article 101(1) TFEU. The concept of an undertaking is not defined in the EU competition rules but needs to be derived from case law. The ECJ applies a functional concept of undertaking. The legal form of an entity is not relevant for the concept. It is the activity of any given entity that makes it qualify as an undertaking or not. Every entity engaged in an economic activity is an undertaking. This includes both natural and legal persons.

An economic activity is any activity that goes beyond private consumption and that does not consist in the exercise of public powers or other public tasks. In recent years, public health insurance organisations have been the subject of several judgments of the ECJ. A health insurance organisation does not exercise an economic activity when it provides services based on the principle of solidarity. This is the case when it provides coverage independent of the premium paid by the respective individual. If it provides additional services which are not based on the principle of solidarity but financed through the premium paid by the insured person this will be considered an economic activity and the organisation will qualify as an undertaking when performing these services.

For any coordination of market behaviour, at least two entities are needed. There are two cases in which two entities are treated as one undertaking: entities belonging to the same corporate group are considered to be a single economic unit if they are not independent in their decision making, i.e. if one of them is controlled by the other or both are controlled by the same third entity. In this case there is no room for independent market behaviour that could be coordinated. Article 101(1) TFEU does not apply. The other case is the principal/agent relationship: if the agent does not bear any appreciable own risk (because of investments in marketing, warehouses etc.) he will not be considered an independent entity but as forming a single economic unit with the principal. Again, there is no room for an application of the EU competition rules under such circumstances.

3. AGREEMENTS, DECISIONS AND CONCERTED PRACTICES

Article 101(1) TFEU prohibits any form of cooperation between independent undertakings assuming that it leads to a distortion or restriction of competition. Although Article 101(1) TFEU lists three forms of prohibited collusion, it is generally accepted that the concepts of 'agreement', 'concerted practice' and 'decision of an association of undertakings' overlap. There is no need to draw a clear-cut distinction between the types of behaviour named above, and the Commission tends to make a general distinction between independent conduct and collusion only. This approach has been upheld by the ECJ in one of the *Polypropylene* cases:

The list in Article [101(1) TFEU] is intended to apply to all collusion between undertakings, whatever the form it takes. There is continuity between the cases listed. The only essential thing is the distinction between independent conduct, which is allowed, and collusion, which is not, regardless of any distinction between types of collusion.[42]

3.1 Agreements

The notion of 'agreement' within the meaning of Article 101(1) TFEU is not restricted to a particular type of contract or deal. It is also not required that an agreement is legally binding.[43] In the *Adalat* case, the General Court stated that

the concept of an agreement within the meaning of Article [101 TFEU] centres around the existence of a concurrence of wills between at least two parties, the form in which it is manifested being unimportant so long as it constitutes the faithful expression of the parties' intention.[44]

Under this broad concept, Article 101(1) TFEU covers a wide range of practices. The following categories shall serve as examples of agreements that may fall into the ambit of EU competition law:

- legally binding and enforceable contracts (or those intended to be binding[45]) irrespective of their form, including expired contracts that are nonetheless adhered to by the parties;[46]
- membership rules of trade associations[47] and certain agreements on common standards;[48]
- settlement agreements such as trade mark delimitation agreements or settlements of patent disputes;[49]

---

[42] ECJ (8 July 1999), Case C-49/92 P – *Commission v Anic Partecipazioni SpA* [1999] ECR I-4125, para. 108.
[43] For a detailed analysis of the concept of agreement under Article 101 TFEU see Lianos, 'Collusion in Vertical Relations', 1027, 1037.
[44] GC (26 October 2000), Case T-41/96 – *Bayer v Commission* [2000] ECR II-3383, para. 69.
[45] According to Article 101(2) TFEU all prohibited agreements are automatically void.
[46] ECJ (15 June 1976), Case 51/75 – *EMI Records v CBS United Kingdom* [1976] ECR 811, para. 30.
[47] GC (2 July 1992), Case T-61/89 – *Dansk Pelsdyravlerforening v Commission* [1992] ECR II-1931.
[48] Commission Guidelines on the applicability of Article 101 TFEU to horizontal co-operation agreements, OJ No. C 11 of 14 January 2011, p. 1, paras. 257 et seq.
[49] See, e.g., XXIInd Report on Competition Policy 1992, paras. 168–76, regarding a 'non-use clause' in a trademark agreement of a brand name to which the Commission objected on grounds of Article 101 TFEU. See also the Commission's Guidelines on the application of Article 81 of the EC Treaty [Article 101 TFEU] to technology transfer agreements; OJ No. C 101 of 27 April 2004, p. 2.

- 'gentlemen's agreements'[50] and all other agreements that are not legally binding or supported by enforcement procedures;[51]
- the constant and systematic use of anticompetitive terms and conditions in sales invoices by one party and their tacit acceptance by the other party;[52]
- agreements establishing a European Economic Interest Grouping or its byelaws;[53]
- collective labour agreements between employers and workers.[54]

3.1.1 Concept of a 'single, overall agreement'

The concept of a 'single, overall agreement' has been developed by the Commission in order to facilitate the enforcement of Article 101 TFEU against complex cartels of a long duration. According to this concept, it is not necessary for the Commission to prove a series of different agreements concluded by the same cartel members over a period of time and to identify each of its parties, especially when they have changed over a period of time. Undertakings can be held responsible for the overall cartel even though they were not involved in all of its operations on a day-to-day basis or did not participate in all of its constituent elements. Participation in the overall agreement is sufficient to establish the responsibility if

it is shown that [the undertaking concerned] knew, or must have known, that the collusion in which it participated [. . .] was part of an overall plan intended to distort competition and that the overall plan included all the constituent elements of the cartel.[55]

It must however be noted that there is no presumption of a single, overall agreement consisting of numerous multi- and bilateral agreements between members of the cartel. Following the *Cement Cartel* cases the Commission is obliged to prove that those particular agreements form one overall agreement:

Bi- or multilateral concerted practices can be regarded as constituent elements of a single anticompetitive agreement only if it is established that they form part of an overall plan pursuing a common objective.

---

[50] Commission decision of 13 December 2000, Case COMP/33.133-B – *Soda-ash*, OJ No. L 10 of 15 January 2003, p. 1, para. 56.

[51] GC (26 October 2000), Case T-41/96 – *Bayer v Commission* [2000] ECR II-3383, para. 68.

[52] Commission decision of 13 June 1987, Case IV/31.741 – *Sandoz*, OJ No. L 222 of 10 August 1987, p. 28, para. 26, confirmed by ECJ (11 January 1990), Case C-277/87 – *Sandoz Prodotti Farmaceutici v Commission* [1990] ECR I-45.

[53] Whish and Bailey, *Competition Law* (Oxford University Press, 7th edn, 2012), p. 100, citing further authorities.

[54] But see limitations in ECJ (21 September 1999), Case C-67/96 – *Albany* [1999] ECR I-5751, para. 59; Commission decision of 30 September 1986, Case IV/31.362 – *Irish Banks' Standing Committee*, OJ No. L 295 of 18 October 1986, p. 28, para. 16.

[55] GC (20 April 1999), Joined Cases T-305/94 to T-307/94, T-313/94 to T-316/94, T-318/94, T-325/94, T-328/94, T-329/94, T-335/94 – *LVM v Commission* [1999] ECR II-931, para. 773.

However, the fact that objects of such concerted practices and such an anticompetitive agreement coincide is not sufficient to establish that an undertaking that was party to those practices participated in that agreement.

Only where the undertaking knew, or ought to have known, when it participated in those concerted practices, that it was taking part in the single agreement, can its participation in those practices constitute the expression of its accession to that agreement.[56]

If the court succeeds in proving these elements, it is entitled to consider that the undertaking in question 'rendered itself co-responsible for the entire infringement committed during its participation'.

It is possible for an undertaking to exonerate itself from the responsibility for the participation in a cartel by publicly distancing itself from what was agreed during the meetings. However, since the notion of 'public distancing' has to be interpreted narrowly it is necessary for the undertaking not only to publicly announce its disapproval but also to inform the other participants of the meeting/cartel that 'it did not wish to be considered to be a member of the cartel nor to participate in the meetings that were a cover for unlawful concerted action'.[57]

In order to prove an undertaking's responsibility in cases where there is no direct evidence of a cartel, the courts apply a two-prong test: first, they have to establish that there has been some contact between the competitors that was likely to reduce the uncertainty about the firms' future conduct. Subsequently, they have to show that the firms' conduct was affected by the prior contact.[58]

While this test has been applied repeatedly, it has also provoked some legitimate criticism.[59] With respect to the first prong it should be borne in mind that, in general, information about future conduct of a competitor is valuable only in an oligopolistic market or in one with high barriers of entry. Otherwise, it is unlikely to have any perceivable effect on competition.

As regards the second requirement, it must be noted that the courts are not required to prove that a firm's conduct was in fact anticompetitive. It suffices for them to show that a particular firm's conduct is *based* on the prior contact with a competitor.[60] It follows that the burden of proof is very low on the side of the authority/court. In contrast, it is very difficult for a company to refute a finding of concerted practice.

---

[56] GC (15 March 2000), Joined Cases T-25/95, T-26/95, T-30/95 to T-32/95, T-34/95 to T-39/95, T-42/95 to T-46/95, T-48/95, T-50/95 to T-65/95, T-68/95 to T-71/95, T-87/95, T-88/95, T-103/95, T-104/95 – *Cimenteries CBR v Commission* [2000] ECR II-491, paras. 4109–12.

[57] GC (5 December 2006), Case T-303/02 – *Westfalen Gassen Nederland BV v Commission* [2006] ECR II-4567, para. 103.

[58] See GC (17 December 1991), Case T-7/89 – *SA Hercules Chemicals NV v Commission* [1991] ECR II-1711, paras. 256 et seq.

[59] See Joshua, 'Single Continuous Infringement of Article 81 EC: Has the Commission Stretched the Concept beyond the Limit of Its Logic?', *European Competition Journal*, 5 (2005), 451, citing Benjamin N. Cardozo.

[60] Monti, *EC Competition Law* (Cambridge University Press, 2007), pp. 327 et seq.

In addition, it has been argued that there is no adequate legal basis for the courts' single overall agreement approach, because neither the legal systems of the Member States[61] nor Art. 101 TFEU fully support such an extensive interpretation.[62] The assumption of one single agreement instead of a number of separate agreements may also lead to the circumvention of the five-year limitation period[63] for competition infringements as has been the case in the Commission's *Choline Chloride*[64] decision.[65]

This last issue has recently been dealt with by the General Court when it partly reversed the Commission's decision in the *Copper Plumbing Tubes*[66] case. The Commission had treated a number of agreements covering a period of more than twelve years as a single, overall agreement. While there had been meetings through-out the entire time, the parties contended that no collusive conduct had taken place for a period of at least sixteen months. Accordingly, they were of the opinion that there were in fact two separate infringements, the first of which terminated more than five years before the Commission's proceedings commenced and which was therefore protected by the statute of limitation.[67] In applying the above-mentioned test, the Commission rejected these claims because, even if there had been no illegal agree-ments during the period in dispute, the Commission considered that the undertaking had failed to 'publicly distance'[68] itself from the practice adhered to so far.

The General Court, however, held that such a finding

cannot become relevant before the Commission has discharged its burden of proof [. . .], namely the submission of evidence of facts sufficiently proximate in time for it to be reasonable to accept that that infringement continued uninterruptedly between two specific dates.[69]

Thus, it came to the conclusion that the undertaking in question had in fact partici-pated in *two separate infringements*. Even though the decision is based on a unique

---

[61] See ECJ (8 July 1999), Case C-235/92 P – *Montecatini SpA v Commission* [1999] ECR I-4539.

[62] Seifert, 'The Single Complex and Continuous Infringement – "Effet" Utilitarism?', *European Competition Law Review*, 29 (2008), 546, 553 et seq.

[63] Council Regulation (EC) No 1/2003 of 16 December 2002 on the implementation of the rules on competition laid down in Articles 81 and 82 of the Treaty, OJ No. L 1 of 4 January 2003, p. 1, Article 25(2).

[64] Commission decision of 9 December 2004, Case COMP/E-2/37.533 – *Choline Chloride*, OJ No L 190 of 22 July 2005, p. 22, para. 9; cf. GC (12 December 2007), Joined Cases T-101/05, T- 111/05 – *BASF and UCB v Commission*, [2007] ECR II-4949, para. 139.

[65] Bailey, 'Single, Overall Agreement in EU Competition Law', *Common Market Law Review*, 47 (2010), 473, 479.

[66] Commission decision of 3 September 2004, Case C.38.069 – *Copper Plumbing Tubes*, OJ No. L 192 of 13 July 2006, p. 21.

[67] Article 25(2) of Council Regulation (EC) No 1/2003 of 16 December 2002 on the implementation of the rules on competition laid down in Articles 81 and 82 of the Treaty, OJ No. L 1 of 4 January 2003, p. 1.

[68] Commission decision of 3 September 2004, Case C.38.069 – *Copper Plumbing Tubes*, OJ No. L 192 of 13 July 2006, p. 21, para. 464.

[69] GC (19 May 2010), Case T-18/05 – *IMI and Others v Commission* [2010] ECR II-1769, para. 86.

set of facts and the timeframe during which collusive action could not be proved is extraordinarily long, it can nonetheless be deduced that 'public distancing' is no longer required in all cases. Rather, the onus to prove the continuity of an infringement is on the Commission.[70]

3.1.2 Unilateral conduct

According to the scheme of the EU competition rules, Article 101 TFEU shall apply only to bi- and multilateral agreements whereas Article 102 TFEU covers all unilateral measures. However, groups of cases may be distinguished in which Article 101(1) TFEU is applicable although the conduct of an undertaking appears to be unilateral. In such cases, whether the measure at issue is truly unilateral needs to be carefully assessed, since its nature and effects may be similar to those of agreements covered by Article 101(1) TFEU.

In particular this may apply to vertical systems of distribution where the supplier tries unilaterally to restrict the number of wholesalers involved in a distribution network or to limit the volume of products sold on a particular market. In such cases, the infringement of Article 101(1) TFEU may result from a tacit and/or express understanding between the supplier and its retailers.

The distinction between unilateral conduct and conduct caught by Article 101(1) TFEU has been subject to several legal disputes before the ECJ. In the leading case of *Adalat*, the General Court and the ECJ had to decide whether an export ban on pharmaceuticals imposed by Bayer on its Spanish and French wholesalers in order to restrict parallel imports to the United Kingdom where the prices were considerably higher, had been tacitly incorporated into the distribution agreements with the distributors and therefore was subject to Article 101 TFEU.

In the Commission's view[71] there was a tacit agreement between Bayer and its dealers not to export to the UK. This finding was supported by the fact that the wholesalers had ceased to supply the UK market in response to Bayer's new policy to cut the supplies. The Commission's decision, however, was annulled by the General Court[72] and this judgment was upheld by the ECJ upon appeal.[73]

---

[70] The decision also contains another interesting issue: the GC was of the opinion that the first infringement was not time-barred because the undertaking 'resumed and repeated' the *same* infringement when it participated in the second agreement. This understanding of Article 25(2) of Regulation (EC) No 1/2003 clearly deviates from prior interpretations of the clause; see Einhaus, 'Water Flowing? News on the Continuous Infringement', *European Law Reporter*, **9** (2010), 289, 295 et seq. Against this background it is surprising that apparently neither of the parties appealed the case before the ECJ.

[71] Commission decision of 10 January 1996, Case IV/34.279/F3 – *ADALAT*, OJ No. L 201 of 9 August 1996, p. 1.

[72] GC (26 October 2000), Case T-41/96 – *Bayer v Commission* [2000] ECR II-3383.

[73] ECJ (6 January 2004), Joined Cases C-2/01, C-3/01 – *BAI and Commission v Bayer* [2004] ECR I-23.

The General Court in its judgment elaborates on the distinction between unilateral conduct and a (tacit) agreement:

[A] distinction should be drawn between cases in which an undertaking has adopted a genuinely unilateral measure, and thus without the express or implied participation of another undertaking, and those in which the unilateral character of the measure is merely apparent. Whilst the former do not fall within Article [101(1) TFEU], the latter must be regarded as revealing an agreement between undertakings and may therefore fall within the scope of that article. That is the case, in particular, with practices and measures in restraint of competition which, though apparently adopted unilaterally by the manufacturer in the context of its contractual relations with its dealers, nevertheless receive at least the tacit acquiescence of those dealers.[74]

The General Court thus acknowledged that the concept of 'agreement' encompasses cases where one of the parties tacitly follows and/or engages in practices established by another party.[75] However, according to the court convincing evidence of a 'meeting of minds' between the supplier and its retailer must be provided by the Commission or national competition authority in order to find Article 101(1) TFEU applicable. In the *Adalat* case the Commission failed to achieve this goal:

The mere fact that the unilateral policy of quotas implemented by Bayer, combined with the national requirements on the wholesalers to offer a full product range, produces the same effect as an export ban does not mean either that the manufacturer imposed such a ban or that there was an agreement prohibited by Article [101(1) TFEU].[76]

Accordingly, for Article 101(1) TFEU to apply in cases of unilaterally imposed restrictions, proof is required that:

- one party had intended to impose a measure contrary to Article 101 TFEU,
- the other party had intended to adhere to the policy introduced by the supplier.

Furthermore, the policy change pursued by one party communicated to the other party must form part of the contractual relationship and the other party's positive reaction to it must be proved. According to the ECJ:

it is necessary that the manifestation of the wish of one of the contracting parties to achieve an anticompetitive goal constitute an invitation to the other party, whether express or implied, to fulfil that goal jointly, and that applies all the more where, as in this case, such an agreement is not at first sight in the interests of the other party, namely the wholesalers.[77]

---

[74] GC (26 October 2000), Case T-41/96 – *Bayer v Commission* [2000] ECR II-3383, para. 71.

[75] For a critical discussion of this judgment and the concept of agreement under Article 101 TFEU in vertical relationships, see Lianos, 'Collusion in Vertical Relations under Article 81 EC', 1051.

[76] ECJ (6 January 2004), Joined Cases C-2/01, C-3/01 – *BAI and Commission v Bayer* [2004] ECR I-23, para. 88.

[77] Ibid., para. 102.

It is, however, not sufficient to argue that non-binding circulars and letters containing, for example, price recommendations and instructions on discount policy sent by a producer in accordance with the distribution agreement automatically become part of the contractual relationship. An (albeit tacit) acquiescence on the side of the distributors must still be proved.[78] On the contrary, the existence of a lawful contract clause, e.g. allowing the retailer to export, does not in itself preclude the existence of a later agreement or concerted practice infringing Article 101 TFEU, in this case prohibiting or restricting the export.[79]

3.1.3 State measures

In principle, national legislative and administrative measures as such may not constitute an 'agreement' within the meaning of Article 101(1) TFEU, although they may be contrary to EU law. In such cases, Member States would be in breach of their obligations under the EU Treaty, in particular the duty to cooperate according to Article 4(3) TFEU in combination with Article 101 and Article 102 TFEU.

EU competition rules do not apply when the national law requires the undertaking to enter into an agreement covered by Article 101(1) TFEU without leaving the undertaking any room for a behaviour that is not restrictive of competition. This is not the case where provisions of national law merely allow or encourage an anti-competitive agreement:

If anticompetitive conduct is required of undertakings by national law or if the latter creates a legal framework eliminating any possibility of competitive conduct on their part, Articles [101 and 102 TFEU] do not apply. In such a situation, the restriction of competition is not attributable, as is implied by those provisions, to the autonomous conduct of the undertakings. Articles [101 and 102 TFEU] may apply, by contrast, if it is found that the national legislation does not preclude undertakings from engaging in autonomous conduct which prevents, restricts or distorts competition.[80]

If there is no room left for the undertakings involved to act in compliance with EU competition law, their behaviour is attributed to the State rather than to themselves.

In the US, this concept is also referred to as the 'State action defence'. The State action defence was first developed in 1943 when the Supreme Court held that a state-run cartel for the production of raisins could not be prohibited, because the Sherman Act applied to '*private* restraints on trade' only (emphasis added). Based

---

[78] GC (3 December 2003), Case T-208/01 – *Volkswagen v Commission* [2003] ECR II-5141; ECJ (13 July 2006), Case C-74/04 P – *Commission v Volkswagen* [2006] ECR I-6585.

[79] Commission decision of 30 October 2002, Cases COMP/35.587, COMP/35.706, COMP/36.321 – *Nintendo*, OJ No. L 255 of 8 October 2003, p. 33, paras. 162–9.

[80] GC (30 September 2003), Joined Cases T-191/98, T-212/98 to T-214/98- *Atlantic Container Line and Others v Commission* [2003] ECR II-3275, para. 1130.

on points of federalism it argued that the (federal) Sherman Act was not designed to nullify a *State's* decision to displace competition through legislation.[81]

In subsequent decisions this precedent was further refined. In 1975 it was decided that the defence was only available in cases where the State '*required* the anticompetitive activities' (emphasis added), but not in cases where it merely *permitted* them.[82] In *Cantor v Detroit Edison Co.*, it found that no antitrust immunity was conferred when a State agency *passively* accepted an agreement that was contrary to antitrust legislation.[83] In 1980 the Supreme Court was confronted yet again with a cartel that was based on State legislation. In summing up some of the earlier case law, it put forward two conditions on which the State action doctrine (both in the US and the EU) still turns today:

These decisions establish two standards for antitrust immunity under Parker v. Brown. First, the challenged restraint must be 'one clearly articulated and affirmatively expressed as state policy'; second, the policy must be 'actively supervised' by the State itself.[84]

Within the EU it has to be borne in mind that every Member State may set its own rules and regulations which can have differing effects on competition. Even though there have been efforts to create awareness for those effects on the part of the legislator,[85] there is still room for improvement and it seems reasonable to demand that national cartel authorities and the Commission be authorised to review future regulations before they enter into force.[86] Thus, while there is little discussion about the conditions under which the 'State action defence' is recognised, analysts are now focusing on how to reduce the very basis of its application – the possibility of preventing the promulgation of laws and regulations which negatively affect competition in the first place.

3.2 Decisions by associations of undertakings

3.2.1 Association

The term 'association' in Article 101(1) TFEU relates to a very broad concept which includes all types of associations, regardless of their structure, whose purpose it is to act in the interest of their members. If their members are profit-driven, it does not

---

[81] US Supreme Court, *Parker v Brown*, 317 US 341 (1943), 351.

[82] US Supreme Court, *Goldfarb v Virginia State Bar*, 421 US 773 (1975), 790.

[83] US Supreme Court, *Cantor v Detroit Edison Co.*, 428 US 579 (1976), 593.

[84] US Supreme Court, *California Retail Liquor Dealers Ass'n v Midcal Aluminium, Inc.*, 445 US 97 (1980), 105.

[85] See, e.g., 'Better Regulation: A Guide to Competition Screening', published by the DG Competition, available at http://ec.europa.eu/competition/publications/advocacy/legis_test.pdf.; 'The Principle of Competition as a Guideline for Legislation and State Action, the Responsibility of Politics, the Role of Competition Authorities', 12th International Conference on Competition held by the German Cartel Authority, available at www.bundeskartellamt.de/wDeutsch/download/pdf/Diskussionsbeitraege/05_IKK_Dokumentation.pdf.

[86] Gal and Faibish, 'Six Principles for Limiting Government-Facilitated Restraints on Competition', *Common Market Law Review*, 44 (2007), 69, 89.

matter whether the associations themselves are for-profit or not-for-profit organisations. Even the public law status of an association or the fact that it has been entrusted with some public functions does not preclude the applicability of Article 101(1) TFEU. Within the scope of the cartel prohibition the term 'association' includes, but is not limited to:

- professional regulatory bodies of the liberal professions;[87]
- architects' associations;[88]
- non-profit-making associations;
- associations of associations;[89]
- associations of undertakings established outside the EU;[90]
- sports associations;[91]
- trade associations;[92]
- associations of wine-growers and wine dealers.[93]

3.2.2 Decision

Associations of undertakings, such as trade associations, perform a myriad of legal functions, many of which are beneficial to consumers. Nonetheless they may also facilitate collusion either between individual undertakings or across the entire association. Against this background, their acts are subject to close scrutiny. Generally speaking, the concept of 'decision' encompasses any measure undertaken by an association which reflects the association's desire to coordinate its members' actions in accordance with its statutes.[94] An act of an association does not have to be legally binding, it is sufficient when the members comply with it. In particular, the following measures are covered by Article 101(1) TFEU:

- articles of association and other rules and regulations governing its constitution;[95]
- common resolutions and supplemental agreements;[96]

---

[87] ECJ (18 June 1998), Case C-35/96 – *Commission v Italy* [1998] ECR I-3851, paras. 39 et seq.; ECJ (15 May 1975), Case C-71/74 – *Fruit-en Groentenimporthandel and Frubo v Commission* [1975] ECR 563, paras. 28–32.

[88] Commission decision of 24 June 2004, Case COMP/A.38549 – *Belgian Architects' Association*, OJ No. L 4 of 6 January 2005, p. 10.

[89] GC (26 January 2005), Case T-193/02 – *Piau v Commission* [2005] ECR II-209, para. 72.

[90] ECJ (27 September 1988), Joined Cases C-89/85, C-104/85, C-114/85, C-116/85, C-117/85, C-125/85, C-126/85 to C-129/85 – *Ahlström Osakeyhtiö and Others v Commission (Woodpulp)* [1988] ECR 5193.

[91] GC (26 January 2005), Case T-193/02 – *Piau v Commission* [2005] ECR II-209, para. 69.

[92] Commission decision of 26 July 1976, Case IV/28.980 – *Pabst Richarz/BNIA*, OJ No. L 231 of 21 August 1976, p. 24.

[93] ECJ (30 January 1985), Case 123/83 – *BNIC v Clair* [1985] ECR 391, p. 416.

[94] Bellamy and Child, *European Community Law of Competition* (Oxford University Press, 6th edn, 2008), p. 138.

[95] Commission decision of 9 June 1989, Case IV/27.958 – *National Sulphuric Acid Association* OJ No. L 190 of 5 July 1989, p. 22, para. 6.

[96] ECJ (11 July 1989), Case 246/86 – *Belasco and Others v Commission* [1989] ECR 2117, para. 5.

- decisions binding upon the members;[97]
- non-binding recommendations;[98]
- codes of conduct.[99]

3.3 Concerted practices

Article 101(1) TFEU prohibits any form of collusion between independent under-takings, and the concept of 'concerted practice' is designated to catch some less intense forms of cooperation than agreements and decisions by associations of undertakings. According to the ECJ, its main purpose is to preclude

co-ordination between undertakings which, without having reached the stage where an agreement, properly so called, has been concluded, knowingly substitutes practical coopera-tion between them for the risks of competition.[100]

The concepts of 'agreements' and 'concerted practices' are intended to cover all forms of collusion of the same nature and distinguishable only by their intensity. It is therefore not necessary to draw a line between them in each case and to provide a precise legal and factual analysis. It is however essential to make a proper distinction between a concerted practice and a parallel behaviour which does not infringe the EU competition rules.

3.3.1 Legal test

The ECJ's judgment in the *Dyestuffs* case read in conjunction with the judgment delivered in the *Sugar Cartel* case gives a full picture as to the elements of the legal test of what constitutes a concerted practice within the meaning of Article 101 TFEU. In the latter case the ECJ ruled that Article 101 TFEU precludes

any direct or indirect contact between such operators, the object or effect whereof is either to influence the conduct in the market of an actual or potential competitor or to disclose to such a competitor the course of conduct which they themselves have decided to adopt or contemplate adopting on the market.[101]

---

[97] ECJ (8 November 1983), Joined Cases 96/82 to 102/82, 104/82, 105/82, 108/82, 110/82 – *NV IAZ International Belgium and Others v Commission* [1983] ECR 3369, para. 20.

[98] ECJ (27 January 1987), Case 45/85 – *Verband der Sachversicherer v Commission* [1987] ECR 405, para. 30.

[99] GC (28 March 2001), Case T-144/99 – *Institute of Professional Representatives before the European Patent Office v Commission* [2001] ECR II-1087, paras. 72–80.

[100] ECJ (14 July 1972), Joined Cases 48/69, 49/69, 51/69 to 57/69 – *ICI v Commission* [1972] ECR 619, paras. 64–5.

[101] ECJ (16 December 1975), Joined Cases 40/73 to 48/73, 50/73, 54/73 to 56/73, 111/73, 113/73, 114/73 – *Suiker Unie v Commission* [1975] ECR 1663, para. 173.

It can be deduced from the case law that any conduct to be classified as a concerted practice must include the following elements:

- a mental consensus;
- a direct or indirect contact between the parties;
- the substitution of competition by cooperation; and
- a causal link between the mental consensus and the concerted practice.

a) Mental consensus

In the *Dyestuffs* case, the ECJ set out that the parties had knowingly substituted practical cooperation between the undertakings concerned. The concept of concerted practice requires a subjective element in the form of a common intention of the undertakings to lessen the competitive pressure between them. This intention does not have to be communicated explicitly; however, it must be clear that the market players involved do want to pursue the same goal.

b) Direct/indirect contact between the parties

Furthermore, there must be some contact between the undertakings. It may consist of meetings, discussions, participation at professional conventions and conferences or even 'soundings out' both orally and in writing. For example, in the *Cement Cartel*[102] case the General Court held that an undertaking was party to a concerted practice because it received information at a meeting on the future pricing by its competitors. Neither a systematic participation in the meetings with competitors nor a constant correspondence is necessary; it must, however, be clear that the undertakings involved in the concerted practice did communicate with each other, including through an intermediary, in order to exchange information which had a detrimental effect on competition. In the *T-Mobile Netherlands*[103] case the ECJ held that a single meeting between undertakings can be sufficient to establish a concerted practice:

[W]hat matters is not so much the number of meetings held between the participating undertakings as whether the meeting or meetings which took place afforded them the opportunity to take account of the information exchanged with their competitors in order to determine their conduct on the market in question and knowingly substitute practical cooperation between them for the risks of competition.[104]

---

[102] GC (15 March 2000), Joined Cases T-25/95, T-26/95, T-30/95 to T-32/95, T-34/95 to T-39/95, T-42/95 to T-46/95, T-48/95, T-50/95 to T-65/95, T-68/95 to T-71/95, T-87/95, T-88/95, T-103/95, T-104/95 – *Cimenteries CBR v Commission* [2000] ECR [2000] II-491.
[103] ECJ (4 June 2009), Case C-8/08 – *T-Mobile Netherlands and Others* [2009] ECR I-4529.
[104] Ibid., para. 61.

c) Substitution of competition by cooperation

The concept of 'concerted practice' includes any form of cooperation that is contrary to the normal competitive process. This refers primarily to any exchange of sensitive information on not otherwise readily accessible market data such as pricing, discount policies or planned changes of prices, business strategies etc. As held in the *British Sugar* case, even the unilateral disclosure of information that is relevant to the market may constitute a concerted practice.[105] Article 101(1) TFEU also covers any other measure that allows the undertakings involved to 'create a climate of mutual certainty as to the future pricing policies'[106] and enables them to pursue the aim of removing in advance any uncertainty about the future conduct of their competitors. In the *Hüls* case the ECJ held:

[A]lthough that requirement of independence does not deprive economic operators of the right to adapt themselves intelligently to the existing and anticipated conduct of their competitors, it does however strictly preclude any direct or indirect contact between such operators, the object or effect whereof is either to influence the conduct on the market of an actual or potential competitor or to disclose to such a competitor the course of conduct which they themselves have decided to adopt or contemplate adopting on the market, where the object or effect of such contact is to create conditions of competition which do not correspond to the normal conditions of the market in question, regard being had to the nature of the products or services offered, the size and number of the undertakings and the volume of the said market.[107]

The market conduct at issue is caught by Article 101(1) TFEU as a concerted practice only when the concertation by undertakings involved has been implemented on the market. This has been ruled on by the ECJ in the *Hüls* case as well:

[T]he concept of concerted practice [. . .] implies, besides undertakings' concerting with each other, subsequent conduct on the market . . .[108]

At the same time the ECJ introduced a rebuttable presumption that once the Commission had adduced evidence of concertation it was for the undertaking to establish that the concertation had not been followed by particular measures implemented on the market.[109]

d) Causal link between mental consensus and concerted practice

According to the *Hüls* judgment, the measures implemented on the market by the undertaking involved in the concerted practice must be the direct result of the already planned coordination of their market conduct. Only then may all the requirements set out by Article 101(1) TFEU be regarded as satisfied:

---

[105] GC (12 July 2001), Joined Cases T-202/98, T-204/98, T-207/98 – *Tate & Lyle and Others* [2001] ECR II-2035.

[106] Ibid., para. 60.   [107] ECJ (8 July 1999), Case C-199/92 P – *Hüls* [1999] ECR I-4287, para. 160.

[108] Ibid., para. 161.   [109] Ibid., para. 162.

It follows, first, that the concept of a concerted practice, as it results from the actual terms of Article 81(1) EC, implies, besides undertakings' concerting with each other, subsequent conduct on the market, and a relationship of cause and effect between the two.[110]

3.3.2 Anticompetitive effects of a concerted practice

Concerted practices are prohibited, regardless of their effect, when they have an anticompetitive object. It is therefore not required to prove the anticompetitive effects of a particular concertation by undertakings as long as its anticompetitive object has been established:[111]

Secondly, contrary to Hüls's argument, a concerted practice as defined above is caught by Article [101(1) TFEU], even in the absence of anticompetitive effects on the market.

First, it follows from the actual text of that provision that, as in the case of agreements between undertakings and decisions by associations of undertakings, concerted practices are prohibited, regardless of their effect, when they have an anticompetitive object.

Next, although the very concept of a concerted practice presupposes conduct by the participating undertakings on the market, it does not necessarily mean that that conduct should produce the specific effect of restricting, preventing or distorting competition.[112]

3.3.3 Burden of proof

As already stated, according to the *Hüls* judgment, the Commission or national competition authorities applying Article 101(1) TFEU are obliged to provide evidence that the concertation between undertakings did take place. Its implementation on the market will be presumed:

subject to proof to the contrary, which it is for the economic operators concerned to adduce, there must be a presumption that the undertakings participating in concerting arrangements and remaining active on the market take account of the information exchanged with their competitors when determining their conduct on that market.[113]

This presumption may be rebutted by the undertaking at any stage of the proceeding, including by appeal before a court of law. Usually a concerted practice may be inferred when parallel behaviour is established and the contact between the parties has been successfully proved.

The sole existence of a parallel market conduct may not be regarded as sufficient proof for a concerted practice when there are other plausible alternative explanations

---

[110] Ibid., para. 161.

[111] For a detailed assessment of the standard of proof in cases of restrictions of competition by object see Bailey, 'Restrictions of Competition by Object under Article 101 TFEU', *Common Market Law Review*, 49 (2012), 559, 587.

[112] ECJ (8 July 1999), Case C-199/92 P – *Hüls*, [1999] ECR I-4287, paras. 163–5.

[113] ECJ (8 July 1999), Case C-49/92 C – *Commission v Anic Partecipazioni SpA* [1999] ECR I-4125, para. 121.

for the steps taken by the undertakings concerned. In such cases a stringent test of parallelism is applied and empirical evidence that there are no other explanations for the measures applied by the parties must be presented.[114]

Summary of Section 3

Article 101(1) TFEU lists three forms of prohibited collusion: 'agreements', 'concerted practices' and 'decisions of an association of undertakings'. The distinction between these types of behaviour is not always clear-cut. However, this does not harm the effectiveness of Article 101(1) TFEU since the key distinction is the distinction between independent conduct and collusive behaviour. Collusive behaviour of any kind is prohibited by Article 101(1) TFEU.

The notion of an 'agreement' covers a wide range of practices. It is not restricted to a particular type of contract or deal. It is also not required that an agreement is legally binding. Agreements do not have to be written.

The concept of a 'single, overall agreement' has been developed by the Commission in order to facilitate the enforcement of Article 101 TFEU against complex cartels of a long duration. According to this concept, it is not necessary for the Commission to prove a series of different agreements concluded by the same cartel members over a period of time and to identify each of its parties, especially when they have changed over a period of time. Undertakings can be held responsible for the overall cartel even though they were not involved in all of its operations on a day-to-day basis or did not participate in all of its constituent elements. However, recent case law suggests that an interruption of anticompetitive behaviour for a significant period of time sets limits to the assumption of a single, overall agreement. The burden of proof rather shifts back to the Commission which has to prove the continuity of the infringement.

Article 101 TFEU applies to bi- or multilateral restrictions of competition. However, there are cases where unilateral conduct seems to be covered by the provision as well. This may occur in particular in vertical distribution partnerships. The supplier of a given product may request the wholesaler to adhere to certain anticompetitive practices. A tacit acquiescence of the wholesaler is required to turn this initially unilateral behaviour into an 'agreement' within the meaning of Article 101(1) TFEU.

Anticompetitive agreements which are required by State actions that do not leave any room for behaviour in compliance with the EU competition rules are considered not to fall into the ambit of Article 101(1) TFEU. They are attributed to the State rather than to the undertakings involved.

---

[114] ECJ (31 March 1993), Joined Cases C-89/85, C-104/85, C-114/85, C-116/85, C-117/85 and C-125/85 to C-129/85 – *Ahlström Osakeyhtiö and Others v Commission (Woodpulp II)* [1993] ECR I-1307, paras. 126, 127.

Associations of undertakings of any kind must not coordinate the market behaviour of their member undertakings through their decisions.

The concept of 'concerted practice' is designed to catch some less intense forms of cooperation than agreements and decisions by associations of undertakings. Any conduct to be classified as a concerted practice must include a mental consensus, a direct or indirect contact between the parties, the substitution of competition by cooperation, and a causal link between the mental consensus and the concerted practice. The burden of proof for these elements rests on the competition authority. The sole existence of a parallel market conduct may not be regarded as sufficient proof for a concerted practice when there are other plausible alternative explanations for the steps taken by the undertakings concerned.

4. THE OBJECT OR EFFECT OF PREVENTING, RESTRICTING OR DISTORTING COMPETITION

Before the concept of restriction of competition and the distinction between 'object' and 'effect' within the meaning of Article 101(1) TFEU are set out in detail, some preliminary comments have to be made.

First, as mentioned above, the prohibition of Article 101(1) TFEU applies to all types of agreements resulting in a distortion of competition regardless of their structure and the number of parties. Both horizontal and vertical agreements are therefore covered.

Secondly, for the purpose of Article 101(1) TFEU it is required to define the relevant market in order to assess the infringement and its effect on trade between Member States. Contrary to Article 102 TFEU, however, market dominance is not a prerequisite for finding a violation of the EU competition rules.

Lastly, the restrictive nature of the agreement at stake must be adequately demonstrated by the Commission or a national competition authority. Account should be taken of all actual conditions, whether of an economic or legal nature, that might influence the market conduct of the parties involved. A 'rubber-stamped' analysis by the Commission or a national competition authority is not sufficient.[115]

4.1 Restriction of competition

Article 101(1) TFEU shall apply only when the market conduct in question has as its object or effect the 'prevention, restriction or distortion of competition'. The

---

[115] Whish and Bailey, *Competition Law*, p. 117.

distinction between the three concepts is however not applied in practice – generally they are referred to collectively as 'restriction of competition' and discussed as a common concept that has to be defined in light of the EU competition law framework.

It must also be noted that the concept of a restriction of competition is of an economic nature. For this reason, a clear-cut line needs to be drawn between contractual restrictions on the one hand and factual restrictions on the other since the latter do not necessarily have to result from the former. Only a limited class of agreements is considered *ex definitione* to have a restriction of competition as its object.[116]

The concept of 'restriction of competition' has to be read in line with the general objective of the EU as stated in Article 3(1)(b) TFEU: 'The Union shall have exclusive competence in [. . .] the establishing of the competition rules necessary for the functioning of the internal market'. The competition referred to in this section shall be understood as 'effective competition' which the General Court described as

the degree of competition necessary to ensure the attainment of the objectives of the Treaty. Its intensity may vary to an extent dictated by the nature of the product concerned and the structure of the relevant market. Furthermore, its parameters may assume unequal importance, as price competition does not constitute the only effective form of competition or that to which absolute priority must in all circumstances be given.[117]

An additional point to consider is whether the agreement or alleged concerted practice results in the restriction of the undertakings' ability to independently follow particular market strategies. It is inherent in the concept of undistorted competition that 'each economic operator must determine independently the policy which he intends to adopt on the common market'.[118]

Another important example of restriction of competition is that of agreements that hinder market integration by isolating national markets or parts of them and sheltering them from effective competition. In its landmark judgment *Consten and Grundig v Commission*, the ECJ held:

Since the agreement thus aims at isolating the French market for Grundig products and maintaining artificially, for products of a very well-known brand, separate national markets within the Community, it is therefore such as to distort competition in the Common Market.[119]

---

[116] For a detailed analysis of the concept of restriction of competition under Article 101(1) TFEU see Nazzini, 'Article 81 EC between Time Present and Time Past', 497.

[117] GC (27 September 2006), Case T-168/01 – *GlaxoSmithKline Services v Commission* [2006] ECR II-2969, para. 109.

[118] ECJ (16 December 1975), Joined Cases 40/73 to 48/73, 50/73, 54/73 to 56/73, 111/73, 113/73, 114/73 – *Suiker Unie v Commission* [1975] ECR 1663, paras. 174–175.

[119] ECJ (13 July 1966), Joined Cases 56/64, 58/64 – *Consten and Grundig v Commission* [1966] ECR 299, p. 343.

4.2 Object or effect

The requirements of 'object' and 'effect' in Article 101(1) TFEU are alternative and not cumulative. They are to be read disjunctively. It is necessary to establish the object of an agreement or a concerted practice. The effects of such an agreement or a concerted practice shall however be scrutinised only when it is not clear that its object is to restrict the competition on the internal market:

The fact that these are not cumulative but alternative requirements, indicated by the conjunction 'or', leads first to the need to consider the precise purpose of the agreement, in the economic context in which it is to be applied. This interference with competition referred to Article [101(1) TFEU] must result from all or some of the clauses of the agreement itself. Where, however, an analysis of the said clauses does not reveal the effect on competition to be sufficiently deleterious, the consequences of the agreement should then be considered and for it to be caught by the prohibition it is then necessary to find that those factors are present which show that competition has in fact been prevented or restricted or distorted to an appreciable extent.[120]

4.3 Object

The object of an agreement shall be considered before analysing its effects. It has to be established by assessing the objective aims of the agreement at stake. An agreement has the object of distorting competition if the actions undertaken at least potentially impede trade between Member States[121] either for economic reasons or because they hinder the integration of the internal market. The parties' subjective intentions are irrelevant.[122] Thus, an agreement is caught by Article 101(1) TFEU even though its parties claim that the distortion of competition resulting from it was not their intention or that it did not have an appreciable effect on competition.[123]

With regard to horizontal agreements, the European courts have underlined in several cases that agreements pursuing objects contrary to Article 101(1) TFEU covered by the cartel prohibition 'cannot be justified by an analysis of the economic context of the anticompetitive conduct concerned'.[124] The following types of

---

[120] ECJ (30 June 1966), Case 56/65 – *Société Technique Minière v Maschinenbau Ulm* [1966] ECR 235, p. 249.

[121] GC (8 July 2004), Joined Cases T-67/00, T-68/00, T-71/00, T-78/00 – *JFE Engineering v Commission* [2004] ECR II-2501, para. 393.

[122] Ibid., para. 249. On the role of subjective intentions for the assessment under Article 101 TFEU, see Bailey, 'Restrictions of Competition by Object under Article 101 TFEU', 578.

[123] GC (8 July 2004), Case T-44/00 – *Mannesmannröhren-Werke AG v Commission* [2004] ECR II-2223, para. 30, 196.

[124] See for example, GC (8 July 2004), Joined Cases T-67/00, T-68/00, T-71/00 and T-78/00 – *JFE Engineering v Commission* [2004] ECR II-2501, para. 184.

horizontal agreements have been found by the ECJ to have, by their nature, the object of restricting competition on the internal market:[125]

- horizontal price fixing – this is the most prominent and most well-known prohibition. The courts' and the Commission's longstanding practice has developed an abundance of cases that cover a broad array of different agreements that have as their object to fix prices.[126] In addition, the General Court has confirmed[127] the Commission's position[128] that the object-based approach also applies to *buyers'* price fixing;
- the partitioning of markets – be it geographically[129] or with respect to certain customers;[130]
- exclusive purchasing arrangements within a cooperative.[131]

The above-mentioned offences are often referred to as *per se*[132] or *hardcore* restrictions.[133]

In addition to horizontal agreements, there are also a number of *vertical* constellations which are illegal on their face. This used to be true for virtually all agreements that limit the purchaser's control over the sold goods or services, such as the fixing of resale prices or the imposition of export bans.[134] A more detailed list of prohibited practices can be found in Article 4 of the Commission's Regulation on vertical restraints.[135]

---

[125] For a detailed discussion of the concept of restriction of competition by object see Bailey, 'Restrictions of Competition by Object under Article 101 TFEU', 559.

[126] See, e.g., Commission decision of 21 February 2007, Case COMP/E-1/38.823 – PO/*Elevators and Escalators*, available at http://ec.europa.eu/competition/antitrust/cases/dec_docs/38823/38823_1340_4.pdf, para. 22; GC (9 July 2003), Case T-224/00 – *Archer Daniels Midland and Archer Daniels Midland Ingredients v Commission* [2003] ECR II-2597; GC (11 March 1999), Case T-141/94 – *Thyssen Stahl v Commission* [1999] ECR II-347, para. 675; GC (6 April 1995), Case T-148/89 – *Tréfilunion SA v Commission* [1995] ECR II-1063, para. 109.

[127] GC (8 September 2010), Case T-29/05 – *Deltafina v Commission* [2011] ECR II-4077, para. 277.

[128] Commission decision of 20 October 2004, Case COMP/C.38.238/B.2 – *Raw Tobacco Spain*, available at http://ec.europa.eu/competition/antitrust/cases/dec_docs/38238/38238_249_1.pdf, paras. 77–83.

[129] GC (29 June 1995), Case T-32/91 – *Solvay v Commission* [1995] ECR II-1825; Commission decision of 24 January 2007, Case COMP/F/38.899 – *Gas Insulated Switchgear*, available at http://ec.europa.eu/competition/antitrust/cases/dec_docs/38899/38899_1030_7.pdf.

[130] Commission decision of 5 December 2001, Case COMP/37.800/F3 – *Luxembourg Brewers*, OJ No. L 253 of 21 September, p. 21; Commission decision of 5 September 1979, Case IV/29.021– *BP Kemi – DDSF*, OJ No. L 286 of 14 November 1979, p. 32.

[131] ECJ (25 March 1981) Case 61/80 – *Coöperatieve Stremsel – en Kleurselfabriek v Commission* [1981] ECR 851, para. 12.

[132] For a general discussion of presumptions in EU competition law, including the notion of *per se* infringement, see Bailey, 'Presumptions in EU Competition Law, *European Competition Law Review*, 31 (2010), 362.

[133] For a discussion of price fixing as a *per se* infringement from an economic point of view, see Kokkoris, 'Purchase Price Fixing: A per se Infringement?', *European Competition Law Review*, 28 (2007), 473.

[134] ECJ (13 July 1966), Joined Cases 56/64, 58/64 – *Consten and Grundig v Commission* [1966] ECR 299.

[135] Commission Regulation (EU) No 330/2010 of 20 April 2010 on the application of Article 101(3) of the TFEU to categories of vertical agreements and concerted practices, OJ No. L 102 of 23 April 2010, p. 1, Article 4.

However, this general notion has been somewhat muddied by the *GlaxoSmithKline* decision of the General Court. The case centred on the question whether a certain provision that limited the purchaser's ability to export drugs bought from the manufacturer was contrary to EU competition law. The court noted that the prices for medicines concerned were not usually established by the interplay of supply and demand and that, therefore, no direct inference could be drawn from the clause:

In this largely unprecedented situation, it cannot be inferred merely from a reading of the terms of that agreement, in its context, that the agreement is restrictive of competition, and it is therefore necessary to consider the effects of the agreement . . . [136]

Although the General Court's judgment obviously deviates from prior decisions, it must be borne in mind that its reasoning is strictly limited to a specific set of facts and an atmosphere which is by-and-large regulated rather than subject to free competition.

In the *Hüls* judgment cited above, the ECJ stated that the 'two-stage' approach also applies to concerted practices insofar as the object of cooperation is a hardcore restriction of competition:

a concerted practice [. . .] is caught by Article [101(1) TFEU], even in the absence of anti-competitive effects on the market. [137]

The Commission's approach concerning the scope of the 'object category' has been reflected in its Guidelines on the application of Article 101(3) TFEU as follows:

21. Restrictions of competition by object are those that by their very nature have the potential of restricting competition. These are restrictions which in light of the objectives pursued by the Community competition rules have such a high potential of negative effects on competition that it is unnecessary for the purposes of applying Article [101(1) TFEU] to demonstrate any actual effects on the market. This presumption is based on the serious nature of the restriction and on experience showing that restrictions of competition by object are likely to produce negative effects on the market and to jeopardise the objectives pursued by the Community competition rules. Restrictions by object such as price fixing and market sharing reduce output and raise prices, leading to a misallocation of resources, because goods and services demanded by customers are not produced. They also lead to a reduction in consumer welfare, because consumers have to pay higher prices for the goods and services in question. [138]

The Commission has made reference to this approach in a number of its publications. For example, its Vertical Block Exemption Regulation defines hardcore restrictions as those agreements that have as their object:

---

[136] GC (27 September 2006), Case T-168/01 – *GlaxoSmithKline Services v Commission* [2006] ECR II-2969, para. 147.
[137] ECJ (8 July 1999), Case C-199/92 P – *Hüls* [1999] ECR I-4287, para. 163.
[138] Commission Guidelines on the application of Article 81(3) of the Treaty, OJ No. C 101 of 27 April 2004, p. 97, para. 21.

- the restriction of the buyer's ability to determine its sale price;
- the restriction of the territory into which a buyer may sell the contract goods or services, except where certain conditions are met;
- the restriction of active or passive sales to end-users by members of a selective distribution system;
- the restriction of cross-supplies between distributors within a selective distribution system;
- the restriction, agreed between a supplier of components and a buyer who incorporates those components, of the supplier's ability to sell the components as spare parts to end-users or to repairers.[139]

Likewise, the Commission's Motor Vehicle Block Exemption Regulation lists a number of hardcore restrictions specific to the automotive industry.[140]

Additional guidance can be sought in the Commission's Technology Transfer Agreements Block Exemption Regulation,[141] the Commission's Guidelines on the Application of Article 101(3) TFEU,[142] as well as in the Commission's notices.

The types of agreements listed in any of these publications (the 'blacklisted restrictions') are most likely to be considered restrictions by object.

4.4 Effects

According to the 'two-stage' test the effects of an agreement have to be scrutinised in the light of Article 101(1) TFEU only when its object has not been found to restrict competition. In general, an agreement is likely to have an adverse effect on competition when it either

- affects actual or potential competition between suppliers of competing products (inter-brand competition) to such an extent that on the relevant market negative effects on prices, output, innovation or the variety or quality of goods and services can be expected with a reasonable degree of probability, or
- restricts the supplier's distributors from competing with each other by imposing some restraints on intra-brand competition.

---

[139] Commission Regulation (EU) No 330/2010 of 20 April 2010 on the application of Article 101(3) of the TFEU to categories of vertical agreements and concerted practices, OJ No. L 102 of 23 April 2010, p. 1, Article 4.
[140] Commission Regulation (EU) No 461/2010 of 27 May 2010 on the application of Article 101(3) of the TFEU to categories of vertical agreements and concerted practices in the motor vehicle sector, OJ No. L 129 of 28 May 2010, p. 52, Article 5.
[141] Commission Regulation (EC) No 772/2004 of 27 April 2004 on the application of Article 81(3) EC to categories of technology transfer agreements, OJ No. L 123 of 27 April 2004, p. 11, Article 4.
[142] Commission Guidelines on the application of Article 81(3) of the Treaty, OJ No. C 101 of 27 April 2004, p. 97, paras. 21–3.

4.4.1 Extensive market analysis

Each analysis of effects imposed on the market by a particular measure must be supported by an in-depth examination of the economic market conditions. In other words, the agreement/concerted practice in question must be considered in the market context in which it occurred. This was held by the ECJ in the *Delimitis* judgment,[143] delivered as an answer to a preliminary question of a German appeal court whether a provision in an agreement between a brewery and a licensee of a public house owned by the brewery imposing on the licensee the obligation to purchase a minimum amount of beer each year, was contrary to Article 101(1) TFEU. After stating that the agreement in question did not have the restriction of competition as its object the ECJ went on to examine its effects.

As the effect of an agreement can only be determined after a full analysis of the economic context in which the undertakings operate, the court decided to scrutinise the following elements:

- definition of the relevant geographical and product market;
- possible limitation of access to the market;
- foreclosure effects of the agreements entered into by the parties.

4.4.2 Analysis of the counterfactual situation

For a complete and proper assessment as to whether an agreement has a restrictive effect on competition the European courts compare the current factual situation to the hypothetical situation which would persist had the agreement at issue not been concluded. This longstanding line of jurisprudence was initiated by the ECJ in *Société Technique Minière*, where it held that

Where an analysis of the said clauses does not reveal the effect on competition to be sufficiently deleterious, the consequences of the agreement should then be considered, and for it to be caught by the prohibition it is then necessary to find that those factors are present which show that competition has in fact been prevented or restricted or distorted to an appreciable extent. The competition must be understood within the actual context in which it would occur in the absence of the agreement in dispute.[144]

This understanding has recently been confirmed by the General Court in the *O2 Germany* case. In its judgment, the court annulled the respective Commission decision because it had failed to present, *inter alia*, an examination of competition in the absence of the roaming agreement in question.[145] Despite requiring such an extensive analysis, the court maintained that 'the taking into account of the competition

---

[143] ECJ (28 February 1991), Case C-234/89 – *Delimitis v Henninger Bräu* [1991] ECR I-935.
[144] ECJ (30 June 1966), Case 56/65 – *Société Technique Minière v Maschinenbau Ulm* [1966] ECR 235, para. 8.
[145] GC (2 May 2006), Case T-328/03 – *O2 (Germany) v Commission* [2006] ECR II-1231, paras. 65–117.

situation that would exist in the absence of the agreement, does not amount to [. . .] applying a *rule of reason* [. . .]'[146] (emphasis added).

It has since been argued that the approach taken by the General Court does not significantly differ from the rule of reason analysis in US antitrust law[147] and that EU courts should apply the same standard under Article 101(1) TFEU.[148]

In *Van den Bergh Foods Ltd* the General Court clearly stated that the existence of a rule of reason is not accepted in EU competition law and that such an approach would be difficult to reconcile with the structure of Article 101 TFEU.[149] Nonetheless, it is widely believed that the requirements set by the court entail an analysis that is quasi-tantamount to such a rule.[150]

4.4.3 Relevant material factors

A proper assessment of both the market context and the counterfactual situation should, according to the ECJ, include:

The nature and quantity, limited or otherwise, of the products covered by the agreement, the position and importance of the grantor and the concessionnaire on the market for the products concerned, the isolated nature of the disputed agreement or, alternatively, its position in a series of agreements, the severity of the clauses intended to protect the exclusive dealership or, alternatively, the opportunities allowed for other commercial competitors in the same products by way of parallel re-exportation and importation.[151]

There are also a number of other issues that must be taken into account when determining the conditions of a specific market. In *Delimitis* the ECJ referred to:

- the number and size of producers present on the market,
- the degree of saturation of that market, and
- customer fidelity to existing brands.[152]

4.4.4 Effects on actual and potential competitors

Article 101(1) TFEU may also apply when an agreement threatens the penetration of a market by a potential *future* competitor.

In *European Night Services*, four national railway companies, each of them dominant in their respective home market, formed a joint venture in order to provide

---

[146] Ibid., para. 69.

[147] Marquis, 'O2 (Germany) v Commission and the exotic mysteries of Article 81(1) EC', *European Law Review*, 32 (2007), 29, 44.

[148] Robertson, 'What is a Restriction of Competition? The Implications of the CFI's Judgment in O2 Germany and the Rule of Reason', *European Competition Law Review*, 28 (2007), 252, 260.

[149] GC (23 October 2003), Case T-65/98 – *Van den Bergh Foods Ltd. v Commission* [2003] ECR II-4653, para. 106.

[150] See also 4.4.8 Rule of Reason below.

[151] ECJ (30 June 1966), Case 56/65 – *Société Technique Minière v Maschinenbau Ulm* [1966] ECR 235, p. 250.

[152] ECJ (28 February 1991), Case C-234/89 – *Delimitis v Henninger Bräu* [1991] ECR I-935, para. 22.

seamless train transportation services between different continental European cities and the UK. Whereas, at the time of the notification, the companies were not 'actual competitors' on any of the proposed routes, it was debated whether or not they were 'potential competitors', because the adoption of Directive 91/440 changed the conditions of competition on the market and, under certain circumstances, allows for the penetration of foreign markets which were previously reserved to the respective national railway undertakings. The Commission had also argued that the agreement raised the barriers of entry for newly established companies that were to enter the market for train transport at night.

The General Court acknowledged the possibility of such potential competition and, in reference to *Delimitis*, stated:

It must [...] be stressed that the examination of conditions of competition is based not only on existing competition between undertakings already present on the relevant market but also on potential competition, in order to ascertain whether, in the light of the structure of the market and the economic and legal context within which it functions, there are real concrete possibilities for the undertakings concerned to compete among themselves or for a new competitor to penetrate the relevant market and compete with the undertakings already established.[153]

However, the General Court noted that the Commission's mere statement that such potential competition was affected by the agreement did not suffice. Rather, it held that an 'economically realistic approach'[154] was necessary to determine whether or not such potential competition really existed.

In the case at hand it was very unlikely that either the existing undertakings were to become actual competitors or that newly established undertakings were to enter the market for night train services. Thus it was held that the joint venture between the national railway companies could not possibly have a negative effect on such potential competition.

Agreements might also be caught by Article 101(1) because they are detrimental to the business interests of third parties. In many instances, these agreements will also be in violation of EU competition law for other reasons. Such limitations may arise from agreements:

- that contain exclusive supply[155] or sale provisions and therefore exclude third parties from the market in question;
- that set up exclusive distribution schemes and thereby impede parallel imports by third parties.[156]

---

[153] GC (15 September 1998), Joined Cases T-374/94, T-375/94, T-384/94, T-388/94 – *European Night Services and Others* [1998] ECR II-3141, para. 137.

[154] Ibid.

[155] GC (2 July 1992), Case T-61/89 – *Dansk Pelsdyravlerforening v Commission* [1992] ECR II-1931.

[156] ECJ (13 July 1966), Joined Cases 56/64, 58/64 – *Consten and Grundig v Commission* [1966] ECR 299, p. 341.

4.4.5 Networks of agreements

The existence of a network of similar agreements may be one of the decisive factors in establishing an infringement of Article 101(1) TFEU. In general, an agreement may be covered by Article 101(1) TFEU if it is established that it constitutes an element of a network of similar agreements which prevents new competitors from entering the particular market. In the *Van den Bergh Foods* case, the General Court held that the network of agreements between an ice cream producer and retailers in Ireland prohibited the distributors from stocking ice creams provided by competitors in the freezers supplied by the manufacturer and therefore created foreclosure effects caught by Article 101(1) TFEU:

In order to determine whether exclusive distribution agreements fall within the prohibition contained in Article [101(1) TFEU], it is appropriate, in accordance with the case-law, to consider whether all the similar agreements entered into in the relevant market and the other features of the economic and legal context of the agreements at issue, show that those agreements cumulatively have the effect of denying access to that market to new competitors. [...] If such examination reveals that it is difficult to gain access to the market, it is then necessary to assess the extent to which the agreements at issue contribute to the cumulative effect produced, on the basis that only those agreements which make a significant contribution to any partitioning of the market are prohibited.[157]

4.4.6 Ancillary commercial restrictions

There are a considerable number of restrictive provisions in agreements which, according to settled case law and Commission practice, do not fall within the scope of Article 101(1) TFEU. Such clauses, often described as 'ancillary restraints', are usually part of broader agreements which have neither the object nor the effect of distorting competition, but for whose execution or the achievement of its main purpose certain limitations are necessary. In order to classify a particular provision as an ancillary restraint, the following two conditions have to be satisfied:

(i) the restriction contained in the examined clause must be objectively necessary for the implementation of the main operation, and

(ii) the restriction in question must be proportionate.[158]

The first stage of this test must be based not on an abstract assessment. Rather, the analysis of the specific context of the main operation made in the light of the competitive situation on the relevant market shall be decisive. The proportionality

---

[157] GC (23 October 2003), Case T-65/98 – *Van den Bergh Foods Ltd v Commission* [2003] ECR II-4653, para. 83.

[158] GC (18 September 2001), Case T-112/99 – *M6 and Others v Commission* [2001] ECR II-2459, para. 106.

requirement shall be met when the duration and scope of the restriction in question do not exceed what is necessary in order to implement the operation at issue.

Applying those principles, the European courts and the Commission (in particular in its corresponding notice[159]) have found the following ancillary restraints to be compatible with Article 101 TFEU:

- non-competition clauses in an agreement for the sale of a business[160] or in a JV agreement in order to protect the parties' individual economic interests;[161]
- restrictions in franchise agreements if they are necessary to prevent free-riding with respect to know-how and assistance provided by the franchisor;[162]
- provisions in the statutes of an association enabling its members to set up an effective purchasing group.[163]

In a more general sense it can be said that ancillary restraints are often included in an agreement to underline the good will of one of the parties and thus to make a transaction effective. For example, the sale of a business may result in its being worth much less to the purchaser if the seller decides to offer the same goods or services in a newly established business next door. Accordingly, such a sale (which, in itself is non-restrictive of competition) might be protected by a non-competition clause ancillary to the main agreement. In its notice the Commission has set out some guidelines as to the circumference of such restrictions, but limitations will always have to be assessed on a case-by-case basis.

4.4.7 Regulatory restraints

A similar approach has been applied by the ECJ in cases where the restriction at issue was not necessary to execute a commercial transaction but was ancillary to a public regulatory function. In the landmark judgment in *Wouters*,[164] the ECJ had to decide, *inter alia*, whether a national Dutch regulation prohibiting lawyers from entering into partnership with non-lawyers was compatible with the EU competition rules, in particular Article 101(1) TFEU.[165] After having stated that the prohibition of multi-disciplinary partnerships aims to limit production and technical development within

---

[159] Commission Notice on restrictions directly related and necessary to concentrations, OJ No. C 56 of 5 March 2005, p. 24.

[160] ECJ (11 July 1985), Case 42/84 – *Remia BV and Others v Commission* [1985] ECR 2545, para. 19.

[161] Commission decision of 5 July 1999, Case No. IV/M.1569 – *Gränges/Norsk Hydro*, available at http://ec.europa.eu/competition/mergers/cases/decisions/m1569_fn.pdf, para. 22.

[162] ECJ (28 January 1986), Case 161/84 – *Pronuptia* [1986] ECR 353, para. 27.

[163] ECJ (15 December 1994), C-250/92 – *Gøttrup-Klim and Others Grovvareforeninger v Dansk Landbrugs Grovvareselskab* [1994] ECR ECR I-5641.

[164] ECJ (19 February 2002), C-309/99 – *Wouters and Others* [2002] ECR I-1577.

[165] On the assessment of rules of professional conduct under the EU competition rules, see Delimatsis, '"Thou shall not . . . (dis)trust": Codes of Conduct and Harmonization of Professional Standards in the EU', *Common Market Law Review*, 47 (2010), 1049, 1080.

the meaning of Article 101(1)(b) TFEU, the court concluded that the regulation at stake did not fall within the scope of Article 101(1) TFEU:

However, not every agreement between undertakings or every decision of an association of undertakings which restricts the freedom of action of the parties or of one of them necessarily falls within the prohibition laid down in Article [101(1) TFEU]. For the purposes of application of that provision to a particular case, account must first of all be taken of the overall context in which the decision of the association of undertakings was taken or produces its effects. More particularly, account must be taken of its objectives, which are here connected with the need to make rules relating to organisation, qualifications, professional ethics, supervision and liability, in order to ensure that the ultimate consumers of legal services and the sound administration of Justice are provided with the necessary guarantees in relation to integrity and experience. It has then to be considered whether the consequential effects restrictive of competition are inherent in the pursuit of those objectives.[166]

Accordingly it is possible to balance non-competition objectives, such as guarantees of integrity and experience to the consumers of legal services and sound administration of Justice, against a restriction of competition and to find out that the former outweighs the latter. Reasonable regulatory rules fall outside the scope of Article 101(1) TFEU when the following three requirements are fulfilled:

(i)   the restriction pursues a legitimate objective;
(ii) the restrictive effects are inherent in the pursuit of that objective;
(iii) the restriction is proportionate.[167]

This three-stage test has to be applied with regard to the overall legal and economic context in which the examined restriction is applied.

The *Wouters* judgment has been confirmed and extended to a partially private regulatory system in the *Meca-Medina* case which concerned the compatibility of the International Swimming Association's anti-doping rules with EU competition law.[168] The ECJ decided that the restrictions on competition leading to the exclusion of an athlete from a sporting event (i) had a legitimate object (safeguarding equal chances for athletes, athletes' health, the integrity and objectivity of competitive sport and ethical values in sport),[169] (ii) were necessary to ensure enforcement of the doping ban,[170] and (iii) were proportionate in relation to that object.[171] Consequently the ECJ confirmed the anti-doping rules' compatibility with Article 101 TFEU.[172]

---

[166] ECJ (19 February 2002), C-309/99 – *Wouters and Others* [2002] ECR I-1577, para. 97.
[167] Ibid.; ECJ (18 July 2006), Case C-519/04 P – *Meca-Medina and Majcen v Commission* [2006] ECR I-6991, para. 42.
[168] ECJ (18 July 2006), Case C-519/04 P – *Meca-Medina and Majcen v Commission* [2006] ECR I-6991.
[169] Ibid., para. 43.   [170] Ibid., para. 44.   [171] Ibid., para. 55.
[172] For another example of restrictions through a regulatory body, see Gorecki and Mackey, 'Hemat v Medical Council: Its Implications for Irish and EU Competition Law', *European Competition Law Review*, 28 (2007), 285.

Commentators have described the *Wouters* test as one of deontological[173] or regulatory ancillarity[174] or called it a 'European style rule of reason'.[175] Whatever name will prevail, the court has made it abundantly clear that certain restrictions are not subject to Article 101 TFEU because their anticompetitive effect is outweighed by *non-competition* objectives.[176] As the first *Wouters* requirement is the pursuit of a legitimate object, all exceptions are most likely to fall within the ambit of public interest.

4.4.8 Rule of reason

Following the approach of the European courts not to apply the EU competition rules to certain classes of agreements, some consideration was given to the question whether Article 101(1) TFEU allows for the adoption of a 'rule of reason'.[177]

The term 'rule of reason' describes a system of analysis utilised to assess the legality of allegedly anticompetitive conduct under the Sherman Act.[178] It was first developed by the US Supreme Court in 1911 when Chief Justice White held that

the standard of reason [. . .] was intended to be the measure used for the purpose of determining whether in a given case a particular act had or had not brought about the wrong against which the statute provided[179]

His approach, to take into account the 'surrounding circumstances'[180] of an agreement in order to consider whether it *unreasonably* restrained trade, was heavily criticised at the time,[181] but nonetheless formed the basis for a broad application of the standard in later cases. In 1918, the court explained the approach in more detail:

[T]he legality of an agreement or regulation cannot be determined by so simple a test, as whether it restrains competition. Every agreement concerning trade, every regulation of trade, restrains. To bind, to restrain, is of their very essence. The true test of legality is whether the restraint imposed is such as merely regulates and perhaps thereby promotes competition or whether it is such as may suppress or even destroy competition. To determine that question the court must ordinarily consider the facts peculiar to the business to which the restraint is

---

[173] Loozen, 'Professional Ethics and Restraints of Competition', *European Law Review*, 31 (2006), 28, 39.
[174] Whish and Bailey, *Competition Law*, pp. 130 et seq.
[175] Monti, 'Article 81 EC and Public Policy', *Common Market Law Review*, 39 (2002), 1057, 1088 et seq.
[176] See Szyszczak, 'Competition and Sport', *European Law Review*, 32 (2007), 95.
[177] For a recent contribution to this discussion, see Lavrijssen, 'What Role for National Competition Authorities in Protecting Non-competition Interests after Lisbon?', *European Law Review*, 35 (2010), 636.
[178] 15 USC § 1, sections 1 and 2 of which are broadly equivalent to Articles 101 and 102 TFEU.
[179] US Supreme Court, *Standard Oil Co. of New Jersey v United States*, 221 US 1 (1911), at 60.
[180] Ibid. at 58.
[181] Cf. Justice Harlan's dissent, ibid. at 88: '[W]e are asked to read into the act *by way of judicial legislation an exception that is not placed there by the lawmaking branch of the Government*, and this is to be done upon the theory that the impolicy of such legislation is so clear that it cannot be supposed Congress intended the natural import of the language it used. *This we cannot and ought not to do.*' (emphasis in the original)

applied; its condition before and after the restraint was imposed; the nature of the restraint and its effect, actual or probable. The history of the restraint, the evil believed to exist, the reason for adopting the particular remedy, the purpose or end sought to be attained, are all relevant facts. This is not because a good intention will save an otherwise objectionable regulation or the reverse; but because knowledge of intent may help the court to interpret facts and to predict consequences.

Under this scheme, there were now two types of agreements: those that were clearly and irrefutably illegal (*per se* illegality for manifestly anticompetitive conduct only) and those that required a full analysis of the facts (rule of reason for all remaining constellations). As the courts tried to avoid the often strenuous efforts required by the rule of reason analysis, many practices were henceforth categorised to be illegal *per se*. In addition, as courts became more familiar with certain issues that had previously been reviewed under the rule of reason, they applied a 'truncated' or 'quick look' rule of reason which aimed to exclude excessive pro-competitive evidence in cases where, without falling under one of the *per se* categories, anticompetitive effects of the agreement were apparent.[182]

The US Supreme Court has subsequently curtailed the application of the quick look analysis and determined that 'no categorical line [can be] drawn between restraints that give rise to an intuitively obvious inference of anticompetitive effect and those that call for more detailed treatment'.[183] As a result the regular 'full-fact' rule of reason review remains the standard applied in the majority of cartel cases in the US.

In the context of EU law the rule of reason concept was thus understood as a case-by-case evaluation of the market conduct at issue, in particular the balancing of positive and negative effects of an undertaking's actions.[184] Consequently, an anti-competitive practice shall fall outside Article 101(1) TFEU if the positive effects, such as opening new markets or technical development, outweigh the negative ones.

This approach has been explicitly rejected by the General Court in its *Métropole* judgment:

According to the applicants, as a consequence of the existence of a rule of reason in Community competition law, when Article [101(1) TFEU] is applied it is necessary to weigh the pro and anticompetitive effects of an agreement in order to determine whether it is caught by the prohibition laid down in that article. It should, however, be observed, first of all, that contrary to the applicants' assertions the existence of such a rule has not, as such, been confirmed by the Community courts. Quite to the contrary, in various judgments the Court of

---

[182] US Supreme Court, *National Soc'y of Prof. Engineers*, 435 U.S. 679 (1978), at 692; US Supreme Court, *National Collegiate Athletic Ass'n v. Board of Regents of Univ. of Okla.*, 468 US 85 (1984), 104–113; US Supreme Court, *Indiana Fed'n of Dentists*, 476 US 447 (1986), 457–65.

[183] US Supreme Court, *California Dental Ass'n v. Federal Trade Commission*, 526 US 756 (1999), 780 et seq.

[184] See Psychogiopoulou, 'EC Competition Law and Cultural Diversity: The Case of the Cinema, Music and Book Publishing Industries', *European Law Review*, 30 (2005), 838; Basaran, 'How Should Article 81 EC Address Agreements that Yield Environmental Benefits?', *European Competition Law Review*, 27 (2006), 479; Szyszczak, 'Competition and Sport' 95.

Justice and the Court of First Instance have been at pains to indicate that the existence of a rule of reason in Community competition law is doubtful.[185]

Thus, under the European framework the balancing of anticompetitive and pro-competitive effects shall be concluded exclusively within the framework laid down by Article 101(3) TFEU.[186]

Summary of Section 4

Article 101(1) TFEU shall apply only when the market conduct in question has as its object or effect the *'prevention, restriction or distortion of competition'*. The distinction between the three concepts is however not applied in practice – generally they are referred to collectively as *'restriction of competition'* and discussed as a common concept that has to be defined in light of the EU competition law framework.

The requirements of 'object' and 'effect' are alternative and not cumulative. The effects of an agreement or a concerted practice need to be assessed only when the object to restrict competition cannot be established.

The object of an agreement or concerted practice has to be analysed by assessing the objective aims of the agreement at stake. The parties' subjective intentions are irrelevant. An agreement has the object of distorting competition if the actions undertaken at least potentially impede trade between Member States either for economic reasons or because they hinder the integration of the internal market. There are a number of practices that are considered to have an anticompetitive object *per se*. This includes price fixing in horizontal agreements and the fixing of minimum resale prices in vertical agreements. Other practices need to be assessed individually.

If no restrictive object can be established it has to be assessed whether the practice in question had a restrictive effect on competition. Article 101 TFEU protects both inter-brand and intra-brand competition. Inter-brand competition occurs for example between suppliers of competing products. Intra-brand competition occurs for example between distributors of the same supplier. To establish a restrictive effect, an extensive analysis of the economic circumstances needs to be carried out. This includes a comparison of the current factual situation to the hypothetical situation which would persist had the agreement at issue not been concluded. Both the effects on actual and potential competitors have to be taken into consideration.

In some cases it is not the individual agreement that has a restrictive effect on competition but it is its being part of a network of similar agreements that gives it an anticompetitive effect. In particular, an agreement may be covered by Article 101(1) TFEU if it is established that it constitutes an element of a network of similar agreements which prevents new competitors from entering the particular market.

---

[185] GC (18 September 2001), Case T-112/99 – *M6 and Others v Commission* [2001] ECR II-2459, para. 72.
[186] But cf. the so-called 'European style rule of reason', discussed at 4.4.7 above.

Ancillary restraints are considered not to fall into the ambit of Article 101(1) TFEU. They are usually part of broader agreements which have neither the object nor the effect of distorting competition, but for whose execution or the achievement of their main purpose certain limitations are necessary. Ancillary restraints have to be objectively necessary and proportionate with regard to the main purpose.

Regulations of associations of undertakings which restrict competition in pursuit of public interest goals may also escape the prohibition of Article 101(1) TFEU (for example anti-doping rules of sports associations). The restrictions of competition need to be inherent in the regulation and proportionate to the legitimate goal of the regulation.

The consideration of non-competition interests in the assessment of restrictions of competition has led to a debate on whether a rule of reason applies also in Europe. However, the ECJ holds that any balancing of restrictions of competition with beneficial effects they may have needs to be carried out within the framework of Article 101(3) TFEU.

5. THE EXAMPLES OF COLLUSION LISTED IN ARTICLE 101(1) TFEU

Article 101(1) TFEU contains a non-exhaustive list of prohibited practices. Consequently, a practice does not necessarily have to fall under one of the listed categories in order to be caught by the provision. Nonetheless, the subsection represents a great variety of different forms of collusion; certain conduct might even be reflected by two or more of the examples stipulated in Article 101 TFEU. The European courts have repeatedly stressed that it is not necessary to differentiate between the examples as the concepts are fluid and often overlap.[187] In any event, for the purpose of a better understanding, it seems appropriate to explain each of the categories in more detail.

5.1 Direct or indirect fixing of purchase or selling prices or other trading conditions

The first subheading of Article 101(1) TFEU describes the most notable example of a cartel. All fixing of prices or conditions falls within the ambit of this section. These practices generally constitute 'hardcore restrictions' which are easier to qualify as being restrictive of competition.[188] The cases that deal with price fixing are often well

---

[187] GC (24 October 1991), Case T-1/89 – *Rhône-Poulenc SA v Commission* [1991] ECR II-867, para. 126; ECJ (8 July 1999), Case C-49/92 P – *Commission v Anic Partecipazioni SpA* [1999] ECR I-4125, para. 108; Commission decision of 21 October 1998, Case IV/35.691/E-4 – *Pre-Insulated Pipe Cartel*, OJ No. L 24 of 30 January 1999, p. 1.

[188] For a discussion of price fixing as a *per se* infringement from an economic point of view, see Kokkoris, 'Purchase Price Fixing: A Per Se Infringement?', 473.

known even in the general public. As they contain some of the most blatant and clear-cut infringements they frequently result in high fines and attract great media coverage. In many instances such cases will concern the direct fixing of selling prices,[189] but the provision also applies to the fixing of purchase prices[190] and other trading conditions.[191] In addition, it also includes more subtle practices including those that indirectly[192] fix prices or conditions, regardless of whether the agreement in question covers all or only certain elements of a price. It covers the fixing of minimum prices[193] as well as maximum prices[194] and prohibits agreements regarding sales margins,[195] rebates and joint price increases.[196]

In *Cartonboard*, for example, the Commission discovered that a number of European producers of carton board had met regularly in order to agree on price increases for each grade of their respective products and to agree on and implement simultaneous price increases throughout the EU.[197] These agreements were part of an overall plan that also included the partitioning of markets, limitation of production and the exchange of detailed business information that led to substantial harm to competition. Given the open and drastic limitations, the Commission held that there could be 'no doubt whatever about the anticompetitive purpose of [. . .] the cartel'. Accordingly, the undertakings who had taken part in the illegal agreements were ordered to end the infringements and to pay significant fines.

5.2 Limiting or controlling production, markets, technical development, investment

In addition to fixing prices or allocating markets, cartel members often agree on limiting or controlling production, technical development or investment. Such additional agreements may, for example, help maintain a specific price level. Even though

---

[189] Commission decision of 28 January 2009, Case 39.406 – *Marine Hoses*, summary decision published in OJ No. C 168 of 21 July 2009, p. 6, para. 9.

[190] Commission decision of 9 June 1989, Case IV/27.958 – *National Sulphuric Acid Association*, OJ No. L 190 of 5 July 1989, p. 22, para. 6; ECJ (15 December 1994), Case C-250/92 – *Gøttrup-Klim and Others Grovvareforeninger v Dansk Landbrugs Grovvareselskab* [1994] ECR I-5641, para. 35.

[191] Commission decision of 22 December 1972, Case IV/243, 244, 245 – *CIMBEL*, OJ No. L 303 of 31 December 1972, p. 24.

[192] Commission decision of 13 July 1994, Case IV/C/33.833 – *Cartonboard*, OJ No. L 243 of 19 September 1994, p. 1, para. 133.

[193] Commission decision of 24 July 2002, Case COMP/E-3/36.700 – *Industrial and Medical Gases*, OJ No. L 84 of 1 April 2003, p. 1, para. 359.

[194] ECJ (6 November 1979), Joined Cases 16/79 to 20/79 – *Danis* [1979] ECR 3327, para. 7.

[195] ECJ (29 October 1980), Joined Cases 209/78 to 215/78 – *Heintz van Landewyck SARL v Commission* [1980] ECR 3125, paras. 106–41.

[196] Commission decision of 5 February 1992, Case IV/31.572, 32.571 – *Building and Construction Industry in the Netherlands*, OJ No. L 92 of 7 April 1992, p. 1, para. 86.

[197] Commission decision of 13 July 1994, Case IV/C/33.833 – *Cartonboard*, OJ No. L 243 of 19 September 1994, p. 1, para. 175; cf. GC (14 May 1998), Case T-295/94 – *Buchmann GmbH v Commission* [1998] ECR II-813.

it is not necessary for any of these measures to be accompanied by other restrictive actions, this is often the case. Such practices include agreements concerning specific quotas or covenants not to produce a certain product at all.[198] They are particularly utilised in times of oversupply when the parties involved try to justify their behaviour by referring to harsh market conditions (crises) and/or ruinous competition. However, such excuses have not been upheld by either the Commission or the European courts. Instead, they have maintained that the existence of a crisis cannot in itself preclude the anticompetitive nature of an agreement.[199]

In *CIMBEL*, the Commission investigated a number of institutionalised cartel agreements covering the Belgian cement market. Besides other prohibited practices they concerned national and international quotas, uniform prices and a compensation fund for cases when a certain supplier exceeded/undershot the quota assigned to him. The notifying parties argued that the contract in question (which derived in large part from earlier, expired agreements) would help the independent cement manufacturers survive in an environment of ruinous competition. Although the Commission recognised the fact that this might indeed have been the case at the time of the Great Depression, at the time of the decision such an argument was insufficient to compensate for the detriment to competition both on a national and European level. In consequence, the Commission unequivocally rejected the application for negative clearance and made it clear that the limitation of production is a serious infringement of competition law which it will not tolerate.[200]

5.3 Sharing markets or sources of supply

The free movement of goods has been and continues to be one of the main pillars of the EU. The sharing (or allocation) of markets clearly restricts this general principle and is therefore prohibited. This subsection applies not only to geographical markets but also to product markets and markets of customers and suppliers.

Many of the early cartel decisions concerned agreements between companies which used to be active on one specific market only. In a number of cases, the offenders tried to maintain national boundaries which previously circumscribed

---

[198] See, e.g., Commission decision of 2 August 1989, Case IV/31.553 – *Welded Steel Mesh*, OJ No. L 260 of 6 September 1989, p. 1, para. 78; Commission decision of 21 December 1988, Case IV/31.865 – *PVC*, OJ No. L 74 of 17 March 1989, p. 1, para. 38; Commission decision of 17 December 1980, Case IV/29.869 – *Italian Cast Glass*, OJ No. L 383 of 31 December 1980, pp. 19, 24.

[199] ECJ (15 October 2003), Joined Cases C-238/99 P, C-244/99 P, C-245/99 P, C-247/99 P, C-250/99 P to C-252/99 P and C-254/99 P – *Limburgse Vinyl Maatschappij and Others v Commission* [2002] ECR I-8375, para. 487; Commission decision of 2 April 2003, Case COMP/C.38.279/F3 – *French Beef*, OJ No. L 209 of 19 August 2003, p. 12, para. 130.

[200] Commission decision of 31 December 1972, Case IV/243, 244, 245 – *CIMBEL*, OJ No. L 303 of 31 December 1972, p. 24, paras. 18–29.

their respective markets.[201] In others, similar intentions were carried out by exclusively dealing with a specific retailer or licensee and by protecting this exclusivity in a specific area.[202]

Sharing of customers and/or suppliers often occurs in major industry businesses such as construction or gas/oil. Customers may, for example, be classified according to the volume/amount of a possible award[203] or according to their geographic location.

Although less common, the prohibition also applies to the sharing of product markets. In *PO/Needles*,[204] for instance, one of the concerned undertakings had agreed to restrict its manufacturing activities to a certain type of needle only (for which it secured a market outlet in exchange), leaving the related markets of other haberdashery items to its competitors.

The partitioning of markets regularly forms part of a complex cartel structure. In *Copper Industrial Tubes* a number of European tube manufacturers regularly attended meetings of an association whose primary purpose was to promote quality standards for cobber tubes. In undocumented sessions of the association's regular meeting agenda, the parties would fix sales prices and commercial terms, coordinate price increases and allocate customers and market shares in the European territories. They also appointed so-called 'market leaders' for the respective customers and territories.[205] This rather recent case demonstrates that, even though in theory there has been a single internal market for over forty years, it is still common practice to agree on maintaining these former markets.

5.4 Applying dissimilar conditions to equivalent transactions

The prohibition of applying dissimilar conditions to equivalent transactions is tantamount to a prohibition of discrimination. It bans all agreements and concerted

[201] Commission decision of 23 November 1984, Case IV/30.907 – *Peroxygen Products*, OJ No. L 35 of 7 February 1985, p. 1, para. 44; Commission decision of 12 June 1978, Case IV/29.453 – *SNPE-LEL*, OJ No. L 191 of 14 July 1978, p. 41, para. 13; cf. ECJ (28 February 1986), Case 161/84 – *Pronuptia* [1986] ECR 353, para. 26; ECJ (16 December 1975), Joined Cases 40/73 to 48/73, 50/73, 54/73 to 56/73, 111/73, 113/73, 114/73 – *Suiker Unie v Commission* [1975] ECR 1663, paras. 550, 553.

[202] ECJ (13 July 1966), Joined Cases 56/64, 58/64 – *Consten and Grundig v Commission* [1966] ECR 322; cf. Commission decision of 20 September 2000, Case COMP/36.653 – *Opel*, OJ No. L 59 of 28 February 2001, p. 1, para. 136.

[203] Commission decision of 5 September 1979, Case IV/29.021 – *BP Kemi – DDSF*, OJ No. L 286 of 14 November 1979, p. 32, para. 80.

[204] GC (12 September 2007), Case T-30/05 – *Prym and Prym Consumer v Commission* [2007] ECR II-107, para. 188, upheld by ECJ (3 September 2009), Case C-534/07 P – *Prym and Prym Consumer v Commission* [2009] ECR I-7415.

[205] Commission decision of 16 December 2003, Case C.38.240 – *Industrial Tubes*, OJ No. L 125 of 28 April 2004, p. 50, paras. 10–11, confirmed by GC (6 May 2009), Case T-116/04 – *Wieland-Werke and Others* [2009] ECR II-1087.

practices that apply dissimilar conditions to equivalent situations which result in constraints of competition for one of the affected parties, unless the differentiation is objectively justified.[206] In this respect, its scope of application may in some cases be similar to that of Article 102(c) TFEU. The notable difference, however, is that Article 101 TFEU requires an agreement whereas Article 102(c) TFEU prohibits discriminatory conduct only if the acting party is an undertaking in a dominant position. Thus, in order for an agreement to be caught by this subheading, the restriction must result from a discriminatory agreement between two or more undertakings and not from the freely determined conduct of one independent undertaking.[207]

Like the rest of the section, the prohibition of applying dissimilar conditions to equivalent transactions applies to both vertical and horizontal restraints. In the area of vertical agreements, one of the most important examples is that of selective distribution systems according to which a manufacturer limits the resale of its products to certain distributors. Such selected distribution systems are not subject to Article 101 TFEU if they comply with certain criteria. One of these conditions is that the distributors are chosen on the basis of objective criteria of a qualitative nature. Thus, a discriminatory selective distribution system between a manufacturer and a limited number of distributors leads to a restriction of competition with respect to other possible distributors.[208]

The subsection also applies to agreements that result in restrictions on upstream or downstream markets. This includes, for example, agreements between a seller and a purchaser not to supply certain (or any) competitors of the purchaser. It also includes agreements by which the purchaser agrees not to resell the obtained goods to certain customers or to grant a specific group of customers worse conditions than others.

In addition, the prohibition also applies to horizontal agreements if they result in competitive disadvantages to third parties.[209]

A well-known example of applying dissimilar conditions to equivalent transactions is that of Hasselblad, a Swedish company that manufactures professional medium format SLR cameras. Starting in 1958, Hasselblad concluded selective distribution agreements with a number of European importers. Initially, the agreements prohibited sales outside the importers' respective territories. Although these prohibitive clauses were later abandoned, Hasselblad sought to stop parallel imports by pressuring the appointed distributors not to sell their products to foreign purchasers. In addition, cameras that had not been imported by an appointed distributor did not benefit from a special guarantee that provided for more rapid repair services. The Commission held that this practice would place parallel imports of Hasselblad

---

[206] ECJ (19 October 1977), Case C-124/76 – *Moulins Pont-à-Mousson v ONIC* [1977] ECR 1795, para. 17.

[207] GC (12 January 1995), Case T-102/92 – *Viho v Commission* [1995] ECR II-17, para. 51.

[208] GC (12 December 1996), Case T-19/92 – *Leclerc v Commission* [1996] ECR II-1851, paras. 112–17.

[209] Commission decision of 15 May 1974, Case IV/400 – *Agreements between Manufacturers of Glass Containers*, OJ No. L 160 of 17 June 1974, p. 1, para. 34.

cameras at a competitive disadvantage in comparison to 'properly' imported cameras and that it would therefore constitute a measure in restraint of competition.[210]

5.5 Tying of contracts

The last subheading of Article 101(1) refers to the bundling or tying of contracts, i.e. situations where customers of one product (the tying product) are required also to purchase another distinct product (the tied product) from the same supplier or someone designated by the latter.[211] The prohibition does not apply to situations where two products that are often and typically bought together are bundled (as would be the case with portable computers and batteries or shoes and laces for example). Whether or not two products are distinct is determined by customer demand, i.e. if a significant number of customers would prefer to acquire the tying product without having to purchase the tied product, the two products are very likely to be distinct.

The vast majority of bundling cases arise under Article 102 TFEU. If the tying undertaking does not have a dominant position, its action might be subject to Article 101 TFEU. However, as a general rule, this provision requires an agreement. Thus, the independent decision by an autonomous undertaking to sell its products in sets is not caught by Article 101 TFEU. It is also legal for an undertaking to give its customers a discount if they buy two or more different products. This leaves a rather limited scope of application for this subheading. The prohibition would, for example, apply when two independent undertakings decide to tie their products to the detriment of their customers.

In *Windsurfing International*, the ECJ investigated a licence agreement between a sailboard company (licensor) and an independent manufacturer of sailboards (licensee). A sailboard consists of a board and a rig. The licence granted to the licensee covered only the rig and not the board. The licence agreement stipulated, *inter alia*, that the licensee could not sell the rig without a board that had previously been approved by the licensor. The Commission held (and the ECJ confirmed) that such a practice would restrict competition as it ties the use of the licence to the condition of securing the licensor's approval for other products sold by the licensee.[212]

---

[210] Commission decision of 2 December 1981, Case IV/25.757 – *Hasselblad*, OJ No. L 161 of 12 June 1982, p. 18, para. 57. On appeal, however, the Commission was unable to prove that owners of cameras which had not been imported by the appointed distributor had to wait longer for their repairs than owners of Hasselblad cameras in other Member States. The Court therefore dismissed this part of the Commission's decision, see ECJ (21 February 1984), Case 86/82 – *Hasselblad v Commission* [1984] ECR 883, para. 34.

[211] Vertical Guidelines, para. 214.

[212] ECJ (25 February 1986), Case 193/83 – *Windsurfing International v Commission* [1986] ECR 611, paras. 54–9.

Summary of Section 5

Article 101(1) TFEU contains a non-exhaustive list of prohibited practices. It is not necessary to differentiate between the examples as the concepts are fluid and often overlap. Again, a teleological approach is applied.

Most prominent examples include cartel agreements on prices, quotas, market allocation or bidding behaviour.

6. EFFECT ON TRADE BETWEEN MEMBER STATES

Article 101 TFEU applies only to agreements, practices or decisions which 'may affect trade' between Member States. The inter-Member State clause has been interpreted broadly as covering all types of trans-border practices having a detrimental effect on competition on the internal market. The requirement defines the scope of the application of Article 101 TFEU and plays a central role when determining whether national competition authorities and national courts examining particular cases are under an obligation to apply the EU competition law according to Regulation 1/2003.

In order to clarify and recapitulate the principles on the meaning of an effect on trade the Commission has published Guidelines on the 'effect on trade' concept contained in Articles 81 and 82 of the Treaty.[213]

6.1 Concept of 'trade'

According to settled case law the concept of trade between Member States

is not limited to traditional exchanges of goods and services. It is a wider concept, covering all cross-border economic activity, including establishment. This interpretation is consistent with the fundamental objective of the Treaty to promote free movement of goods, services and capital.[214]

The concept of trade also covers situations when agreements at issue are supposed to be implemented in only one Member State. This especially may be the case where national cartels cover the whole or a large part of the national market, which reinforces compartmentalisation of the market and makes it difficult for competitors

---

[213] Commission Guidelines on the effect on trade concept contained in Articles 81 and 82 of the Treaty, OJ No. C 101 of 27 April 2004, p. 81.

[214] Ibid., para. 19.

from other Member States to enter the market.[215] The same approach applies to a network of agreements operating only in one Member State.

6.2 'Effect on trade'

Trade between Member States is or may be affected when the three criteria set out in *Société Technique Minière* are fulfilled:

it must be possible to foresee with a sufficient degree of probability on the basis of a set of objective factors of law that the agreement in question may have an influence, direct or indirect, actual or potential, on the pattern of trade between Member States.[216]

Against this background a subjective intention to affect trade is not necessary. The concept of effect on trade is neutral and it is not required that the trade is reduced. Moreover Article 101(1) TFEU also applies when there is an increase in trade that results from the anticompetitive agreement.[217]

6.3 Concept of appreciability

The trade pattern between Member States must be affected in an appreciable way. When examining the appreciability of the effects resulting from the agreements/ practices in question, the general legal and economic context of the scrutinised agreement and, if required, the cumulative effect of parallel networks in case of vertical restraints should be taken into account.

The Commission's guidelines on the 'effect on trade' concept provide precise instructions as to the applicability of the concept. A negative rebuttable presumption of non-appreciability applies when:

- the aggregate market share of the parties on any relevant market within the Union affected by the agreements does not exceed 5%,[218] and
- the parties' turnover is below €40 million in the case of horizontal agreements, or the aggregate Union turnover of the suppliers involved is smaller than €40 million in the case of vertical agreements.[219]

---

[215] ECJ (13 July 2006), Case C-295/04 to C-298/04 – *Manfredi* [2006] ECR I-6619, paras. 50–2.
[216] ECJ (30 June 1966), Case 56/65 – *Société Technique Minière v Maschinenbau Ulm* [1966] ECR 235, p. 249.
[217] ECJ (13 July 1966), Joined Cases 56/64, 58/64 – *Consten and Grundig v Commission* [1966] ECR 299, p. 341.
[218] Commission Guidelines on the effect on trade concept contained in Articles 81 and 82 of the Treaty, OJ No. C 101 of 27 April 2004, p. 81, para. 52(a).
[219] Ibid., para. 52(b).

On the other hand, a positive rebuttable presumption of appreciability shall apply when the above-mentioned turnover and market share thresholds are exceeded.

Summary of Section 6

Article 101 TFEU applies only to agreements, practices or decisions which may affect trade between Member States. The inter-Member State clause defines the scope of the application of Article 101 TFEU and plays a central role when determining whether national or EU competition law applies. The clause has been interpreted broadly as covering all types of trans-border practices having a detrimental effect on competition on the internal market. The effect needs to be appreciable to cause EU competition law to apply.

7. *DE MINIMIS* DOCTRINE

The concept of appreciability also applies to the effects of an agreement, concerted practice or a decision by an association on the relevant market. Hence, those measures which have only insignificant influence on competition are not covered by Article 101(1) TFEU:

[A]n agreement falls outside the prohibition in Article [101 TFEU] when it has only an insignificant effect on the markets, taking into account the weak position which the persons concerned have on the market of the product in question.[220]

More detailed information on the agreements and practices deemed to fall outside the scope of Article 101(1) TFEU can be found in the Commission's Notice on Agreements of Minor Importance[221] which creates a 'safe harbour' for agreements that do not exceed the following thresholds:

- aggregate market share amounts to less than 10% on any relevant market in the case of agreements between competitors, or
- market share held by each of the parties does not exceed 15% on any of the relevant markets in the case of agreements between non-competitors.

It is important to note that the Commission's Notice is only of an instructive nature and its applicability may be limited depending on the facts of the case. It is settled case law that the *de minimis* doctrine does not apply when the parties to an

---

[220] ECJ (9 July 1969), Case 5/69 – *Völk* [1969] ECR 295, paras. 5 and 7.
[221] Commission Notice on Agreements of Minor Importance which do not appreciably restrict competition under Article 81(1) of the Treaty establishing the European Community (de minimis), OJ No. C 368 of 22 December 2001, p. 13.

agreement have small market shares but the market is a fragmented one and the market shares exceed significantly those of most competitors.[222]

The Notice contains a list of 'hardcore' restrictions which are not encompassed by the 'safe harbour' benefit. The most important are agreements on price fixing, market sharing, resale price maintenance and export restrictions.

Summary of Section 7

Restrictions of competition are covered by Article 101(1) TFEU only if they have an appreciable anticompetitive effect. A number of particularly severe restrictions (*per se* restrictions) are considered always to have an appreciable effect. For other restrictions quantitative considerations apply.

8. ARTICLE 101(2) TFEU – NULLITY OF THE AGREEMENT

Article 101(2) TFEU provides that any agreement restricting competition which is caught by Article 101(1) TFEU is automatically void unless it meets the requirements laid down in Article 101(3) TFEU. The sanction of automatic nullity has been introduced into the system of competition rules in order to reinforce the effects of the cartel prohibition. It 'constitutes a fundamental provision being essential for the accomplishment of the tasks entrusted to the Union and, in particular, for the functioning of the internal market'.[223]

8.1 General principles

The main aim of Article 101(2) TFEU is to ensure and reinforce independent undertakings' compliance with the Treaty regulations on competition law. For this reason the provision of Article 101(2) TFEU can only be interpreted with reference to its purpose in Union law and it must be limited to this context.[224] Thus, no effect will be given to exemptions or defences based on national law.

Although the *consequences* of the nullity of the relevant contractual provisions are determined by national law, it is a matter of EU law to decide whether the agreement in question is void or not. Since the law of the EU takes precedence over national regulations it is not, under any circumstances, the competence of national administrative and legislative bodies to change the scope of Article 101(2) TFEU.

---

[222] ECJ (7 June 1983), Joined Cases 100/80 to 103/80 – *Musique Diffusion française (re Pioneer) v Commission* [1983] ECR 1825; ECJ (10 July 1980), Case 30/78 – *Distillers Company (re Pimms) v Commission* [1980] ECR 2229.

[223] ECJ (1 June 1999), Case C-126/97 – *Eco Swiss v Benetton* [1999] ECR I-3055, para. 36.

[224] ECJ (30 June 1966), Case 56/65 – *Société Technique Minière v Maschinenbau Ulm* [1966] ECR 235, p. 250.

8.1.1 *Ex lege* effect

The sanction of nullity applies directly and without notice. Therefore, neither the Commission nor the national competition authorities are required to specifically declare an agreement void.[225] Such administrative decisions have no binding force and are only of a declaratory nature. National authorities and courts are under a legal duty to respect the nullity of an agreement covered by Article 101(1) TFEU and to safeguard the rights of the individuals arising from the nullity of an agreement or part of it. A void agreement has no legal effect as between the contracting parties and establishes no rights or duties of third parties.[226]

8.1.2 *Ex tunc* effect

Article 101(2) TFEU renders agreements and decisions caught by Article 101(1) TFEU automatically void. The sanction of nullity covers all past and future effects of the agreement or decision in question as long as an infringement of the competition rules exists.[227]

It is not clear however whether the nullity sanction applies transiently. Under Regulation 17/1962 one of the major questions in this area related to whether the mere act of notifying an agreement could have a provisional effect on its legality or whether no such effect could be presumed until the Commission decided on the application of Article 101(3) TFEU. With the entry into force of Regulation 1/2003, this concern has become irrelevant as the Commission no longer grants negative clearance.[228]

Today, the discussion centres around the question of whether the legality of an agreement is affected by its passing above or below the market share thresholds established by the Commission's *de minimis* notice. If the market shares of the parties to an agreement change and they exceed (or fall below) the values laid down in the Commission's notice, an agreement which used to be illegal may become legal and, vice versa, an agreement which was previously viewed by the Commission as not restricting competition may become incompatible with the internal market due to the changing positions of the parties.

To date, there does not seem to be any decision by a European court that has dealt with this issue. Following an interpretation with reference to the purpose of EU competition law, it seems reasonable to say that an agreement shall become void the very moment that Article 101 TFEU applies to it. Conversely, it could no longer be

---

[225] ECJ (6 February 1973), Case 48/72 – *SA Brasserie de Haecht v Wilkin Janssen* [1973] ECR 77, para. 6; Council Regulation (EC) No 1/2003 of 16 December 2002 on the implementation of the rules on competition laid down in Articles 81 and 82 of the Treaty, OJ No. L 1 of 4 January 2003, p. 1, Article 1(1).

[226] ECJ (25 November 1971), Case 22/71 – *Béguelin Import v G.L. Import Export* [1971] ECR 949, para. 29.

[227] ECJ (6 February 1973), Case 48/72 – *SA Brasserie de Haecht v Wilkin Janssen* [1973] ECR 77, para. 26.

[228] See section 9 below.

considered to be restrictive of competition as soon as it falls below the aforementioned thresholds. This view has also been expressed by the English Court of Appeal when in its judgment in *Passmore v Morland & Ors* it stated:

> Article [101(2) TFEU] has to be construed in conjunction with Article [101(1) TFEU]. In particular, Article [101(2) TFEU] has to be construed in the light of an appreciation that the prohibition in Article [101(1) TFEU] is not an absolute prohibition; but rather a prohibition which arises when, and continues for so long as (and only for so long as), it is needed in order to promote the freedom of competition within the common market which is the stated objective of Article [101(1) TFEU]. The prohibition is temporaneous (or transient) rather than absolute; in the sense that it endures for a finite period of time – the period of time for which it is needed – rather than for all time [. . .] [T]he nullity imposed by Article [101(2) TFEU] is an exact reflection of the prohibition imposed by Article [101(1) TFEU]. If the prohibition is temporaneous (or transient) then so is the nullity.

While such an interpretation seems to be in line with the condition set out in *Société Technique Minière v Maschinenbau Ulm* that Article 101(2) TFEU be limited to the context of EU law[229] it also has other less desirable effects. For example, courts might have to specify the exact point in time at which an agreement was first caught by Article 101(1).[230] In addition, such a 'European' interpretation would affect national interpretations according to which the validity of an agreement is determined (only) at the time of its inception. In Germany, for example, a once void agreement may not become valid and enforceable due to a change of law or circumstances unless it is reconfirmed by the parties.[231]

8.1.3 *Erga omnes* effect

Agreements caught by Article 101(2) TFEU have no effects as between the contracting parties and cannot be invoked against third parties.[232] This nullity is absolute in nature and binding on all relevant courts.[233]

Despite the precise wording of Article 101(2) TFEU, there is a general consensus that some exceptions apply to this concept. For example, the void part of an agreement may be severed from the (otherwise valid) remainder and in some instances an illegal clause might be amended by a court so as not to infringe Article 101 TFEU.[234]

In contrast, parties cannot rely on the principle of 'unclean hands' (*venire contra factum proprium* in some jurisdictions): if one party to an agreement tries to fend off

---

[229] ECJ (30 June 1996), Case 56/65 – *Société Technique Minière v Maschinenbau Ulm* [1996] ECR 235.
[230] Smith, *Competition Law: Enforcement and Procedure* (Butterworths, 2001), p. 446, section 19.07.
[231] Hirsch, Montag and Säcker (eds.), *Competition Law: European Community Practice and Procedure, Article-by-Article Commentary* (Sweet & Maxwell, 2007), section H. margin number 2–8–056.
[232] ECJ (13 June 2006), Joined Cases C-295/04 to 298/04 – *Manfredi* [2006] ECR I-6619, para. 57.
[233] ECJ (20 September 2001), Case C-453/99 – *Courage Ltd and Bernard Crehan* [2001] ECR I-6297, para. 22.
[234] See Section 8.2 below.

its contractual obligations arguing that the agreement violates competition law, the other (disadvantaged) party cannot rely on the first party's bad faith in order to insist on performance. This proactive rescission of a contract due to the violation of competition law is sometimes referred to as 'invoking the Euro defence' and has been accepted by the ECJ.[235]

8.2 Severance

The nullity sanction applies only to the provisions of the agreement that fall under the prohibition of Article 101(1) TFEU. The agreement as a whole is void only when the void clauses cannot be severed from the remaining provisions of the contract[236] or when the remaining provisions have no autonomous legal content.[237] In one judgment the ECJ concluded that while the question whether the void clause can be severed from the rest of the agreement must be decided by Union law, the consequences of the nullity for other parts of the agreement are a matter for national law[238] and will be determined by the national court resolving the dispute. This leads to the (undesirable) effect that a void international agreement may have varying effects in different Member States.[239]

Following the reasoning of severability, contractual clauses which stipulate that an agreement shall not become invalid as a whole when one of its clauses is invalid (severability clauses), are compatible with Article 101 TFEU. The nullity sanction only applies to the entire agreement insofar as the application of the remainder of the agreement would lead to results incompatible with Article 101(1) TFEU.

Agreements that are generally susceptible to fall within the ambit of a block exemption regulation forfeit *all* of its benefits if they contain a so-called 'black' clause. These clauses usually describe hardcore restrictions, such as the limitation of output or sales, the fixing of prices, and the restriction of customers.[240] If an agreement contains a single black clause it renders the entire block exemption inapplicable.[241]

---

[235] ECJ (20 September 2001), Case C-453/99 – *Courage Ltd and Bernard Crehan* [2001] ECR I-6297, para. 24.

[236] ECJ (30 June 1966), Case 56/65 – *Société Technique Minière v Maschinenbau Ulm* [1966] ECR 235, p. 250.

[237] Hirsch, Montag and Säcker (eds.), *Competition Law*, section H. margin number 2–8–061.

[238] ECJ (14 December 1983), Case 319/82 – *Société de Vente de Ciments et Bétons de l'Est v Kerpen&Kerpen* [1983] ECR 4173, para. 11.

[239] See Smith, *Competition Law: Enforcement and Procedure*, p. 446, section 19.06.

[240] Commission Regulation (EC) No. 2659/2000 of 29 November 2000 on the application of Article 81(3) of the Treaty to categories of research and development agreements, OJ No. L 304 of 5 December 2000, p. 7, Article 5; see also Commission Regulation (EU) No. 330/2010 of 20 April 2010 on the application of Article 101(3) TFEU to categories of vertical agreements and concerted practices, OJ No. L 102 of 23 April 2010, p. 1, para. 10.

[241] Commission Guidelines on the applicability of Article 81 of the EC Treaty to horizontal cooperation agreements, OJ No. C 3 of 6 January 2001, p. 2, para. 37; the term 'black clause' does not appear in the new Guidelines on the applicability of Article 101 TFEU to horizontal cooperation agreements, OJ No. C 11 of 14 January 2011, p. 1, but see para. 128.

Summary of Section 8

Although the *consequences* of the nullity of an anticompetitive agreement are determined by national law, it is a matter of EU law to decide whether the agreement in question is void or not.

The sanction of nullity applies directly and without notice. A void agreement has no legal effect as between the contracting parties and establishes no rights or duties of third parties.

The sanction of nullity covers all past and future effects of the agreement or decision in question so long as an infringement of the competition rules exists.

The nullity sanction applies only to the provisions of the agreement that fall under the prohibition of Article 101(1) TFEU. The agreement as a whole is void only when the void clauses cannot be severed from the remaining provisions of the contract or when the remaining provisions have no autonomous legal content.

9. ARTICLE 101(3) TFEU – LEGAL EXCEPTION

Agreements or practices that fall within the scope of Article 101(1) TFEU are not necessarily unlawful. Article 101(3) TFEU provides a legal exception to the cartel prohibition and excludes agreements satisfying four conditions listed therein from the scope of Article 101(1) TFEU.

9.1 General

9.1.1 Purpose of the provision

The main aim of EU competition law is to protect competition on the market in order to enhance consumer welfare and ensure the optimal allocation of resources. Since some of the agreements restricting competition may also have some pro-competitive effects, it is necessary to balance the possible efficiency gains against anticompetitive effects and to assess the net effect of an agreement. In this way, the above-mentioned aim of the EU competition rules may be achieved by ensuring that market conduct, optimal from a competition policy point of view, is not classified as unlawful. This approach is reflected in Article 101(3) TFEU which expressly states that some anticompetitive agreements may generate net economic benefits.

9.1.2 Legal nature

Before the entry into force of Regulation 1/2003, an undertaking that wished to have a certain agreement excluded from the scope of application of Article 101 TFEU had to notify the agreement to the Commission and apply for individual exemption.[242] The Commission had the sole power to declare Article 101(1) TFEU inapplicable.[243] This system of obligatory notification of agreements to the Commission has been replaced by a system of 'legal exception'. According to Article 1(2) Regulation 1/2003, Article 101(3) TFEU has become directly applicable; not only may it be applied by the Commission, but also by the competition authorities of the Member States and national courts. At the same time the Commission lost its exclusive power to grant individual exemptions pursuant to Article 101(3) TFEU.

Under the new regime, undertakings can no longer notify agreements they find restrictive of competition to the Commission and rely on its decisions or 'comfort letters' to confirm the compatibility of the market conduct at issue with EU competition law. This means that the companies themselves are responsible for the assessment of the measures to be undertaken and implemented on the market and that the competition authorities may at any time scrutinise them in the light of Article 101 TFEU and impose sanctions in case of an infringement.

9.1.3 Scope of application

Article 101(3) TFEU applies to all types of agreements found to infringe Article 101(1) TFEU, regardless of whether it has the restriction of competition as its object or effect. Even measures referred to as 'hardcore' restrictions may escape the prohibition in Article 101(1) TFEU:

the Court considers that, in principle, no anticompetitive practice can exist which, whatever the extent of its effects on a given market, cannot be exempted, provided that all the conditions laid down in Article [101(3) TFEU] are satisfied . . .[244]

9.1.4 Burden of proof

Article 2 of Regulation 1/2003 sets out that the burden of proof for the application of Article 101(3) TFEU rests on the undertaking seeking to demonstrate that an agreement is compatible with the EU competition rules. In such a case, the undertaking

---

[242] Council Regulation No. 17/1962 of 6 February 1962: First regulation implementing Articles 85 and 86 of the Treaty, OJ No. 13 of 21 February 1962, p. 204, Article 4(1).

[243] Ibid., Article 9(1).

[244] GC (15 June 1994), Case T-17/93 – *Matra Hachette v Commission* [1994] ECR II-595, para. 85.

concerned must prove that all four conditions laid down in Article 101(3) TFEU are satisfied.

The burden of proving an infringement of Article 101(1) TFEU is on the authority or party alleging the infringement at issue.

9.1.5 Purpose and nature of block exemptions

Article 101(3) TFEU can be applied either to individual agreements or to categories of agreements by way of a block exemption regulation. Most of the existing block exemption regulations have been adopted by the Commission acting under powers delegated by the Council. Different block exemptions cover classes of agreements providing legal certainty for the undertakings concerned. Parties to agreements covered by a block exemption are relieved of the burden of presenting that their individual conduct meets the requirements set out in Article 101(3) TFEU. Since the application of a block exemption is based on the presumption that all restrictive agreements covered by it fulfil the conditions of Article 101(3) TFEU, the parties merely have to prove that they fall within the general scope of application of the block exemption.

An agreement covered by a block exemption may not be declared invalid by a national court. However, under certain circumstances, the Commission and national competition authorities are empowered to withdraw the benefit of a block exemption.

9.2 Application of Article 101(3) TFEU

The exception of Article 101(3) TFEU applies when an agreement meets the following four cumulative[245] conditions:

(i)   it must contribute to improving the production or distribution of goods or to promoting technical or economic progress;
(ii) it must allow the consumers a fair share of the resulting benefit;
(iii) it must not impose on the undertakings restrictions which are not indispensable to the attainment of these objectives;
(iv) it must not afford undertakings the possibility of eliminating competition in respect of a substantial part of the products in question.[246]

---

[245]   GC (19 March 2003), Case T-213/00 – *CMA GCM and Others v Commission*, [2003] ECR II-913, para. 226; cf. Commission Guidelines on the application of Article 81(3) of the Treaty, OJ No. C 101 of 27 April 2004, p. 97, para. 42.
[246]   Article 101(3) TFEU.

The most relevant practical issues regarding the application of the four criteria have been discussed by the Commission in its Guidelines on the application of Article 81(3) of the Treaty.[247]

According to these guidelines, the assessment of Article 101(3) TFEU is made within the confines of each relevant market.[248] The Commission is thus of the opinion that the negative effects of an agreement on one market may not be outweighed by benefits observed on another market. However, in *Compagnie Générale Maritime* the General Court held that positive effects on other markets *should* be taken into account, regardless of whether or not there is a specific link to the relevant market in question.[249] The Commission has tried to limit the court's interpretation to the facts of this case.[250] Therefore, it remains to be seen what position the ECJ will take with respect to this issue.

In any event, Article 101(3) TFEU has to be applied within the actual economic context in which the agreement operates. The exception applies as long as its requirements are met.[251]

9.2.1 First condition – efficiency gains

An efficiency claim may be raised only when the benefit produced by the agreement at issue is of an objective nature and value to the Union. Since only objective benefits can be taken into account, Article 101(3) TFEU does not encompass agreements which only benefit its parties.[252] The assessment of positive effects must not necessarily be limited to the relevant product markets – it may include all markets benefiting from the scrutinised agreement.

The purpose of the first condition is to identify and define the nature of the efficiencies that are to be analysed in the light of the second and third conditions. Therefore it is necessary to establish a link between the agreement and the claimed benefits and to specify their objective value. In order to achieve this goal the Commission proposes to apply the following 'four-step' test to each efficiency claim, according to which the claim made by an undertaking must specify:

(i)   the nature of the agreement in order to verify whether the claimed efficiencies are objective in nature;

(ii) the link between the agreement and the efficiencies, in order to verify that the efficiencies result from the economic activity that forms the object of the agreement;

[247] Commission Guidelines on the application of Article 81(3) of the Treaty, OJ No. C 101 of 27 April 2004, p. 97.

[248] Ibid., para. 43.

[249] GC (28 February 2002), Case T-86/95 – *Compagnie Générale Maritime and Others v Commission* [2002] ECR II-1011, para. 343.

[250] Commission Guidelines on the application of Article 81(3) of the Treaty, OJ No. C 101 of 27 April 2004, p. 97, footnote 57.

[251] Ibid., para. 10.

[252] ECJ (13 July 1966), Joined Cases 56/64, 58/64 – *Consten and Grundig v Commission* [1966] ECR 299, 348.

(iii)   the likelihood and magnitude of each claimed efficiency, in order to establish its objective value;

(iv)   how and when each claimed efficiency would be achieved.[253]

Article 101(3) TFEU covers all types of economic efficiencies and its scope may not be limited to the categories listed therein. The main distinction shall be drawn between cost and quantitative efficiencies.

a) Cost efficiencies

The sources of possible cost savings are discussed in detail in paras. 64–68 of the Guidelines on the application of Article 81(3). They include: the development of new production technologies and methods, synergies resulting from the integration of existing assets, economies of scale, economies of scope and better planning of the production.

b) Qualitative efficiencies

Some qualitative efficiencies generated by an agreement falling under Article 101(3) TFEU may also be subject to the assessment in light of Article 101(1) TFEU. The Commission specifies the following types of benefits which are most likely to influence the outcome of the overall analysis: the introduction of new or improved goods and services, quality improvements and the development of novel features, a more rapid dissemination of new technology and the provision of services that are better tailored to customer needs.[254] The examples given by the Commission primarily cover agreements in the area of research and development.

Article 101(3) TFEU is not necessarily limited to enhancements in economic efficiency. The first condition named therein also allows for other objectives to be scrutinised. In *Métropole Télévision* the General Court conceded quite a broad scope of interpretation to the Commission when it held that

in the context of an overall assessment, the Commission is entitled to base itself on considerations connected with the pursuit of the public interest in order to grant the exemption under Article.[255]

According to the jurisprudence of the ECJ and the Commission's decisional practice, these may include:

- infrastructure and employment policy;[256]
- environmental objectives;[257]

---

[253] Ibid., para. 51.   [254] Ibid., paras. 69–72.

[255] GC (11 July 1996), Joined Cases T-528/93, T-542/93, T-543/93, T-546/93 – *Métropole Télévision v Commission* [1996] ECR II-649, para. 118.

[256] Commission decision of 29 April 1994, Case IV/34.456 – *Stichting Baksteen*, OJ No. L 131 of 26 May 1994, p. 15, para. 27.

[257] Commission decision of 17 September 2001, Case COMP/34493 etc. – *DSD and others*, OJ No. L 319 of 4 December 2001, p. 1, para. 144; Commission decision of 24 January 1999, Case IV.F.1/36.718 – *CECED*, OJ No. L 187 of 26 July 2000, p. 47, paras. 47–57.

- regional policy and regional development;[258]
- public health.[259]

As follows from the decisional practice of the General Court, it is often difficult to decide upfront whether a certain agreement will have more positive or more negative effects. The assessment frequently centres around questions of probability;[260] accordingly the 'balancing exercise' gives much leeway for either party to present a convincing case in their favour. However, given the limited number of cases and the restrictive interpretation by the General Court, all non-economic reasoning should be treated as additional or corroborating evidence which, by itself, would only in very exceptional circumstances justify an exemption under Article 101(3) TFEU.[261]

9.2.2 Second condition – fair share for consumers

Article 101(3) TFEU applies only when a fair share of the benefit resulting from the agreement at issue will accrue to the consumers. For the purpose of Article 101(3) TFEU the concept of 'consumer' shall be understood as 'all direct or indirect users of the products covered by the agreement, including producers that use the products as an input, wholesalers, retailers and final consumers'.[262]

Since an overall assessment is required, there is no need to prove that each efficiency caught by the first condition benefits the consumers. The focus should be on the overall impact on the consumers of the particular products on the relevant market and the question whether the benefits compensating consumers for any actual or likely negative impact caused by the competition restriction at issue have been passed on to them. The exemption of Article 101(3) TFEU applies only when the net effect of the agreement is at least neutral from the point of view of consumers directly or indirectly affected by the agreement.

As with the first condition, a distinction can be made between cost efficiencies on the one hand and qualitative efficiencies on the other. Cost efficiencies may, for example, arise from increased output which also leads to lower prices for consumers. In such a constellation the following factors should be taken into account:

- the characteristics and structure of the market;
- the nature and magnitude of the efficiency gains;

---

[258] Commission decision of 23 December 1992, Case IV/33.814 – *Ford Volkswagen*, OJ No. L 20 of 28 January 1993, p. 14, para. 23 and limitations set out in para. 36; confirmed to the same extent by the GC (15 July 1994) in Case T-17/93 – *Matra Hachette v Commission* [1994] ECR II-595.

[259] Commission decision of 6 October 1994. Case IV/34.776 – *Pasteur Mérieux-Merck*, OJ No. L 309 of 2 December 1994, p. 1, para. 89.

[260] GC (27 September 2006), Case T-168/01 – *GlaxoSmithKline Services v Commission* [2006] ECR II-2969, paras. 301 et seq.

[261] For a detailed analysis of the issue of non-economic enhancements, see, Sufrin, 'The Evolution of Article 81 (3) of the EC Treaty', *Antitrust Bulletin*, 51 (2006), 915, 952–67.

[262] Commission Guidelines on the application of Article 81(3) of the Treaty, OJ No. C 101 of 27 April 2004, p. 97, para. 84.

- the elasticity of demand;
- the magnitude of the restriction of competition.[263]

The passing-on of qualitative efficiencies in the form of new and improved products requires a value judgment approach and needs to involve analysis of the whole economic context in which the agreement at stake operates. In particular, it should be assessed whether the claimed efficiencies will create benefits that will compensate for the negative effects resulting from the restrictions on competition.[264]

9.2.3 Third condition – indispensability of restrictions

The indispensability condition is of essential importance. According to the Commission Guidelines it requires a twofold test:

(i)   whether the agreement at issue is necessary to achieve the analysed efficiencies, and

(ii)   whether the particular restrictions resulting from the agreement are reasonably necessary for the attainment of the efficiencies.

Under (i) it should be assessed if there are other economically practicable and less restrictive means of achieving the claimed efficiencies. The second limb of the test (ii) is designed to exclude any individual restrictions which are not necessary to produce the claimed benefits from the scope of Article 101(3) TFEU. In order to establish whether this is the case, a test shall be conducted to show whether the absence of the agreement would eliminate or significantly reduce the volume of efficiencies or make it less possible that they materialise.

In *BNP-Dresdner Bank*[265] the Commission has exempted an agreement between two major banks from the application of Article 101(1) TFEU. The French Banque Nationale de Paris and the German Dresdner Bank had agreed to cooperate with each other on a worldwide and exclusive basis. The cooperation agreement, which aimed at reducing costs and strengthening the banks' respective presence in third countries, was held by the Commission to considerably restrict both actual and potential competition between the two entities. The Commission, *inter alia*, considered that the exclusivity clauses contained in the agreement would limit the banks' ability to cooperate with third party financial institutions. Nonetheless, it was of the opinion that these stipulations were indispensable, because they were the only

---

[263] Ibid., para. 96.   [264] Ibid., paras. 103–4.
[265] Commission decision of 24 June 1996, Case IV.34.607 – *BNP-Dresdner Bank*, OJ No. L 188 of 27 July 1996, p. 37.

available tool for the banks to protect their business secrets and the know-how they had shared.[266]

9.2.4 Fourth condition – no elimination of competition in a substantial part of the market

The last condition of Article 101(3) TFEU recognises the priority of rivalry and competitive process over pro-competitive efficiencies. It has been designed to prevent the elimination of competition and is based on the evaluation of the extent to which competition will be reduced as a result of the agreement. The general principle is that the more competition is already weakened on the relevant market, the slighter the further reduction of competition has to be in order for the agreement to fall outside the scope of Article 101(3) TFEU.[267] This assessment should be made based on a realistic analysis of both actual and potential competition on the market concerned, including factors such as: sources of competition in the market, existence of entry barriers into the market, competitive strength of actual/potential competitors and the regulatory framework.[268]

Despite the fact that market shares alone are insufficient to establish the magnitude of competition in the market, they are often used as a starting point when determining whether or not sufficient competition remains. However, an in-depth analysis of the actual market conditions must be undertaken in order to verify such a first impression. Declining any intention to set firm thresholds, the Commission uses in its examples a combined market share of 70% as being indicative of the elimination of competition, absent specific circumstances.[269]

There is no direct relation between the elimination of competition and the concept of dominance as expressed in Article 102 TFEU. It is widely accepted that competition can be substantially eliminated without there being a dominant undertaking in the market. In addition, the General Court has recently clarified the inverse situation when it held that

the prohibition on eliminating competition is a narrower concept than that of the existence or acquisition of a dominant position, so that an agreement could be regarded as not eliminating competition within the meaning of Article [101(3)(b)] TFEU, and therefore qualify for exemption, even if it established a dominant position for the benefit of its members.[270]

---

[266] Ibid., para. 20(c); see also a similar example in the Commission Guidelines on the application of Article 81(3) of the Treaty, OJ No. C 101 of 27 April 2004, p. 97, para. 77.

[267] Commission Guidelines on the application of Article 81(3) of the Treaty, OJ No. C 101 of 27 April 2004, p. 97, para. 107.

[268] In-depth analysis of the most important factors: ibid., paras. 109–15.   [269] Ibid., para. 116.

[270] GC (28 February 2003), Case T-395/94 – *Atlantic Container Line and Others v Commission* [2002] ECR II-875, para. 330.

Summary of Section 9

Restrictions of competition may be exempted from Article 101(1) TFEU if their negative effects on competition are outweighed by efficiency gains. Article 101(3) TFEU provides the framework for the balancing of these effects.

Both cost efficiencies and qualitative efficiencies can outweigh the negative effects on competition of a certain practice.

An exemption is available only if consumers benefit from the efficiency gains sufficiently. Furthermore, the restrictions in question need to be proportionate and indispensable in relation to the efficiency gains.

Competition must not be totally eliminated through a restrictive practice even if it creates efficiency gains. The more competition is already weakened on the relevant market, the more unlikely it is that a restriction benefits from Article 101(3) TFEU.

QUESTIONS ON CHAPTER 2

1. In what sense is the concept of undertaking a functional concept? (2.1.2)
2. What is the key feature of an undertaking? (2.1.3)
3. Is the exercise of public powers subject to the EU competition rules? (2.2.2)
4. Does EU competition law apply to restriction between entities belonging to the same corporate group? (2.3)
5. Can gentlemen's agreements constitute a violation of Article 101(1) TFEU? (3.1)
6. Under what conditions is uniform conduct caught by the cartel prohibition? (3.3)
7. Can an agreement have a restriction of competition as its object although the parties to it do not have any intention to restrict competition? (4.3)
8. What are ancillary restraints? (4.4.6)
9. Can you give some examples of restrictive practices that are covered by Article 101(1) TFEU? (5)
10. Does a restriction of competition have to be appreciable to fall under Article 101(1) TFEU? Under which aspects is this relevant? (6.3; 7)
11. What are the civil law sanctions in case of a violation of Article 101(1) TFEU? (8)
12. Under what conditions is an exemption from the cartel prohibition possible? (9.2)
13. Who will decide whether an exemption is available for a given practice? (9.1.2)

SUGGESTED ESSAY TOPICS

1. The role of consumer welfare in EU competition policy
2. The concept of a single, overall agreement
3. Is there a European rule of reason?

3

Possibilities for cooperation under Article 101 TFEU

1. INTRODUCTION

Article 101(1) TFEU prohibits any kind of cooperation between undertakings which leads to a distortion of competition within the internal market. However, Article 101(3) TFEU provides for an exemption from this general prohibition. Some agreements, while having anticompetitive effects, will also lead to substantial pro-competitive benefits, such as market entry by new players or the introduction of new products. In this case an exemption may be available. For a complete assessment of the effects on competition resulting from a particular agreement, all relevant market factors must be considered in detail. In particular, material conditions under which competitive forces operate on the market must be taken into account: size and number of competitors, customer fidelity to existing brands, existing intellectual property rights (hereinafter: IPRs) etc. These agreements do not fit perfectly into one analytical pattern and their proper assessment requires an in-depth analysis, not only of the factual circumstances, but also of economic data pertaining to particular market conduct.

Different block exemptions cover categories of agreements to increase legal certainty for the undertakings concerned. Parties to agreements qualifying for block exemption are relieved of the burden of showing that their individual conduct meets the requirements set out in Article 101(3) TFEU. Since the application of a block exemption is based on the presumption that all restrictive agreements covered by it fulfil the conditions of Article 101(3) TFEU, the parties merely have to prove that they fall within the general scope of application of the block exemption. An agreement benefiting from a block exemption may not be declared invalid by a national court. However, under certain circumstances, the Commission and national competition authorities are empowered to withdraw the block exemption.

For cases where no block exemption is applicable, the Commission has issued guidelines, for example on horizontal cooperation,[1] on vertical agreements[2] or on technology transfer agreements.[3] Their purpose is to provide all interested parties with a comprehensive analytical framework and to improve the level of legal certainty by giving undertakings, national courts and competition authorities guidance on the application of Article 101 TFEU to those types of cooperation.

Summary of Section 1

Although Article 101(1) TFEU prohibits any kind of agreement restrictive of competition an exemption may be available under Article 101(3) TFEU. The assessment of an agreement under Article 101(3) TFEU requires a comprehensive review of the economic setting of the cooperation to determine its effects on competition and the efficiency gains that may outweigh any anticompetitive effects. To facilitate the self-assessment that has to be carried out in this respect the Commission has adopted a number of block exemption regulations that govern common types of agreements. For agreements that satisfy the criteria set out in a block exemption no individual assessment of the effects in the particular case is required. They benefit from an exemption under Article 101(3) TFEU. The Commission provides guidance for self-assessment in a number of guidelines for agreements that do not fall within the scope of a block exemption.

2. HORIZONTAL AGREEMENTS

Not every agreement entered into by competitors is prohibited. Under certain circumstances efficiency gains resulting from the cooperation may outweigh the restriction of competition resulting from the agreement at issue. In the following, the possibilities of horizontal cooperation will be explored.

2.1 Definition

According to the Horizontal Guidelines issued by the Commission, the notion of horizontal cooperation comprises all agreements or concerted practices entered into between companies operating at the same level of the economy. Horizontal cooperation can occur between actual or potential competitors.

---

[1] Commission Guidelines on the applicability of Article 101 TFEU to horizontal cooperation agreements, OJ No. C 11 of 14 January 2011, p. 1 (hereinafter: Horizontal Guidelines).

[2] Commission Guidelines on Vertical Restraints, OJ No. C 130 of 19 May 2010, p. 1 (hereinafter: Vertical Guidelines).

[3] Commission Guidelines on the application of Article 81 of the EC Treaty to technology transfer agreements, OJ No. C 101 of 27 April 2004, p. 2.

2.2 Actual and potential competitors

Two companies are treated as actual competitors if they are active on the same relevant market.[4]

A company is treated as a potential competitor of another company if, in the absence of the agreement, in case of a small but permanent increase in relative prices it is likely that the former, within a short period of time, would undertake the necessary additional investments or other necessary switching costs to enter the relevant market on which the latter is active. This assessment has to be based on realistic grounds, the mere theoretical possibility to enter a market being insufficient.[5]

In *Air France/Alitalia*,[6] the two airlines wanted to establish a far-reaching strategic alliance. This alliance would have created a European multi-hub system in order to interconnect their worldwide networks and the coordination of passenger service operations, including extensive use of code-sharing, coordination of their scheduled passenger network, sales revenue management, mutual recognition of their frequent flyer programmes and marketing coordination and also coordination in other areas.

To assess whether the cooperation agreement would have an effect on competition, the Commission did not just examine actual competition between the airlines, but also potential competition. In case of airlines, this means especially potential competition on non-overlap flight routes:

In order to determine whether or not the non-operating Party was a potential entrant on a given non overlap route, an economic approach has been applied, based on a set of objective criteria which make it possible to determine whether entry on this route would be commercially realistic for the non-operating Party. According to this approach, an airline will, in principle, only be considered as a potential competitor on a specific route if that route is either directly linked to one of its hubs or is sufficiently large and frequented by local traffic to allow market entry on a point-to-point basis, while taking into account the operational requirements and benchmarks of the respective business strategy. As benchmarks, the Commission has notably examined whether the carrier in question operates routes of similar size/characteristics, whether it has already a local market presence and whether it operates appropriate aircraft.[7]

In assessing those prerequisites, the Commission came to the conclusion that potential competition between the two parties had not been restricted by the agreement. As the Commission had concerns about actual competition, the parties had to make commitments to remedy those concerns, but eventually the airlines could form their alliance.

---

[4] Horizontal Guidelines, para. 10.   [5] Ibid.
[6] Commission, decision of 7 April 2004, Case COMP/38.284/D2 – *Société Air France/Alitalia Linee Aeree Italiane*, available at http://ec.europa.eu/competition/antitrust/cases/dec_docs/38284/38284_104_1.pdf.
[7] Ibid., para. 111.

2.3 Types of cooperation

Although the Horizontal Guidelines explicitly address only seven types of horizontal cooperation, it has to be noted that other forms of cooperation agreements are also covered by Article 101(1) TFEU and must be assessed with regard to their possible anti- and pro-competitive effects. The most common types of cooperation, also discussed by the Commission in the Guidelines, are:

- information exchange;
- research and development agreements (R&D);
- specialisation agreements;
- production agreements;
- purchase agreements;
- commercialisation agreements;
- standardisation agreements.

2.4 Form of cooperation

Depending on the goals pursued by the parties to a cooperation agreement, their collaboration may have different forms. In principle, from a competition law point of view the choice of one or another form of collaboration does not play any role. The undertakings are therefore free to develop different structures as basis for their cooperation. These may be periodic meetings to discuss matters of common interest, pooling the results of research works or establishing a common committee to oversee the collaboration. They may also establish a joint venture company that would carry out a common task of both partners.[8]

2.5 Legal framework

Forms of horizontal collaboration have to be analysed within the framework of Article 101(1) TFEU. Agreements caught by the cartel prohibition may be exempted if they fulfil the requirements laid down in Article 101(3) TFEU. Certain types of horizontal agreements may be covered by one of two block exemption regulations issued by the Commission:

---

[8] See also Whish and Bailey, *Competition Law* (Oxford University Press, 7th edn, 2012), p. 572.

- block exemption regulation for specialisation agreements (Regulation 1218/2010),[9]
- block exemption regulation for research and development (Regulation 1217/2010).[10]

Agreements falling outside the scope of the above-mentioned block exemptions and all other types of horizontal agreements are covered by the Horizontal Guidelines issued by the Commission. The Horizontal Guidelines provide a framework for analysing agreements concluded by competitors. They concentrate on the assessment of pro- and anticompetitive effects resulting from particular market conduct both in the light of Article 101(1) as well as Article 101(3) TFEU. The Horizontal Guidelines do not relate to horizontal agreements containing hardcore restrictions such as price fixing, output limitations or market sharing. Such hardcore restrictions are presumed to always have negative effects and are therefore caught in principle by Article 101(1) TFEU.

2.6 General approach by the Union courts

There are very few judgments of the Union courts on the application of Article 101 TFEU to horizontal cooperation agreements. According to the ECJ, the central point of the analysis of horizontal cooperation agreements shall be the assessment of the actual conditions in which companies function and the economic context in which they operate.

In the *European Night Services* case,[11] the General Court had to review upon appeal a Commission decision holding that a joint venture (ENS) between the British, German, French and Dutch railways violated Article 101(1) TFEU. ENS had been formed to provide and operate overnight passenger rail services through the Channel Tunnel. The railway companies agreed to provide ENS with certain services like traction over their networks, in particular locomotives, train crews and paths. To operate the night passenger services, the railway undertakings concerned acquired specialised rolling stock through ENS which was suitable for running on the different rail systems, financed by long-term leasing arrangements. The Commission decided to exempt those agreements from the application of the competition rules under the

---

[9] Commission Regulation (EU) No 1218/2010 of 14 December 2010 on the application of Art. 101(3) TFEU to certain categories of specialisation agreements, OJ No. L 335 of 18 December 2010, p. 43 (hereinafter: Specialisation Block Exemption).

[10] Commission Regulation (EU) No 1217/2010 of 14 December 2010 on the application of Art. 101(3) TFEU to certain categories of research and development agreements, OJ No. L 335 of 18 December 2010, p. 36 (hereinafter: R&D Block Exemption).

[11] GC (15 September 1998), Joined Cases T-374/94, T-375/94, T-384/94 and T-388/94 – *Euro Night Services and Others v Commission* [1998] ECR II-3141.

condition that the concerned railway undertakings had to supply to any competitor wishing to operate night passenger trains through the Channel Tunnel the same necessary rail services they agreed to supply to ENS on the same terms. The railway companies challenged the decision with regard to the imposed conditions.

In para. 136 of its judgment, the General Court stressed the significance of economic context and competition conditions as assessment factors when applying Article 101(1) TFEU:

Before any examination of the parties' arguments as to whether the Commission's analysis as regards restrictions of competition was correct, it must be borne in mind that in assessing an agreement under [Article 101(1) TFEU], account should be taken of the actual conditions in which it functions, in particular the economic context in which the undertakings operate, the products or services covered by the agreement and the actual structure of the market concerned, unless it is an agreement containing obvious restrictions of competition such as price-fixing, market-sharing or the control of outlets. In the latter case, such restrictions may be weighed against their claimed pro-competitive effects only in the context of [Article 101(3) TFEU], with a view to granting an exemption from the prohibition in [Article 101(1) TFEU].

This approach has been confirmed in *O2 Germany*.[12]

This case concerned a cooperation agreement between two German mobile tele-communication operators. O2 and T-Mobile concluded a framework agreement on infrastructure sharing and national roaming for 3G services (third generation of GSM mobile telecommunications) on the German market. The Commission concluded that it had no grounds for action with regard to the agreed-on site sharing. Furthermore, it declared the provisions relating to roaming to benefit from an exemption under Article 101(3) TFEU. O2 brought an action before the General Court seeking the annulment of that part of the decision relating to the exemption insofar as this exemption implies that the concerned provision restricts competition (although those restrictions are outweighed by efficiency gains).

The General Court rejected the Commission's legal assessment with the argument that it had failed to analyse the factual effects of the agreement on competition. The Court also developed the test applied in the *Euro Night Services* case further by pointing out that a counterfactual analysis of the case was required under Article 101(1) TFEU in order to properly assess all pro- and anticompetitive effects flowing from a horizontal agreement:

Moreover, in a case such as this, where it is accepted that the agreement does not have as its object a restriction of competition, the effects of the agreement should be considered and for it to be caught by the prohibition it is necessary to find that those factors are present which show that competition has in fact been prevented or restricted or distorted to an appreciable extent. The competition in question must be understood within the actual context in which it would

---

[12] GC (2 May 2006), Case T-328/03 – *O2 (Germany) v Commission* [2006] ECR II-1231.

occur in the absence of the agreement in dispute; the interference with competition may in particular be doubted if the agreement seems really necessary for the penetration of a new area by an undertaking [. . .]

The examination required in the light of [Article 101 TFEU] consists essentially in taking account of the impact of the agreement on existing and potential competition and the competition situation in the absence of the agreement, those two factors being intrinsically linked.[13]

This new approach based on a more economically realistic assessment of potential effects on competition resulting from the creation of a joint venture is reflected in the horizontal block exemptions and the Horizontal Guidelines.

2.7 US approach to horizontal agreements

The US Supreme Court uses two types of analysis to determine whether an agreement between competitors is lawful: *per se* and rule of reason.[14] Agreements that are very likely to harm competition and have no significant positive effect on competition are considered *per se* unlawful.[15] *Per se* illegal agreements between competitors include agreements to fix prices or output, to rig bids, or to share or divide markets by allocation of customers, suppliers, territories, or lines of commerce.[16] Other agreements are assessed under the rule of reason. This means that there will be a factual inquiry into the agreement's overall competitive effects in those cases.[17] This analysis compares the state of competition on the relevant market with and without the agreement in question. It focuses on the question whether the agreement is likely to harm competition by increasing the ability or the incentive to profitably raise prices above what would probably be possible without the agreement or reduce output, quality, service or innovation below that level.[18] The rule of reason analysis consists of flexible inquiries and varies in focus and detail depending on the agreement in question and the affected market.

In certain cases, the US agencies[19] treat competitor collaborations as horizontal mergers and analyse the collaboration according to the US Horizontal Merger Guidelines when the following prerequisites are fulfilled: (a) the collaboration has to be amongst competitors in that relevant market; (b) the collaboration involves an efficiency-enhancing integration of economic activity in that market; (c) all competition is eliminated between the participants in that market through the

---

[13] Ibid., paras. 68/71.

[14] US Supreme Court, *National Society of Professional Engineers v United States*, 435 US 679 (1978), 692.

[15] US Supreme Court, *FTC v Superior Court Trial Lawyers Association*, 493 US 411 (1990), 432–6.

[16] Federal Trade Commission (FTC) and Department of Justice (DoJ), Antitrust Guidelines for Collaborations among Competitors, April 2000, p. 3.

[17] Ibid., p. 3.   [18] Ibid., p. 4.   [19] Antitrust investigations in the US are either pursued by the FTC or the DoJ.

integration; and (d) the collaboration does not terminate within a sufficiently limited period by its own specific and express terms.[20]

Comparably to market share thresholds in the EU, the US agencies have set out so-called 'Antitrust Safety Zones'. According to those rules, they do not challenge competitor collaboration when the combined market shares of the collaboration and its participants is 20% or lower on the relevant markets.[21]

Summary of Section 2

Horizontal agreements relate to cooperation between actual or potential competitors. The types and forms of horizontal cooperation are manifold. Cooperation can relate to activities such as joint research and development or joint purchase of products. The level of integration resulting from a horizontal cooperation can reach from a mere coordination of the use of pre-existing assets to the establishment of a joint venture. There is limited case law of the EU courts on horizontal cooperation. What can be derived is that the entire economic context and the conditions of competition need to be analysed to assess the compatibility of a horizontal cooperation with Article 101 TFEU.

The Commission has adopted a R&D Block Exemption and a Specialisation Block Exemption. These provisions are complemented by the Horizontal Guidelines.

3. INFORMATION EXCHANGE

3.1 Definition

Many types of horizontal cooperation include a certain degree of information exchange. Such information exchange may take different forms. Data can be shared either directly between competitors, indirectly through a common agency (like trade associations) or through a third party (like market research organisations, companies' suppliers or retailers).[22]

Information exchange may solve problems of information asymmetries and make markets more efficient. This may happen when undertakings compare their best practices and improve their internal efficiency or consumers may directly benefit by reducing their search costs and improving choice.

The Commission sets out its approach to the assessment of information exchange in section 2 of the Horizontal Guidelines.

---

[20] FTC and DoJ, Antitrust Guidelines for Collaborations among Competitors, April 2000, p. 5.

[21] Ibid., p. 26.

[22] Horizontal Guidelines, para. 55; with regard to the development of the Information Exchange chapter of the Guidelines, see Camesasca, Schmidt and Clancy, 'The EC Commission's Draft Horizontal Guidelines: Presumed Guilty when Having a Chat', *Journal of European Competition Law and Practice*, 1 (2010), 405.

3.2 Restrictive effects on competition

To have restrictive effects on competition, an information exchange must be likely to have an appreciable adverse impact on at least one of the parameters of competition (such as price, output, product quality, product variety or innovation). There is a higher probability of companies achieving a collusive outcome in markets that are transparent, concentrated, non-complex, stable and symmetric.[23] Collusive outcomes can also be achieved in other market situations through information exchanges where they would not be possible without those information exchanges. Overall, collusive outcomes are more likely on markets where demand and supply conditions are relatively stable and on markets with symmetric structures, for example tight oligopolies.

The exchange of strategic data is more likely to be caught by Art. 101 TFEU than other kinds of data as it reduces the companies' incentives to compete. Information about prices and quantities is considered most strategic, followed by information about costs and demand.[24]

In *T-Mobile Netherlands*,[25] five operators of mobile telephone networks held a meeting where they discussed, *inter alia*, the reduction of standard dealer remunerations for post-paid subscriptions. During those discussions, confidential information came up. The Dutch competition authority found that they had concluded an agreement or entered into a concerted practice that restricted competition and thus were prohibited under national law. This case went to appeal before a Dutch court, which asked the ECJ to clarify the concept of concerted practices. The ECJ held:

a concerted practice pursues an anticompetitive object for the purpose of Article [101(1) TFEU] where, according to its content and objectives and having regard to its legal and economic context, it is capable in an individual case of resulting in the prevention, restriction or distortion of competition within the common market. It is not necessary for there to be actual prevention, restriction or distortion of competition or a direct link between the concerted practice and consumer prices. An exchange of information between competitors is tainted with an anticompetitive object if the exchange is capable of removing uncertainties concerning the intended conduct of the participating undertakings.[26]

The ECJ referred the case back to the Dutch court to determine whether the information exchanged at the meeting was capable of removing such uncertainties.

In the US, agreements that involve the exchange or disclosure of information are treated as agreements that may facilitate collusion.[27] Benefits and problems with these kinds of agreements are evaluated similarly to the Commission's approach. They are analysed under the rule of reason.

---

[23] Horizontal Guidelines, para. 77.   [24] Ibid., para. 86.
[25] ECJ (4 June 2009), Case C-8/08 – *T-Mobile Netherlands and Others* [2009] ECR I-4529.
[26] Ibid., para. 43.
[27] FTC and DoJ, Antitrust Guidelines for Collaborations among Competitors, April 2000, p. 15.

3.3 Potential efficiency gains

Information exchange may lead to efficiency gains. Knowing their competitors' costs, companies can benchmark their performance against the best practices in their industry to become more efficient. It may help companies to allocate production towards high-demand markets or low-cost companies. Exchange of consumer data in markets with asymmetric information about consumers (banking and insurance sector) may raise efficiency. Genuinely public information exchange can benefit consumers as it allows them to make more informed choices.[28]

In *John Deere Ltd v Commission*,[29] the General Court had to decide about such an information exchange system. In this case, the Agricultural Engineers Association Limited (AEA) was a trade association open to all manufacturers or importers of agricultural tractors operating in the United Kingdom (UK). The AEA initiated an agreement establishing an information exchange system also open to non-members who were manufacturers or importers of agricultural tractors to the UK. The information exchange system was based on data held by the UK Department of Transport. Under UK law, all vehicles including tractors had to be registered with this department if they were to be used on public roads. The department collected different kinds of information like the aggregate industry information, information concerning the sales of each member (number of units sold by each manufacturer and their market shares in various geographical areas) and information concerning the sales made by the dealers in the distribution network of each member (imports and exports in their respective territories). The AEA got this information through a data-processing company responsible for the processing and handling of some of the data obtained by the UK Department of Transport.

The AEA argued that this information exchange system did not infringe the EU competition rules. The General Court held that:

on a truly competitive market transparency between traders is in principle likely to lead to the intensification of competition between suppliers, since in such a situation, the fact that a trader takes into account information made available to him in order to adjust his conduct on the market is not likely, having regard to the atomized nature of the supply, to reduce or remove for the other traders any uncertainty about the foreseeable nature of its competitors' conduct. On the other hand, the Court considers that, as the Commission argues this time, general use [. . .] of exchanges of precise information at short intervals, identifying registered vehicles and the place of their registration is, on a highly concentrated oligopolistic market such as the market in question and on which competition is as a result already greatly reduced and exchange of information facilitated, likely to impair substantially the competition which exists between traders [. . .]. In such circumstances, the sharing, on a regular and frequent basis, of information

---

[28] Para. 97 of the Horizontal Guidelines.

[29] GC (27 October 1994), Case T-35/92 – *John Deere Ltd v Commission* [1994] ECR II-957.

concerning the operation of the market has the effect of periodically revealing to all the competitors the market positions and strategies of the various individual competitors.[30]

This case is a good example of an information exchange system although Article 101(3) TFEU did not apply here. It shows that the exchange of customer data in an oligopolistic market may raise competition concerns, even if it does not concern prices and was not concluded to underpin another anticompetitive agreement.

Summary of Section 3

Information exchange between competitors may occur in many ways. Some industry associations may operate market information systems or competitors may exchange information in meetings at industry conferences or trade fairs. The exchange of information will be regarded as restricting competition if it relates to information that is of relevance for the current or future market conduct of undertakings. Any exchange of strategic information such as price increases or capacity reductions will be regarded as leading to a concerted practice in the sense of Article 101(1) TFEU. Only aggregate or historical data may be exchanged. Potential efficiency gains of information exchanges can take the form of cost benchmarks that result in lower costs or the elimination of information asymmetries. It has to be kept in mind that any such information exchange has to be limited to a strict minimum to satisfy the test under Article 101(3) TFEU.

4. R&D AGREEMENTS

4.1 Definition

In principle R&D cooperation may reduce unnecessary costs and lead to significant cross-fertilisation of ideas. This may lead to better and more efficient development of new products to the benefit of consumers. On the other hand, such agreements may have foreclosure effects and cause other competition problems like reduction of output or increase of prices. R&D agreements may be covered by the R&D Block Exemption. They are also discussed in section 3 of the Horizontal Guidelines.

R&D agreements may vary in form and scope of cooperation between parties. Generally speaking, their 'centre of gravity' is cooperation concerning research, development and marketing of new products and technologies. Joint improvement of existing technologies is also included.

The R&D Block Exemption applies to six types of R&D agreements in relation to goods and services:

---

[30] Ibid., para. 51.

(i) *Joint R&D of products and/or technologies and joint exploitation of the results.* Example: A and B, producers of carglass, agree to combine their R&D departments into a joint venture to develop a new formula to increase heat reflection. After the new formula is ready for marketing, the joint venture will produce and distribute the resulting new carglass.

(ii) *Joint exploitation of the results of R&D of products or technologies jointly carried out pursuant to a prior agreement.* Example: A and B are companies in the business of producing components for the computer industry. A and B agree that they will join their R&D efforts to develop a new component for the production of harddrives. After the R&D has been successfully concluded, A and B agree to jointly exploit the results.

(iii) *Joint R&D of products and technologies excluding joint exploitation of the results.* Example: A and B are two companies on the market for the manufacture of pigments for coatings and other applications. They agree to coordinate their previous R&D efforts by setting up a joint venture to complete the R&D and produce the pigments. Those pigments will be sold back to A and B, who will commercialise them separately.

(iv) *Paid-for R&D of products and technologies and joint exploitation of the results.* Example: A and B produce carglass. They ask C, a company specialised in this kind of research, to develop for payment a new kind of carglass with greater heat reflection, as they do not have R&D departments that would be able to do so on their own and they have limited financial resources that keep them from contracting alone with a third party for the R&D. The agreement between A, B and C provides for A and B to exploit the results of C's R&D jointly.

(v) *Joint exploitation of the results of paid-for R&D of products or technologies pursuant to a prior agreement between the same parties.* Example: A is a company that primarily is in the business of developing new pigments for colour companies, but sometimes also produces and distributes pigments itself. B asks A to do R&D for a new pigment. After A succeeds in developing that pigment, A and B agree to jointly exploit the results of the R&D.

(vi) *Paid-for R&D of products and technologies excluding joint exploitation of the results.* Example: A is a company focused on research in the automotive sector. B is a producer of automotives with its own R&D department. As its own R&D department is not able to carry out a planned R&D project within a reasonable timeframe, B instructs A with the R&D project. A grants B the licence for the exclusive production and distribution of the resulting innovation for the duration of the patent.

Since the notion of joint exploitation is not defined in Article 1 of the Regulation, it is necessary to consult Recital 9 of the Regulation, according to which joint exploitation can take various forms of cooperation including manufacture, the exploitation of IPRs or even the marketing of new products.

4.2 Specificities of market definition in the R&D context

Proper assessment of the impact of a horizontal R&D agreement on competition depends on the definition of the relevant product market. In case of improvements to existing products those existing products and their substitutes form the relevant market. A totally different methodology will be applied if R&D is conducted in relation to entirely new products and/or technologies.

Under certain circumstances,[31] the assessment of effects on competition in relation to existing markets may prove insufficient. Two scenarios can be distinguished depending on different kinds of innovation in given industries. Firstly, there are sectors where the process of innovation is structured in a way that makes it possible to identify competing R&D poles. Competing R&D poles are directed towards the same new products or technologies or substitutes for those products or technologies with a similar timing. Therefore, it has to be analysed whether, after an R&D agreement, there will remain a sufficient number of R&D poles. An example of this kind of sector is the pharmaceutical industry. Secondly, in other industries, innovative efforts are not that clearly structured and therefore do not allow for an identification of R&D poles. Normally, in this situation the Commission would not try to assess the impact of an R&D cooperation on innovation. The assessment would be limited to existing product and/or technology markets which are close or related to the specific R&D agreement.

For this reason the analysis should concentrate on the question whether the R&D agreements merely intended or already put into operation will leave free space for other market players willing to conduct similar R&D programmes. In other words it must be investigated whether after the conclusion of the agreement there will be a sufficient degree of competition in innovation. There can be a certain interrelation between competition and innovation. Innovation markets comprise markets where no product market yet exists and companies compete in innovation and R&D to create and enter this new market. Sometimes, potential competition and competition in innovation are not clearly distinguishable.

4.3 Main competition concerns raised by R&D agreements

In principle, R&D cooperation may cause the following three types of negative effects: (i) restriction of innovation, (ii) coordination of the parties' behaviour, (iii) foreclosure problems depending on the market power of the collaborating undertakings.

---

[31] See scenarios described in Horizontal Guidelines, paras. 119–22.

In *Asahi/Saint-Gobain*,[32] both companies set up a joint venture to coordinate their respective R&D and the production of bi-layer products. These new products were intended to be used in safety glazing for ground transportation vehicles and architectural applications. Those new bi-layer products were supposed to have advantages over conventional laminated glass, such as greater resistance to impact or scratches and weight savings. The joint venture agreement provided for a joint R&D programme and two pilot plants to start the industrial application. The agreement restricted the parties from constructing other plants prior to the two pilot plants and from expanding their capacities without prior consent of the other party. Otherwise, nothing would prevent the parties from competing with each other in the production and sale of the bi-layer products. The joint venture also comprised the joint exploitation of the IPRs and it would be the exclusive licensor of technology to its parents but also to third parties during the R&D and the production period covered by the joint venture.

Both parties were strong market players in the glass industry and the production of safety glass for vehicles and therefore also major competitors on the market for the result of the R&D. The Commission was of the opinion that each could have carried out the R&D on their own. Due to this market situation and the joint exploitation, the Commission saw a restriction of competition within the meaning of Article 101(1) TFEU even if there was a competitive production and sales process.

But the Commission found that even though there were competitive risks with regard to the joint venture, it contributed to improving the production, the technical and economic progress and consumer benefit according to Article 101(3) TFEU:

The new product will be a technically advanced and innovative one, the development of which will entail great financial risk for the parties, as its commercial viability is still uncertain. Substantial research and development still has to be done in order to make commercial sales of bi-layer products possible. Given the strength of the demand side ... considerable effort has to be made to minimize costs or, should costs prove to be above those of conventional windshields, to realize substantial advantages in quality and performance that will justify the higher price. The efforts and risks involved, if undertaken independently by the parties, would most certainly not lead to results as rapid, efficient and economic as those envisaged.

This shows that even if a R&D agreement is likely to have negative effects on competition because strong market players are parties to the agreement, those effects may be outweighed by the overall benefit to consumers.

---

[32] Commission decision of 16 December 1994, Case IV/33.863 – *Asahi/Saint-Gobain*, OJ No. L 354 of 31 December 1994, p. 87.

4.4 R&D agreements not restricting competition

Many R&D agreements do not fall within the ambit of Article 101(1) TFEU. Such agreements include:

- R&D agreements at a rather theoretical stage and far from exploitation of possible results;[33]
- R&D cooperation between non-competitors – if the parties are not able to carry out the necessary R&D separately;[34]
- outsourcing of R&D to entities not active in the exploitation of the results, e.g. research institutes and universities;[35]
- 'pure' R&D agreements not extended to joint exploitation of results.[36]

An example of a 'pure' R&D agreement can be found in *Canon/Kodak*[37]:

In this case, Canon, Kodak and three other companies entered into an agreement for the development and licensing of a new advanced photographic system for films, cameras and photo-finishing equipment. This system was supposed to become an alternative to existing systems and benefit consumers by reducing the size of the equipment and making it easier to handle. The cooperation itself was limited to the development of the system as the agreement was supposed to terminate once the joint R&D had been successfully completed. The developed technologies were not only available to the parties, but also to third party manufacturers through licences.

Even though the parties had very high market shares, a restriction of competition could not be assumed as there was no foreclosure risk due to the open licensing and the cooperation between the parties was strictly limited.

Another example of an R&D agreement that would not fall under Article 101(1) TFEU and can be described as an outsourcing of R&D could be the following scenario:[38]

A small research company (A) discovers and patents a pharmaceutical substance that will revolutionise the treatment of a certain disease based on a new technology. As A does not have its own marketing organisation, it enters into an R&D agreement with B, a big pharmaceutical producer. So far B's products were used to cure that disease. B would not be able to build an expertise equivalent to A's within a reasonable timeframe. For the existing products, B has a market share of around 75% in each Member State, but its patents will expire within five years. There are two other research pools with other companies at about the same stage of development

---

[33] Horizontal Guidelines, para. 129.   [34] Ibid., para. 130.   [35] Ibid., para. 131.   [36] Ibid., para. 132.
[37] Commission Notice pursuant to Article 19(3) of Council Regulation No 17 concerning Case IV/34.796 – *Canon/Kodak*, OJ No. C330 of 1 November 1997, p. 10.
[38] Horizontal Guidelines, para. 147, Example 2.

for the same technology. B agreed to provide funding and know-how for product development, as well as future access to the market. B will have a licence for exclusive production and distribution of the resulting product for the patent duration. The product is expected to be brought to the market within five to seven years.

It is likely that the resulting product will belong to a new market. The parties bring complementary resources and skills to this cooperation which significantly increases the probability of the product entering the market. Although B has considerable market power on the existing market, this market power will decrease shortly. As B has no expertise in this field, the agreement will not lead to a loss in R&D. Furthermore, the existence of two other R&D pools reduces the incentive to reduce R&D efforts. The exploitation rights are necessary for B to recoup the needed investments and it has to be taken into account that A has no marketing resources of its own. Restrictive effects according to Article 101(1) TFEU are therefore unlikely. If there were restrictive effects, the conditions of Article 101(3) TFEU would probably be fulfilled.

4.5 Conditions for exemption under Article 101(3) TFEU

The conditions for an exemption of an R&D agreement are stipulated in Article 3 secs. (2)–(5) of the R&D Block Exemption. All of them must be fulfilled for an exemption to apply.

Article 3(2) R&D Block Exemption requires that all parties to the R&D agreement have access to the results of the R&D for the purpose of further research or exploitation. However, universities and other research institutes may limit their rights to use the results of R&D for further research.

Article 3(3) R&D Block Exemption provides that in case of agreements limited to joint R&D or paid-for R&D each party must be granted access to any pre-existing know-how of the other parties, if this is necessary for the exploitation of the results. Compensation for giving access to the pre-existing know-how may be foreseen, but it must not be so high as to impede access.

Article 3(4) R&D Block Exemption permits cooperation only where it relates to results protected by IPRs or constituting know-how which contributes to technical or economic progress. The results of R&D must be decisive for the manufacturing of the contract products.

Pursuant to Article 3(5) R&D Block Exemption, undertakings charged with manufacture by way of specialisation in production must be obliged to fulfil orders for supplies from other parties to the R&D agreement unless there is joint distribution. This way it is secured that all parties have access to the products produced by the others.

4.6 Duration of the agreement and market share threshold

According to Article 4(1) R&D Block Exemption the exemption shall apply for the duration of the R&D when the parties are not competitors. In case of a joint exploitation, the exemption shall continue to apply for seven years. This is meant to give them the possibility to await stabilisation of their market shares and to guarantee a minimum period of return on their investments.[39]

It is assumed that negative effects are not likely to appear with R&D agreements in the absence of significant market power. Although there are no clear-cut thresholds for market power indicating the high probability of infringement, it is assumed that a combined market share of less than 25% is a safe harbour.[40] Therefore, where the parties are competitors, according to Article 4(2) R&D Block Exemption the exemption shall apply for the periods specified above only if:

- in case of R&D agreements involving joint R&D, their combined market share does not exceed 25% on the relevant products or technology market;
- in case of R&D agreements involving paid-for R&D, the combined market share of the financing party and all parties with which the financing party has entered into R&D agreements with regard to the same products or technologies does not exceed 25% on the relevant products or technology market.

4.7 Agreements not covered by the exemption (hardcore restrictions)

The block exemption does not apply to severe anticompetitive restraints which directly or indirectly, in isolation or in combination with other factors under the control of the parties have as their object restrictions listed in Article 5 (1) (a)–(j). The most relevant ones are:

- restriction of the freedom to carry out R&D independently or with third parties in unrelated fields, or after the completion of the R&D agreement or the paid-for R&D, in the field to which it relates or in a connected field;
- limitation of output or sales;
- price fixing;
- prohibition of passive sales into certain territories or to certain customers.

---

[39]   Recital 14 R&D Block Exemption.
[40]   25% market share is a condition for application of the block exemption regulation for research and development.

4.8 Restrictions excluded from exemption

Contrary to hardcore restrictions, the presence of an excluded restriction does not mean that the rest of the R&D agreement cannot be exempted. Pursuant to Article 6, the exemption in Article 2 shall not apply to obligations not to challenge IPRs and the obligation not to grant licences to third parties to manufacture contract products or apply contract technologies unless the agreement provides for the exploitation of the results of the R&D by at least one of the parties and such exploitation takes place in the internal market vis-à-vis third parties.

In this context, contract technology means a technology or product arising out of joint R&D and contract product is a product arising out of the joint R&D or manufactured or provided applying the contract technologies.[41]

4.9 US approach

In the US, R&D agreements are considered as agreements that limit decision making or combine control or financial interests, but also mostly as pro-competitive. Therefore, they are analysed under the rule of reason.[42] R&D is considered less likely to facilitate collusion, as R&D conduct is often conducted in secret. It would thus be difficult to monitor agreements to coordinate R&D.

The US agencies have set a special safety zone for R&D competition in terms of innovation markets. Generally, the agencies do not challenge a R&D collaboration on the basis of effects on competition in innovation markets, where three or more independently controlled research efforts possess the required specialised assets or characteristics and the incentive to engage in R&D that is a close substitute for the collaboration's R&D activity, additional to those of the collaboration.[43]

Summary of Section 4

R&D cooperation may be covered by the R&D Block Exemption. It may take various forms ranging from pure R&D to joint exploitation of the results. As a general rule, R&D agreements between competitors benefit from the block exemption up to a combined market share of 25%. The exemption applies only if the R&D agreement does not include any hardcore restrictions of competition such as a prohibition of R&D in areas unrelated to the joint R&D project. Innovation must not be limited by R&D cooperation but rather facilitated.

---

[41] Article 1 (e) and (f) R&D Block Exemption.
[42] FTC and DoJ, Antitrust Guidelines for Collaborations among Competitors, April 2000, p. 14.
[43] Ibid, pp. 26 et seq.

R&D cooperation may have effects on different markets: at the very early stage of a R&D project it may affect an innovation market. In this market different approaches to a certain problem may compete with each other. Often there are several R&D poles, one of which may be eliminated by the cooperation. R&D cooperation may also restrict competition on the technology market which is further downstream from the innovation market. R&D has already reached the stage of a technology that may compete with other technologies that serve the same purpose. Finally, when the technologies are developed into products ready for market launch, R&D cooperation may also affect a product market.

5. SPECIALISATION AGREEMENTS

Specialisation agreements are another type of horizontal cooperation that is governed by a block exemption. In a specialisation agreement competitors pool certain activities but remain independent with regard to others. This type of cooperation may create efficiencies that outweigh the restrictions of competition involved in such practices and that may justify an exemption from Article 101(1) TFEU.

The Specialisation Block Exemption applies to the following three types of specialisation agreements (Article 2(1), Article 1(1)(a–d) Specialisation Block Exemption):

(i)   unilateral specialisation agreements – one party agrees to cease production of certain goods or services and to purchase them from a competing undertaking;

(ii) reciprocal specialisation agreements – two or more parties on a reciprocal basis agree to cease or refrain from producing different products and to purchase those products from other parties;

(iii) joint production agreements – two or more parties agree to produce certain products jointly.

The Specialisation Block Exemption applies only to agreements between competitors.[44] Agreements between non-competitors are in principle vertical supply agreements and fall within the scope of Regulation 330/2010, the block exemption regulation for vertical agreements.[45]

---

[44] Specialisation Block Exemption, Recital 8.
[45] Commission Regulation (EU) No. 330/2010 of 20 April 2010 on the application of Article 101(3) TFEU to categories of vertical agreements and concerted practices, OJ No. L 102 of 23 April 2010, p. 1.

5.1 Extended scope of the exemption

Pursuant to Article 2(3) Specialisation Block Exemption the exemption also applies if one of two conditions listed below is fulfilled:

(i)   the parties accept an exclusive purchase and/or exclusive supply obligation;
(ii) the parties do not independently sell the specialisation products but jointly distribute those products.

An exclusive purchase obligation is an obligation to purchase the specialisation product only from a party to the agreement,[46] while an exclusive supply obligation means an obligation not to supply a competing company other than a party to the agreement with the specialisation product.[47]

In *BP Kemi/DDSF*,[48] the Commission had to decide about an exclusive purchasing agreement concerning the distribution of synthetic ethanol in Denmark. There are two kinds of ethanol, synthetic and agricultural, but they can be used for the same purposes. Ethanol is used in the production of drinkable spirits, vinegar, pharmaceutical products, cosmetics or for chemical synthesis. BP Kemi was a subsidiary of the BP Group, at the time the largest producer of synthetic ethanol in the EU. DDSF was a company active in Denmark that primarily produced agricultural ethanol and stopped producing synthetic ethanol after the agreement with BP Kemi. The agreement provided for DDSF to buy all of its requirements of synthetic ethanol from BP Kemi. BP Kemi would have no obligation to supply DDSF with more than a certain amount of synthetic ethanol, while DDSF would be free to buy synthetic ethanol in excess of that amount from other suppliers, if it first gave BP Kemi the opportunity to supply under the original conditions. The agreement was to run for six years and could be terminated on twelve months' written notice. In an associated agreement, BP Kemi agreed to keep the listed prices of DDSF for ethanol and in principle to apply the same payment conditions as DDSF. BP Kemi also agreed to compensate DDSF if annual sales exceeded 25% of the two companies' combined sales.

Generally, the Commission's view on exclusive supply and purchasing agreements was the following:

Exclusive supply and purchasing agreements concluded with a view to the resale of the goods are exempted under Article [101(3) TFEU] from the general prohibition on restrictive practices, in spite of their restrictive effects, because in general they facilitate the general sale of the product, make it possible to carry out more intensive marketing, and ensure continuation of supplies to customers while at the same time rationalizing distribution. However, such improvements in distribution exist only where the parties apply a clear vertical separation

---

[46] Article 1 lit. p Specialisation Block Exemption.   [47] Article 1 lit. o Specialisation Block Exemption.
[48] Commission decision of 5 September 1979, Case IV/29.021 – *BP Kemi/DDSF*, OJ No. L 286 of 14 November 1979, p. 32.

of activities. The economic justification for exclusive arrangements applies where the supplier is not developing his own active sales activities in the territory allocated to the dealer and thus does not enter into competition with him there.[49]

The Commission then applied those conditions to the given purchasing agreement:

The Purchasing Agreement concluded by the parties does not meet these conditions. In DDSF's main sales area, Denmark, DDSF and BP Kemi compete in respect of goods covered by the agreement. Both take their offers to what is, essentially, the same category of customers. This fact also explains why protective clauses in DDSF's favour were included in the cooperation agreement, stating that BP Kemi should follow DDSF's list prices and that BP Kemi should compensate DDSF if its annual sales were to exceed a quarter of the two undertakings' combined sales. The Purchasing Agreement is therefore partly a 'horizontal' agreement, concluded between two undertakings at the same level of trade, limiting the commercial freedom of the party undertaking to purchase exclusively from the other and the access of other suppliers to the Danish market, without however introducing any improvement in the distribution of goods which would tend to outweigh these disadvantages.[50]

This shows that generally, the Commission regards purchasing agreements as exempted under Article 101(3) TFEU from the prohibition of restrictive practices, but certain additional terms in an agreement may transform a purchasing agreement into a forbidden horizontal agreement.

5.2 Market share threshold

The block exemption applies only to agreements concluded by parties that have a combined market share not exceeding 20% (Article 3 Specialisation Block Exemption) on the relevant market. In accordance with Article 5 Specialisation Block Exemption, the market share generally has to be calculated on the basis of the sales data of the preceding calendar year. There are also rules for the situation where the parties outgrow the market share cap. If they are initially below 20% but rise above that level without exceeding 25%, the exemption continues to apply for two consecutive calendar years. If they also exceed 25%, the exemption continues to apply for one more year.

5.3 Agreements not covered by the exemption

Article 4 contains a 'black list' of competition restraints. If a specialisation agreement has any of the following restraints directly or indirectly as its object, the exemption does not apply:

[49] Ibid., para. 95.   [50] Ibid., para. 96.

- fixing of prices when selling the products to third parties;[51]
- limitation of output or sales;[52]
- allocation of markets or customers.

However, the parties may agree on the level of output of a joint venture or the level of prices it will charge from its immediate customers – Article 4(2) Specialisation Block Exemption.

Summary of Section 5

Specialisation agreements relate to a type of cooperation where undertakings rely on a competitor for a certain function. This may generate efficiencies, for example through a better use of capacities. Specialisation benefits from the Specialisation Block Exemption up to a combined market share of 20%. A specialisation agreement must not contain any hardcore restrictions such as price fixing or output limitations.

6. PRODUCTION AGREEMENTS

Production agreements are a type of specialisation agreement that may be covered by the Specialisation Block Exemption. This category of agreement is also discussed by the Commission in section 4 of the Horizontal Guidelines.

According to the Horizontal Guidelines[53] there are three main categories of production agreements:

- production agreements where the production is carried out by only one party;
- joint production agreements – the parties agree to produce certain products jointly;
- horizontal subcontracting agreements:
  - specialisation agreements[54] – parties agree unilaterally or reciprocally to cease production of a product and to purchase it from the other party
  - subcontracting agreements – one party entrusts the other with the production of a product. Subcontracting agreements are in principle vertical agreements unless concluded between competitors.

Vertical subcontracting agreements are not covered by the Horizontal Guidelines. They fall within the scope of the Vertical Guidelines.

---

[51] With the exception of the fixing of prices charged to immediate customers in the context of joint distribution.

[52] With the exception of provisions on the agreed amount of products in the context of unilateral or reciprocal specialisation agreements or the setting of the capacity and production volume in the context of a joint production agreement; and the setting of sales targets in the context of joint distribution.

[53] Horizontal Guidelines, paras. 150–3.

[54] Specialisation Block Exemption Regulation for specialisation agreements.

One of the main risks resulting from production agreements is the possibility of coordination of the parties' competitive behaviour as suppliers. This problem may arise when the collaborating parties are actual competitors on one of the relevant markets including potential spill-over markets. Furthermore production agreements may also give rise to foreclosure problems. In particular, an in-depth analysis should be made when one of the parties has a strong market position or joint production of an important component is planned.

Production agreements are in principle restrictions of competition by object if their main goal is to restrict competition by limiting output, price fixing or market allocation. However, the parties may agree on the level of output of a joint venture or on the level of prices it will charge.[55]

Whether a production agreement has restrictive effects on competition depends on a number of factors such as the characteristics of the market as well as the nature and market coverage of the cooperation and the product. Production agreements between companies that have no market power or agreements between non-competitors are generally not covered by Article 101(1) TFEU unless foreclosure effects arise. Agreements entered by competitors may also be excluded from the scope of cartel prohibition if the cooperation is the only justifiable way to enter the new market or to launch a new product. Anticompetitive effects are also unlikely if the parties to a production agreement have a small proportion of their total costs in common.

Companies below a certain market share are unlikely to have a significant degree of market power. If the combined market share exceeds 20%,[56] the restrictive effects have to be analysed as the agreement does not fall within the scope of the Specialisation Block Exemption. In general, a production agreement in a concentrated market is more likely to lead to restrictive effects than in a non-concentrated market. Furthermore, some competition concerns may also arise when cooperation between strong potential competitors is concerned.

Production agreements not covered by the Specialisation Block Exemption may be exempted under Article 101(3) TFEU if the parties manage to demonstrate improvements to production or other efficiencies. Claimed efficiencies must not result from output reductions or market allocation.

The US agencies consider that production collaborations may be anticompetitive as they may involve agreements on the level of output, the use of key assets, or on the price of the product of the collaboration.[57] They are considered to limit independent decision making or combine control or financial interests and are therefore analysed under the rule of reason.

---

[55] Horizontal Guidelines, para. 160.
[56] Maximum market share allowed for application of the Specialisation Block Exemption Regulation for specialisation agreements.
[57] FTC and DoJ, Antitrust Guidelines for Collaborations among Competitors, April 2000, p. 13.

Summary of Section 6

Production cooperations are a type of specialisation agreement that is covered by the Specialisation Block Exemption. Competitors may cease production of certain components of their production and source them from a competitor. This may trigger investment in new production facilities or create other efficiencies. Such agreements may be reciprocal or non-reciprocal. They benefit from the exemption up to a combined market share of the parties involved of 20%.

7. PURCHASING AGREEMENTS

Purchasing agreements are often concluded by associations of small and medium-sized undertakings to create buyer power by achieving volumes and discounts similar to their bigger competitors. From a certain level, such buying power may give rise to competition concerns. The Horizontal Guidelines provide a framework for the assessment of purchasing agreements. They are not, however, covered by any block exemption regulation.

If there are no competition concerns on the horizontal level, vertical agreements between the association and individual association members and between the association and suppliers have to be assessed. Those agreements may be subject to the block exemption regulation on vertical restraints.[58]

Article 101(1) TFEU applies to purchasing agreements only if they are concluded by undertakings competing on the same retail market or serve as a tool to engage in price fixing, market allocation or other hardcore restrictions of competition. Generally, purchasing agreements may lead to increased prices, reduced output, product quality or innovation, or anticompetitive foreclosure of other possible purchasers. Joint purchasing may lead to a concentration of significant buyer power and lower purchasing costs. When downstream competitors purchase a large amount of their products through a purchasing association, they may not be inclined to compete for prices on the selling market. The cost savings may not, however, be necessarily transferred to consumers if the purchasers have power on the selling markets. If such an association of purchasers has a significant degree of buying power, there is a risk that they may force suppliers to reduce the range or quality of products. When there is only a limited number of suppliers, purchasing agreements may also cause some foreclosure effects.

---

[58] Commission Regulation (EU) No. 330/2010 of 20 April 2010 on the application of Article 101(3) TFEU to categories of vertical agreements and concerted practices, OJ No. L 102 of 23 April 2010, p. 1.

In cases where purchasing agreements do not primarily concern joint purchasing, but are a tool to engage in price fixing, output limitation or market allocation, they are considered to restrict competition by object. However, if members of purchasing associations agree on the purchasing prices the association may pay to suppliers, this does not apply. In those cases, the whole purchasing agreement and not just the price agreement has to be assessed on whether it has restrictive effects on competition.

If purchasing agreements do not have the restriction of competition as their object, they have to be analysed with regard to their likely effects on competition on both the purchasing and selling markets.

For this analysis, market power has to be taken into consideration. It is assumed that no significant market power exists when the parties to the purchasing agreement have a combined market share of less than 15% on the selling market and less than 15% in the purchasing market.[59] A market share above this threshold does not necessarily indicate that a purchasing agreement has restrictive effects on competition. A detailed assessment is required in those cases, taking into account factors such as market concentration and possible countervailing power of strong suppliers.

Purchasing agreements may also lead to collusive outcomes as they generally facilitate the coordination of the parties' behaviour on selling markets. This is likely to be due to the fact that the parties have the same costs for the products they purchase together, but they also need to have market power and market characteristics need to be conducive to coordination. Collusive behaviour may also result from information exchange that is necessary to implement a purchasing agreement such as an agreement on purchase prices and volumes.

The exemption under Article 101(3) TFEU applies to purchasing agreements if the agreement brings about economies of scale. In particular, this can be efficiency gains like lower purchase prices or reduced costs of transaction, transportation and storage. But those efficiency gains have to be passed on to consumers to a certain extent to outweigh restrictive effects on competition. This may happen through lower prices on the selling markets; cost savings cannot just benefit the parties to the purchasing agreement.

In the US, buying collaborations are considered as agreements limiting independent decision making or combining control or financial interests under certain conditions. It is also accepted that they may be pro-competitive and many of them do not raise competitive concerns.[60] They are therefore assessed under the rule of reason.[61]

---

[59] Horizontal Guidelines, para. 208.
[60] FTC and DoJ, Antitrust Guidelines for Collaborations among Competitors, April 2000, p. 14.
[61] For a further discussion of purchasing agreements in the US, see Eaton, 'Joint Purchasing: Assisting the Survival of Small Retailers in Small Markets', *European Competition Law Review*, 30 (2009), 301.

Summary of Section 7

Joint purchasing is considered compatible with the EU competition rules if the combined market share of the parties involved does not exceed 15%. Accordingly, joint purchasing gives smaller undertakings the possibility to obtain better conditions when sourcing products from third parties. This improves their competitive chances in relation to their bigger rivals. Joint purchasing may lead to a high commonality of costs if the price of the purchased good amounts to a substantial part of the price of the end product. Prices for the end product may be very similar in such a case. This may affect the assessment under Article 101(3) TFEU.

8. COMMERCIALISATION AGREEMENTS

Commercialisation agreements involve cooperation of competitors in the selling, distribution or promotion of their products. This kind of agreement can vary in scope depending on the commercialisation functions that are covered. They can go from joint selling agreements that lead to joint determination of all commercial aspects of the sale of a product to more limited agreements addressing only specific commercialisation functions, such as distribution, after-sales service or advertising.

The Commission had to assess a commercialisation agreement in the *UEFA Champions League* case.[62] The joint selling arrangement granted UEFA the exclusive right to jointly sell certain commercial rights, including media rights for the UEFA Champions League as a whole and for all matches in the league on behalf of the participating football clubs.

The Commission concluded that this arrangement restricted competition:

UEFA's joint selling arrangement has the effect that through the agreement to jointly exploit the commercial rights of the UEFA Champions League on an exclusive basis through a joint selling body, UEFA, prevents the individual football clubs from individually marketing such rights. This prevents competition between the football clubs and also between UEFA and the football clubs in supplying in parallel media rights to the UEFA Champions League to interested buyers in the upstream markets. [...] Third-party commercial operators are therefore forced to purchase the relevant rights under the conditions jointly determined in the context of the invitation to bid, which is issued by the joint selling body. [...] In the absence of the joint selling agreement the football clubs would set

---

[62] Commission decision of 23 July 2003, Case COMP/C.2–37.398 – *Joint Selling of the Commercial Rights of the UEFA Champions League*, OJ No. L 291 of 8 November 2003, p. 25.

such prices and conditions independently of one another and in competition with one another.[63]

Despite the restriction of competition, the Commission also saw benefits for consumers that outweighed its negative effects and Art. 101(1) TFEU was therefore inapplicable with regard to Art. 101(3) TFEU. Those benefits were the improvement of production and distribution by creating a quality branded league focused product sold via a single point of sale, and the competitive restrictions were found indispensable for achieving those benefits.

Commercialisation agreements can lead to price fixing, output limitation, market and customer allocation, and exchange of strategic information.[64]

Commercialisation agreements, in particular joint selling agreements, give rise to anticompetitive concerns when they introduce any form of price fixing. Since such agreements have in principle the object of coordinating the pricing policy, it is very likely that they restrict competition by object.[65] But such agreements may not only restrict price competition, they may also restrict the total volume of products to be delivered within the limits of the agreement.

Commercialisation agreements between non-competitors fall outside the scope of cartel prohibition unless they contain some vertical restraints such as restrictions on passive sales[66] or resale price maintenance.[67]

Joint commercialisation agreements are potentially relevant from the competition point of view when they allow for the exchange of sensitive commercial information or they influence a significant part of the parties' final costs. Agreements entered into by competitors active on different geographical markets may also cause some anticompetitive effects. Such a risk exists when reciprocal agreements to distribute each other's products are concluded since they may facilitate or result in market allocation.[68] However, if the combined market share of the parties to an agreement does not exceed the threshold of 15%, no market power of the participating undertakings is assumed. In such cases Article 101(1) TFEU does not apply as long as the agreement does not involve price fixing. If the combined market share is greater than 15% the impact of the agreement on the market must be assessed together with the degree of market concentration.[69]

The availability of an exemption under Article 101(3) TFEU depends on the size of the efficiencies generated by a commercialisation agreement. Only the efficiencies that result directly from integration of economic activities of the concerned parties

---

[63] Ibid., para. 114.   [64] Horizontal Guidelines, paras. 230 et seq.   [65] Ibid., paras. 234 et seq.

[66] 'Passive sales' means to respond to unsolicited requests from individual customers. See Vertical Guidelines, para. 51.

[67] A manufacturer forces or persuades retailers to sell his product at the same price. See *Black's Law Dictionary* (West Group, 8th edn, 2004), p. 1332

[68] Horizontal Guidelines, para. 236.   [69] Ibid., paras. 240 et seq.

may be taken into account. Moreover, claimed efficiencies, such as for example cost savings through reduced duplication of resources, must be clearly demonstrated.[70]

The Commission had to assess efficiencies generated by a commercialisation agreement in the *UEFA* case:

It is concluded that UEFA's joint selling arrangement leads to the improvement of production and distribution by creating a quality branded league focused product sold via a single point of sale. Moreover, consumers receive a real fair share of the benefits deriving from it. Furthermore, the restrictions inherent in UEFA's joint selling arrangement are indispensable for achieving these benefits, save for the provision prohibiting individual football clubs from selling live TV rights to free-TV broadcasters.[71]

Summary of Section 8

Commercialisation agreements relate to the joint selling, distribution or promotion of goods or services. For some products an expansive distribution network with highly trained staff may be required that smaller suppliers cannot afford. Cooperation with others may improve their access to the market in such a case. Joint commercialisation is likely to benefit from an exemption under Article 101(3) TFEU up to a combined market share of 15%.

9. STANDARDISATION AGREEMENTS

Agreements on standards aim at defining technical or quality requirements with which current or future products, production processes or methods should comply.[72] This can be standards for a wide variety of issues, such as different grades or sizes of particular products or technical specifications in product markets. Furthermore, the terms of access for a particular quality mark or standards on the environmental performance of products can be considered standardisation agreements. Ensuring access to standards is crucial for the standard to produce positive economic effects as access to the standard may be required for market access.[73]

Usually, standardisation agreements produce positive economic effects such as economic interpenetration and encouraging the development of new and improved products.[74] Therefore, they generally do not fall within the scope of Article 101(1)

---

[70] Horizontal Guidelines, paras. 246 et seq.

[71] Commission decision of 23.6.2003, Case COMP/C.2-37.398 – *Joint selling of the commercial rights of the UEFA Champions League*, OJ No. L 291 of 8 November 2003, p. 25, para. 201.

[72] Horizontal Guidelines, para. 257.

[73] Sattler, 'Standardisation under EU Competition Rules: The Commission's New Horizontal Guidelines', *European Competition Law Review*, 32 (2011), 343, 346; details about standard setting in the US can be found in: Koenig and Spiekermann, 'EU Competition Law Issues of Standard Setting by Officially-entrusted versus Private Organisations', *European Competition Law Review*, 30 (2009), 449, 451.

[74] Horizontal Guidelines, para. 263.

TFEU if the participation in the setting of standards is unrestricted and transparent or the standards are adopted by recognised standardisation bodies on a non-discriminatory basis. Anticompetitive effects will arise when the standard setting pursues the objective of excluding potential or actual competitors from the relevant market. Standardisation agreements may have the effect of restricting competition where they limit parties' freedom to develop their own standards or grant them joint control over production and/or innovation.

In cases where agreements on standards are used as part of a broader agreement that is meant to exclude actual or potential competitors, a restriction of competition by object can be assumed.[75] This is also true for agreements where the disclosure of restrictive licensing terms prior to the adoption of a standard functions as a cover to fix prices.[76]

Where companies have no market power, a standardisation agreement is unlikely to restrict competition.[77] As a negative definition, it can be said that a standardisation agreement has no restrictive effects on competition if participation in the standard-setting process is unrestricted, the procedure for adopting the standard is transparent, there is no obligation to comply, and access to the standard is granted on fair, reasonable and non-discriminatory terms.[78] Phrased differently, to comply with competition law, standard-setting processes would have to recognise 'five golden rules':[79] firstly, there would have to be an open, transparent and non-discriminating access to the standardisation organisation; secondly, there could be no predefinition of standards during standard-setting processes; thirdly, there would be a need for an open, transparent and non-discriminating access to the results of the standardisation in the form of licensing; fourthly, an open and non-discriminating access to potential membership categories; and fifthly, the possibility to develop competing standards or products.

Standards are often set by formal or informal standard-setting organisations.[80] In order to ensure access to a standard, the IPR policies of most formal standard-setting organisations require participants who want their IPR to be included in the standard to irrevocably commit to offer the licence to that IPR on fair, reasonable and non-discriminatory terms, a so-called 'FRAND' commitment.[81] Particularly, they function to prevent IPR holders from impeding the implementation of a standard by refusing to license their IPR or licensing it only by requesting excessive fees after an industry has been locked into a particular standard.[82] To assess whether fees charged for access to an IPR in this context are unfair or unreasonable, it is necessary to examine whether the fees bear a reasonable relationship to the economic value of the IPR.[83] This may be done by comparing licensing fees charged by the company in question

---

[75] Ibid., para. 273.   [76] Ibid., para. 274.   [77] Ibid., paras. 277 et seq.   [78] Ibid., para. 280.
[79] Koenig and Spiekermann, 'EU Competition Law Issues of Standard Setting', 454 et seq.
[80] Sattler, 'Standardisation under EU Competition Rules', 343, 345.   [81] Horizontal Guidelines, para. 285.
[82] Ibid., para. 287.
[83] ECJ (16 July 2009), Case C-385/07 P – *Der Grüne Punkt – Duales System Deutschland GmbH v Commission* [2009] ECR I-6155, para. 142.

for the relevant patents before the industry had been locked into the standard (i.e. a competitive environment) and, afterwards, assuming that the comparison can be made in a consistent and reliable manner.[84] Royalty rates charged for the same IPR in other comparable standards may also be used to assess whether the rates are 'FRAND', or independent expert assessment could be obtained.

Even if IPR holders agreed to a 'FRAND' commitment, problems can arise when the IPRs are transferred to a new holder and the commitment no longer applies. Irrevocability of the commitment is not enough to ensure the availability of an IPR; the IPR holders would also have to commit to ensure that any company to which the IPR is transferred is also bound by the commitment.[85] Especially with regard to licensing IPRs in standard setting, the Commission seems to follow a preventive approach.[86] Normally, competition authorities can only intervene after an infringement of competition occurred, but in the given context this will often be too late as IPR holders will only start to claim excessive licensing fees once users are locked into the standards in question.[87] But such a prevention-based approach would need effective enforcement mechanisms to ensure compliance.[88] Standard-setting organisations would have to monitor compliance and provide for effective enforcement, but are most likely not inclined to do so due to competition between them and liability issues.[89]

For Article 101(3) TFEU to apply it must be demonstrated that the information necessary to apply the standard is available to all interested undertakings and that all market players involved had the opportunity to participate in the process of standard setting. Standards should not limit innovation, and foreclosure of third parties must be avoided.

Summary of Section 9

Some industries are based on standards in order for the products of the individual suppliers to be compatible with each other. In such cases a restriction of competition is accepted at the level of the competing standards for the sake of more effective competition on the market for the respective product. For example, data storage devices usually are based on the same standard so that they can be read by computers or players of competing manufacturers. To be compatible with the EU competition rules, standard setting needs to meet a number of criteria. Participation in the standard-setting process has to be unrestricted and the procedure for adopting the standard has to be transparent. There must not be any obligation to comply with the standard. Finally, access to the standard has to be granted on fair, reasonable and non-discriminatory terms that have to be defined in each individual case.

---

[84] Horizontal Guidelines, para. 289.   [85] Ibid., para. 285.
[86] Sattler, 'Standardisation under EU Competition Rules', 343, 349.   [87] Ibid.   [88] Ibid.
[89] Ibid.; a further discussion of the 'FRAND' or 'RAND' issue can be found in Välimäki, 'A Flexible Approach to RAND Licensing', *European Competition Law Review*, 29 (2008), 686.

10. VERTICAL AGREEMENTS

The cartel prohibition of Article 101(1) TFEU applies also to agreements entered into by undertakings acting on different levels of the distribution chain,[90] e.g. by producers and distributors or wholesalers and retailers. The block exemption regulation for vertical agreements (hereinafter: the Vertical Block Exemption)[91] defines this term in Article 1(1)(a) as follows:

agreement or concerted practice entered into between two or more undertakings each of which operates, for the purposes of the agreement or the concerted practice, at a different level of the production or distribution chain, and relating to the conditions under which the parties may purchase, sell or resell certain goods or services.

The Commission takes the view that vertical restraints are in general less harmful to competition than horizontal agreements.[92] Their effects on competition depend primarily on the market context and the barriers to entry:

For most vertical restraints, competition concerns can only arise if there is insufficient competition at one or more levels of trade, that is, if there is some degree of market power at the level of the supplier or the buyer or at both levels. Vertical restraints are generally less harmful than horizontal restraints and may provide substantial scope for efficiencies.[93]

Vertical agreements usually affect intrabrand competition, i.e. competition between distributors selling the same products. EU competition law does not only protect interbrand competition, i.e. competition between the manufacturers of different brands, but also seeks to ensure efficient distribution of the products made by one manufacturer. Intrabrand competition gives distributors an incentive to reduce their margins, improve their services or to excel by other parameters of competition. Furthermore, intrabrand competition is closely related to the EU policy goal of market integration. The exclusive allocation of the territory of a Member State to a single distributor may contribute to maintaining national markets with different price levels, which undermines any efforts to create one pan-European market. In general, vertical agreements attract the scrutiny of the competition rules if they either contain hardcore restrictions of intrabrand competition or if they affect interbrand competition.

Risks for interbrand competition may arise for example if an undertaking with a strong market position tries to strengthen its market position by preventing distributors from selling products of its competitors. The *Repsol* case[94] illustrates this consideration.

---

[90] ECJ (13 July 1966), Joined Cases 56/64 and 58/64 – *Consten and Grundig v Commission* [1966] ECR 299.
[91] Commission Regulation (EU) No. 330/2010 of 20 April 2010 on the application of Article 101(3) TFEU to categories of vertical agreements and concerted practices, OJ No. L 102 of 23 April 2010, p. 1.
[92] Vertical Guidelines, paras. 98 et seq.   [93] Vertical Guidelines, para. 6.
[94] Commission decision of 12 April 2006, Case COMP/B-1/38.348 – *Repsol C.P.P.*, available at http://ec.europa.eu/competition/antitrust/cases/dec_docs/38348/38348_998_1.pdf.

In this case the Commission had to assess non-compete clauses included in supply agreements between Repsol, a company active mainly in the distribution of fuel and lubricants in Spain, and service station operators. The non-compete clauses prohibited the distribution of competing products by service station operators. In its preliminary assessment, the Commission found that the non-compete clauses might cause the foreclosure of third party competitors on the Spanish fuel retail market as other suppliers in the market could not sell to the service station operators. By raising the barriers to entry, other suppliers would be excluded from the market:

the Commission considered thus that the non-compete clauses in the agreement in question, [. . .] might help significantly to create a foreclosure effect on the fuel retail market in Spain. Having regard to the economic and legal context of these agreements, the Commission noted that the market was accessible only with difficulty by competitors wishing to enter it or increase their market share there. This was due notably to the significant vertical integration of operators, the cumulative effect of the parallel networks of vertical restraints, difficulties in setting up an alternative network and other competitive conditions (principally the saturation of the market and the nature of the product).[95]

In the Commission's view, the agreements containing the non-compete clauses contributed significantly to the foreclosure effect as the tied market share of Repsol's sales was considerable at 25–35%, the non-compete commitments were of a substantial duration (between 25 and 40 years) and service station operators and consumers were in a weak position in comparison to Repsol which enjoyed a substantial market share. The case illustrates the importance of market power for the effect of restrictive clauses in vertical agreements. It also shows how foreclosure effects can arise from vertical agreements.

The potential restrictive effects of vertical agreements may be outweighed by possible benefits to competition. The Commission identified the following beneficial effects of vertical agreements:[96]

(i) Solution of the 'free-rider' problem – exclusive distribution may help to avoid the free-riding understood as situations in which distributors use (free-ride) promotion and investment efforts of other distributors and offer the same products for lower prices since they have lower costs;[97]

(ii) vertical agreements may provide local distributors with territorial protection which enables them to make 'first-time investments' and open up new markets for the product at issue;[98]

---

[95] Ibid., para. 23.   [96] Vertical Guidelines, para. 107.

[97] Example: Distributors A, B, and C sell branded cosmetics in the same region. A and B launch an advertising campaign in local media. C does not participate but sells the advertised cosmetics at lower prices than A and B as he has no costs for advertising.

[98] Example: Distributor A is the only sales outlet in a region that offers a certain machine. The machine needs regular maintenance that can be carried out only with the help of special tools that A bought. A is the

(iii) protection granted to distributors by producers enables the wholesalers and/or retailers to make client-specific investments (purchase of special equipment, employee training etc.) which would not otherwise be possible – avoidance of the 'hold-up' problem[99];

(iv) economies of scale on the side of distributors may result in lower prices;[100]

(v) promotion of uniformity and common standards – vertical agreements may help to create a brand image and thereby increase the attractiveness of a product to end-users.[101]

EU competition law aims at balancing those pro- and anticompetitive effects of vertical agreements. The legislative framework pertaining to vertical agreements consists of the following provisions:

- the Vertical Block Exemption;
- the Vertical Guidelines; and
- Regulation 461/2010 on motor vehicle distribution.[102]

10.1 General pattern of the Vertical Block Exemption

The Vertical Block Exemption applies to various types of vertical agreements and adopts an approach based not only on the terms of the agreement but also on the market power of the participating undertakings. The Vertical Block Exemption is designed in a way that it declares all restrictions of competition in vertical agreements as qualifying for an exemption under Article 101(3) TFEU provided that neither party to the agreement has a market share exceeding 30%. This reflects the

---

exclusive distributor for the machine and the exclusive provider of maintenance services in the region for a certain period to allow him to recoup his investments in the tools.

[99] Example: A manufacturer of electronic components has to invest into a new production line to execute the order of a customer. An exclusive supply agreement will give the manufacturer the certainty that he will recoup his investments.

[100] Example: A manufacturer of an electronic component sells the component only to distributors who order a certain minimum quantity of it. The minimum quantity reduces the costs for packaging, shipping etc. As a result the manufacturer can offer the component at lower prices.

[101] Example: A runs a franchise shoe business. His licensees agree to follow certain common standards with regard to the design of the shops, the training of the personnel and the variety of shoes offered. This contributes to the attractiveness for consumers since they can expect a uniform offering from every licensee.

[102] Commission Regulation (EU) No. 461/2010 of 27 May 2010 on the application of Article 101(3) TFEU to categories of vertical agreements and concerted practices in the motor vehicle sector, OJ [2010] L 129 of 28 May 2010, p. 52. Further information on the application of this regulation can be found in Clark and Simon, 'The New Legal Framework for Motor Vehicle Distribution: A Toolkit to Deal with Real Competition Breakdowns', *Journal of European Competition Law and Practice*, 1 (2010), 478; and Zuehlke and De Stefano, 'EC Motor Vehicle Block Exemption Reform: Are You Ready for the New Regime?', *European Competition Law Review*, 31 (2010), 93.

consideration that vertical agreements may have an impact on interbrand competition only from a certain degree of market power of one of the parties. Another condition for the exemption is that the respective agreement must not contain any hardcore restrictions of intrabrand competition identified in Article 4 of the Vertical Block Exemption. Otherwise the entire agreement will be void. Excluded restrictions as defined in Article 5 of the Vertical Block Exemption do not benefit from the exemption but do not render the entire agreement void. They are invalid and the validity of the remainder of the agreement depends on the national severability rules. Those excluded restrictions aim at protecting interbrand competition.

The most important issues relating to interpretation of the Vertical Block Exemption are discussed in the Vertical Guidelines.[103] Moreover, they provide guidance for self-assessment with regard to vertical agreements that do not benefit from the block exemption.

10.2 Scope

The definition of 'vertical agreement' can be found in Article 1(1)(a) Vertical Block Exemption. Its scope encompasses agreements between two or more non-competitors[104] relating to both purchase and sale or resale of services and goods. Agreements between associations of undertakings and their members or suppliers may also benefit from the block exemption under the conditions set out in Article 2(2) Vertical Block Exemption. Finally, the exemption shall apply to agreements that assign the buyer or grant him the right to use certain IPRs as long as this is not the primary object of the agreement and the granted/assigned rights are directly related to the purchase, sale or resale of goods or services – Article 2(3) Vertical Block Exemption.

10.3 The market share cap

An exemption granted pursuant to Article 2(1) Vertical Block Exemption applies only under the condition that the market share held by both the supplier (in the market he sells into) and the buyer (on the market in which he purchases) does not exceed 30% in each case. In vertical agreements involving exclusive supply arrangements[105] the purchaser's market share should be taken into account as there is a concern that the

---

[103] A discussion with regard to the differentiation of unilateral and multilateral conduct in vertical restraints can be found in Jedličková and McCabe, 'Boundaries between Unilateral and Multilateral Conducts in Vertical Restraints', *European Competition Law Review*, 29 (2008), 600.

[104] However, according to Art. 2(4), the exemption may also be applicable to agreements between competitors if the conditions laid down therein are fulfilled.

[105] Vertical Guidelines, para. 176.

supply market may be foreclosed by an agreement. Some commentators argue that the threshold is too low or improperly cast.[106] The opinion that the market share cap is too low can be based on the fact that there is a need for a dominant firm for anticompetitive effects to arise. Non-dominant firms cannot raise competitor's costs or harm consumers as there still is interbrand competition. Those arguing that the threshold is improperly cast would agree with such assumptions and additionally point out that there can be anticompetitive effects in cases of oligopolistic interdependence. Therefore, it is argued that it would be better to assess the market concentration and not the market share of one market participant. There are even voices who consider a detailed analysis necessary to assess whether a certain practice is to the consumer's detriment as there are always uncertainties about market definitions due to inconclusive evidence and therefore uncertainties about market share thresholds.[107] On the other hand, the procedural efficiency of the current safe harbour rule would be lost, if a detailed analysis were to be practised.

The market share cap for the buyer has been criticised since it creates a requirement to assess the buyer's market share which may lead to uncertainty and higher compliance costs.[108] Originally, the Commission had planned to consider market share on the buyer's selling markets, which normally number more than markets on which he buys. The implemented threshold thus can be seen as a compromise between avoiding undue complexity and not ignoring the market power of buyers.[109]

Detailed guidance on the calculation of the market share can be found in Article 7 Vertical Block Exemption. According to this provision, the supplier's market share is generally calculated on the basis of sales data and the buyer's market share is calculated on the basis of purchase value, each relating to the preceding year. If no market data is available, estimates have to be made based on reliable market information. Some additional issues relating to market share are discussed in the Vertical Guidelines where further instructions on definition of the relevant market and calculation of the market share are given.[110]

10.4 Resale price maintenance

Article 4(a) Vertical Block Exemption prohibits the imposition of a fixed or minimum resale price. The parties to a vertical agreement may however set a recommended or maximum resale price as long as they do not indirectly enforce the recommendation

[106] Monti, *EC Competition Law* (Cambridge University Press, 2007), p. 360.
[107] Bishop and Ridyard, 'EC Vertical Restraints Guidelines: Effects-Based or Per Se Policy?', *European Competition Law Review*, 23 (2002), 35, 37.
[108] Whish and Bailey, 'Regulation 330/2010: The Commission's New Block Exemption for Vertical Agreements', *Common Market Law Review*, 47 (2010), 1757, 1773.
[109] Ibid.   [110] Vertical Guidelines, paras. 86–95.

as a de facto minimum resale price. A non-exhaustive list of indirect means that may lead to prohibited resale price maintenance is given in para. 48 of the Vertical Guidelines:

agreement fixing the distribution margin, fixing the maximum level of discount the distributor can grant from a prescribed price level, making the grant of rebates or reimbursement of promotional costs by the supplier subject to the observance of a given price level, linking the prescribed resale price to the resale prices of competitors, threats, intimidation, warnings, penalties, delay or suspension of deliveries or contract terminations in relation to observance of a given price level.

Even measures taken to monitor and identify price-cutting distributors may be regarded as 'indirect pressure' to fix prices.

With regard to the anticompetitive or pro-competitive effects of resale price maintenance (RPM), there have been controversial discussions. Some commentators hold that RPM can have pro-competitive effects because it can help to prevent retailers from free-riding on other retailers' pre-sale promotional services.[111] Promotional services can be product demonstrations, test drives or consultations. If one retailer offers such services while the other one does not, this other retailer could free-ride on the services provided by his competitor by saving the costs of those services and therefore being able to offer the product for a lower price. Once the retailers providing the services realise this, they will stop providing those services, which leads to a decline of the manufacturer's sales. By establishing a minimum resale price, manufacturers can prevent retailers from going below a certain price limit and thereby attracting consumers by lowering prices.

Furthermore, there is the argument that RPM forces retailers to compete on non-price parameters like the pre-sale services instead of the price, therefore stimulating interbrand competition by eliminating intrabrand price competition.[112] This may maximise the provision of pre-sale services and it may benefit producers as it increases demand for their products.[113] On the other hand, it can be criticised that there is no way to make sure that RPM leads to better services provided by the retailers as they may decide not to offer any and just keep the higher resale margin.[114]

RPM may also facilitate the entry of new brands into the market by guaranteeing a sufficient return which induces retailers to market the new product aggressively.[115]

---

[111] Kneepkens, 'Resale Price Maintenance: Economics Call for a More Balanced Approach', *European Competition Law Review*, 28 (2007), 656, 657; Buttigieg, 'Lingering Uncertainty over the Antitrust Approach to Resale Price Maintenance', *Journal of European Competition Law and Practice*, 1 (2010), 397, 398.

[112] Gey and Kamann, 'The Assessment of Minimum Resale Price Maintenance in Europe in the Aftermath of Leegin', *Zeitschrift für Wettbewerbsrecht* (2008), 208, 213.

[113] Kneepkens, 'Resale Price Maintenance', 656, 658.   [114] Ibid.

[115] Gey and Kamann, The Assessment of Minimum Resale Price Maintenance', 208, 214.

A potential anticompetitive effect of RPM may be the facilitation of retailer cartels and therefore higher prices for consumers.[116] A resale price above the competitive level enforced by the manufacturer may have the same effect as a cartel of retailers. The benefit for the retailers in that case is that they do not even have to monitor and enforce the cartel themselves as the manufacturer does it for them.

Furthermore, RPM may facilitate manufacturer cartels.[117] If manufacturers co-ordinately establish RPM, it prevents retail prices from going lower. Thus it takes away an incentive for manufacturers to offer their products at a lower wholesale price and therefore prevents manufacturers from cheating on a cartel. However, RPM does not function as a cartel of manufacturers itself.

RPM may also be used by manufacturers with market power to incentivise retailers not to sell a rival's or new entrant's product and therefore the manufacturer may forestall innovation to the consumer's detriment.[118]

As RPM can also have pro-competitive effects under certain circumstances, it is argued that it should not be considered as anticompetitive in any case but that the specifics of each case should be thoroughly assessed.[119] Nonetheless, the Commission considers RPM to be a hardcore restriction which is 'unlikely to fulfil the conditions of Article [101(3) TFEU]'.[120] However, in the Vertical Guidelines,[121] the Commission recognises RPM efficiencies, *inter alia*, in cases of new product launches to induce promotional efforts of retailers and expand overall demand or in cases of coordinated short-term low-price campaigns to the benefit of consumers.

The Commission dealt with RPM in the *Yamaha* case[122] concerning a Japanese company mainly active in the production and trade of musical instruments and audio products. Yamaha distributed its products according to agreements between Yamaha's European subsidiaries and 'official' dealers. To some agreements guidelines were added requesting dealers to apply the recommended retail prices of Yamaha. Furthermore, Yamaha tried to prevent retailers from granting rebates exceeding 15% of the recommended retail price. Even though the prices were formally 'recommended', the Commission considered this clause to amount to resale price maintenance and imposed a fine against Yamaha.[123]

---

[116] Kneepkens, 'Resale Price Maintenance', 656, 660.   [117] Ibid., 661.

[118] Gey and Kamann, 'The Assessment of Minimum Resale Price Maintenance', 208, 214.

[119] Kneepkens, 'Resale Price Maintenance', 656, 664.

[120] Commission Regulation (EU) No 330/2010 of 20 April 2010 on the application of Article 101(3) TFEU to categories of vertical agreements and concerted practices, OJ No L 102 of 23 April 2010, p. 1, Art. 4(a).

[121] Para. 225.

[122] Commission decision of 16 July 2003, Case COMP/37.975 – *PO/Yamaha*, available at http://ec.europa.eu/competition/antitrust/cases/dec_docs/37975/37975_91_3.pdf.

[123] Ibid., para. 126.

10.5 Exclusive distribution

The Vertical Block Exemption allows only a limited degree of territorial or customer exclusivity. Such agreements may restrict intrabrand competition and cause market partitioning. The Commission is particularly sensitive to exclusive distribution since it may shelter national markets from imports from other Member States. Pursuant to Article 4(b) Vertical Block Exemption, the Vertical Block Exemption shall 'not apply to agreements having as their object the restriction of the territory into which, or of the customers to whom, the buyer may sell the contract goods or services'. It has to be noted that the Vertical Block Exemption allows the restriction of active sales though. Active sales are sales that can be traced back to active promotion activities of the buyer. A supplier may allocate a territory exclusively to a distributor and request other distributors not to effect any active sales into that territory. However, a distributor may not be protected from passive sales of other distributors (so-called 'absolute territorial protection'). Passive sales are sales that are effected based on unsolicited orders. For example, if the exclusive distributor of a product in France receives an enquiry from Spain he may not reject the enquiry or forward it to the distributor in Spain. However, the French distributor may not engage in any promotion activities in Spain. The prohibition of the restriction of passive sales ensures a minimum degree of parallel trade between Member States and tries to strike a balance between the beneficial effects of exclusive distribution and the goal of market integration. The same considerations apply to the allocation of customers or customer groups.

Indirect measures restricting the buyer's freedom such as a refusal or reduction of bonuses or discounts, a reduction of supplied volumes or a threat of contract termination fall also within the scope of Article 4(b) Vertical Block Exemption.[124]

In the Yamaha case discussed above, Yamaha had also imposed indirect territorial restrictions on its retailers.

For example, Yamaha imposed an obligation on retailers only to sell to final customers. The Commission found that this prevented supplies to other authorised retailers in other Member States and thereby frustrated the goal of market integration in particular since price levels in different Member States for Yamaha products varied appreciably.[125]

Another obligation was to only buy from the Yamaha national subsidiary. The Commission found this clause also to have the object to prevent cross-supplies between authorised dealers within a country and between all Member States. The Commission held that it resulted in a sheltering of the distribution networks from cross-supplies and thereby restricted competition.[126]

---

[124] A more extensive list of indirect restrictions is provided in para. 50 of the Vertical Guidelines.
[125] Ibid., para. 89.   [126] Ibid., para. 99.

Furthermore, Yamaha caused its distributors to supply only distributors that were authorised by the Yamaha national subsidiary. The Commission considered this clause to have the object of partitioning national markets and sheltering the concerned markets from cross-supplies and therefore restricting competition as well.[127]

Yamaha, moreover, imposed territorial restrictions with regard to guarantees it was granting, resulting in guarantees only being valid in the country of the purchase. The Commission held in this regard:

> not extending the guarantee to parallel imports and exports might constitute a major obstacle to the development of trade within the Community and must consequently be prohibited.[128]

In *JCB Service*,[129] the ECJ had to assess the distribution network of the JCB Group. This group manufactured and marketed construction site and agricultural machinery, earthmoving and construction equipment as well as spare parts for their products. JCB's distribution network was structured on a national basis. It had one subsidiary or one exclusive importer per Member State.

The Commission took the view that the agreements establishing JCB's distribution network had as their effect a partitioning of national markets and absolute territorial protection. According to the Commission, the following practices were caught by Article 101(1) TFEU: the prohibition/restriction on official distributors to sell outside their allotted territories (to other Member States; active or passive sales to end-users and authorised and unauthorised resellers were covered); the imposition of a service fee on sales made by official distributors outside their territory; the implementation of a remuneration system which makes allowances granted to distributors dependent on the destination of sales and limits them to end-user sales; the determination of resale/retail prices or discounts for goods purchased from JCB for resale by official distributors; and the obligation for official distributors to purchase exclusively from JCB for resale to prevent purchasers from buying from distributors in other Member States.

The General Court and the ECJ upheld the Commission's decision with regard to those points.

Territorial restrictions may also take the form of direct or indirect export bans. The Commission has classified the following types of vertical agreements to amount to indirect export bans incompatible with Article 4(b) Vertical Block Exemption:

- the limitation of the producer's guarantee only to consumers in Member States that have bought the product in the same Member State (*Yamaha, Zanussi*[130]);

---

[127] Ibid., para. 102.
[128] Ibid., para. 111; see also Commission decision of 23 October 1978, Case IV/1.576 – *Zanussi*, OJ No. L 322 of 16 November 1978, p. 36.
[129] ECJ (21 September 2006), Case C-167/04 – *JCB Service v Commission* [2006] ECR I-8935.
[130] Commission decision of 23 October 1978, Case IV/1.576 – *Zanussi*, OJ No. L 322 of 16 November 1978, p. 36. Zanussi produced domestic electrical appliances. Under the Zanussi guarantee, users of their appliances were only entitled to service under the guarantee from the Zanussi subsidiary which imported the appliance. The service was refused when the appliance had been used in a country other than that into which

- monitoring clauses enabling the producer to trace the movement of products from one Member State to another (*Hasselblad*[131]);
- purchasing of supplies of product imported to one Member State in order to prevent its sale to other Member States (*Konica*[132]);
- requirement that foreign customers must pay a 15% deposit when buying a new car (*Mercedes-Benz*[133]).

The prohibition of Article 4(b) Vertical Block Exemption does not apply when one of the exceptions set out therein is available:

- it is permissible to restrict active sales to an exclusive territory or an exclusive group of customers as long as passive sales are possible;
- it is not prohibited to restrict passive and active sales to end-users by a buyer operating at the wholesale level of trade;
- it is permissible to restrict both passive and active sales by members of selective distribution systems to unauthorised distributors within the territory reserved by the supplier to operate that system;
- restrictions on buyers of components are permitted if the components were to be sold to manufacturers producing goods competing with the ones of the supplier.

In cases where the Vertical Block Exemption does not apply, an individual assessment of the exclusive distribution agreement is necessary. According to the jurisprudence of the ECJ, exclusive distribution agreements do not necessarily fall within the scope of Article 101(1) TFEU.[134] However, an infringement of the cartel prohibition should be assumed if the agreement confers absolute territorial protection on the distributor.

---

it was originally imported by the local subsidiary. Guarantee service was also refused when the appliance had been modified or alterations had been carried out by non-approved persons. This has been affirmed by the Commission decision of 16 July 2003, Case COMP/37.975 – *PO/Yamaha*, available at http://ec.europa.eu/competition/antitrust/cases/dec_docs/37975/37975_91_3.pdf.

[131] Commission decision of 2 December 1981, Case IV/25.757 – *Hasselblad*, OJ No. L 161 of 12 June 1982, p. 18. Hasselblad was the leading manufacturer of a certain kind of single-lens roll-film reflex cameras. It affixed serial numbers on every item of equipment. In its standard agreement, it prohibited distributors from directly or indirectly selling or offering Hasselblad cameras outside their allotted territories. The Commission found that Hasselblad and its distributors applied this policy and the serial numbers to monitor market compartmentalisation. Systematic checks of the products were part of an overall system of market partitioning.

[132] Commission decision of 18 December 1987, Case IV/31.503 – *Konica*, OJ No. L 78 of 23 March 1988, p. 34. This decision concerned a Konica practice aimed at preventing the export of colour films from the UK to other Member States and the resale of parallel imported colour film on the German market. Because of changes in currency exchange rates, there were incentives for parallel exports from the UK to Germany. In letters, Konica asked UK wholesalers not to engage in such export business and threatened to stop supplying them or to raise their prices. Furthermore, Konica bought up its own discounted film in Germany to protect German dealers against competition from parallel imports, thus eliminating interbrand competition.

[133] Commission decision of 10 October 2001, Case COMP/36.264 – *Mercedes-Benz*, OJ No. L 257 of 25 September 2002, p. 1. DaimlerChrysler, manufacturer of motor vehicles, foreclosed parallel trading between Member States by instructing its agents to require a 15% deposit in cases of parallel exports of cars, i.e. when EU costumers ordered cars outside their own country with their domestic specifications.

[134] ECJ (30 June 1966), Case 56/65 – *Société Technique Minière v Maschinenbau Ulm* [1966] ECR 235; ECJ (13 July 1966), Joined Cases 56/64 and 58/64 – *Consten and Grundig v Commission* [1966] ECR 299.

For the proper assessment under Article 101(1) TFEU the market positions of the supplier and its competitors are of great importance. As the Commission states in its Vertical Guidelines, the loss of intrabrand competition may give rise to competitive concerns if interbrand competition is limited.[135] Foreclosure problems are a potential threat only if the distributors have significant market power in the downstream buyer market. This may be the case when the distributors are given very large exclusive territories. The cumulative effect of several comparable agreements must also be considered. A combination of exclusive distribution agreements with single branding or exclusive purchasing may cause anticompetitive effects such as foreclosure to other suppliers or a significant limitation of intrabrand competition.

Exclusive distribution agreements may lead to efficiencies relevant from the perspective of Article 101(3) TFEU. In its Vertical Guidelines the Commission states that this particular type of agreement may lead to savings in logistic costs due to economies of scale in production and transportation.[136] Additionally, they may enable distributors to make investments required to protect or build up the brand image.

10.6 Selective distribution

Selective distribution agreements are often adopted by producers of branded or sophisticated consumer goods such as jewellery, hi-tech products or luxury goods. The producer sells his products only to officially appointed distributors and retailers that fulfil certain criteria. This practice gives the supplier control over the distribution channels and enables him to decide on the level of technical expertise possessed by the outlets or their location and interior design. A distinction has to be made between qualitative selective distribution and quantitative selective distribution.

In a qualitative selective distribution system the dealers are selected on the basis of objective criteria corresponding to the nature of the product to be sold. In a quantitative selective distribution system the distributors have to fulfil some additional requirements such as an obligation to order a certain amount of products on a regular basis or a minimum sales target.[137] There may also be a combination of qualitative and quantitative selection criteria.

Selective distribution agreements may restrict the number of authorised distributors and thus lead to reduction of intrabrand competition. Other potential negative effects are the risks of foreclosure and collusion between suppliers and/or buyers.

---

[135] Vertical Guidelines, paras. 153 and 154.   [136] Ibid., para. 164.
[137] For further discussion, see Velez, 'Recent Developments in Selective Distribution', *European Competition Law Review*, 32 (2011), 242.

Selective distribution systems based on objective qualitative criteria fall out-side the scope of Article 101(1) TFEU. Accordingly, there is no need for any exemption under Article 101(3) TFEU. In the *Metro I*[138] decision the ECJ defined three criteria which must be fulfilled for a selective system to be compatible with Article 101 TFEU:

selective distribution systems constituted, together with others, an aspect of competition which accords with [Article 101(1) TFEU], provided that resellers are chosen on the basis of objective criteria of a qualitative nature relating to the technical qualifications of the reseller and his staff and the suitability of his trading premises and that such conditions are laid down uniformly for all potential resellers and are not applied in a discriminatory fashion.[139]

Those criteria are:

(a) The product in question requires selective distribution

According to the jurisprudence of the ECJ and decisions by the Commission[140] three categories of goods meeting this requirement may be named: (i) technically complex products requiring special technical assistance – cars, hi-tech, computers, (ii) luxury goods, brand image of which is very important – perfumes, jewellery, cosmetic products etc., (iii) products with extremely short shelf-life necessitating particularly careful distribution – newspapers.

(b) Qualitative selection criteria

Criteria applied by the supplier have to be solely qualitative in nature and must be applied in a uniform way without discrimination towards any potential distributors. Such criteria may be the requirements to hire highly trained staff, to have suitable premises in an appropriate location, and the provision of high-standard after sales services.

(c) Necessity

Qualitative restrictions imposed on the distributors may, according to *Metro I*, not go beyond what is necessary to protect the quality of product sold within the distribution system. In other words the suppliers may not be granted power to control the market conduct of their distributors in a way that would facilitate price fixing or indirect imposing of resale prices.

Selective systems not fulfilling one of those requirements fall into the ambit of Article 101(1) TFEU but benefit from the Vertical Block Exemption if the market share threshold is not exceeded.

---

[138] ECJ (25 October 1977), Case 26/76 – *Metro v Commission (Metro I)* [1977] ECR 1875; for facts of the case, see the description of the appeal, *Metro II*, above.

[139] Ibid., para. 20.

[140] See, for example, GC (12 December 1996), Case T-88/92 – *Leclerc v Commission* [1996] ECR II-1961.

However, some specific clauses that may be included in selective distribution agreements are classified as hardcore restrictions of competition in Article 4 Vertical Block Exemption.

Article 4 (c) Vertical Block Exemption prohibits any restriction of passive or active sales to end-users by members of a selective distribution system. Consequently, no exclusivity can be given to the members of a selective distribution system with regard to customer groups. Distributors are free to sell to any customer. As can be derived from para. 56 of the Vertical Guidelines this provision is to be understood as also ensuring that members of a selective distribution system are free to sell via the internet.

Article 4 (d) Vertical Block Exemption provides for another restriction with regard to selective distribution systems. Cross-supplies between distributors must not be prohibited. Therefore, agreements may not have as their effect or object the restriction of active or passive sales of contract products between selected distributors. These distributors must have the option to purchase contract products from other distributors within the network. Distributors cannot be forced to buy contract products exclusively from one source and there can be no restrictions imposed on appointed wholesalers with respect to sales of the product to appointed retailers within a selective distribution network. The prohibition aims at preventing market partitioning and the establishment of different price levels through restrictions on members of a selective distribution system that have effects similar to an export ban.

Any direct or indirect obligation not to sell the brands of a particular competing supplier is excluded from the block exemption under Article 5(1)(c) Vertical Block Exemption. Accordingly, members of a selective distribution system remain free to sell products of competing manufacturers in their premises.

Agreements not covered by the Vertical Block Exemption have to be considered in the light of Article 101(1) TFEU. The main factor to be included in such an assessment is the market position of the supplier and its competitors. According to the Commission the loss of intrabrand competition is problematic only if interbrand competition is weak.[141] The number of selective distribution networks present in the same market may also have some relevance for the analysis of anticompetitive effects. Quantitative selective distribution does not cause any competition concerns if it is adopted only by one supplier not having a dominant position or by only a small number of producers. Market power of competitors may also play a significant role since the presence of strong competitors and a high level of interbrand competition may outweigh the reduction in intrabrand competition. Other factors to be considered are entry barriers and the existence of buyer power.

In its Vertical Guidelines, the Commission states that selective distribution systems may lead to savings in logistic costs due to economies of scale, solution of the

---

[141] Ibid., para. 177.

free-rider problem or the creation of a brand image.[142] The criteria set out in Article 101(3) TFEU must, however, be applied individually in each case considering the specifics of the economic background.[143]

10.7 Non-compete obligations

The term 'non-compete obligation' refers to any obligation on the buyer not to manufacture, purchase, sell or resell goods which compete with the contract goods, or any obligation on the buyer to purchase from the supplier more than 80% of the buyer's total purchases of the contract goods (this type of clause being referred to as 'quantity forcing').[144] Non-compete obligations and quantity forcing agreements may have similar effects.[145] These practices are also referred to as 'single branding'.

Significant restrictions of competition may also result from so called 'English clauses'. They permit the buyer to purchase the required products from other sellers offering lower prices only if the regular supplier decides not to match them after being properly informed.

Non-compete clauses are exempted under Article 5(1)(a) Vertical Block Exemption if the supplier's market share is less than 30% and the non-compete obligation is limited to five years. Tacitly renewable agreements do not benefit from the block exemption if they can extend to a period exceeding five years. Non-compete clauses that extend to a longer period can be block-exempted under Article 5(2) Vertical Block Exemption if the goods or services are sold by the buyer from premises owned by the supplier or leased from third parties.[146] This may be the case for example with regard to beer supply or petrol distribution agreements.

Obligations not to manufacture, purchase, sell or resell goods or services after the termination of the agreement do not benefit from the block exemption – Article 5(1)(b) Vertical Block Exemption.

Non-compete clauses that do not comply with Article 5 Vertical Block Exemption are excluded from the block exemption and thus void but do not render the entire supply agreement void. The validity of the remainder of the agreement depends on the severability rules under national law.

---

[142] Ibid., para. 185.

[143] For a recent example of selective distribution in the motor vehicle sector, see ECJ (14 June 2012), Case C-158/11 – *Auto 24*, nyr.

[144] Commission Regulation (EU) No. 330/2010 of 20 April 2010 on the application of Article 101(3) TFEU to categories of vertical agreements and concerted practices, OJ No. L 102 of 23 April 2010, p. 1, Article 1(1)(d).

[145] For a further discussion of single branding agreements, see also Dethmers and Posthuma de Boer, 'Ten Years On: Vertical Agreements under Article 81', *European Competition Law Review*, 30 (2009), 424.

[146] In ECJ (28 February 1991), Case C-234/89 – *Delimitis v Henninger Bräu* [1991] ECR I-935, a publican leased a pub from the brewery that also exclusively supplied him with beer.

Agreements not falling within the scope of the block exemption must be individually assessed in the light of Article 101(1) TFEU. Some guidance on the application of the cartel prohibition to such agreements can be found in the Vertical Guidelines at paras. 138–160 where factors relevant in the assessment are set out and discussed. Generally the Commission follows the approach developed by the ECJ that non-compete clauses do not necessarily have the object or effect of restricting competition. Each case should be analysed individually in the light of its economic and legal context. In the already mentioned *Henninger* case, the court introduced a two-step test to establish whether the agreement at issue infringed Article 101 TFEU:

agreement is prohibited by Article 85(1) of the EEC Treaty [Article 101(1) TFEU], if two cumulative conditions are met. The first is that, having regard to the economic and legal context of the agreement at issue, it is difficult for competitors who could enter the market or increase their market share to gain access to the national market [...]. The second condition is that the agreement in question must make a significant contribution to the sealing-off effect brought about by the totality of those agreements in their economic and legal context. The extent of the contribution made by the individual agreement depends on the position of the contracting parties in the relevant market and on the duration of the agreement.[147]

If non-compete agreements are concluded in a great number by large suppliers and small purchasers it may be essential to assess the cumulative effect of the network of such agreements.

The most important factors to be taken into account when considering possible anticompetitive effects stemming from non-compete obligations are the market position of the supplier and the duration of the agreement. According to the Vertical Guidelines, the higher the market share and the longer the duration, the more likely are the foreclosure effects.[148] In principle, agreements concluded by non-dominant companies for less than a year are unlikely to cause anticompetitive effects. Agreements concluded for less than five years must be investigated carefully and a proper balancing of pro- and anticompetitive effects is required. Agreements concluded for a period of more than five years are generally not considered to bring significant efficiencies. Foreclosure effects are likely when a significant number of suppliers enters into vertical agreements with buyers on the relevant market. It is assumed that cumulative foreclosure effects are not likely to appear when the market share of the largest supplier is below 30% and the market share of the five largest suppliers does not exceed the threshold of 50%.

---

[147] Ibid., para. 27.   [148] Vertical Guidelines, para. 133.

10.8 E-commerce

The internet can reach a far bigger number of customers than traditional forms of sale. Therefore, restrictions of the use of the internet are usually restrictions with regard to resale. Generally, every distributor must be allowed to sell products over the internet. If a customer visits a distributor's website and purchases a product from this website and the distributor delivers it, this is considered a passive sale. Even the availability of different language options on a website alone does not change the passive character of a sale.[149]

The Commission considers certain restrictions of passive sales as hardcore restrictions.[150] One example is an agreement where an exclusive distributor is obliged to re-route customers from areas that are exclusive to other distributors to their websites or the manufacturer's website. Furthermore, distributors must not be asked to limit their amount of overall sales over the internet or to pay a higher price for products to be resold online.

A restriction of active sales over the internet is possible, i.e. a supplier may prevent a distributor from actively soliciting customers of areas allocated to other distributors over the internet, e.g. by putting advertisements on the websites of local newspapers in those other areas. Furthermore, a supplier may require the distributor to observe certain quality standards for an online shop where his products are sold.[151]

In *Pierre Fabre*[152] the ECJ gave a preliminary ruling on the question whether suppliers may prohibit or limit internet sales by their selective distributors. The luxury cosmetics and personal care products company Pierre Fabre imposed a de facto ban on internet sales on its independent selective distributors by requiring them to have outlets with qualified pharmacists physically present. The ECJ held that

Article 101(1) TFEU must be interpreted as meaning that, in the context of a selective distribution system, a contractual clause requiring sales of cosmetics and personal care products to be made in a physical space where a qualified pharmacist must be present, resulting in a ban on the use of the internet for those sales, amounts to a restriction by object within the meaning of that provision where, following an individual and specific examination of the content and objective of that contractual clause and the legal and economic context of which it forms a part, it is apparent that, having regard to the properties of the products at issue, that clause is not objectively justified.[153]

Furthermore, the court pointed out that selective distribution systems are restrictions by object unless they are objectively justified. Certain types of selective distribution that are capable of improving competition with regard to factors other than price are

---

[149] Ibid., para. 52.   [150] Ibid., paras. 52 (a)–(d).   [151] Ibid., para. 54.
[152] ECJ (13 October 2011), Case C-439/09 – *Pierre Fabre Dermo-Cosmétique* [2011] ECR nyr.
[153] Ibid., para. 47.

objectively justified and therefore do not infringe Article 101(1) TFEU. The ban on internet sales also does not benefit from the Vertical Block Exemption as it at least restricts passive sales. An individual exemption under Article 101(3) TFEU is generally available, but in this case was a matter for the national court to assess.

10.9 Agency agreements

Article 101(1) TFEU is only applicable to agreements between independent undertakings, not between persons or entities forming a 'single economic entity'.[154] Therefore, agency agreements can escape Article 101(1) TFEU under certain conditions. In this case, clauses that are prohibited in other vertical agreements can be legally included in the agency agreement.

An agent is a person vested with the power to negotiate and/or conclude contracts for the purchase of goods or services by the principal or the sale of goods or services supplied by the principal on behalf of the principal, either in the agent's own name or in the name of the principal.[155] Whether or not an agreement is an agency agreement depends on the financial or commercial risk the agent has to bear. An agreement will be qualified as an agency agreement for competition law purposes in cases where the agent does not bear any or only insignificant risks with regard to the contracts concluded on behalf of the principal. Risks that naturally come with offering agency services, such as the risk of the agent's income depending on his success as an agent, are not material to this assessment.[156]

Obligations imposed on the agent in relation to negotiated or concluded contracts fall outside the scope of Article 101(1) TFEU since the principal bears the commercial and financial risks with regard to the sale or purchase of the contract goods and services. Limitations on the territory in which the agent may sell or the prices and conditions at which the agent must sell or purchase are considered to form an inherent part of the agency agreement as they are necessary for the principal to determine the scope of the agent's activity.[157]

In *DaimlerChrysler*[158] the General Court had to decide whether there was a principal–agent relationship between Mercedes-Benz and the agents/workshops that were part of its passenger car distribution network in Germany. The Commission held that this was not the case as the Mercedes-Benz agents had to bear significant commercial risks that were inextricably linked to their function as an

---

[154] Henty, 'Agency Agreements – What are the Risks? THE CFI's Judgment in DaimlerChrysler AG v Commission', *European Competition Law Review*, 27 (2006), 102.

[155] Vertical Guidelines, paras. 12 et seq.   [156] Ibid, para. 15.

[157] For a more detailed illustration of the criteria necessary to define an agency agreement, see Dieny, 'The Relationship between a Principal and its Agent in the Light of Article 81(1) EC: How Many Criteria?', *European Competition Law Review*, 29 (2008), 5.

[158] GC (15 September 2005), Case T-325/01 – *DaimlerChrysler v Commission* [2005] ECR II-3319.

agent. According to the Commission, the fact that the agents had to bear a considerable share of the price risk had to be considered such a commercial risk as discounts on the sale of the car were deducted in entirety from their commission. Moreover, the agents had to bear the risk of transport costs for new vehicles. The agents were required to pass on the costs of transport and the transport risk to the customer. The agents also had to use their own financial resources for sales promotion purposes. They had to acquire demonstration vehicles at their own expense. In addition, there were a number of other commercial risks the agents had to bear.

The court annulled the Commission's decision in this regard and held that the Commission had overstated the risks involved in the activities of the German agents. The court took the view that the price risk was not significant enough to qualify the agent as an undertaking distinct from Mercedes-Benz. The court argued that the situation would be different if the agent had to hold a certain stock of new cars and to sell them at his own risk. In that case he could set prices independently and thus determine his own market conduct. However, this was not the case since the German dealers did not have to bear any risk of cars remaining unsold:

As the [. . .] agent is not required to hold a stock of cars, it is wrong to treat him, for economic purposes, as being in the same position as a dealer in cars who receives from the manufacturer, by way of remuneration, a margin which he uses not only to fund his new-car sales business in general, but also [. . .] to grant discounts to car buyers [. . .] [An] agent is not obliged, either under the agency agreement or in practice, to give up part of his commission in order to sell a car which he has in stock. That would represent a real price risk, as he would already have had to bear the costs associated with the purchase of the car and of holding it in stock. [. . .] Therefore, if the agent does not wish to forgo a part of his commission, he does not take an order for a car.[159]

The other risks identified by the Commission were also not recognised by the court as significant enough to consider the agents independent undertakings. Therefore, the court did not apply Article 101(1) TFEU to the relationship between Mercedes-Benz and the German agents. This has the effect that any restrictive clauses could be validly included in the agency agreements that the Commission had tried to establish.

10.10 Withdrawal of the exemption

The Commission may withdraw the benefit of the block exemption pursuant to Article 29 Regulation 1/2003 when it finds that the vertical agreement has effects incompatible with Article 101(3) TFEU. In case of the Vertical Block Exemption, this may occur where the buyer has significant market power in a downstream market or

---

[159] Ibid., para. 97.

access to the relevant market or competition therein is restricted by a cumulative effect of parallel networks of similar vertical restraints implemented by competing buyers or suppliers.

Should a vertical agreement have effects incompatible with Article 101(3) TFEU within the territory of a Member State a national competition authority may withdraw the block exemption as stated in Recital 13 Vertical Block Exemption.

In the *Henninger*[160] case a publican and a brewery argued about a contract that required the publican to obtain supplies of different kinds of beer and soft drinks from the brewery's subsidiaries. The contract also provided for the publican to lease the pub from the brewery. The product range was determined on the basis of current price lists of the brewery, and the publican had to purchase a minimum quantity to avoid a penalty for non-performance. Furthermore, the publican was permitted to purchase beer and soft drinks from companies in other Member States.

This was a standard agreement between breweries and publicans at this time in Germany. Therefore, one issue of the case was whether a bundle of agreements could cumulatively have an appreciable effect on competition that one single agreement would not have, so that all similar agreements would have to be prohibited. The ECJ decided that such a supply agreement is prohibited by Article 101(1) TFEU if an agreement in question makes 'a significant contribution to the sealing-off effect brought about by the totality of those agreements in their economic and legal context'[161] and that it is difficult for competitors who could enter the market or increase their market share to gain access to the national market.

10.11 US policy

In the US the Supreme Court decided in 1977 in *GTE Sylvania*[162] that all vertical restraints, except for fixing minimum prices as resale price maintenance, should be assessed under a rule of reason analysis. Only in cases where the vertical restraints adversely affect interbrand competition should they be prohibited. This opinion is based on the assumption that vertical restraints are designed to encourage distributors to promote products more efficiently. As a conclusion it can be assumed that if a producer has no market power he needs to invest in the most effective distribution network to stand a chance against his competitors.[163] It is the Supreme Court's opinion that antitrust law has to protect interbrand competition[164] and only where there is a lack of interbrand competition and therefore market power present should vertical restraints be considered unlawful.

---

[160] ECJ (28 February 1991), Case C-234/89 – *Delimitis v Henninger Bräu* [1991] ECR I-935.
[161] Ibid., para. 27.   [162] US Supreme Court, *Continental TV Inc. v GTE Sylvania Inc.*, 433 US 36 (1977).
[163] Monti, *EC Competition Law*, p. 356.   [164] US Supreme Court, *State Oil Co. v Kahn*, 522 US 3 (1997).

Summary of Section 10

The concept of vertical agreement encompasses agreements between undertakings that are active at different levels of the economy such as distribution agreements. EU competition law does not only protect interbrand competition but also intrabrand competition, i.e. competition between distributors of products of the same brand to ensure efficient distribution. As a general rule, competition problems are unlikely to arise in the absence of a certain degree of market power. The Vertical Block Exemption therefore provides for a market share threshold of 30% individual market share of either the supplier or the distributor. Furthermore, a vertical agreement must not contain any hardcore restrictions of competition to benefit from the block exemption.

Resale price maintenance is considered one such hardcore restriction since it may eliminate price competition between distributors. Suppliers may recommend prices, however, so long as they do not seek to enforce such recommendations.

EU competition law for reasons of market integration does not allow absolute territorial or customer protection. Distributors may be appointed exclusively for a territory or a customer group but passive sales into such territory or to such group must not be restricted. Passive sales are sales that are made after receiving an unsolicited order.

Selective distribution usually does not fall into the ambit of Article 101(1) TFEU if it relies on purely qualitative selection criteria and those criteria are necessary and proportionate in light of the specific properties of the product. Quantitative selective distribution inherently leads to a restriction of the number of retailers and is subject to review under Article 101(3) TFEU.

Non-compete clauses impose an obligation on the distributor to purchase all or almost all of its total demand for a certain product from the supplier. Such clauses are block-exempted for a maximum duration of five years. They may affect interbrand competition if a large share of the distributors is tied and thus not available for other suppliers as a sales channel.

The stipulations of the Vertical Block Exemption extend also to e-commerce. Restrictions of passive sales via the internet are prohibited. Also, limitations of internet sales in general may give rise to competitive concerns if such limitations are not objectively justified by the specific properties of the product in question.

Agency agreements are not covered by Article 101(1) TFEU if the agent does not carry any appreciable entrepreneurial risk. In this case the agent is not considered a distinct undertaking in the sense of the EU competition rules but rather a part of the undertaking of the principal.

The benefit of a block exemption may be withdrawn by the Commission or a national competition authority if a vertical agreement that nominally meets the criteria of the block exemption in an individual case generates adverse effects that outweigh the efficiencies induced by it. This may be the case if a supplier enters into a large number of similar agreements that collectively have a restrictive effect on competition.

11. TECHNOLOGY TRANSFER AGREEMENTS

Technology transfer agreements relate to the licensing of technology.[165] In principle such agreements have pro-competitive effects as they reduce duplication of R&D efforts, strengthen the incentive for initial R&D and facilitate competition on the respective product market. However, under certain circumstances technology transfer agreements may have also detrimental effects on competition. In particular this may be the case where the restrictive agreements are concluded by undertakings with a high degree of market power.

In order to provide an adequate level of legal certainty the Commission issued a block exemption regulation for technology transfer agreements (hereinafter: the Technology Transfer Block Exemption).[166] Following an economics-based approach the Technology Transfer Block Exemption places great emphasis on the market power of the participating enterprises. The Technology Transfer Block Exemption follows a pattern similar to the Vertical Block Exemption. Any technology transfer agreement benefits from a block exemption under Article 101(3) TFEU provided that certain market share thresholds are not exceeded and provided that no hardcore restrictions of competition are included in the agreement. Those hardcore restrictions are listed in Article 4 Technology Transfer Block Exemption. The Technology Transfer Block Exemption also identifies a number of clauses in Article 5 that are excluded from the block exemption but do not render the entire licence void.

The Technology Transfer Block Exemption is accompanied by guidelines[167] which provide guidance on the interpretation of the concepts of the Technology Transfer Block Exemption and for licences that do not fall into its scope. With regard to such licences a self-assessment with the help of the guidelines has to be carried out.

---

[165] For a discussion of competition law problems with regard to software licensing agreements, see Välimäki, 'Copyleft Licensing and EC Competition Law', *European Competition Law Review*, 27 (2006), 130.

[166] Commission regulation (EC) No. 772/2004 of 27 April 2004 on the application of Article 81(3) of the Treaty to categories of technology transfer agreements, OJ No. L 123 of 27 April 2004, p. 11.

[167] Commission Guidelines on the application of Article 81(3) of the Treaty to technology transfer agreements, OJ No. C 101 of 27 April 2004, p. 2 (hereinafter: the Technology Transfer Guidelines).

11.1 Scope

In order for an agreement to fall within the scope of the block exemption it has (i) to qualify as a technology transfer agreement, (ii) to be entered into between two undertakings and (iii) to permit the production of contract products. Agreements between more than two undertakings are not covered by the Technology Transfer Block Exemption as the Commission is not empowered to block-exempt multilateral technology transfer agreements under Council Regulation 19/65.[168]

The notion of technology transfer agreement is defined in Article 1 (b) Technology Transfer Block Exemption and covers different types of intellectual property licences such as patent licences, know-how licences and software copyright licences. Licences for other intellectual property rights such as trade marks or copyright covering other items than software do not fall within the scope of the definition.

The concept of 'transfer' requires that the technology flows from one undertaking to another. Such transfers normally take the form of licensing one party with a right to use certain technology against royalty payments. The definition of a technology transfer agreement also covers ancillary licences for other IPRs such as trade marks under the condition that the licence of these rights is not the primary objective of the agreement and that they are directly related to the production of products.

As a result of the agreement the licensee must be granted the right to produce goods using the licensed rights. Pursuant to Article 2 Technology Transfer Block Exemption the exemption applies as long as the IPR granted has not expired, lapsed or been declared invalid.

11.2 Market share thresholds

According to Article 3(1) Technology Transfer Block Exemption, where the parties to the technology transfer agreement are competitors the block exemption shall apply only if their combined market share does not exceed 20% of the affected relevant technology and product markets. This market share threshold corresponds to the market share thresholds defined by the Commission for certain types of horizontal cooperation agreements.

Agreements concluded between non-competitors are covered by the block exemption if each of the parties' individual market share does not exceed 30% of the affected relevant technology and product markets. This threshold is stipulated in Article 3(2) Technology Transfer Block Exemption. The Commission accepts a much

---

[168] Council Regulation (EEC) No. 19/65 of 2 March 1965 on application of Article 85(3) of the Treaty to certain categories of agreements and concerted practices, OJ No. P 36 of 6 March 1965, p. 35.

higher degree of market power in vertical technology transfer agreements, which is consistent with the approach under the Vertical Block Exemption.

Article 8 Technology Transfer Block Exemption provides for the relevant market share to be calculated on the basis of market sales value data relating to the preceding year. If no market data is available, estimates have to be made based on reliable market information. If the market share initially did not exceed 20% or 30% respectively but later rises above those thresholds, the exemption continues to apply for two more calendar years following the year in which the threshold was first exceeded.[169]

11.3 Hardcore restrictions

Article 4 Technology Transfer Block Exemption contains a 'black list' of hardcore restrictions, the inclusion of which results in the exemption not being applicable to the whole agreement. For agreements between competitors Article 4(1) Technology Transfer Block Exemption shall apply whereas Article 4(2) Technology Transfer Block Exemption lists restrictions unacceptable in agreements between non-competitors.

11.3.1 Agreements between competitors

a) Restrictions on the price set for the sale of products to third parties
Any kind of price fixing is prohibited – agreements on maximum, minimum or recommended prices are not exempted if they directly or indirectly serve the purpose of fixing minimum resale prices. Also price fixing in cross-licences is anticompetitive, e.g. in situations where competitors use cross-licensing combined with royalties calculated on the basis of individual product sales as a means of price coordination.

b) Output limitation
An output limitation may have similar effects to resale price maintenance. The quantity of a specific good available on the market has direct influence on the price of this good. Output limitations therefore are likely to establish a minimum price in the market. Reflecting this consideration, the prohibition does not apply to limitations imposed on the licensee in a non-reciprocal agreement or imposed only on one of the licensees in a reciprocal agreement.[170] In these cases one of the parties remains free to increase output and thus supply extra quantities to the market.

---

[169]   Further information can be found in the Technology Transfer Guidelines, paras. 65–73.
[170]   For a definition of reciprocal and non-reciprocal agreements, see Art. 1(c) and (d) Technology Transfer Block Exemption.

c) Allocation of markets or customers

Market and customer allocation between competing undertakings is generally prohibited – Article 4(1)(c) Technology Transfer Block Exemption. However the Regulation provides for a number of exceptions from this principle. They are listed in Article 4(1)(c) Technology Transfer Block Exemption and may be grouped in three subcategories: restrictions relating to field of use, territorial restrictions and customer group restrictions.[171]

Exceptions listed here include: cases where a licensor grants the licensee in a non-reciprocal agreement a territorially exclusive licence to manufacture on the basis of the licensed technology and therefore agrees not to produce himself the products in that territory; cases where the licensor appoints the licensee as his sole licensee in a particular territory; cases where restrictions in agreements between competitors limit the licence to certain product markets or technical fields of use; or cases with captive use restrictions.[172]

It has to be noted that the Technology Transfer Block Exemption allows a higher degree of territorial protection than the Vertical Block Exemption. The IPR holder may reserve to himself a territory or a customer group and agree with the other party on absolute territorial protection, provided that the agreement is non-reciprocal. In this case even passive sales into the exclusive territory or to the exclusive customer group can be prohibited. This is a significant concession in light of the market integration policy goal. It is based on the consideration that the IPR holder is not obliged to grant any licences and thus disseminate his secret knowledge at all. In order to encourage licensing, the IPR holder retains the right to reserve territories or customer groups entirely to himself.

d) Restrictions on use and development of technology between competing undertakings

Any limitation of the licensee's ability to exploit its own technology or restriction of the ability of any of the parties to the agreement to carry out R&D is not covered by the block exemption. The parties must be free to carry out independent R&D, but they can agree to provide each other with future improvements of their respective technologies. This provision also does not extend to restrictions on a party's ability to carry out R&D with third parties, where restrictions are necessary to protect a licensor's know-how against disclosure, although the protecting measure must be necessary and proportionate. In order not to reduce the licensee's incentive to invest in the improvement of its technology the licensee must be unrestricted in using its

---

[171] All of them are also discussed in the Technology Transfer Guidelines, paras. 84–93.

[172] Captive use restrictions are requirements whereby the licensee may produce the products incorporating the licensed technology for his use only. Therefore, the licensee can be obliged to not sell the components to other producers. See Technology Transfer Guidelines, para. 92.

own competing technology, so long as in doing so it does not use the technology licensed from the licensor.[173]

11.3.2 Agreements between non-competitors

a) Price restrictions

Non-competitors are also not allowed to fix prices or to set minimum prices. An exception applies to agreements stipulating recommended resale prices provided that such recommendations are not indirectly enforced as minimum prices.

b) Restrictions with regard to territory or customers

As they are serious restrictions of competition, generally any restriction of the territory into which, or of the customers to whom, the licensee may passively sell the contract products results in the loss of the block exemption unless it falls within one of the exceptions listed in Article 4(2)(b) Technology Transfer Block Exemption.[174]

For example, a licensee may be granted absolute territorial protection for a duration of two years. This reflects the consideration that absolute territorial protection may be necessary to encourage a licensee to make the investments necessary to use the licensed technology. Territorial protection increases the chances for recoupment of such initial investments and thus gives an incentive to innovate by licensing-in new technology.

c) Restrictions of active or passive sales to end-users by members of a selective distribution system

Licensees, being members of a selective distribution system and operating at the retail level, shall not in any way be restricted in selling the contract products either passively or actively to end-users. They can only be prohibited from selling out of an unauthorised place of establishment. This follows the stipulations under the Vertical Block Exemption.

11.4 Excluded restrictions

Article 5 Technology Transfer Block Exemption provides a 'grey list' of restrictions that are not block-exempted. Inclusion of any of the listed provisions in a licence agreement does not prevent the application of the block exemption to the rest of the

---

[173] Technology Transfer Guidelines, paras. 94 et seq.
[174] A detailed description of each exception can be found in the Technology Transfer Guidelines, paras. 98–105.

agreement, assuming that it is severable from the provision covered by Article 5 Technology Transfer Block Exemption. The 'grey list' contains the following restrictions:

- Any obligation on the licensee to grant an exclusive licence or assign rights to the licensor or a third party designated by the licensor in respect of its own severable improvements or its own new applications to the licensed technology.
- Any obligation on the licensee to assign to the licensor or a third party rights to its own severable improvements or its own new applications of the licensed technology.

Both of the provisions above concern severable improvements of the licensed technology. An improvement is severable if exploitation is possible without infringing upon the licensed technology. The rationale behind these provision is that they reduce the licensee's incentive to innovate as they would prevent him from effectively exploiting his improvements as he could not license them to third parties or keep the right on his improvement at all. But non-exclusive grant-back obligations with regard to severable improvement are block-exempted.

- 'No-challenge' clause – an obligation preventing the licensee from challenging the validity of the rights held by the licensor in the internal market. The licensor is however permitted to terminate the agreement in case the licensee decides to challenge the validity of one or more rights in question.

These clauses are excluded as licensees are usually best positioned to determine whether an IPR is valid. Generally, invalid IPRs stifle innovation rather than promoting it.

In *Bayer*[175] the ECJ had to assess a no-challenge clause under Article 101(1) TFEU in a rather specific setting. Bayer and Süllhöfer argued about patents with regard to foamable, polyurethane-based substances. The legal proceedings were concluded with an agreement of the parties granting each other non-exclusive licences. Bayer also agreed not to challenge the validity of one of Süllhöfer's patents. As Süllhöfer later terminated the agreement, the question of the compatibility of the no-challenge clause with the EU competition rules arose.

The ECJ decided that:

a no-challenge clause in a patent licensing agreement may, depending on the legal and economic context, restrict competition within the meaning of Article [101(1) TFEU]. Such a clause does not, however, restrict competition when the agreement in which it is contained granted a free licence and the licensee does not, therefore, suffer the competitive disadvantage involved in the payment of royalties or when the licence was granted subject to payment of

---

[175] ECJ (27 September 1988), Case 65/86 – *Bayer v Süllhöfer* [1988] ECR 5249.

royalties but relates to a technically outdated process which the undertaking accepting the no-challenge agreement did not use.[176]

Although no-challenge clauses do not benefit from the block exemption the licensor may reserve a right to terminate the licence if the licensor challenges the licensed intellectual property rights.

11.5 Withdrawal of the block exemption

According to Article 6 Technology Transfer Block Exemption the Commission may under certain conditions withdraw the benefit of the block exemption pursuant to Article 29 Regulation 1/2003. This may be the case if an agreement proves to have effects incompatible with Article 101(3) TFEU, in particular where barriers to entry arise from a network of similar licensing agreements, the agreement at issue prohibits the licensor to license other licensees or where the parties do not exploit the licensed technology. National competition authorities have similar powers if a licence has such effects in a territory of a Member State – Article 6(2) Technology Transfer Block Exemption.

11.6 US approach

The US agencies consider restraints in the vast majority of intellectual property licensing agreements under the rule of reason. But there are some cases where American courts conclude that a restraint's 'nature and necessary effect are so plainly anticompetitive' that it should be treated as unlawful *per se*.[177] Among those restraints are naked price fixing, output restraints, and market division among horizontal competitors, as well as certain group boycotts and resale price maintenance.[178]

11.7 Settlements in licensing disputes

Disputes over IPRs may be solved by licensing. In the context of settlement agreements, licensing as such is not a restriction of competition since it enables parties to

---

[176] Ibid., para. 21.
[177] US Supreme Court, *FTC v Superior Court Trial Lawyers Association*, 493 US 411, 433 (1990).
[178] DoJ and FTC, Antitrust Guidelines for Licensing of Intellectual Property, 1995, p. 16. For a detailed comparison of the European and the US approach towards technology licensing, especially with regard to exclusive licensing, see Baches Opi, 'The Approaches of the European Commission and the U.S. Antitrust Agencies towards Exclusivity Clauses in Licensing Agreements', *Boston College International and Comparative Law Review*, 24 (2000), 85.

use their technologies after the agreement is implemented. But certain terms of such an agreement may be caught under Article 101(1) TFEU, as licensing within settlement agreements is treated like any other licence agreement.[179] To assess competitive threats of such a licensing agreement, it has to be determined whether or not the parties are competitors. If they are in a one-way or two-way blocking position (i.e. when a technology cannot be exploited without infringing upon another or neither technology can be exploited without each infringing upon the other), they are not considered competitors.[180]

Licensing agreements are generally considered competitive, as in the absence of a licence the licensee would be excluded from the market. Usually, the Technology Transfer Block Exemption applies. Where no blocking position exists and the parties are therefore to be considered competitors, settlements are likely to be considered a means to restrict competition.[181] Furthermore, where the parties have significant degrees of market power and the restrictions imposed in the agreement clearly go beyond what is necessary to unblock, the agreement is likely to be caught by Article 101(1) TFEU, particularly where the parties share markets or fix reciprocal royalties that impact market prices.[182]

In *Bayer*[183] the ECJ did not consider the settlement as a reason for a more lenient treatment of potential restrictions of competition. The ECJ held that there is 'no distinction between agreements whose purpose is to put an end to litigation and those concluded with other aims in mind'[184] with regard to their treatment under Article 101(1) TFEU.

In the US, licence settlements are analysed under the rule of reason.[185] Generally, genuine licensing agreements seem to be welcomed by focusing on the lack of competition without the agreement so long as there are no clear anticompetitive effects.[186] Licensing agreements are only considered unlawful if they are collusive and their anticompetitive effects outweigh their beneficial competitive aspects. When courts have held that such agreements had anticompetitive effects, this has not been about resolving IPRs disputes, but about other inappropriate terms of the agreements in question. Cases are usually analysed under an effects-based inquiry which makes it more fact-driven.[187]

---

[179] Technology Transfer Guidelines, para. 204. [180] Ibid. [181] Ibid., para. 205. [182] Ibid., para. 207.
[183] See Section 11.4 above.
[184] ECJ (27 September 1988), Case 65/86 – *Bayer v Süllhöfer* [1988] ECR 5249, para. 15.
[185] Robert and Falconi, 'Patent Litigation Settlement Agreements in the Pharmaceutical Industry: Marrying the Innovation Bride and the Competition Groom', *European Competition Law Review*, 27 (2006), 524, 527; Phan, 'Leveling the Playing Field: Harmonization of Antitrust Guidelines for International Patent Licensing Agreements in the United States, Japan, and the European Union', *American University International Law Review*, 10 (1994), 447, 452 et seq.
[186] Ibid., p. 528. [187] Ibid.

Summary of Section 11

The Technology Transfer Block Exemption covers production licences for intellectual property rights such as patents, know-how and software copyright. The dissemination of new technologies is considered beneficial for competition since it fosters innovation and thus may outweigh certain restrictions of competition that may result from a licence agreement at the same time. The block exemption follows the general pattern of stipulating a market share threshold and certain hardcore restrictions that must not be included in a technology transfer agreement. In the case of a licence between competitors a combined market share of 20% must not be exceeded. In the case of non-competitors a market share threshold of 30% individual market share applies.

The Technology Transfer Block Exemption allows for a higher degree of territorial and customer protection. Under certain conditions absolute territorial or customer protection may be permissible at least for a certain period of time. However, the block exemption does not allow price fixing or output limitations.

No-challenge clauses are classified as excluded restrictions, i.e. as restrictions that do not benefit from the block exemption but do not render the entire licence void. However, licensors may reserve the right to terminate the licence in case licensed intellectual property rights are challenged by the licensee.

Settlements of intellectual property right infringement procedures under EU competition law are subject to the same standards as other intellectual property licences. If they contribute to resolve blocking positions they may be pro-competitive. If no blocking position exists they will be assessed as a licence between competitors. Obviously, the outcome of the infringement action cannot be predicted easily. According to competition authorities this makes such settlements susceptible to serve as a disguise for market sharing or other illicit arrangements.

QUESTIONS ON CHAPTER 3

1. What types of competition can be restricted by horizontal agreements? (2.2)
2. What are the risks for competition resulting from information exchange between competitors? (3.2)
3. What are the potential pro-competitive effects of information exchange? (3.3)
4. What are the markets on which R&D cooperations may have a restrictive effect? (4.2)

5. Under what conditions do specialisation agreements benefit from a block exemption? (5)
6. To what extent are production agreements permissible under the EU competition rules? (6)
7. What are the risks for competition involved in a purchasing agreement? (7)
8. What are the efficiencies that may justify the exemption of a commercialisation agreement? (8)
9. What are the pro-competitive effects of a standardisation agreement? (9)
10. What are the types of competition that may be affected by vertical agreements? (10)
11. Why is resale price maintenance prohibited under the EU competition rules? (10.4)
12. To what extent is territorial or customer protection permissible under the Vertical Block Exemption? (10.5)
13. What are the potential detrimental effects of non-compete clauses on competition? (10.7)
14. What types of agreements are covered by the Technology Transfer Block Exemption? (11.1)
15. What is the pattern of the Technology Transfer Block Exemption? (11)

SUGGESTED ESSAY TOPICS

1. The assessment of information exchange under EU competition law
2. Are there economic justifications for resale price maintenance?
3. The competition rules applicable to e-commerce

4 Article 102 TFEU – abuse of a dominant position

1. INTRODUCTION

Article 102 TFEU complements the regulations of EU competition law dealing with agreements between two or more undertakings. The provision restricts certain conduct by undertakings which have a dominant position in a given market. Although dominant undertakings are in principle free to engage in diverse economic activities exactly as their competitors do, they have a 'special responsibility' not to hinder competition on the market. This term was first used in one of the ECJ's landmark decisions on the abuse of a dominant position. It concerned the tyre manufacturer Michelin. During the administrative procedure, the Commission established that Michelin had a dominant position on the market for new replacement tyres for lorries, buses and similar vehicles and that it had abused this position by way of its rebate and bonus system. In the subsequent appeal proceedings the ECJ confirmed the Commission's finding that *Michelin* had a dominant position on the market for replacement tyres and added:

A finding that an undertaking has a dominant position is not in itself a recrimination but simply means that, irrespective of the reasons for which it has such a dominant position, the undertaking concerned has a *special responsibility* not to allow its conduct to impair genuine undistorted competition on the common market.[1] (emphasis added)

Thus, Article 102 TFEU does not prohibit dominance as such. It merely places specific restrictions on companies that have a dominant position.

Summary of Section 1

While Article 101 TFEU covers bi- or multilateral restrictions of competition, Article 102 TFEU governs unilateral conduct that restricts competition. Dominant undertakings have a special responsibility not to impair competition by their smaller rivals. Article 102 TFEU does not prohibit dominance as such though.

---

[1] ECJ (9 November 1983), Case 322/81 – *Michelin v Commission* [1983] ECR 3461, para. 57.

2. ELEMENTS OF ARTICLE 102 TFEU

Article 102 TFEU governs abusive conduct by dominant undertakings. The possession or strengthening of a dominant position by way of competition does not fall within the scope of the prohibition. Dominance alone is never an offence. The dominance of many global players (such as Microsoft or Intel) is a direct result of their inventions and entrepreneurship. The competition regime generally encourages such efforts as they form the basis of our society's competitive layout. Therefore, unless there is an abuse, there can be no finding of an infringement of Article 102 TFEU. On the other hand, the provision specifies that the concerned undertaking must have a dominant position in the relevant product market. Accordingly, it does not apply to abusive practices by non-dominant undertakings. Such practices may, of course, be subject to other prohibitions. In essence, Article 102 TFEU stipulates two major requirements: a *dominant position* and an *abuse*. If the Commission finds such a dominant position and an abuse it may impose a fine on the dominant undertaking.[2]

The wording of Article 102 TFEU requires that the following conditions are met to establish a violation:

(i)   a dominant position on the relevant market must be held by one or more undertakings;
(ii) the position must be held in the internal market or a substantial part of it;
(iii) abuse of the dominant position;
(iv) actual or potential effect on trade between Member States.

It is not necessary to demonstrate that the abusive conduct is a result of the exercise of the dominant position in the relevant market. The undertaking must not even be aware of its dominant position. In other words no causal link between points (i) and (iii) is required.[3] Moreover, the abusive conduct may also take place on a different market than the market dominated by the undertaking. Thus in *Tetra Pak*[4] the ECJ noted that the undertaking in question had a quasi-monopoly on the market for *aseptic* cartons for liquids ('tetra briks') and a 'leading', albeit not dominant, position on the market for *non-aseptic* cartons. Even though these products serve different purposes and form distinct product markets, both the General Court and the ECJ put considerable weight on the fact that Tetra Pak appeared to have a dominant position on a (hypothetical) overall market for cartons. It also noted that many of Tetra Pak's

---

[2] The fining policy has been criticised as unpredictable and therefore not meeting the required standard of legal certainty, see Dethmers and Engelen, 'Fines under Article 102 of the Treaty on the Functioning of the European Union', *European Competition Law Review*, 32 (2011), 86.

[3] ECJ (21 February 1973), Case 6/72 – *Europemballage Corporation and Continental Can Company v Commission* [1973] ECR 215, para. 27.

[4] ECJ (14 November 1996), Case C-333/94 P – *Tetra Pak v Commission* [1996] ECR I-5951.

customers bought both aseptic and non-aseptic cartons and that the two markets were therefore closely related. Against this background, the ECJ was of the opinion that the 'associative links' between the two markets constituted a sufficient nexus for a finding that the undertaking had abused its dominant position.[5]

Summary of Section 2

A violation of Article 102 TFEU has several prerequisites: The provision is addressed to entities qualifying as undertakings and which hold a dominant position in the internal market or a substantial part of it. A dominant position can be held by one undertaking alone or collectively by several undertakings. Article 102 TFEU applies only to abuses of a dominant position while the attainment of a dominant position as such is not prohibited. Finally, the abuse has to have an effect on trade between Member States, i.e. a cross-border element that gives it relevance for the functioning of the internal market.

3. UNDERTAKING

In principle, the notion of 'undertaking' shall be interpreted in the same way as in the case of Article 101 TFEU, i.e. it covers all persons and entities engaged in an economic activity.[6]

3.1 Non-application of the 'single economic entity' doctrine

There is, however, an important difference between Article 101 TFEU and Article 102 TFEU and their respective notions of the term 'undertaking'. This difference concerns the application of the single economic entity doctrine. As has been explained in Chapter 2 above in connection with the concept of undertaking under Article 101 TFEU,[7] agreements between parent companies and their wholly owned subsidiaries in general are not caught by the cartel prohibition, because the related companies are considered to form one single undertaking.[8]

This concept has not been applied to Article 102 TFEU cases. Dominant companies may not favour their own subsidiaries or group companies over third parties. The leading case on this issue is *GT-Link*.[9] It concerned the operation of a commercial port and the shipping duties that its users, i.e. the shipping companies that berthed within the port's limits, were charged. The port operator, which had a dominant position

---

[5] Ibid., paras. 21–31.   [6] For a more detailed discussion, see Chapter 2, section 2.

[7] See Chapter 2, Section 2.3.

[8] ECJ (4 May 1988), Case 30/87 – *Corinne Bodson v Pompes funèbres des régions libérées* [1988] ECR 2479, para. 19.

[9] ECJ (17 July 1997), Case C-242/95 – *GT Link v De Danske Statsbaner* [1997] ECR I-4449.

on the market for ferry port services between Denmark and Germany, was the subsidiary of the publicly owned Danish national railway company Danske Statsbaner. In addition to its railway and port business Danske Statsbaner also operated a ferry service between Denmark and Germany. Unlike its competitors, the operator of this ferry service did not have to pay any of the shipping duties usually charged by the port operator. The ECJ held that such practices are capable of constituting an abuse under Article 102 TFEU insofar as they entail the application of dissimilar conditions to equivalent trans-actions.[10] It did not give weight to the fact that both the port operator and the ferry services operator were subsidiaries of the same parent company. Accordingly, the single economic entity doctrine does not apply to Article 102 TFEU cases.

3.2 Exceptions for undertakings entrusted with the operation of services of general economic interest and revenue-producing monopolies (Article 106(2) TFEU)

Article 102 TFEU also applies to state-owned and private companies having a monopoly conferred upon them by statute. However, the personal scope of the prohibition is limited by Article 106(2) TFEU which grants Member States the right to confer immunity on undertakings from Article 102 TFEU in limited cases. Undertakings may only be exempted from the application of Article 102 TFEU if they have been entrusted with the performance of services of 'general economic interest' or if they are a 'revenue-producing monopoly' and if the application of the competition rules would make the provision of the services more difficult. The Member States are generally free to define the services they consider to be of 'general economic interest' and their decision is only subject to control for manifest error.[11] Services to which Article 102 TFEU has been applied include, *inter alia*, public television and radio stations,[12] suppliers of electricity,[13] public employment agen-cies,[14] universal postal services,[15] and mooring operators.[16] In any event, the provi-sion should be interpreted narrowly since it constitutes an exception to a general rule and the European courts have been very reluctant to extend their rulings to similar or related undertakings.

---

[10] Ibid., paras. 42, 46.

[11] Commission Communication regarding Services of general interest in Europe, OJ No. C 17 of 19 January 2001, p. 04, para. 22.

[12] ECJ (30 April 1974), Case 155–73 – *Sacchi* [1974] ECR 409, paras. 14–15.

[13] ECJ (27 April 1994), Case C-393/92 – *Municipality of Almelo and others v NV Energiebedrijf Ijsselmij* [1994] ECR I-1477, para. 48.

[14] ECJ (23 April 1991), Case C-41/90 – *Höfner and Elser v Macrotron* [1991] ECR I-1979, para. 24.

[15] ECJ (17 May 2001), Case C-340/99 – *TNT Traco*, [2001] ECR 4109, paras. 52–53; ECJ (18 December 2007), Case C-220/06 – *Asociación Profesional de Empresas de Reparto y Manipulado de Correspondencia* [2007] ECR I-12175, paras. 78–9.

[16] ECJ (18 June 1998), Case C-266/96 – *Corsica Ferries II* [1998] ECR I-3949, para. 45.

Summary of Section 3

Article 102 TFEU applies only to undertakings. In general, the concept of undertaking as defined for purposes of delimiting the scope of Article 101 TFEU is valid also for Article 102 TFEU. There is an exception, however, with regard to the single economic entity doctrine. This doctrine does not apply under Article 102 TFEU, which means that a dominant undertaking may violate the competition rules by giving its subsidiaries preferential treatment in relation to third parties. In addition, Article 102 TFEU does not apply to undertakings that are entrusted by the state with a service of general economic interest or if they are a revenue-producing monopoly and have been granted immunity from Article 102 TFEU by the respective Member State.

4. EFFECTS ON INTER-STATE TRADE

For the purpose of Article 102 TFEU an understanding of this requirement similar to that in the case of Article 101(1) TFEU should be adopted. The decisive point is whether the conduct in question causes a change in the structure of competition in the internal market. Yet, as the following example illustrates, it is not necessary that the illegal conduct has a negative effect on European customers. In *Commercial Solvents*, the defendant had a world monopoly in a specific raw material that was used for the production of anti-tuberculosis drugs. When it entered the market for the downstream product (i.e. the market of anti-tuberculosis drugs) it ceased to supply the raw material to a number of former customers. The Commission had found that this refusal to supply was tantamount to an abuse of a dominant position. In its defence before the ECJ, the defendant alleged that the vast majority (approx. 90%) of the purchaser's anti-tuberculosis drugs were sold outside the EU (where tuberculosis has largely disappeared). Therefore, the dominant undertaking asserted, the refusal to supply had no effect on trade between Member States. But the defendant's reasoning did not convince the ECJ which was of the opinion that in order for Article 102 TFEU to apply it was sufficient that an undertaking that does business within the internal market was being put at a disadvantage. It held that

[w]hen an undertaking in a dominant position within the common market abuses its position in such a way that a competitor in the common market is likely to be eliminated, it does not matter whether the conduct relates to the latter's exports or its trade within the common market, once it has been established that this elimination *will* have repercussions on the competitive structure within the common market.[17]

---

[17] ECJ (6 March 1974), Joined Cases 6/73, 7/73 – *Commercial Solvents v Commission* [1974] ECR 223, para. 33.

In an effort to clarify the implications that certain activities related to the EU's competition law regime may have on trade, the Commission has published a guidance document that summarises the relevant case law of the European courts.[18] The document is quite comprehensive and contains a number of detailed examples. Nonetheless, as a general rule it can be said that, unless an 'abuse is purely local in nature or involves only an insignificant share of the sales of the dominant undertaking',[19] it is very likely that the Commission and the courts will find trade between Member States to be affected.

For example, the Commission states that the mere 'existence of a dominant position in several Member States implies that competition in a substantial part of the internal market is already weakened.'[20] In cases where an abuse covers only a *single* Member State, it has been argued, for example, that the practice has foreclosed competitors from other Member States.[21] Even if an agreement or abuse covers only part of a Member State, the Commission might still see sufficient grounds to justify EU jurisdiction.[22]

This interpretation by the Commission and the European courts may seem exhaustive only at first sight. Regard must be given to the overall competition regime envisaged by the TFEU: Article 3(1)(b) grants the Union exclusive competence in the area of establishing the competition rules necessary for the functioning of the internal market. This difficult task can only be achieved if the European institutions are given the ability to address all relevant competition concerns, however small their effect on inter-state trade may be.

Summary of Section 4

The concept of effect on trade between Member States under Article 102 TFEU does not differ from the concept under Article 101 TFEU. It is applied broadly and any potential cross-border effect will suffice to give a certain practice a nexus to EU competition law. The conduct does not necessarily have to affect consumers in the EU but an effect on trade between Member States may also consist in a change of the market structure in the EU, for example by reducing the number of manufacturers of a certain product that is mainly exported to non-EU markets.

---

[18] Commission Guidelines on the effect on trade concept contained in Articles 81 and 82 of the Treaty, OJ No. C 101 of 27 April 2004, p. 81.

[19] Ibid., para. 99.   [20] Ibid., para. 76.

[21] Ibid., para. 93 with reference to ECJ (9 November 1983), Case 322/81 – *Michelin v Commission* [1983] ECR 3461, para. 103.

[22] Commission Guidelines on the effect on trade concept contained in Articles 81 and 82 of the Treaty, OJ No. C 101 of 27 April 2004, p. 81, para. 76.

5. DOMINANT POSITION

Article 102 TFEU applies only to undertakings having a dominant position on the relevant market.[23] The assessment in each individual case requires a two-stage test to be completed. First, the relevant market must be established by defining the proper product, geographic and temporal markets. In other words an in-depth analysis of the category of products that consumers regard as substitutes because of their characteristics, use and price should be made.[24] In the next step the dominant position of the undertaking should be investigated. At this point it is necessary to consider among other factors the market power of the company, its market share and the significance of barriers to entry.

5.1 Four concepts of market power

There is no conclusive definition of what exactly the term 'market power' describes. Obviously, it refers to the position of a specific undertaking in a given market, but it is not entirely clear under what conditions it can be said that an undertaking has market power. Indeed, one would assume that *every* undertaking has *some* power on the market in which it is active, at least with respect to its own behaviour. For example, every vendor is usually free to raise or lower its prices or to change its products. Nonetheless, the concept of market power seems to refer to a more specific situation.

There are a number of different theories that aim to explain market power. The most important four approaches – all of which have had some influence on the Commission's and the European courts' case law on dominance – can be summarised as follows.[25]

The first and most well-known concept defines market power as the ability to raise prices. It is based on the assumption that prices are set by consumers' demand and that an undertaking may only deviate from such a 'competitive price' if it has significant power on the relevant market.

The second approach uses commercial power as an indicator of market power. It relates to situations where one undertaking has significant advantages in comparison to other undertakings. Such advantages can be of an economic nature (if, for

---

[23] For a discussion of the differences between the concept of dominance under EU competition law and the concept of monopolisation under US antitrust law, see De Smet, 'The Diametrically Opposed Principles of US and EU Antitrust Policy', *European Competition Law Review*, 29 (2008), 356.

[24] Commission Notice on the definition of the relevant market for the purposes of Community competition law, OJ No. C 372 of 9 December 1997, p. 5.

[25] The discussion of the four concepts of market power is largely based on an analysis conducted by Monti. For a more detailed overview see Monti, *EC Competition Law* (Cambridge University Press, 2007), pp. 124 et seq.; Monti, 'The Concept of Dominance in Article 82', *European Competition Journal* (Special Supplement), 9 (2006), 31.

example, one company has significantly more monetary resources than its competitors) or may result from specific situations that place one company in a considerably better situation than its competitors (this might be the case, for example, when a long-time trade relationship between two companies leads to the de facto exclusion of competition).

Under the third concept it is assumed that an undertaking has a dominant position if it is able, in whichever way, to hurt its competitors, as any harm done to a competitor augments the undertaking's chances to later raise prices above a competitive level. This would be the case, for example, where a company devises a strategy to raise a competitor's input costs for a product that is interchangeable with its own.[26]

Lastly, it has been argued that an undertaking has market power whenever it meets the market shares or other requirements established by the relevant jurisdiction. However, such a stringent approach would have the effect that undertakings below the threshold are not subject to penalties even if, for whatever other reason, they actually have much more market power than their market share suggests.[27]

5.2 Indicators of dominance as established by the European courts

All of the above-cited theories have had some effect on how the Commission and the European courts interpret the notion of market power. The basic legal test of dominance has been established by the ECJ in the *United Brands* case.

The case concerned the conduct of the EU's largest importer of bananas, United Brands (hereinafter: UBC), who sold its products under the popular Chiquita brand. UBC imported its products from outside the EU and unloaded them in two central ports in the Netherlands and Germany from where they were passed on to distributors and ripeners throughout the Union. Despite the central dispatch, the prices UBC charged its customers in the EU varied considerably. For example, the price paid by Danish customers was 2.38 times the price paid by Irish customers.[28] These price differences (together with complaints relating to other abuses) led to an investigation by the Commission. Before analysing the conduct in question, the Commission first analysed UBC's position on the relevant market. It started its assessment with a general remark, stating that dominance

relates to a position of economic strength enjoyed by an undertaking which enables it to prevent effective competition being maintained in the relevant market by giving it the power

---

[26] See Krattenmaker, Lande and Salop, 'Monopoly Power and Market Power in Antitrust Law', *Georgetown Law Journal*, 76 (1987), 241, 250, who call their approach 'Bainian Market Power'.

[27] On the concept of dominance in the energy sector, see Pype, 'Dominance in Peak-term Electricity Markets', *European Competition Law Review*, 32 (2011), 99.

[28] See ECJ (14 February 1978), Case 27/76 – *United Brands v Commission* [1978] ECR 207, para. 65.

to behave to an appreciable extent independently of its competitors, customers and ultimately of its consumers.[29]

The court's definition comprises two elements: the ability to prevent competition and the ability to behave independently of competitors.

This concept has been reaffirmed and supplemented by the judgment in the *Hoffmann-La Roche* case (also referred to as *Vitamins I*), another landmark decision in the ambit of Article 102 TFEU. Hoffmann-LaRoche is an international pharmaceutical company that manufactured and sold at the time of the judgment, among many other products, bulk vitamins used in food and animal feed. The Commission investigated the respective markets for a number of vitamins and came to the conclusion that Hoffmann-LaRoche had a dominant position on many of these markets.[30] In addition, it found that it had abused this position by way of fidelity rebates and by applying dissimilar conditions to equivalent transactions. On appeal, the ECJ rejected some of the Commission's findings, but confirmed the general notion of dominance and abuse with respect to some vitamins. With respect to dominance in general, it held that:

such a [dominant] position [...] enables the undertaking [...] if not to determine, at least to have an appreciable influence on the conditions under which that competition will develop, and in any case to act largely in disregard of it so long as such conduct does not operate to its detriment.[31]

The ECJ has always stressed that dominance may derive from a combination of several factors[32] and that an undertaking's position must therefore be assessed in the light of all relevant market circumstances. This requires a comprehensive survey which usually encompasses the following three-step approach:

(i)   assessment of the undertaking's market strength based on its market share;
(ii) analysis of barriers to entry or expansion. This concept refers to an actual competitor's or potential future competitor's possibility to enter or expand on the relevant product market;
(iii) evaluation of countervailing market power, i.e. investigation whether competitors or purchasers may offset the undertaking's power.

In an effort to provide substantive guidance on the policy underlying Article 102 TFEU, the Commission issued in 2008 an interpretative note about the enforcement of this provision.[33] Although the guidance papers published by the Commission are not

---

[29] Ibid.
[30] Commission decision of 9 June 1976, Case IV/29.020 – *Vitamins*, OJ No. L 223 of 16 August 1976, p. 27.
[31] ECJ (13 February 1979), Case 85/76 – *Hoffmann-La Roche v Commission* [1979] ECR 461, para. 39.
[32] ECJ (14 February 1978), Case 27/76 – *United Brands v Commission* [1978] ECR 207, para. 66.
[33] Commission Communication Guidance on the Commission's enforcement priorities in applying Article 82 EC to abusive exclusionary conduct by dominant undertakings, OJ No. C 45 of 24 February 2009, p. 7

binding on the European courts, the Commission itself may only depart from them for good reason.[34] Much weight can thus be given to the Commission's following statement:[35]

[A]n undertaking which is capable of profitably increasing prices above the competitive level for a significant period of time does not face sufficiently effective competitive constraints and can thus generally be regarded as dominant.[36]

The Commission takes up some of the notions explained above and clearly relies on the ECJ's decisions in *United Brands* and *Hoffmann-LaRoche*. However, it also leaves sufficient room for a broader interpretation of the concept in specific cases. In any event, the Commission and the courts will almost always base their findings on (i) the undertaking's market share, (ii) whether or not there are barriers to entry and (iii) the existence of countervailing market power (as outlined above). For this reason, each of these three areas will be explored in more detail below.

5.3 Market position of the undertaking – market share

One of the most important criteria in establishing a finding of dominance is the market share of the undertaking in question. However, it must be borne in mind that the proof of even a significant market share does not in itself provide sufficient information on the position of an undertaking in the relevant market.[37] Moreover, market share assessment is not necessarily conclusive in analysing the competitive process in the market and does not give any hint on the potential competition that may arise therein. Therefore the existence of a large market share shall not be deemed

---

(hereinafter: Article 102 Guidance Paper). For a discussion of the paper from an economic point of view see Ridyard, 'The European Commission's Article 82 Guidelines: Some Reflections on the Economic Issues', *European Competition Law Review*, 30 (2009), 230; Motta, 'The European Commission's Guidance Communication on Article 82', *European Competition Law Review*, 30 (2009), 593; Gravengaard and Kjarsgaard, 'The EU Commission Guidance on Exclusionary Abuse of Dominance – and its Consequences in Practice', *European Competition Law Review*, 31 (2010), 285; Kellerbauer, 'The Commission's New Enforcement Priorities in Applying Article 82 EC to Dominant Companies' Exclusionary Conduct: A Shift Towards a More Economic Approach?' *European Competition Law Review*, 31 (2010), 175.

[34] GC (25 October 2005), Case T-38/02 – *Groupe Danone v Commission* [2005] ECR II-4407, para. 523.

[35] The legal nature of the Article 102 Guidance Paper is, however, different from that of the Commission's various guidelines. While guidelines limit the Commission's discretion and allow deviations only if they are well reasoned, the Guidance Paper will only influence the advance identification of cases that will be treated with priority, see Kjolbye, 'Rebates under Article 82 EC: Navigating Uncertain Waters', *European Competition Law Review*, 31 (2010), 66. The issuance of the Commission's considerations with regard to Article 102 TFEU in the form of enforcement priorities has been criticised by Lovdahl Gormsen, 'Why the European Commission's Enforcement Priorities on Article 82 EC Should be Withdrawn', *European Competition Law Review*, 31 (2010), 45.

[36] Article 102 Guidance Paper, para. 11.

[37] Nonetheless the Commission's approach is criticised by commentators as relying 'mechanically' on market shares, see Dethmers and Dodoo, 'The Abuse of Hoffmann-La Roche: The Meaning of Dominance under EC Competition Law', *European Competition Law Review*, 27 (2006), 537.

decisive for the application of Article 102 TFEU. It should rather be examined whether such market share is likely to confer lasting market power on the allegedly dominant undertaking.

Although market shares are not regarded to be a decisive factor, the practice of the European courts and the Commission suggests that certain market share thresholds are helpful when assessing the market power of an undertaking. They should, however, be understood as mere indicators of dominance rather than rigid rules.

- **Statutory monopoly** – possession of a statutory monopoly in the provision of goods and services does not immunise the undertaking from the application of Article 102 TFEU. However, in cases where the monopoly has been conferred by virtue of national legislation the exemption of Article 106(2) TFEU may apply.
- **Market share exceeding 70%** – in principle very high market shares are evidence of the existence of a dominant position. In the *Hilti* case the ECJ stated, for example, that a market share between 70% and 80% is in itself a 'clear indication of the existence of a dominant position'.[38] It can be assumed that no additional evidence is required in order to establish dominance.[39]
- **Market share between 50% and 70%** – in cases where the market share exceeds 50%, a rebuttable presumption of dominance applies, as has been held by the ECJ in *Akzo*.[40] Although market shares are considered to be sufficient evidence of dominance in such cases, some additional economic factors should also be taken into account. The 50% presumption has been subject to criticism because it establishes that even undertakings falling well short of being monopolists in the strict sense of the term, must prove that they do not have market power.[41]
- **Market share between 40% and 50%** – may indicate a dominant position, but further economic factors, such as changes in the market share over time, the market share of the closest competitor, and the number and strength of other competitors etc. have to be taken into consideration.[42]
- **Market share between 25% and 40%** – dominance may not be assumed unless some exceptional circumstances are apparent, for example, substantial disparities in market shares or significant barriers to entry.[43]
- **Market share less than 25%** – dominance is very unlikely to be created and may only be assumed in exceptional circumstances. This threshold has been confirmed

---

[38] GC (12 December 1991), Case T-30/89 – *Hilti AG v Commission* [1991] ECR II-1439, para. 92.

[39] GC (23 December 2003), Case T-65/98 – *Van den Bergh Foods Ltd v Commission* [2003] ECR II-4653, para. 154.

[40] ECJ (3 July 1991), Case C-62/86 – *Akzo v Commission* [1991] ECR I-3359, para. 60.

[41] Whish and Bailey, *Competition Law* (Cambridge University Press, 7th edn, 2012), p. 182; Cour and Møllgaard, 'Meaningful and Measurable Market Dominance', *European Competition Law Review*, 24 (2003), 132.

[42] ECJ (14 February 1978), Case 27/76 – *United Brands v Commission* [1978] ECR 207, paras. 108–10.

[43] ECJ (15 December 1994), Case C-250/92 – *Gøttrup-Klim and Others Grovvareforeninger v Dansk Landbrugs Grovvareselskab* [1994] ECR I-5641, para. 48; cf. GC (17 December 2003), Case T-219/99 – *British Airways v Commission* [2003] ECR II-5917, paras. 211–24.

by the Commission in its *guidelines on the assessment of significant market power.*[44]

- Market shares **below** 10% typically 'rule out the existence of a dominant position'.[45]

Market shares should always be analysed in conjunction with the shares of the undertaking's largest competitors. In principle the smaller the shares of the competitors the likelier is the existence of a dominant position. In cases where the 'dominant' undertaking's market share is relatively low, the Commission tends to apply Article 102 TFEU only where there is a major difference between the undertaking's and the competitors' market share.[46] Thus in *British Airways* the General Court specifically noted that British Airways' market share was a 'multiple of the market shares of each of its five main competitors'.[47] A similar approach had been taken by the Commission in *Vitamins I* when it noted that, with respect to various groups of Vitamins, Hoffmann-LaRoche's competitors had market shares from 'slightly more than half' to 'slightly less than one-quarter' of Hoffmann-LaRoche's share.[48]

Other factors that can be taken into account in the assessment of an undertaking's position include the stability of its market share, its product range, its overall financial situation and whether or not it forms part of a larger group of companies. These aspects may not only affect the way in which an undertaking is viewed by its competitors, but also its ability to compensate for losses. Such circumstances may contribute to an undertaking's position as an indispensable trading partner.

5.4 Barriers to entry and expansion

As has been indicated above, the market power of an undertaking does not depend solely on its market share. There are a variety of other factors that can be considered by the courts. One group of particular importance is that of the so-called barriers to entry and expansion. The term comprises a multitude of factors that can have negative effects on the competitive environment. This variety makes it difficult to define the concept. Nonetheless, today, it is understood that barriers to entry refer to costs 'which must be borne by a firm which seeks to enter the industry but [are] not borne by firms already in the industry'.[49] Thus, if there are high barriers to entry, an

---

[44] Commission Guidelines on market analysis and the assessment of significant market power under the Community regulatory framework for electronic communications networks and services, OJ No. C 165 of 11 July 2002, p. 6, para. 75.

[45] ECJ (25 October 1977), Case 26/76 – *Metro v Commission (Metro I)* [1977] ECR 1875, para. 17.

[46] ECJ (9 November 1983), Case 322/81 – *Michelin v Commission* [1983] ECR 3461, para. 35.

[47] GC (17 December 2003), Case T-219/99 – *British Airways v Commission* [2003] ECR II-5917, para. 211.

[48] Commission decision of 9 June 1976, Case IV/29.020 – *Vitamins*, OJ No. L 223 of 16 August 1976, p. 27, para. 5.

[49] Stigler, *The Organization of Industry* (University of Chicago Press, 1968), p. 67.

undertaking's market share will not usually have to be excessively high in order to prove a dominant position. Conversely, if there are no or very low barriers to entry, an undertaking's high market share is not necessarily meaningful. Economic, technical and legal difficulties in entering the market may impede the competitor in expanding his production or discourage potential competitors in providing effective competition to the dominant undertaking. It follows that the existence of barriers to entry is an important factor which always needs to be examined when applying Article 102 TFEU.[50]

In para. 17 of its Article 102 Guidance Paper the Commission has listed numerous situations which could limit or bar competitors' entry into a market. Even though the paper is not legally binding, the examples listed therein serve as a good basis for a general understanding of the concept. They include:

- **Legal barriers** – such as government concessions, patents, licences or other intellectual property rights.

  In *Decca Navigator System*[51] the Commission considered the market position of a provider of navigational aids for use at sea. The Decca Navigator System (DNS) was an international navigation system based on hyperbolic low-frequency waves which was invented at the end of the Second World War. The system consisted of land-based transmission stations that emitted positioning signals and portable receivers (in a way, it was similar to the satellite-based GPS system by which it was later replaced). Racal Decca, the company who had invented the system and emitted the signals, was also for a long time the only manufacturer of receivers. In addition, and due to frequency restrictions, it was also the only provider of DNS services in a number of European countries. When competing companies on the market for navigation systems tried to enter the market for receivers of DNS signals, Racal Decca started to make changes in the transmission so as to render the competitors' products useless. Later on, it concluded agreements with its competitors to allocate markets. The Commission, which eventually came to the conclusion that Racal Decca had infringed both Articles 101 and 102 TFEU, particularly stressed the fact that there were very high barriers to entry.[52] The frequencies used to emit DNS signals were conceded to Racal Decca by public authorities and it therefore had a monopoly on the market for such transmissions.

- **Capacity constraints** – large investment costs must be committed in order to enter the market/expand the production and those costs will not be recovered at market exit (e.g. the erection of a new production facility).

---

[50] The concept of barrier to entry as applied by the European courts is criticised as too broad by commentators, see Heit, 'The Justifiability of the ECJ's Wide Approach to the Concept of "Barriers to Entry"', *European Competition Law Review*, 27 (2006), 117.

[51] Commission decision of 21 December 1988, Case IV/ 30.979, 31.394 – *Decca Navigator System*, OJ No. L 43 of 15 February 1989, p. 27.

[52] Ibid., para. 92, 8.

In the decision that prohibited the acquisition of Aer Lingus by its main competitor Ryanair, the Commission noted that the resulting company would have had a dominant position on some fifty flight routes. In its assessment, the Commission put a special emphasis on the fact that some airports were simply not big enough to allow for new entrants as they were unable to provide a sufficient number of starting and landing slots. According to the Commission, these capacity constraints hindered any potential competitors from entering the market.[53]

- **Economies of scale** and scope – large-scale production may give the allegedly dominant undertaking an advantage over smaller actual and potential competitors as it can spread a one-time investment over a larger quantity of products, leading to lower average (per item) costs.

In 1988 the Commission issued a decision concerning the abuse of a dominant position by a manufacturer and seller of plasterboard in the United Kingdom. Plasterboard is used in the construction of ceilings and the lining of walls in housing and in commercial and administrative buildings. The undertaking in question, a traditional domestic company called BPB, had a 92–100% market share on the relevant market. This was due mostly to the fact that up until 1982 BPB was the only major plasterboard manufacturer in Great Britain and that there were no regular imports of plasterboard. When three European manufacturers entered the market for plasterboard, BPB adopted a variety of exclusionary practices including exclusive supply arrangements with distributors, special discounts and other measures to exclude imports. Obviously, BPB's immense market share was a major indicator of dominance. But the Commission also took into account that BPB enjoyed 'substantial economies in producing on a large scale'. The sheer quantity of plasterboard sold – BPB's sales amounted to more than 100 million m^2 compared to less than 4 million m^2 by the second biggest supplier – conferred on BPB a major advantage in terms of magnitude.[54]

- **Absolute cost advantages** – such as preferential access to essential facilities, natural resources, R&D or capital, for example, as a result of longstanding contractual relations.

Thus in *Soda-ash* the Commission investigated the pricing policy of Solvay, an international manufacturer of soda-ash. Soda-ash is a naturally occurring carbonate, but can also be produced synthetically. It is one of the important elements in the production of glass. In the market concerned, Solvay had a market share of approximately 70% which it tried to maintain by deploying a pricing strategy that made it largely unprofitable for its competitors to sell to Solvay's customers.

---

[53] Commission decision of 27 June 2007, Case Comp/M.4439 – *Ryanair/Aer Lingus*, available at http://ec.europa.eu/competition/mergers/cases/decisions/m4439_20070627_20610_en.pdf, paras. 672–700.

[54] Commission decision of 5 December 1988, Case IV/31.900 – *BPB Industries plc*, OJ No. L 10 of 13 January 1989, p. 50, para. 116, confirmed by GC (1 April 1993), Case T-65/89 – *BPB Industries and British Gypsum v Commission* [1993] ECR II-389.

Among other strategies, Solvay granted rebates to its customers that effectively augmented in relation not to the absolute quantity sold, but to the percentage of the customer's total demand. These rebates were mostly applied to 'marginal tonnage', i.e. a customer's purchases that exceeded the quantity envisaged in a previous supply contract. The prices for such 'additional supplies' were considerably lower than Solvay's average prices, but its competitors would have had to match these lower prices in order to win even part of the business. In establishing Solvay's dominance on the market for soda-ash, the Commission took into account a number of specific advantages that the undertaking had on the European market. For example, it considered Solvay's particular manufacturing strength, with plants in six different European countries, and the improbability of a new manufacturer entering the market.[55]

- **Privileged access to supply** – the allegedly dominant undertaking is vertically integrated and/or has control over supply of inputs required by (potential) competitors.

  In the above-mentioned plasterboard case, vertical integration was an additional factor in establishing dominance. BPB not only sold plasterboards, it also manufactured the base and intermediate products of gypsum and plaster. As BPB either owned or factually controlled all gypsum mines and quarries, any potential competitor wishing to manufacture plasterboard in the UK would have had to either import the raw materials or develop new mines.[56] In addition, BPB employed architects and engineers who ensured a constant link to building companies' distributors.

  In *United Brands* the ECJ noted that UBC was integrated to a very high degree: it owned large banana plantations in Central and South America, had its own fleet, managed wagons and lorries in the ports of delivery and largely controlled ripeners and distributors.[57]

- A **highly developed distribution and sales network** may confer commercial advantages over rivals of the dominant undertaking and may constitute an obstacle for potential competitors.

  The highly developed distribution network of an ice-cream manufacturer was a major issue in the *Van den Bergh* decision. The company, which was originally known as HB Ice Cream, was Ireland's principal manufacturer of ice-cream products, particularly of so-called 'impulse ice cream', i.e. single wrapped items that were designed for immediate consumption, where it had a market share of well over 75%. Impulse ice cream was almost always stored in freezers prominently

---

[55] Commission decision of 19 December 1990, Case IV/33.133-C – *Soda-ash – Solvay*, OJ No. L 152 of 15 June 1991, p. 21, para. 45.

[56] Commission decision of 5 December 1988, Case IV/31.900 – *BPB Industries plc*, OJ No. L 10 of 13 January 1989, p. 50, para. 45.

[57] ECJ (14 February 1978), Case 27/76 – *United Brands v Commission* [1978] ECR 207, paras. 71, 80.

positioned in or just outside the retailer's premises, for example, at garage fore-courts, kiosks and grocery stores. The freezers were generally made available to the retailers free of charge under the condition that they would only be used to store a certain manufacturer's products. Given the constraints of surface area typical for places where impulse ice cream was sold, once a manufacturer managed to install a freezer at a specific retail outlet, it was practically impossible for other manufacturers to sell ice cream at that specific retailer. HB Ice Cream was the only company that had a national distribution network and was therefore present in most retail outlets. Its strategy of exclusivity resulted in the exclusion of competitors and was tantamount to an abuse of its dominant position.[58]

- **The established position of the incumbent firms on the market** – market entry may prove difficult if specific experience or a good reputation is required to compete effectively. Customer loyalty, tight relationships between suppliers and customers and high costs of promotion and advertising may hinder market entry as well.

  In *Long-term contracts France* the Commission examined the market conduct of EDF, the incumbent operator in electricity markets in France. It came to the conclusion that EDF had maintained much of the near-monopoly it had prior to the liberalisation of the electricity markets. In particular, it found that EDF held a dominant position in the market for the supply of electricity to large industrial customers in France and that it had abused this position by, *inter alia*, concluding long-term contracts with large industrial customers which contained resale restrictions.[59] In its decision regarding the specific commitments imposed on EDF, the Commission referred to a number of barriers to entry including the regulatory framework, access to information on customers and EDF's vertical integration. In addition it placed a special emphasis on EDF's client portfolio and its established position with large industrial customers[60] which resulted from longstanding contractual relations.

- **Other strategic barriers** – situations where it is costly for customers to switch to another product, for example, because switching would require new investments or costly training for employees. This might be the case for example where a manufacturer's product is incompatible with those of its competitors or where a customer has concluded a long-term contract that is difficult to rescind. As a consequence, customers may be 'locked in' to a specific supplier because switching would not be economically viable.

---

[58] Commission decision of 11 March 1998, Case No IV/34.073, 34.395, 35.436 – *Van den Bergh Foods Limited*, OJ No. L 246 of 4 September 1998, p. 1, confirmed by GC (23 October 2003), Case 65/98 – *Van den Bergh Foods v Commission* [2003] ECR II-4653.

[59] Commission decision of 17 March 2010, Case COMP/39.386 – *Long-term contracts France*, available at http://ec.europa.eu/competition/antitrust/cases/dec_docs/39386/39386_1536_3.pdf, paras. 25–29.

[60] Ibid., paras. 26, 89.

Such a strategic barrier has been touched upon, for example, in the US Supreme Court's *Eastman Kodak*[61] decision. Eastman Kodak manufactured and sold photocopiers and related equipment. In addition, it sold services and replacement parts for all of its products. On this secondary (after-sales) market of servicing its machines Eastman Kodak competed with independent service organisations. The suit was commenced by a group of these independent service organisations claiming that Eastman Kodak would only sell replacement parts for their machines to customers who agreed not to buy repair services from independent service providers. The case is best known as an example for tying practices, but it also illustrates a manufacturer's strategic advantage in comparison with its competitors. Due do the initial investment in a photocopier from Eastman Kodak, purchasers were locked in as far as replacement parts and services were concerned. In the case at hand, this situation was intensified by the inability of independent service providers to provide original parts. However, the same would be true for other situations where an initial investment makes switching expensive.

5.5 Countervailing buyer power

As has been shown, the question of whether or not an undertaking has a dominant position depends largely on its position on the market, i.e. its market power, and on the structure of the market on which it does business, i.e. barriers to entry and expansion. Nonetheless, an undertaking's position which, based on these aspects, is likely to be dominant might still be offset by other factors, so-called 'countervailing powers'.[62]

The most important countervailing power is that of the undertaking's customers, also referred to as countervailing buyer power. As a result, a dominant position may not be assumed as long as the customers are able to influence the terms and conditions on which they acquire goods from allegedly dominant undertakings. In such cases the seller is unable to behave independently of its customers, which is one of the requirements set out in the *United Brands* test.[63] This might be the case for example where a single purchaser buys large percentages of a manufacturer's production.

In *Italian Flat-Glass*[64] the Commission had found that three glass manufacturers, in addition to fixing prices, had a collective dominant position in the Italian market for flat-glass used in the automotive industry. It asserted that

---

[61] US Supreme Court, *Eastman Kodak Co. v Image Technical Services, Inc.*, 504 US 451 (1992).

[62] For an appraisal of buyer power under the EU competition rules from an economic point of view, see Doyle and Inderst, 'Some Economics on the Treatment of Buyer Power in Antitrust', *European Competition Law Review*, 28 (2007), 210; Dobson and Inderst, 'Differential Buyer Power and the Waterbed Effect: Do Strong Buyers Benefit or Harm Consumers?', *European Competition Law Review*, 28 (2007), 393.

[63] ECJ (14 February 1978), Case 27/76 – *United Brands v Commission* [1978] ECR 207.

[64] Commission decision of 7 December 1988, Case IV/31.906 – *flat glass*, OJ No. L 33 of 4 February 1989, p. 44.

The business conduct of [the three manufacturers] constitutes an abuse of a collective dominant position, because it restricts the consumers' ability to choose sources of supply and limits the market outlets of the Community's other flat-glass producers. The conduct of the undertakings has involved methods other than those on which normal competition in products or services between economic operators is based, thus further weakening the degree of competition on a market in which, precisely because of the collective dominant position of these undertakings, the degree of competition is already reduced.[65]

The decision was subsequently annulled by the General Court[66] which held that, among other errors of assessment, the Commission had failed to take into account the specific situation on the market for flat-glass. It noted that the vast majority of the entire production of flat-glass was purchased by a single car manufacturer, namely Fiat, but that the Commission had not taken into account the countervailing effect that Fiat's position might have had:

It follows that, even supposing that the circumstances of the present case lend themselves to application of the concept of 'collective dominant position' (in the sense of a position of dominance held by a number of independent undertakings), the Commission has not adduced the necessary proof. The Commission has not even attempted to gather the information necessary to weigh up the economic power of the three producers against that of Fiat, which could cancel each other out.[67]

Thus, the purchasers' economic power must be weighed against the economic power of the allegedly dominant undertaking. On the other hand, the presence of potent purchasers may only offset an undertaking's otherwise dominant position if the purchaser's conduct not only serves its own interest, but also paves the way for a more competitive situation as a whole or, as the Commission puts it, 'strong buyers should not only protect themselves, but effectively protect the market'.[68]

5.6 Super-dominance

According to the ECJ's jurisprudence the scope of responsibility of a dominant undertaking depends on the degree of its dominance. Therefore some dominant companies have further-reaching obligations than other firms that also fall within the scope of Article 102 TFEU. For this reason a behaviour which in one case is

[65] Ibid., para. 80.
[66] GC (10 March 1992), Joined Cases T-68/89, T-77/89 and T-78/89 – *SIV and Others v Commission* [1991] ECR II-1403.
[67] Ibid., para. 366.
[68] Commission, DG Competition discussion paper on the application of Article 82 EC to exclusionary abuses, December 2005, available at: http://ec.europa.eu/competition/antitrust/art82/discpaper2005.pdf, para. 41.

deemed to be abusive may be legal in another situation as the special responsibility of each dominant undertaking has to be considered in the light of the individual circumstances.

In *DPAG – Interception of Cross-Border Mail*[69] the Commission's analysis centred around the conduct of Deutsche Post, the incumbent provider of postal services in Germany. Deutsche Post had intercepted large quantities of mass mailings that originated from the UK and that were supposed to be delivered to German addressees. The mailings were written in German, often referred to German products or stores and usually included reply envelopes with German addresses. On this basis, Deutsche Post argued that even though they were sent from the UK the material originated from Germany. This would have given Deutsche Post the right to claim full domestic postage for each of the mailings rather than a (significantly lower) 'terminal due' for the final delivery of cross-border mail. The terminal due system was installed by the Universal Postal Union to compensate national postal services for the delivery of cross-border mail. But Deutsche Post feared that the system was being used to circumvent its national tariffs. It alleged that the content of the mail was prepared in Germany and that it was sent from the UK only in order to mail it back to Germany (so-called virtual A-B-A remailing). In a first step of its analysis, the Commission (which ultimately rejected Deutsche Post's arguments and came to the conclusion that it had abused its dominant position) looked at the German market for postal services which, at the time, was liberalised only to a limited extent.

DPAG [Deutsche Post] has managed to keep approximately 99% of [the] total letter market turnover, despite the partial opening of this market. In practice, most senders of bulk mail have no alternative but to use the delivery services of DPAG. The Commission thus concludes that virtually all incoming cross border letter mail in Germany is forwarded and delivered by the incumbent.[70]

Deutsche Post's quasi-monopoly on the market for the forwarding and delivery of incoming cross-border mail led the Commission to the following statement:

An undertaking in a dominant position has a special responsibility not to allow its conduct to impair undistorted competition in the common market. The actual scope of the dominant firm's special responsibility must be considered in relation to the degree of dominance held by that firm and to the special characteristics of the market which may affect the competitive situation.[71]

In the assessment of the case, the Commission concluded that Deutsche Post therefore had a '*prima facie* obligation to ensure that [its] service is provided in a non-discriminatory manner'.[72] Thus, companies enjoying a position of dominance

---

[69] Commission decision of 25 July 2001, Case COMP/C-1/36.915 – *Deutsche Post AG – Interception of Cross-Border Mail*, OJ No. L 331 of 15 December 2001, p. 40.
[70] Ibid., para. 94.   [71] Ibid., para. 103.   [72] Ibid., para. 124.

coming close to a monopoly must be aware that the risk of being found to act contrary to Article 102 TFEU may be higher than in case of other 'regular' dominant undertakings.[73]

5.7 Application of Article 102 TFEU to small undertakings

Article 102 TFEU applies to every undertaking having a dominant position on a properly defined relevant market. The absolute size of the company is of no relevance. As a consequence, even a small firm can be found to have acted contrary to Article 102 TFEU. In any event, in order for Article 102 TFEU to apply, it is still necessary even for a small undertaking to have significant power on the market in question and that its conduct affects inter-state trade.

The General Court's decision in *Merci Convenzionali Porto di Genova*[74] illustrates just how narrowly a market may be defined: according to national law the unloading of goods in Italy's ports was reserved to specifically authorised unloading undertakings, prohibiting other companies as well as the ships' crews from performing this task. In the port of Genoa, the concessionaire was Merci Convenzionali. When a strike impeded the unloading of an incoming ship by this company, the owner demanded reimbursement of the charges it had paid and compensation for the damages it had suffered. The Italian court referred the dispute to the ECJ, because it questioned the compatibility of national law with the EU's competition policy, particularly Article 102 TFEU. In a rather short decision, the court considered the statutory monopoly conferred on Merci Convenzionali by the Italian authorities and defined the relevant market as 'that of the organization on behalf of third persons of dock work relating to ordinary freight in the Port of Genoa and the performance of such work'. Merci Convenzionali was the only company active in this market and it was its only business activity. But neither of these peculiarities prevented the ECJ from finding that the company had abused its dominant position on the market. Neither the size nor the limited economic strength of Merci Convenzionali was considered in the court's assessment.

A similar approach has also been taken by the Commission in other cases relating to ground handling services traditionally performed by airport operators.[75]

---

[73] See also GC (17 September 2007), Case T-201/04 – *Microsoft v Commission* [2007] ECR II-3601, para. 775; Commission decision of 3 July 2001, Case COMP/D3/38.044 – *NDC Health/IMS Health: Interim measures*, OJ No. L 59 of 28 February, p. 18, paras. 57–8.

[74] ECJ (10 December 1991), C-179/90 – *Merci Convenzionali Porto di Genova v Siderurgica Gabrielli* [1991] ECR I-5889.

[75] Commission decision of 14 January 1998, Case IV/34.801 – FAG – *Flughafen Frankfurt/Main AG*, OJ No. L 72 of 11 March 1998, p. 30; Commission decision of 11 June 1998, Case IV/35.613 – *Alpha Flight Services/ Aéroports de Paris*, OJ No. L 230 of 18 August, p. 10.

5.8 Collective dominance

Article 102 TFEU prohibits the abuse of a dominant position by one or more undertakings. The provision confirms that two or more undertakings may jointly hold a dominant position (duopoly/oligopoly). The primary requirement of a finding of collective dominance is the existence of a connection between the undertakings alleged to jointly infringe Article 102 TFEU.

Such a connection was referred to by the ECJ in its *Almelo* decision. The case concerned, *inter alia*, an electricity distributor's ability to unilaterally determine prices and impose conditions on its purchasers. The undertaking in question (IJM) was one of several regional electricity distributors in the Netherlands. Its contractual relations with the other regional electricity distributors and with its customers, the local providers of electricity, contained a number of purchase/sale restrictions which made it impossible for local suppliers to buy electricity from a different regional distributor. After its assessment under Article 101 TFEU the court went on to consider the question of whether the regional electricity providers might have abused a position of collective dominance. It observed that IJM did not have a dominant position of its own, but asserted that

a different assessment must apply where that undertaking belongs to a group of undertakings which collectively occupy a dominant position. However, in order for such a collective dominant position to exist, the undertakings in the group must be linked in such a way that they adopt the same conduct on the market.[76]

After a long-running discussion on the nature and content of this requirement[77] some precise guidance on the issue has been delivered by the General Court in its *Airtours* judgment.[78]

The case concerned the acquisition of First Choice by Airtours, both of which were active on the UK market for package holidays, i.e. packages of travel and accommodation. The Commission had prohibited the merger on the ground that it would create a collective dominance of three vertically integrated operators. It noted that the four largest integrated suppliers already had a market share of approximately 80% on the market and assumed that the merger would further strengthen this concentration. The General Court found the Commission's analysis to be insufficient, because it did not adequately consider the characteristics and the structure of the market and therefore drew incorrect conclusions with respect to the creation of collective dominance. The court annulled the Commission's decision and established

---

[76] ECJ (27 April 1994), Case C-393/92 – *Municipality of Almelo and others v NV Energiebedrijf Ijsselmij* [1994] ECR I-1477, paras. 41–2.

[77] See Bellamy and Child, *European Community Law of Competition* (Oxford University Press, 6th edn, 2008), pp. 940 et seq.

[78] GC (6 June 2002), Case T-342/99 – *Airtours v Commission* [2002] ECR II-2585.

a three-prong test that must be met in order to find that two or more undertakings collectively hold a dominant position:

(i) **Market transparency** –

each member of the dominant oligopoly must have the ability to know how the other members are behaving in order to monitor whether or not they are adopting the common policy. As the Commission specifically acknowledges, it is not enough for each member of the dominant oligopoly to be aware that interdependent market conduct is profitable for all of them but each member must also have a means of knowing whether the other operators are adopting the same strategy and whether they are maintaining it. There must, therefore, be sufficient market transparency for all members of the dominant oligopoly to be aware, sufficiently precisely and quickly, of the way in which the other members' market conduct is evolving.[79]

The Commission had argued, *inter alia*, that the market for short-haul flight packages was transparent because all tour operators based their capacity on the programmes of previous seasons and that there were only insignificant changes between two seasons. In addition it found that if there were substantial capacity additions, such circumstances could not be kept secret, as they would usually entail purchases or long-term leases of aircraft. After an analysis of the applicants' arguments the General Court considered that even though the total capacity might not vary significantly, there can still be immense changes within the subcategories of the market:

So, contrary to the Commission's contention, capacity decisions do not involve merely increasing or reducing overall capacity, without taking account of the differences between the various categories of package holidays, which are differentiated by destination, departure date, departure airport, aircraft model, type and quality of accommodation, length of stay and, finally, price. [...] It follows that, on the face of it, the complexity of the capacity planning procedure, the development of the product and its marketing is a major obstacle to any attempt at tacit coordination. [T]he Commission wrongly formed the view [...] that market transparency is high for the four major integrated operators [...].[80]

(ii) **Existence of credible retaliatory measures in order to prevent departure from common policy** –

the situation of tacit coordination must be sustainable over time, that is to say, there must be an incentive not to depart from the common policy on the market. As the Commission observes, it is only if all the members of the dominant oligopoly maintain the parallel conduct that all can benefit. The notion of retaliation in respect of conduct deviating from the common policy is thus inherent in this condition. In this instance, the parties concur that, for a situation of collective dominance to be viable, there must be adequate

---

[79] Ibid., para. 62.   [80] Ibid., paras. 167, 169, 180.

deterrents to ensure that there is a long-term incentive in not departing from the common policy, which means that each member of the dominant oligopoly must be aware that highly competitive action on its part designed to increase its market share would provoke identical action by the others, so that it would derive no benefit from its initiative.[81]

According to the Commission, if one tour operator significantly increased its capacity, the other operators could make use of various retaliatory instruments: the threat of a situation of oversupply; increasing their capacity during the selling season; increasing their capacity for the next season; and de-racking or directional selling during the selling season in order to force the operator which has broken ranks to sell a larger share of its holidays at discount prices. The General Court in turn took the view that the characteristics of the market made it very difficult for any of the tour operators to make effective use of such 'deterrents'. First, due to the limited market transparency, it would be difficult to detect capacity boosts. Secondly, increasing capacity for the same season is possible only to a very limited extent. Thirdly, all capacity increases bear major financial risks as it is highly unpredictable how demand evolves from one year to the next. In essence, the General Court rejected all of the Commission's arguments and concluded that 'the Commission erred in finding that the [mentioned factors] would [...] be a sufficient incentive for a member of the dominant oligopoly not to depart from the common policy'.[82]

(iii) **Inability of competitors and consumers to jeopardise advantages expected from the common policy** – 'to prove the existence of a collective dominant position to the requisite legal standard, the Commission must also establish that the foreseeable reaction of current and future competitors, as well as of consumers, would not jeopardise the results expected from the common policy'.[83]

In the *Airtours* setting there were several hundred smaller, secondary tour operators that competed with the four large undertakings. Nonetheless, the Commission was of the opinion that they would be unable to overcome a coordinated capacity restriction on the part of the oligopolists. In addition it declared that consumers had no buyer power and that they had difficulty in comparing competing products. The General Court performed a detailed assessment to refute these findings. it considered, for example, that as almost 60% of all package holidays were sold in agencies that were not controlled by any of the large tour operators, small operators would most likely take advantage of any situation of undersupply. It also found that for 85% of all customers, price was the single most important factor in choosing their holiday package and that there was ample consumer choice in neighbouring markets which led to major countervailing forces. In the end, the General Court declared:

---

[81] Ibid., para. 62.   [82] Ibid., para. 207.   [83] Ibid., para. 62.

In view of the foregoing observations, the Court concludes that the Commission's assessment of the foreseeable reaction of smaller tour operators, potential competitors, consumers and hotel-owners was incorrect and that it underestimated their reaction as a countervailing force capable of counteracting the creation of a collective dominant position.[84]

The *Airtours* test has later been endorsed by the ECJ when it decided on certain issues concerning the proposed merger of Bertelsmann and Sony. However, the court was reluctant to simply adopt the test. Rather, it noted that

[i]n applying those criteria, it is necessary to avoid a mechanical approach involving the separate verification of each of those criteria taken in isolation, while taking no account of the overall economic mechanism of a hypothetical tacit coordination.[85]

Summary of Section 5

Dominance describes a position of economic strength which enables an undertaking to behave to an appreciable extent independently of its competitors. In such a situation the market mechanism is not exercising its disciplining function on the market conduct of that undertaking and has to be complemented by legal rules to ensure effective competition. There are several indicators of market power, the most important being market share. Under EU case law, a market share above 50% is seen as justifying a presumption of dominance that can be rebutted in individual cases. Barriers to entry may reinforce market power by making market entry of rivals difficult. Low entry barriers may reduce the significance of market share since market entry of rivals is likely, for example, if the undertaking enjoying a high market share raises prices above a competitive level. Countervailing buyer power may also diminish the market power usually conferred by market share. Super-dominant undertakings with a market position close to monopoly may be subject to obligations in favour of their rivals that are even more extensive than for dominant undertakings with a lower degree of market power. The concept of dominance does not require a company to be very large to be in a dominant position in terms of absolute turnover. On a small relevant market an undertaking with a relatively low turnover may possess a dominant position. The question is rather whether such a market qualifies as a substantial part of the internal market which is likely to be found where there is a strong cross-border element in the respective conduct.

Under EU law there is no presumption of collective dominance if a small number of undertakings jointly exceed a certain market share. Collective dominance may occur

---

[84] Ibid., para. 277.
[85] ECJ (10 July 2008), Case 413/06 P – *Bertelsmann and Sony Corporation of America v Impala* [2008] ECR I-4951, para. 125.

in concentrated markets if there is a certain connection between the biggest market participants, which may exist where the market is transparent, retaliatory instruments are available and customers are unable to counterbalance the common policy of the collectively dominant undertakings.

6. SUBSTANTIAL PART OF THE INTERNAL MARKET

Article 102 TFEU applies only when the dominant position is held 'within the internal market or a substantial part of it'. Despite the fact that this requirement is mentioned in almost every Article 102 TFEU case, it is not entirely clear what needs to be established in order for a 'substantial part of the internal market' to be affected.

First, the geographical factors are not decisive. This fact has been established by the ECJ in *Suiker Unie*.[86] The case concerned the conduct of some of the largest European producers of sugar. While the decision primarily related to a cartel between the manufacturers, it also dealt with an abuse of dominance implemented by one of the companies. With regard to the market in question, the ECJ stated that:

For the purpose of determining whether a specific territory is large enough to amount to a 'substantial part of the common market' within the meaning of Article [102 TFEU] the pattern and the volume of the production and consumption of the said product as well as the habits and economic opportunities of the vendors and purchasers must be considered.[87]

It then gave a quick overview of the production of sugar within the market in question and its share with respect to the total production in the EU and declared that

these market shares are sufficiently large for the area [...] to be considered [...] as a substantial part of the common market in this product.[88]

Accordingly, the physical size of the geographical market alone is not necessarily the decisive factor in determining whether an undertaking's dominant position is held in a 'substantial part of the market'. Likewise, there are no clearly defined market share thresholds which would make it easier to assess the question of substantiality. The Commission and the European courts seem to apply a rather expansive interpretation of the concept.[89] This was demonstrated in the *Merci Convenzionali Porto di Genova*

---

[86] ECJ (16 December 1975), Joined Cases 40/73 to 48/73, 50/73, 54/73 to 56/73, 111/73, 113/73, 114/73 – *Suiker Unie v Commission* [1975] ECR 1663.

[87] Ibid., para. 371.   [88] Ibid., para. 375.

[89] See ECJ (26 November 1998), Case C-7/97 – *Oscar Bronner* [1998] ECR I-7791, paras. 32-3; ECJ (17 July 1997), Case C-242/95 – *GT-Link v De Danske Statsbaner* [1997] ECR I-4449, paras. 36 et seq.

case[90] where the Commission found that a single maritime port qualified as a 'substantial part of the market':

Regard being had in particular to the volume of traffic in that port and its importance in relation to maritime import and export operations as a whole in the Member State concerned, that market may be regarded as constituting a substantial part of the Common Market.[91]

In its Guidelines on the effect on trade concept, the Commission explicitly notes that in addition to ports, '[r]egions [and] airport[s] situated in a Member State may, depending on their importance, constitute a substantial part of the common market', but that 'it must be taken into account whether the infrastructure in question is used to provide cross-border services and, if so, to what extent'.[92]

Given the Commission's inclusive interpretation in such narrow markets, a market covering the territory of an entire Member State will almost always amount to a substantial part of the internal market.[93] As a result, the assessment of a dominant position is unlikely to fail because the undertaking's position is not related to a substantial part of the market.

Summary of Section 6

The concept of substantial part of the internal market is broadly interpreted. The key point is that EU competition law covers only conduct that has some nexus to the internal market. A relatively small market such as an airport may qualify as a substantial part of the internal market since it is of relevance for the performance of cross-border services and market integration. At the same time a bigger market may not qualify as substantial if conduct on that market has no impact on cross-border competition.

7. CONCEPT OF ABUSE

There is no clear-cut definition of 'abuse' within the meaning of Article 102 TFEU. The provision merely provides a non-exhaustive list of market practices that are deemed to be abusive. But Article 102 TFEU may also be applied to types of market conduct not specifically mentioned.

---

[90] ECJ (10 December 1991), Case C-179/90 – *Merci Convenzionali Porto di Genova v. Siderurgica Gabrielli* [1991] ECR I-5889.

[91] Ibid., para. 15.

[92] Commission Guidelines on the effect on trade concept contained in Articles 81 and 82 of the Treaty, OJ No. C 101 of 27 April 2004, p. 81.

[93] Commission decision of 17 March 2010, Case COMP/39.386 – *Long-term contracts France*, available at http://ec.europa.eu/competition/antitrust/cases/dec_docs/39386/39386_1536_3.pdf, para. 28 with reference to ECJ (09 November 1983), Case 322/81 – *Michelin v Commission* [1983] ECR 3461, paras. 25-8.

Although the Union courts have not provided a general definition of what constitutes an abuse of a dominant position the explanations delivered by the ECJ in the *Hoffmann-La Roche* case give some guidance with regard to the scope of Article 102 TFEU:

The concept of abuse is an objective concept relating to the behaviour of an undertaking in a dominant position which is such as to influence the structure of a market where, as a result of the very presence of the undertaking in question, the degree of competition is weakened and which, through recourse to methods different from those which condition normal competition in products or services on the basis of the transactions of commercial operators, has the effect of hindering the maintenance of the degree of competition still existing in the market or the growth of that competition.[94]

Accordingly, the purpose of Article 102 TFEU is to protect such competition as remains from being reduced by a dominant company. Actions of dominant companies will be measured under Article 102 TFEU by their effect on the market structure, i.e. by their effect on the ability of the remaining competitors on the markets to maintain or increase their market position.

It must be noted that since the adoption of the judgment the concept of abuse has been influenced by the Commission's 'more economic approach', a concept which was first applied in cartel and merger cases. With respect to Article 102 TFEU it focuses on the effect of the conduct in question and the corresponding consumer welfare goals of competition policy. Some of these goals have been explained by the Commission in its Article 102 Guidance Paper. The Commission tries to put more emphasis on the actual harm of a certain practice for consumer welfare.[95] For example, it has decided to reform its attitude towards exclusionary practices and to intervene only where 'the allegedly competitive conduct is likely to lead to anticompetitive foreclosure'.[96] As this approach requires a detailed economic analysis of each case, there seems to be little room for the application of *per se* rules under Article 102 TFEU.[97]

In line with this more consumer welfare oriented approach the Commission states in its Article 102 Guidance Paper:

---

[94] ECJ (13 February 1979), Case 85/76 – *Hoffmann-La Roche v Commission* [1979] ECR 461, para. 91.

[95] This has been welcomed as bringing in line the Commission's approach to Article 101 TFEU, merger control and Article 102 TFEU. At the same time it has been criticised as not compatible with case law that did not require a practice to harm consumers to be abusive. See Witt, 'The Commission's Guidance Paper on Abusive Exclusionary Conduct: More Radical than it Appears?', *European Law Review*, 35 (2010), 214.

[96] Article 102 Guidance Paper, para. 20.

[97] For reasons for which *per se* rules should be rejected see Whish and Bailey, *Competition Law*, pp. 199–200. The requirement of a detailed economic analysis is seen by commentators as creating legal uncertainty, see Witt, 'The Commission's Guidance Paper on Abusive Exclusionary Conduct', 214, 233.

The aim of the Commission's enforcement activity in relation to exclusionary conduct is to ensure that dominant undertakings do not impair effective competition by fore-closing their competitors in an anticompetitive way, thus having an adverse impact on consumer welfare, whether in the form of higher price levels than would have otherwise prevailed or in some other form such as limiting quality or reducing consumer choice.[98]

This understanding of the concept of abuse implies that the purpose of Article 102 TFEU is not only to ensure a competitive market structure by protecting the remaining competition from being eliminated by a dominant company but also to foster consumer welfare.[99] In consequence, to find an abuse of a dominant position, the Commission will have to establish not only an adverse effect on market structure but also an adverse effect on consumer welfare.[100]

It has to be noted that the mere existence of a dominant position does not amount to an abuse. In order to violate Article 102 TFEU a dominant under-taking has to engage in an activity that negatively affects market structure and consumer welfare and thus is abusive. Dominant undertakings have a special responsibility to avoid any behaviour that might have detrimental effects on competition and consumer welfare in the relevant market. The ECJ stated in this regard:

Therefore, whilst the finding that a dominant position exists does not in itself imply any reproach to the undertaking concerned, it has a special responsibility, irrespective of the causes of that position, not to allow its conduct to impair genuine undistorted competition on the common market.[101]

Summary of Section 7

There are several aspects to the concept of abuse. An abuse may consist in a behaviour that impairs effective competition from smaller rivals. Dominant under-takings have an obligation not to eliminate rivals by means resulting from their market power. An abuse may also consist in conduct directed at customers that the dominant company could not afford under conditions of effective competition. The concept of abuse is an objective concept. The intentions of the dominant company do not have to be established to find an abuse.

---

[98] Article 102 Guidance Paper, para. 19.

[99] Commentators hold that evaluating the change in consumer welfare in each individual case will, however, give rise to significant economic and legal issues. See Schmidt, 'The Suitability of the More Economic Approach for Competition Policy: Dynamic v Static Efficiency', *European Competition Law Review*, 28 (2007), 408.

[100] On the burden of proof with regard to consumer welfare, see Nazzini, 'The Wood Began to Move: An Essay on Consumer Welfare, Evidence and Burden of Proof in Article 82 EC Cases', *European Law Review*, 31 (2006), 518.

[101] ECJ (9 November 1983), Case 322/81 – *Michelin v Commission* [1983] ECR 3461, para. 57.

8. DEFENCES

Article 102 TFEU, contrary to Article 101(3) TFEU, does not provide for a legislative framework for an exemption from the prohibition on abusing a dominant position. However, the Commission and the European courts have accepted a number of objective justifications for conduct of a dominant undertaking that at first sight appears to be abusive. Some of these justifications have developed into constant lines of jurisprudence such as the meeting competition defence. Other objective justifications are more case-specific and have not developed into a constant concept.[102]

8.1 Meeting competition defence

Dominant companies have an obligation not to eliminate by abusive practices such competition as remains. At the same time, markets on which a dominant company operates are intended to be efficient in the sense that dominant companies do not have an obligation to protect inefficient competitors. The meeting competition defence contributes to striking this balance of protecting the competitors of dominant companies and promoting efficiency also in markets where one company is dominant.[103]

The meeting competition defence refers to a line of jurisprudence in which the Union courts considered that defending one's own commercial and economic interests in the face of action taken by certain competitors may be a legitimate aim even for a dominant undertaking.[104] For example, a dominant operator is not prohibited from aligning its prices with those of competitors. The dominant operator must not, however, undercut prices of its competitors in an effort to deprive a smaller company of business. Moreover, the meeting competition defence will only apply if it is shown that the response is suitable, indispensable and proportionate.[105] It has to be noted

---

[102] They reflect that the Commission has to consider the counterfactual situation in each individual case. See Sinclair, 'Counterfactuals in Anticompetitive Contracts and Abuse of Dominance Cases under Articles 101 and 102 TFEU', *European Competition Law Review*, 31 (2010), 509.

[103] The meeting competition defence is one aspect of the consideration that dominant undertakings are allowed to compete on the merits by using methods of 'normal' competition. See Metikopoulou, 'DG Competition's Discussion Paper on the Application of Article 82 EC to Exclusionary Abuses: The Proposed Economic Reform from a Legal Point of View', *European Competition Law Review*, 28 (2007), 241.

[104] Under the US Robinson–Patman Act there is also a meeting competition defence. The Act allows price discrimination where it is used to meet competition from other firms. See Monti, *EC Competition Law*, p. 205. On the origins of the meeting competition defence under EU law see Gravengaard, 'The Meeting Competition Defence Principle: A Defence for Price Discrimination and Predatory Pricing?', *European Competition Law Review*, 27 (2006), 658.

[105] ECJ (14 February 1978), Case 27/76 – *United Brands v Commission* [1978] ECR 207, paras 189–91; GC (1 April 1993), Case T-65/89 – *BPB Industries Plc and British Gypsum Ltd v Commission* [1993] ECR II-39, para. 69; GC (7 October 1999), Case T-228/97 – *Irish Sugar v Commission* [1999] ECR II-2969, para. 112.

that the European courts have made reference to the meeting competition defence in general terms in several judgments but that so far the defence has not been successfully invoked by a party in any decided case. In the *United Brands* case, the banana supplier UBC had stopped supplying a distributor in Denmark which had participated in advertising campaigns for competing banana brands and had become the exclusive distributors for one such brand. UBC invoked the meeting competition defence in the action for annulment of the Commission's decision which found a violation of Article 102 TFEU. The ECJ recognised the concept of the meeting competition defence but held that a refusal to supply an existing customer was not a suitable response to efforts of a competitor to increase sales through common distributors.[106]

In one rather specific case the ECJ discussed the meeting competition defence in relation to behaviour of collectively dominant companies. Thus in the *Atlantic Container Line* case major container shipping lines which operated on the trans-Atlantic routes had entered into a number of agreements which were reviewed by the Commission under Articles 101 and 102 TFEU. The Commission found two measures taken jointly by the shipping lines to have violated Article 102 TFEU: an agreement to place restrictions on the availability and content of service contracts and an agreement altering the remuneration of freight forwarders and thus affecting the competitive structure of the market. The shipping companies maintained that those restrictions of competition were necessary to protect themselves against competition from shipping lines operating under a different legal regime (certain US provisions), making it impossible to compete with them in an uncoordinated way. The Commission rejected those arguments and found the shipping companies' self-protection went against competition rules. Upon appeal the General Court again recognised the meeting competition defence in general terms. It held that the meeting competition defence allows an undertaking involved in allegedly abusive practices to show that

the purpose of those [abusive] practices is reasonably to protect its commercial interests in the face of action taken by certain third parties and that they do not therefore in fact constitute an abuse.[107]

However, the court followed the Commission in finding that the practices in question did not meet these standards but clearly aimed at imposing unfair trading conditions on the customers of the shipping lines.

In conclusion, the meeting competition defence so far has been a rather theoretical defence that has never been successfully invoked.[108]

---

[106] ECJ (14 February 1978), Case 27/76 – *United Brands v Commission* [1978] ECR 207, paras. 189–91.

[107] GC (30 September 2003), Joined Cases T-191/98, T-212/98 to T-214/98 – *Atlantic Container Line and Others v Commission* [2003] ECR II-3275, para. 1114.

[108] On the risks involved for dominant undertakings in reprisals see Temple Lang, 'Reprisals and Overreaction by Dominant Companies as an Anticompetitive Abuse under Article 82(b)', *European Competition Law Review*, 29 (2008), 11.

8.2 Efficiency defence

The efficiency defence is not expressly referred to in the case law of the European courts. The concept encompasses conduct of a dominant undertaking that restricts competition to the detriment of its competitors but is justified by efficiencies that outweigh its negative effects.[109] This line of reasoning can be found in a number of judgments. The *Gøttrup-Klim* case[110] may serve as an example. In this reference for a preliminary ruling a Danish court had raised the question whether an agricultural cooperative purchasing association that was dominant on a number of markets violated Article 102 TFEU when it changed its statutes in a way that prohibited its members from also purchasing through other cooperatives. The purpose of purchasing cooperatives in the agricultural sector was to bundle the (relatively small) purchases of the individual members into larger orders and to achieve better prices and conditions for the members. In this sense the purchasing cooperative generated efficiencies to the benefit of its members. If a member of the cooperative simultaneously had become a member of another cooperative and had channelled part of its purchases through that other cooperative, the order volume of the first cooperative would have decreased and all members would have obtained less favourable conditions. The membership in another cooperative consequently jeopardised the efficiencies created by collective purchasing through a dilution of buyer power. In its judgment the ECJ held that the efficiencies created by a purchasing cooperative outweigh the restrictions of competition that result from a change of the articles of association of the cooperative which prohibits members from becoming a member of a competing cooperative. Accordingly, the ECJ found the change of the articles of association not to violate Article 102 TFEU:

> The answer to the third set of questions referred by the national court must therefore be that even if a cooperative purchasing association holds a dominant position on a given market, an amendment of its statutes prohibiting its members from participating in other forms of organized cooperation which are in direct competition with it does not constitute an abuse of a dominant position contrary to Article 86 of the Treaty [Article 102 TFEU], so long as the abovementioned provision is limited to what is necessary to ensure that the cooperative functions properly and maintains its contractual power in relation to producers.[111]

In its Article 102 Guidance Paper the Commission set out the concept of an efficiency defence that has many similarities with the criteria for an exemption from the cartel prohibition under Article 101(3) TFEU. It comprises the following cumulative

---

[109] For an economic discussion of the efficiency defence see Monti, *EC Competition Law*, p. 208.

[110] ECJ (15 December 1994), Case C-250/92 – *Gøttrup-Klim and Others Grovvareforeninger v Dansk Landbrugs Grovvareselskab* [1994] ECR I-5641.

[111] Ibid., para. 52.

elements for the justification of conduct of a dominant undertaking that would otherwise be considered abusive:[112]

(i)   the efficiencies such as technical improvement or reduction in the cost of production have been or are likely to be realised as a result of the conduct;

(ii) the conduct is indispensable to the realisation of the above-mentioned efficiencies;

(iii) the likely efficiencies outweigh any negative effect on competition or consumer welfare;

(iv) the conduct does not eliminate effective competition by removing all or most existing sources of actual or potential competition.[113]

It has to be noted, however, that the parties to the TFEU and the predecessor treaties have refrained from including a framework for exemption in the treaty provision prohibiting the abuse of a dominant position. Any efficiencies created by the behaviour of dominant companies can be taken into consideration only for the assessment whether the relevant behaviour is abusive. Under the Treaty there is no possibility of justifying abusive behaviour of dominant companies by accepting that they are abusive but claiming that they still merit an exemption from the prohibition of Article 102 TFEU. There is no legal basis for such exemption. The Commission's Article 102 Guidance Paper just sets out the Commission's enforcement priorities in the area of exclusionary conduct but does not amount to a basis to grant exemptions from a Treaty provision.

8.3 Objective justification

Article 102 TFEU is open for objective justifications of allegedly abusive behaviour. In its decisional practice the Commission has accepted very diverse objective justifications for behaviour of a dominant company that has a restrictive effect on competition.[114]

In an early case it was accepted that a supplier treats its contractual customers more favourably than occasional customers in a situation of shortage.[115] A company from the Netherlands during the oil crisis of 1973/1974, when oil-producing countries had dramatically reduced production, complained that subsidiaries of BP had

---

[112] Commentators have argued that the efficiency defence has no basis in the case law of the EU courts and therefore is incompatible with the EU competition rules. See Dreher and Adam, 'Abuse of Dominance under Reform: Sound Economics and Established Case Law', *European Competition Law Review*, 28 (2007), 278.

[113] Article 102 Guidance Paper, para. 30.

[114] For an overview of the various types of objective justifications accepted in the case law, see Albors-Llorens, 'The Role of Objective Justification and Efficiencies in the Application of Article 82 EC', *Common Market Law Review*, 44 (2007), 1727, 1736.

[115] ECJ (29 June 1978), Case 77/77 – *B.P. v Commission* [1978] ECR 1514.

not delivered to it the entire quantity of oil it had ordered and that other customers had received a higher share of their orders. The Dutch company took the view that this constituted a violation of Article 102 TFEU in the form of discrimination.

The Commission had established that the Dutch company had already reduced its purchases from BP prior to the crisis and had been an occasional customer since. During the oil crisis BP was not able to supply to all customers the quantities of oil they had ordered. BP therefore decided to reduce all deliveries by a certain percentage. Deliveries to contractual customers were reduced less than deliveries to occasional customers.

The Commission accused BP in its decision of having abused its dominant position by reducing its supplies to the Dutch complainant substantially and proportionately to a much greater extent than in relation to all its other customers and of having been unable to provide any objective reasons for its behaviour.

The ECJ annulled the decision and held that since the Dutch company's position in relation to BP had been that of an occasional customer several months before the crisis occurred, BP had objective reasons to reduce deliveries to a greater extent than to contractual customers. Otherwise, BP would not have been able to meet its contractual obligations even to a larger extent. The distinction between contractual long-term customers and occasional customers was accepted as an objective justification for a different treatment.[116]

In the *General Motors* case[117] the ECJ accepted very specific reasons as an objective justification for allegedly excessive prices. The circumstances were that the Belgian subsidiary of General Motors had charged a fee for the inspection for conformity of motor vehicles manufactured in another Member State. Under the applicable legal provisions the manufacturer of a motor vehicle had to confirm conformity of motor vehicles manufactured in another Member State with the specifications contained in the approval certificate prescribed by the Belgian authorities. According to the Commission the fee charged for this inspection was excessive in relation to its economic value. A dominant position was attributed to General Motors since this company was the only one empowered by Belgian law to confirm conformity of General Motors cars. The Commission therefore found an abuse of a dominant position under Article 102 TFEU.

The ECJ did not concur with the Commission on the abusive nature of the fees charged for the inspection. The ECJ accepted the argument that the conformity inspections represented an unusual activity on the part of General Motors since such inspections had previously been carried out by state testing-stations. Previously, the inspections only constituted an occasional activity of minute importance in relation to the inspections normally carried out on the vehicles which are put

---

[116] Ibid., para. 32.
[117] ECJ (13 November 1975), Case 26/75 – *General Motors Continental NV v Commission* [1975] ECR 1367.

directly on the market and which are manufactured in accordance with Belgian standards. General Motors applied the charge which was until then normal for the inspection of the vehicles which it imported. The ECJ accepted the only recent entrustment of the conformity inspections to General Motors and the extraordinary nature of the inspections as an objective justification for the allegedly excessive prices.[118] It may have contributed to this assessment by the court that General Motors reduced prices substantially following the Commission's intervention.

This illustrates that it is important for an undertaking to show that the anticompetitive behaviour it has applied was in fact justified by reasons other than the (subjective) interests of the dominant undertaking.

Summary of Section 8

Article 102 TFEU does not provide for a framework for exemption such as Article 101 (3) TFEU. Nonetheless, conduct will not be considered abusive if it is justified by objective reasons. A dominant undertaking is free to compete on the merits and to react to market action taken by its smaller rivals by appropriate means under the meeting competition defence. There may be case-specific reasons for the behaviour of a dominant company other than to restrict competition. The Commission has suggested a framework for an efficiency defence that is similar to the framework of Article 101(3) TFEU and under which efficiency gains and losses of consumer welfare would be balanced.

9. EXPLOITATIVE ABUSES

Article 102 TFEU applies to exploitative practices such as the imposition of unfair purchase or selling prices or other unfair trading conditions. Generally speaking, each abuse of a dominant position may be classified as exploitative if monopoly profits are earned at the expense and to the detriment of other market participants.

9.1 Excessive pricing

The scope of Article 102(2)(a) TFEU encompasses situations where the prices offered to consumers are excessively high. It is not required that the market conduct of the dominant undertaking has negative effects on the market structure and competitors. Economic advantages for the dominant company resulting from the prohibited practice do not have to be demonstrated either. It has to be proved that consumer

---

[118] Ibid., para. 18.

welfare is affected. In its leading case on excessive pricing (the *United Brands* case discussed above) the ECJ stated that, *inter alia*:

charging a price which is excessive because it has no reasonable relation to the economic value of the product supplied is [...] an abuse.[119]

In the same case the ECJ introduced a two-stage test for determining whether a price is reasonable and sufficiently related to the economic value of the supplied product.

- First, the court requires a comparison of actual costs and prices. At this stage it has to be investigated whether the difference between the costs actually incurred by the dominant undertaking and the prices actually charged is excessive. Where a detailed costs analysis may prove difficult, e.g. because of a large scale of operation or a broad range of products supplied, alternative benchmarks such as costs of comparable goods or services may be applied. Excessive or disproportionate costs should however not be taken into account at this stage.
- Second, it has to be determined whether the price is excessive in itself or by comparison to competitors' products and services.

In the *United Brands* case the court indicated that price differences of 100% between Member States and price differences between branded and unbranded bananas of 30–40% could be excessive. However, the court found that the Commission had failed to establish the costs incurred by United Brands sufficiently and to put the prices into relation with costs.[120]

It is questionable whether the difference between costs and prices is a reliable indicator of excessive pricing. The court's concept of excessive pricing rests on the assumption that prices are primarily cost-driven. However, in many industries prices are rather market-driven. This means that prices may deviate substantially from the costs depending on the market situation. Airline tickets, for instance, for the same flight connection may be sold at widely varying prices depending on the time of the booking, the number of available alternatives and other factors. Some tickets may be sold at prices slightly above costs while others are sold far above costs. From an economic point of view the court's reasoning therefore appears overly simplistic. The ECJ has sought to remedy this problem of its initial concept of excessive pricing in later judgments.

The background facts in *Bodson*[121] were that a single company held exclusive concessions of many communes in France for the performance of particular services related to funerals. A competitor started to offer similar services in those communes, which gave rise to a legal dispute resulting in a referral to the ECJ for a preliminary ruling.

---

[119] ECJ (14 February 1978), Case 27/76 – *United Brands v Commission* [1978] ECR 207, para. 250.
[120] Ibid., para. 254.
[121] ECJ (4 May 1998), Case 30/87 – *Corinne Bodson v Pompes Funèbres des régions libérées* [1988] ECR 2479.

In its judgment in *Bodson* the court applied a method referred to as 'yardstick competition'. Its basic concept is not to compare prices of the dominant undertaking with costs but to compare the prices of the dominant undertaking with prices charged by other suitable suppliers of the respective goods or services. In the words of the court:

The French Government and PFRL have denied that the prices charged by the subsidiaries of Pompes Funèbres Générales are unfair. The documents before the Court do not contain any information enabling that problem to be resolved. Since over 30,000 communes in France have not granted to an undertaking the concession to provide 'external services' for funerals, but have left that service unregulated or operate it themselves, it must be possible to make a comparison between the prices charged by the group of undertakings which hold concessions and prices charged elsewhere. Such a comparison could provide a basis for assessing whether or not the prices charged by the concession holders are fair.[122]

9.2 Unfair trading conditions

Exploitative practices may also have the form of unfair trading conditions. Dominant undertakings are not allowed to put into agreements with their suppliers or purchasers clauses designated to restrict economic freedom of their business partners.

According to the ECJ the fact that a particular clause is widely recognised and used in the industry may not serve as a justification for an abusive practice:

conduct cannot cease to be abusive merely because it is the standard practice in a particular sector; to hold otherwise would deprive Article 82 [Article 102 TFEU] of the Treaty of any effect.[123]

The case law on abusive trading conditions is very diverse. The following categories of abusive trading conditions have been identified by commentators:[124]

- restrictions on export of goods;
- restrictions on resale of goods;
- restrictions on the freedom to innovate;
- restrictions on the provision of guarantees;
- restrictive terms of a licence of intellectual property rights.

These categories largely coincide with practices excluded from the Vertical Block Exemption or the Technology Transfer Block Exemption. Practices that may be permissible up to the respective market share threshold may be abusive if applied by a dominant undertaking.

---

[122] Ibid., para 31.

[123] GC (30 September 2003), Joined Cases T-191/98 and T-212/98 to T-214/98 – *Atlantic Container Line and Others v Commission* [2003] ECR II-3257, para. 1124.

[124] See O'Donoghue and Padilla, *The Law and Economics of Article 82 EC* (Hart Publishing, 2006), pp. 648 et seq.

Summary of Section 9

Exploitative abuses are directed against the customers of dominant undertakings. Due to the market power of such undertakings their customers have only limited possibilities to evade exploitation. This may enable dominant undertakings to charge prices that are excessive in relation to the prices charged by them in other territories or that strongly deviate from industry benchmarks. Market power may also enable dominant undertakings to impose other unfair trading conditions on their customers such as restrictions on the resale of goods or overly restrictive terms of an intellectual property rights licence.

10. EXCLUSIONARY ABUSES

Another category of practices covered by Article 102 TFEU are exclusionary abuses. Pursuant to Article 102(2)(b) TFEU it is illegal to limit production, markets or technical development to the prejudice of consumers. Exclusionary conduct makes the products offered by competitors less attractive or less available by limiting their competitors' competitive chances.

A comprehensive framework for the assessment of exclusionary practices has been provided by the Commission in its Article 102 Guidance Paper. According to this document the presence of foreclosure effects shall play a central role in the assessment of individual cases. Foreclosure effects are defined in the document as:

a situation where effective access of actual or potential competitors to supplies or markets is hampered or eliminated as a result of the conduct of the dominant undertaking whereby the dominant undertaking is likely to be in a position to profitably increase prices to the detriment of consumers.[125]

Several types of exclusionary conduct are discussed in the Article 102 Guidance Paper. The Commission's approach reflects its previous decisional practice and the jurisprudence of the EU courts. In this sense the document represents also a compendium of the case law on exclusionary practices. A selection of abusive practices is discussed below.

10.1 Tying and bundling

Tying and bundling may expand the market power of a dominant undertaking to markets on which it is not dominant. This will have detrimental effects for competitors in those markets and thus may be considered abusive.

---

[125] Article 102 Guidance Paper, para. 19.

10.1.1 Definitions

Tying and bundling are very similar economic concepts referring to the combined sale of more than one product. A distinction between the following variants has to be drawn:

- **Tying** refers to a situation where customers purchasing one product (tying product) have to purchase another product from the dominant undertaking (tied product). In the *Microsoft* case[126] the software company has been found to infringe Article 102 TFEU by selling its Windows operating system together with the Windows Media Player. There was no option to buy the Windows operating system without the Windows Media Player.[127]

  The products may be tied physically (technological tie) or through a contract stipulating joint sale (contractual tie).
- **Bundling** – is a joint sale of different products in fixed proportions.
- **Pure bundling** – products are sold jointly and none of them may be purchased separately. They are also always offered in fixed proportions.
- **Mixed bundling** – products may be sold either as a package or individually. However, the price for the package is lower than the sum of the individual prices.

10.1.2 Legal test

As the wording of Article 102(2)(d) TFEU suggests, tying or bundling refers to a situation where two distinct products are sold together that have no connection 'by their nature or according to commercial usage'. According to the Commission it is, however, not required that the products belong to different product markets.[128]

In the *Hilti* case[129] the appellant claimed that the allegedly tied products – nail guns and nails – did not represent two distinct products but only one product, a 'PAF' or 'powder actuated fastening system'. This argument was rejected by the General Court since it would give the dominant undertaking the possibility to prevent any other company from offering consumables for nail guns by claiming that nail guns and nails represent a single indivisible product.[130] If buyers tend to buy the two products separately in the absence of the tying or bundling practice, this is a strong indication of distinct products.

---

[126] GC (17 September 2007), Case T-201/04 – *Microsoft v Commission* [2007] ECR II-3601.

[127] For a detailed discussion of the *Microsoft* cases see Petit and Neyrinck, 'Back to Microsoft I and II: Tying and the Art of Secret Magic', *Journal of European Competition Law and Practice*, 2 (2011), 117; Hobbelen and Jablan, 'Presentational Issues in the Microsoft II Case: Fair Chance for All Browsers or a European Commission Imposed Advantage for Existing Market Players?', *European Competition Law Review*, 32 (2011), 206; Baudenbacher, 'The CFI's Microsoft Judgment: Three Seconds that Changed the IT World', *European Law Review*, 32 (2007), 342; Finbank, 'A Landmark Judgment: The Commission's Long Awaited Victory in the Microsoft Case', *European Law Review*, 32 (2007), 443.

[128] Article 102 Guidance Paper, para. 51.

[129] GC (12 December 1991), Case T-30/89 – *Hilti v Commission* [1991] ECR II-1441.   [130] Ibid., para. 68.

The tying of certain devices and the consumables to be used in those devices is a frequent occurrence in various industries and the subject of a number of judgments of the EU courts. In the *Tetra Pak II* case[131] a manufacturer of packaging machines for beverages had put customers under an obligation to source the packaging material used in the machines exclusively from him. The General Court did not exclude that tying may be justified by objective reasons in individual cases, for example where the proper functioning of a machine requires the use of specific consumables, but did not find these criteria to be met in the case to be decided. The court rather held that Tetra Pak could as well disclose the technical requirements for the consumables to its customers and leave it to them to find a source of supply matching these requirements.[132]

The court in this judgment also made a noteworthy statement on the justifying effect of the concept of commercial usage under Article 102(2)(d) TFEU:

A usage which is acceptable in a normal situation, on a competitive market, cannot be accepted in the case of a market where competition is already restricted.[133]

This statement suggests that there are limits to the justifying force of commercial usage when invoked by a dominant undertaking. However, the wording of Article 102(2)(d) TFEU does not suggest that dominant companies are barred from selling products together if this corresponds with commercial usage. To the contrary, Article 102(2)(d) TFEU is specifically addressed to dominant undertakings and has to be understood as excluding an abuse if the sale of two products together is in conformity with commercial usage. The court's statement therefore appears to go beyond the boundaries of its power to interpret the Treaty.

10.2 Rebates

Rebates can be relevant under Article 102 TFEU in two different ways: Rebates may create foreclosure effects and thus limit 'production, markets or technical development to the prejudice of consumers' in the sense of Article 102(2)(b) TFEU since competitors of a dominant undertaking may find it difficult to sell their products due to the rebates granted by the dominant undertaking. Rebates may also result in the application of 'dissimilar conditions to equivalent transactions with other trading parties, thereby placing them at a competitive disadvantage' in the sense of Article 102(2)(c) TFEU where they are applied in a discriminatory manner.[134] Nonetheless, rebates are also open to objective justifications such as cost savings. These different types of rebates will be discussed below.

---

[131] GC (6 October 1994), Case T-83/91 – *Tetra Pak v Commission* [1994] ECR II-755.   [132] Ibid., para. 138.
[133] Ibid., para. 137.
[134] On the different interpretation of this aspect of rebates by EU and English courts, see Webb, 'Different Views on Discrimination', *European Competition Law Review*, 28 (2007), 620.

10.2.1 Loyalty-inducing rebates

Rebates may give customers incentives to purchase their entire requirements for a particular product from one supplier. If that supplier is dominant and thus a large proportion of the customers are supplied by him on an exclusive basis, competitors will find it difficult to sell their products. Rebates aiming at de facto exclusivity are also referred to as loyalty-inducing rebates or fidelity rebates since they give customers incentives to be loyal to the dominant supplier. It has to be noted that such rebates are problematic under the competition rules only if applied by a dominant undertaking. Other undertakings are free in their rebate policies.

The ECJ had to assess the rebate schemes of dominant undertakings on several occasions. In the *Hoffmann-La Roche* case[135] a dominant manufacturer of vitamins had concluded 'fidelity agreements' with customers which provided that the customers obtain from the manufacturer all or most of their vitamin requirements and that the manufacturer paid a rebate every year or every six months calculated on total purchases by those customers who had obtained all or most of their requirements from the manufacturer. The rebates varied between the customers. The court made some very clear statements on the assessment of such rebates under Article 102 TFEU:

The fidelity rebate, unlike quantity rebates exclusively linked with the volume of purchases from the producer concerned, is designed through the grant of a financial advantage to prevent customers from obtaining their supplies from competing producers.

Furthermore the effect of fidelity rebates is to apply dissimilar conditions to equivalent transactions with other trading parties in that two purchasers pay a different price for the same quantity of the same product depending on whether they obtain their supplies exclusively from the undertaking in a dominant position or have several sources of supply.[136]

The statements do not only set out what the detrimental effects of fidelity rebates on the competitors and customers of a dominant undertaking may be but also indicate that dominant undertakings may grant rebates that are justified by cost savings such as volume rebates that reflect reduced transaction costs.

In the *Irish Sugar* judgment the General Court added another point to the analysis of fidelity rebates:

[it is necessary] to appraise all the circumstances, and in particular the criteria and detailed rules for granting rebates, and determine whether there is any tendency, through an advantage not justified by any economic service, to remove or restrict the buyer's choice as to his sources of supply, to block competitors' access to the market, to apply dissimilar conditions to equivalent transactions with other trading parties, or to reinforce the dominant position by distorting competition.[137]

---

[135] ECJ (13 February 1979), Case 85/76 – *Hoffmann-La Roche v Commission* [1979] ECR 461.
[136] Ibid., para. 90.
[137] GC (7 October 1999), Case T-228/97 – *Irish Sugar v Commission* [1999] ECR II-2969, para. 197.

This statement reflects that a practice can be abusive also if it limits the economic freedom of the counterpart of a dominant undertaking such as the freedom to choose sources of supply. Fidelity rebates may have that effect.

10.2.2 Target rebates

Target rebates function in a similar way to fidelity rebates. They can be used as another instrument to achieve de facto exclusivity. The dominant undertaking will agree with its customers on sales targets to be reached in certain periods of time. If the customer reaches the target, a rebate will be granted. Some rebate schemes will only reward any incremental quantities, i.e. a rebate will be granted on the quantities that exceed the sales target. The sales target may be fixed in such a way that it covers a large part or all of the customer's estimated requirements. However, it may have detrimental effects as well if it covers a smaller proportion of the customer's purchases.

In the scenario underlying the *British Airways* case[138] British Airways concluded agreements with travel agents which included not only a basic commission system for sales by those agents of tickets on British Airways flights ('BA tickets') but also three distinct systems of financial incentives: 'marketing agreements', 'global agreements' and, subsequently, a 'performance reward scheme'.

The marketing agreements enabled certain travel agents to receive payments in addition to their basic commission, in particular a performance reward calculated on a sliding scale, based on the extent to which a travel agent increased the value of its sales of BA tickets, and subject to the agents increasing its sales of such tickets from one year to the next.

The second type of incentive agreements, known as global agreements, was concluded with three travel agents, entitling them to receive additional commissions calculated by reference to the growth of BA's share in their worldwide sales.

Under the third system, the basic commission rate was reduced for all BA tickets but each agent could earn an additional commission. The size of the additional variable element depended on the travel agents' performance in selling BA tickets. The agents' performance was measured by comparing the total revenue arising from the sales of BA tickets issued by an agent in a particular calendar month with that achieved during the corresponding month in the previous year.

The ECJ in its judgment set out two general criteria for the assessment of rebate schemes of dominant undertakings under Article 102 TFEU that do not fall into the category of fidelity rebates discussed in the *Hoffmann-La Roche* case:

It first has to be determined whether those discounts or bonuses can produce an exclusionary effect, that is to say whether they are capable, first, of making market entry very difficult or impossible for competitors of the undertaking in a dominant position and, secondly, of

---

[138] ECJ (15 March 2007), Case C-95/04 P – *British Airways v Commission* [2007] ECR I-2331.

making it more difficult or impossible for its co-contractors to choose between various sources of supply or commercial partners.

It then needs to be examined whether there is an objective economic justification for the discounts and bonuses granted.[139]

Referring to its earlier *Michelin* judgment[140] the court confirmed that goal-related rebates are capable of having such an exclusionary effect since attainment of the sales progression objectives gave rise to an increase in the commission paid on all BA tickets sold by the travel agent concerned, and not just on those sold after those objectives had been attained. It could therefore be of decisive importance for the commission income of a travel agent as a whole whether or not he sold a few extra BA tickets after achieving a certain turnover. The court considered that the progressive nature of the increased commission rates had a very noticeable effect at the margin and emphasised the radical effects which a small reduction in sales of BA tickets could have on the rates of performance-related bonus.

The court furthermore held that in a situation where the dominant undertaking has a much higher market share than its competitors it is particularly difficult for competitors of that undertaking to outbid it in the face of rebates based on overall sales volume. By reason of its significantly higher market share, the undertaking in a dominant position generally constitutes an unavoidable business partner in the market. Most often, rebates granted by such an undertaking on the basis of overall turnover largely take precedence in absolute terms, even over more generous offers of its competitors. In order to attract the co-contractors of the undertaking in a dominant position, or to receive a sufficient volume of orders from them, those competitors would have to offer them significantly higher rates of discount or bonus.[141]

The General Court in its first instance judgment rejected the objective reasons put forward by British Airways.[142] The company had argued that the high level of fixed costs in air transport and the importance of aircraft occupancy rates justified the rebate schemes. However, the court doubted that the benefits from higher occupancy outweighed the extra costs incurred by the rebate schemes. This judgment was confirmed by the ECJ upon appeal.[143]

10.2.3 Permissible rebates

Not all rebates granted by dominant undertakings are prohibited by Article 102 TFEU.[144] The European courts have emphasised in the judgments discussed above

---

[139] Ibid., para. 68/69.
[140] ECJ (9 November 1983), Case 322/81 – *Michelin v Commission* [1983] ECR 3461.   [141] Ibid., para. 75.
[142] GC (17 December 2003), Case T-219/99 – *British Airways v Commission* [2003] ECR II-5925, para. 285.
[143] For an economic discussion of the *British Airways* case, see Monti, *EC Competition Law*, p. 162.
[144] Still, economists are criticising the Commission's policy for imposing a *per se* prohibition against many types of rebates that are considered normal business behaviour. See Monti, *EC Competition Law*, p. 184.

that dominant undertakings may grant rebates that are justified by objective reasons. Such objective reasons may consist in cost savings on the part of the undertaking that may result from larger orders due to reduced transfer costs. A rebate may also reflect lower transport costs caused by larger deliveries. Introductory rebates to launch a new product also have an objective justification.[145]

10.3 Predatory pricing

Predatory pricing refers to a market strategy of a dominant undertaking by which it seeks to drive competitors out of the market through excessively low prices. The dominant undertaking usually has larger resources and can afford the low prices for a longer period than its rivals. The intention typically is to raise prices above competitive level once the goal of disciplining or eliminating competitors has been attained.[146] Predatory pricing is not specifically addressed in Article 102(2) TFEU but can be regarded as one instrument to limit production and markets in the sense of Article 102(2)(b) TFEU.

Since low prices as such are welcomed by competition law the key question is under which circumstances low prices can be regarded as restricting competition. The ECJ developed a test to make a distinction between competitive and anticompetitive pricing in the *AKZO* case.[147] The two-limbed test concerns two different scenarios:

- In the first scenario, a dominant undertaking charges prices below average variable cost.[148] Such a pricing policy is presumed to be abusive. The ECJ assumed that a dominant undertaking has no interest in applying such prices except that of eliminating competitors so as to enable it subsequently to raise its prices by taking advantage of its monopolistic position, since each sale generates a loss.[149]
- In the second scenario, a dominant undertaking charges prices above variable cost but below average total cost.[150] Such a pricing policy is considered abusive if there is additional evidence suggesting that it is part of a strategy seeking to discipline or eliminate a competitor. According to the ECJ such prices can drive from the market undertakings which are perhaps as efficient as the dominant undertaking but which, because of their smaller financial resources, are incapable of withstanding the competition waged against them.[151]

---

[145] For a discussion of the Commission's approach to rebates under the Article 102 Guidance Paper see Kjolbye, 'Rebates under Article 82 EC', 66.
[146] On the economic considerations underlying the recoupment aspect, see Glöckner and Bruttel, 'Predatory Pricing and Recoupment under EU Competition Law – Per se Rules, Underlying Assumptions and the Reality: Results of an Experimental Study', *European Competition Law Review*, 31 (2010), 423.
[147] ECJ (3 July 1991), Case C-62/86 – *AKZO v Commission* [1991] ECR I-3359.
[148] The costs which vary depending on the quantities produced.
[149] ECJ (3 July 1991), Case C-62/86 – *AKZO v Commission* [1991] ECR I-3359, para. 71.
[150] Comprising variable and fixed costs, i.e. which remain constant regardless of the quantities produced.
[151] ECJ (3 July 1991), Case C-62/86 – *AKZO v Commission* [1991] ECRI-3359, para. 72.

In the underlying Commission decision the Commission had not only established prices and costs but had also relied on documentary evidence found during an inspection. In the documents it was clearly stated that AKZO had the intention to force certain competitors out of the market. The ECJ confirmed the Commission's decision in this regard and even included in the second part of the test the requirement that an abusive strategy has to be established in order to find a violation of Article 102 TFEU in the case of prices below average total costs but above average variable cost.

This concept of predatory pricing conflicts with the objective nature of Article 102 TFEU that does not require any subjective element to be established for an abuse. The Commission in its decision makes the subjective intentions expressed in documentary evidence part of its argument in favour of an abuse of a dominant position. This approach appears to have been endorsed by the ECJ. However, in light of the objective concept of abuse under Article 102 TFEU the judgment has to be construed in the sense that it requires the establishment of objective facts that support the finding of a strategy to force a competitor out of the market rather than to establish subjective intentions.

In the *Wanadoo* judgment[152] the ECJ added another aspect to its case law on predatory pricing. It held that Article 102 TFEU does not require the Commission to demonstrate that the dominant undertaking would have the possibility of recouping its losses incurred due to the pricing strategy.[153] The concept of predatory pricing was developed further in the ECJ's *Post Danmark* judgment.[154] The court held that prices charged by a dominant undertaking that do not cover the average variable cost of an entire business area but are above variable cost of the custom at issue are not necessarily abusive.

The Commission in its Article 102 Guidance Paper has largely endorsed the ECJ's case law but prefers to use long-run average incremental cost as a benchmark instead of average total cost. The Commission believes that long-run average incremental cost is a more suitable benchmark for multi-product undertakings that may have economies of scope.[155]

In the US, courts have been sceptical about the concept of predatory pricing. The US Supreme Court considers that 'predatory pricing schemes are rarely tried, and even more rarely successful'.[156] The court held that a decision to engage in below-cost pricing is very costly, as it is unclear how long the prices have to be set below cost in order to drive out competitors. Furthermore, the dominant company remaining on the market must be able to raise prices above competitive level to recoup the losses it has incurred. Those high prices create an incentive for potential competitors to enter

---

[152] ECJ (2 April 2009), Case C-202/07 P – *France Télécom v Commission* [2009] ECR I-2369. For a summary and comment see Alemanno and Ramondino, 'The ECJ France Telecom/Wanadoo Judgment: "To recoup or not to recoup? That was the question for a predatory price finding under Article 82 EC"', *European Law Review*, 34 (2009), 202.

[153] Ibid., para. 44.   [154] ECJ (27 March 2012), Case C-209/10 – *Post Danmark*, nyr.

[155] Article 102 Guidance Paper, para. 26.

[156] *Matsushita Elec. Industrial Co. v Zenith Radio* 475 US 574 (1986).

the market, which reduces the dominant company's profits and makes the strategy unworkable. However, these economic considerations have had little impact on case law in the EU.[157]

10.4 Interaction of jurisprudence on rebates and on predatory pricing

The ECJ's *Tomra* judgment[158] brought some clarification of the jurisprudence on rebates and on predatory pricing. The case concerned rebate schemes applied by Tomra that the Commission found to have a loyalty-inducing effect and aimed at creating de facto exclusivity of Tomra for the supply of the products in question to its customers. Tomra claimed that its rebate scheme was not abusive since the prices resulting from the rebates were above average total costs and therefore not 'predatory' in the sense of the *AKZO* judgment. However, the ECJ held that it is not necessary to examine the relation of prices and costs in a case involving a rebate scheme which has an exclusionary or 'suction' effect and for this reason is already capable of restricting competition.[159] The argument brought by Tomra illustrates the frictions in the case law of the European courts on the different types of abuse under Article 102 TFEU: while it is expected of competitors of a dominant undertaking to be able to compete with the dominant undertaking if it charges prices above average total costs, it is assumed that competitors of dominant undertakings are unable to compete with them if they grant rebates that are not objectively justified but still result in (discounted) prices above average total costs. The tests applied in the two different scenarios therefore appear somewhat arbitrary since the compatibility of a certain practice of a dominant undertaking with Article 102 TFEU depends on whether it is classified as a rebate scheme or as a predatory pricing strategy. Undertakings would be better off 'disguising' their rebate scheme as a pricing strategy. Under policy considerations this is a dissatisfying result.[160]

10.5 Refusal to supply

Freedom of contract is one of the principles underpinning market economy. In general, undertakings are free to select their business partners and to enter into a business relationship or not. Nonetheless, competition law may override this principle where undertakings are dependent on supplies by a dominant undertaking and

---

[157] On the reception of the recoupment considerations in EU competition law, see Moura e Silva, 'Predatory Pricing under Article 82 and the Recoupment Test: Do Not Go Gentle into that Good Night', *European Competition Law Review*, 30 (2009), 61.

[158] ECJ (19 April 2012), Case C-549/10 P – *Tomra and Others v Commission*, nyr.   [159] Ibid., para. 78.

[160] The decisions in the Tomra case have been criticised as overly legalistic, see Federico, 'Tomra v Commission of the European Communities: Reversing Progress on Rebates?', *European Competition Law Review*, 32 (2011), 139.

the refusal to supply or the refusal to enter into a business relationship is capable of restricting competition. In such cases a refusal to supply may violate Article 102 TFEU.

In its early judgments the ECJ applied a very strict policy to the refusal to continue to supply an existing customer. In the *Commercial Solvents* case[161] it held that the manufacturer of a raw material is not entitled to discontinue supplies to a customer which uses the raw material to manufacture the finished product if the supplier intends to enter the market for the finished product itself. The court held:

an undertaking which has a dominant position in the market in raw materials and which, with the object of reserving such raw material for manufacturing its own derivatives, refuses to supply a customer, which itself is a manufacturer of these derivatives, and therefore risks eliminating all competition on the part of this customer, is abusing its dominant position.[162]

This line of jurisprudence was confirmed in a later judgment and even expanded to cover slightly different scenarios. Thus in the *Telemarketing* case[163] a company that was dominant on the broadcasting market for TV advertising refused to accept advertisers that did not want to use the telephone lines and team of telephonists of the dominant company. This case could be seen as a tying practice which tied the telephone services to the TV advertising and the ECJ applied some concepts usually applied to tying cases. Still, the judgment refers to the conduct at issue as a refusal to deal. The ECJ referred to the *Commercial Solvents* judgment and held that it applied to the *Telemarketing* scenario as well:

That ruling also applies to the case of an undertaking holding a dominant position on the market in a service which is indispensable for the activities of another undertaking on another market. If, as the national court has already held in its order for reference, telemarketing activities constitute a separate market from that of the chosen advertising medium, although closely associated with it, and if those activities mainly consist in making available to advertisers the telephone lines and team of telephonists of the telemarketing undertaking, to subject the sale of broadcasting time to the condition that the telephone lines of an advertising agent belonging to the same group as the television station should be used amounts in practice to a refusal to supply the services of that station to any other telemarketing undertaking. If, further, that refusal is not justified by technical or commercial requirements relating to the nature of the television, but is intended to reserve to the agent any telemarketing operation broadcast by the said station, with the possibility of eliminating all competition from another undertaking, such conduct amounts to an abuse prohibited by Article 86 [Article 102 TFEU], provided that the other conditions of that article are satisfied.[164]

---

[161] ECJ (6 March 1974), Joined Cases 6/73, 7/73 – *Commercial Solvents v Commission* [1974] ECR 223.
[162] Ibid., para. 25.
[163] ECJ (3 October 1985), Case 311/84 – *CBEM v CLT and IPB (Telemarketing)* [1985] ECR 3261.
[164] Ibid., para. 26.

In light of the importance of the freedom of contract the ECJ's case law on refusal to supply appears very strict. It has to be noted though that both the *Commercial Solvents* and the *Telemarketing* judgments concerned cases in which a dominant company refused to supply a customer active on a market on which the dominant company either intended to become active or already was active. The dominance on the upstream market by way of the refusal was leveraged to a downstream market. The ECJ apparently is very sensitive to such leveraging of market power. The ECJ possibly would adopt a more lenient approach in a scenario where a dominant undertaking discontinues supplies to a customer which is active on a market on which the dominant undertaking is not present. It would appear appropriate to allow dominant undertakings to terminate a supply relationship with a reasonable notice period in such a case.

Another aspect has been added to the jurisprudence on refusal to supply by the ECJ's judgment in the *Lelos* case.[165] The case is noteworthy in several respects: the court had to strike a balance between the interest of pharmaceutical companies to prevent parallel trade and the goal of market integration. Moreover, the court had to rule under which conditions a refusal to supply is objectively necessary and proportionate to protect the legitimate commercial interests of a dominant undertaking and thus justified under Article 102 TFEU. The circumstances were that the Greek subsidiary of GlaxoSmithKline had stopped supplying wholesalers with certain medicines for which it enjoyed a dominant position. The background was that wholesalers had increased their orders far beyond the requirements of the Greek markets and sold the extra quantities to Member States in which the prices for the medicine were significantly higher due to the differences in the national regulatory provisions for the pricing of pharmaceuticals. GlaxoSmithKline started to supply hospitals and pharmacies in Greece directly in order not to give wholesalers the opportunity to export excess quantities. The wholesalers claimed that such refusal to supply violated Article 102 TFEU. The ECJ recognised that pharmaceutical companies have a certain legitimate interest in limiting parallel trade. However, such interest does not justify a refusal to supply wholesalers at all. The court held that a dominant company has a right to refuse to fulfil orders 'out of the ordinary'.[166] However, given that the question was raised in a procedure for a preliminary ruling, it was left to the national court to determine which orders are 'out of the ordinary'. The ECJ apparently aimed at a solution that obliges dominant companies to meet domestic demand but not to enable parallel exports.[167]

---

[165] ECJ (16 September 2008), Joined Cases C-468/06 to C-478/06 – *Lelos et al. v GlaxoSmithKline* [2008] ECR I-7139. For a summary and analysis see Fountoukakos and Piotrowski, 'Parallel Trade in Pharmaceuticals and Abuse of Dominance after the ECJ's Judgment in Syfait II', *European Law Review*, 34 (2009), 2.

[166] Para. 70.

[167] For an in-depth analysis of the assessment of parallel trade under the EU competition rules, see Tsoufoulas, 'Limiting Pharmaceutical Parallel Trade in the European Union: Regulatory and Economic Justifications', *European Law Review*, 36 (2011), 385.

10.6 Refusal to grant a licence for an intellectual property right

In some exceptional cases the refusal to grant a licence for an intellectual property right (hereinafter: IPR) may represent a violation of EU competition law. Compulsory licensing under the EU competition rules has to be distinguished from compulsory licensing under the laws governing IPRs. The patent laws of many jurisdictions, for instance, provide for compulsory licensing under conditions that are different from those stipulated by EU competition law.

IPRs in individual cases may confer a dominant position on the right holder. In such a situation the right holder is subject to Article 102 TFEU. There are scenarios in which the right holder is not only able to eliminate competition on the market for the protected product due to the exclusive nature of the IPR but also on a downstream market, to be active on which it is necessary to use the protected product.[168] In the *IMS* case,[169] for instance, an undertaking was active on the market for data on the sale of pharmaceuticals in particular territories in Germany. Such sales data is purchased by pharmaceutical companies to monitor performance of their sales force. IMS had subdivided the territory of Germany into a number of 'bricks' and tracked sales in those geographical units. The units corresponded largely with the postal codes, i.e. sales data was provided broken down by postal code. When a competitor entered the market and offered data also by brick or postal code area it was sued by IMS for copyright infringement. The national court held that the 'brick structure' qualified for copyright protection and referred to the ECJ the question whether the refusal to grant a copyright licence under such circumstances could violate Article 102 TFEU. The court first confirmed its general case law on the relationship of Article 102 TFEU and IPRs:

According to settled case-law, the exclusive right of reproduction forms part of the rights of the owner of an intellectual property right, so that refusal to grant a licence, even if it is the act of an undertaking holding a dominant position, cannot in itself constitute abuse of a dominant position.[170]

However, there are exceptions to this general rule. The court stipulated the following conditions for a refusal to license an IPR to be abusive under Article 102 TFEU:

– the undertaking which requested the licence intends to offer, on the market for the supply of the data in question, new products or services not offered by the owner of the IPR and for which there is a potential consumer demand;
– the refusal is not justified by objective considerations; and

---

[168] For an economic discussion of refusals to license intellectual property, see Monti, *EC Competition Law*, p. 227.
[169] ECJ (29 April 2004), Case C-418/01 – *IMS Health*, [2004] ECR I-5039.   [170] Ibid., para. 34.

– the refusal is such as to reserve to the owner of the IPR the market for the supply of data on sales of pharmaceutical products in the Member State concerned by eliminating all competition on that market.[171]

The ECJ left it to the national court to assess whether these conditions were fulfilled in the case at hand. Again, it has to be noted that the refusal of the licence eliminated competition on a downstream market on which the dominant company was active. The exclusionary power of the IPR was leveraged to that market. The case law on refusal to grant an intellectual property licence is limited to such scenarios.[172] Furthermore, it appears that the ECJ has a tendency to soften copyright in cases where copyright is very easily obtained under national law and thus slightly corrects copyright law where it believes it is over-inclusive. The ECJ's judgment in the *Magill* case[173] also supports this impression.

10.7 Essential facility doctrine

Dominant undertakings sometimes base their market position on an exclusive access to certain infrastructure or facilities. Although it is not prohibited under EU competition law to operate such facilities and without granting access to third parties, in certain circumstances a refusal to do so may constitute an abuse of dominant position within the meaning of Article 102 TFEU. The practice of Union institutions gives some guidance on the application of the 'essential facility' doctrine in EU law.[174]

There is no clear-cut definition of what constitutes an essential facility. The Commission defines this term as 'a facility or infrastructure, without access to which competitors cannot provide services to their customers'.[175] A more detailed explanation has been provided by Attorney General Jacobs in the *Bronner* case:[176]

An essential facility can be a product such as a raw material or a service, including provision of access to a place such as a harbour or airport or to a distribution system such as a telecommunications network. In many cases the relationship is vertical in the sense that the dominant undertaking reserves the product or service to, or discriminates in favour of, its own

---

[171] Ibid., para. 52.

[172] For a discussion of compulsory licensing under US law, see Kanter, 'IP and Compulsory Licensing on Both Sides of the Atlantic: An Appropriate Antitrust Remedy or a Cutback on Innovation?', *European Competition Law Review*, 27 (2006), 351.

[173] ECJ (6 April 1995), Joined Cases C-241/91 P and C-242/91 P – *RTE and ITP v Commission* [1995] ECR I-743.

[174] The essential facilities doctrine has been developed first in the US, see Stratakis, 'Comparative Analysis of the US and EU Approach and Enforcement of the Essential Facilities Doctrine', *European Competition Law Review*, 27 (2006), 434.

[175] Commission decision of 21 December 1993, Case IV/34.689 – *Sea Containers/Stena Sealink – Interim measures*, OJ No. L 15 of 18 January 1994, p. 8, para. 66.

[176] ECJ (26 November 1998), Case C-7/97 – *Bronner v Mediaprint* [1998] ECR I-7791.

downstream operation at the expense of competitors on the downstream market. It may however also be horizontal in the sense of tying sales of related but distinct products or services.[177]

A refusal to grant access to an essential facility infringes Article 102 TFEU only when it hinders market entry on a downstream market. This is a common element of the EU competition rules with regard to refusal to supply, refusal to grant an intellectual property licence or refusal to give access to an essential facility. Moreover, it must be demonstrated that access to the facility or infrastructure is objectively necessary for the petitioner to compete effectively on a downstream market. The access to the essential facility must therefore be indispensable to the applicant's business and there must not be any actual or potential substitutes for it. The requirement of indispensability is met when it is economically not viable for the market entrant to duplicate the facility on its own cost. In the *Bronner* case the ECJ held that a newspaper home delivery system developed and operated by a newspaper publishing company does not qualify as an essential facility since it can be either duplicated by competing newspaper publishing companies (potentially in cooperation with further newspapers without home delivery system) or circumvented through other forms of delivery such as the postal system or sales through newspaper stands.[178] The refusal to give access to his home delivery system therefore was considered not to violate Article 102 TFEU.

The owner of an essential facility may, however, refuse access for objective reasons. Capacity constraints, compatibility problems and other technical reasons may justify a refusal.[179]

10.8 Margin squeeze

The liberalisation of the telecommunications sector has brought about a number of cases involving abusive conduct referred to as 'margin squeeze'. Such conduct typically occurs where the previous monopolist still has a monopoly for parts of the telecommunications infrastructure but competes downstream with newcomers on the market. The competitors have to purchase certain services from the incumbent at a wholesale level but compete with the incumbent at the retail level. A pricing strategy of the dominant undertaking that leaves competitors no margin at the retail level may constitute an abusive practice under Article 102 TFEU. In some cases the

---

[177] AG Jacobs, opinion of 28 May 1998 in the case C-7/97 – *Bronner v Mediaprint* [1998] ECR I-7791, para. 50.
[178] Ibid., paras. 43 and 44.
[179] For a detailed discussion of the essential facilities doctrine, see Müller and Rodenhausen, 'The Rise and Fall of the Essential Facility Doctrine', *European Competition Law Review*, 29 (2008), 310.

incumbent has charged higher prices to his competitors at the wholesale level than to his customers at the retail level to frustrate any efforts to compete with it on the downstream market.

The most recent example is the *Telefónica* case.[180] Telefónica was the former state-owned monopoly telecommunication operator in Spain. To offer broadband internet access to customers at the retail level, providers in Spain had to purchase broadband internet access from Telefónica at the wholesale level. The background of the dependence from Telefónica is that there was only one operator of local landline telephone networks, which needed to give access to this network for other operators to offer their services. The tariffs charged by Telefónica to rival providers did not allow them to cover their costs, which led them to complain against the incumbent for an infringement of Article 102 TFEU. Confirming previous case law[181] the General Court upheld a Commission decision imposing a fine against Telefónica for abuse of a dominant position.

Obviously those margin squeeze cases concern a very specific situation where a dominant company acts as a supplier on the wholesale level and at the same time as a rival on the retail level. Under normal conditions, the dominant undertaking would probably not sell at the wholesale level at all. However, under the regulatory environment in the telecommunications industry and the limited possibilities to build competing telephone networks the operator of the network has to offer certain services in order to enable competition on a downstream market.[182]

10.9 Vexatious litigation

In some cases the Commission has considered litigation commenced by a dominant undertaking against a rival to be abusive under Article 102 TFEU. This type of litigation is also referred to as vexatious litigation. The key legal issue with regard to such cases is to determine under which conditions litigation initiated by a dominant undertaking against a rival is 'normal' litigation and when it is abusive. Dominant undertakings are not barred from seeking legal redress in general and

---

[180] GC (29 March 2012), Case T-336/07 – *Telefónica and Telefónica de España v Commission*, nyr.

[181] ECJ (14 October 2010), Case C-280/08 P – *Deutsche Telekom v Commission* [2010] ECR I-9555; ECJ (17 February 2011), Case C-52/09 – *TeliaSonera Sverige*, nyr. On the *Deutsche Telekom* judgment see Bay and De Stefano, 'ECJ Rules on Margin Squeeze Appeal', *Journal of European Competition Law and Practice*, 2 (2011), 128; Bjorgan, 'Margin Squeeze as an Abuse under Article 82 EC', *European Law Review*, 33 (2008), 289. For a discussion of the margin squeeze cases in general, see Hou, 'Some Aspects of Price Squeeze within the European Union: A Case Law Analysis', *European Competition Law Review*, 32 (2011), 250.

[182] For an appraisal of margin squeeze cases under US law, see Grimes, 'US Supreme Court Rejects Price Squeeze Claim: A High Point for Divergence between US and European Law?', *Zeitschrift für Wettbewerbsrecht* (2009), 343.

enjoy the right of access to a judge like any other undertaking. However, in some cases the Commission has found litigation abusive.

To single out the cases of abusive litigation the Commission has defined two criteria that have been confirmed by the General Court:

- litigation is abusive if it cannot reasonably be considered as an attempt to establish the rights of the dominant undertaking and can therefore only serve to harass the opposite party, and
- if the litigation is conceived in the framework of a plan whose goal is to eliminate competition.[183]

Both elements of the test are very problematic. The first element includes some very broad concepts that leave much room for interpretation and involve a risk of deviating decisions. The second element appears to take into consideration the subjective intentions of the dominant undertaking. However, the concept of abuse under Article 102 TFEU is an objective one that does not take into account the subjective intentions of an undertaking. Accordingly, only objective criteria may be used to establish that the litigation was part of a plan to eliminate competition. This is a difficult task to accomplish for competition authorities or private litigants. However, any other interpretation of the second element would run counter to the Treaty.

Similar issues may arise where a dominant company makes use of regulatory procedures to the detriment of a smaller rival. In the *AstraZeneca* case,[184] for example, a pharmaceutical company had withdrawn a registration of a specialty in a specific form and at the same time obtained a registration for that specialty in a slightly different form.[185] This strategy delayed the market entry of generics appreciably. Without considering subjective intentions it will be difficult to establish that the dominant undertaking abused its dominant position by withdrawing and obtaining regulatory approvals without any false statement or other misrepresentation towards the regulatory body. The General Court nonetheless confirmed a Commission decision in this regard which had found a violation of Article 102 TFEU.

---

[183] GC (17 July 1998), Case T-111/96 – *ITT Promedia v Commission* [1998] ECR II-2937, para. 55.

[184] GC (1 July 2010), Case T-321/05 – *AstraZeneca v Commission* [2010] ECR II-2805. For an analysis of the judgment, see Marschollek and Steinbarth, 'How the Application of Patent Law May Upset the Stomach of the European Commission: Delaying or Limiting the Market Entry for Competing Generics is an Abuse of a Dominant Position', *European Law Review*, 36 (2011), 13.

[185] For a detailed discussion of the decision and the 'vexatious' use of regulatory procedures, see Negrinotti, 'Abuse of Regulatory Procedures in the Intellectual Property Context: The AstraZeneca Case', *European Competition Law Review*, 29 (2008), 446; Murphy and Liberatore, 'Abuse of Regulatory Procedures: The AstraZeneca Case', *European Competition Law Review*, 30 (2009), 223, 289, 314; Westin, 'Defining Relevant Market in the Pharmaceutical Sector in the Light of the Losec Case: Just How Different is the Pharmaceutical Market?', *European Competition Law Review*, 32 (2011), 57.

Summary of Section 10

Exclusionary abuses are directed against the smaller rivals of dominant undertakings. Dominant undertakings have an obligation not to eliminate the remaining sources of competition. Exclusionary abuses may take various forms.

Tying and bundling practices limit the competitive chances of the rivals of a dominant undertaking in a market in which it is not dominant. The dominant undertaking will sell a product for which it is dominant together with a product for which it is not dominant. Market power will be leveraged from one market to the other. Furthermore, competitors on the market in which the dominant position exists may find it difficult to sell their products if the dominant undertaking offers a package of products at conditions they cannot match with their individual offer.

Rebates may have both an exclusionary and an exploitative effect. If they are granted by a dominant undertaking arbitrarily this may amount to a discrimination of customers. If rebates are applied uniformly they are unlikely to be discriminatory but they may have a loyalty-inducing effect in the sense that they give customers an incentive to buy all or a large share of their demand for a given product from the dominant undertaking for a certain reference period in order to reach a sales target defined by the dominant undertaking. In such a scenario smaller rivals will find it difficult to sell their products. As a general rule, dominant undertakings may grant rebates only if they reflect cost savings or other efficiencies.

Predatory pricing describes a scenario where a dominant undertaking seeks to drive a smaller rival out the market by applying prices below certain cost benchmarks. It is assumed that such low prices are part of an abusive strategy that will lead to monopoly prices at a later stage to recoup the losses incurred during the low price period.

In some cases a refusal to supply may amount to an abuse of a dominant position. In principle a dominant undertaking is free to choose its trading partners. However, it may be abusive to terminate an existing supply relationship if this leads to the elimination of market participants in a downstream market.

The refusal to license an intellectual property right has been considered an abuse of a dominant position in exceptional cases. They have in common that access to the intellectual property right was indispensable to compete with the right holder in a downstream market.

Similar considerations apply under the essential facilities doctrine. According to this line of jurisprudence the owner of a facility may be obliged to grant rivals access to that facility if it is technically or economically impossible to duplicate it. Another condition is that access to the facility is a prerequisite to compete with the owner in a downstream market.

Abuses in the form of a margin squeeze typically occur in markets where a dominant undertaking supplies rivals with certain goods or services at wholesale level and at the same time competes with them on a downstream market. Wholesale prices that do not give competitors a fair chance to compete on the downstream market are considered abusive.

Vexatious litigation is a type of abuse that involves court or other procedures which are used as an instrument to stifle competition by smaller rivals. It is difficult to distinguish between 'normal' and 'vexatious' litigation without resorting to subjective concepts such as the intention of the dominant undertaking. However, there are some cases where it was concluded that the relevant procedures could not have been initiated with any intention other than to impede competition.

QUESTIONS ON CHAPTER 4

1. What are the prerequisites of a violation of Article 102 TFEU? (2)
2. How can market power be described? (5.2)
3. On which indicators does EU competition law rely to establish market power? (5.3)
4. What is the role of entry barriers? (5.4)
5. Under what circumstances can small undertakings violate Article 102 TFEU?
6. What are the distinctive elements of collective dominance? (5.8)
7. Please explain the concept of abuse under Article 102 TFEU. (7)
8. When is the meeting competition defence available? (8.1)
9. At which market participants are exploitative abuses directed? (9)
10. What are the elements of an abusive tying practice? (10.1)
11. What are the potential negative effects of rebates granted by dominant undertakings? (10.2)
12. Under what conditions can a pricing strategy amount to predatory pricing? (10.3)
13. Which facilities can be considered an essential facility under Article 102 TFEU? (10.7)

SUGGESTED ESSAY TOPICS

1. The concept of market power
2. The notion of collective dominance
3. Defences under Article 102 TFEU

5 Merger control

1. INTRODUCTION

Merger control is the third pillar of EU competition law. At EU level the Commission plays the central role in the control of concentrations. Subject to judicial review by the General Court and the ECJ the Commission decides whether a merger notified by the interested parties may be implemented. In most jurisdictions, including the EU, merger control is designed as an *ex ante* control which shall primarily prevent merging undertakings from reinforcing or establishing a dominant position enabling them to exercise market power that could be harmful for the process of undisturbed competition.

1.1 The purpose of merger control

The main aim of merger control is to prevent mergers leading to the creation or reinforcement of a dominant position and thus depriving consumers of benefits resulting from effective competition such as low prices, high-quality products, wide selection of goods and services, and innovation. Mergers may impede effective competition by altering the market structure in such a way that companies on a relevant market are more likely to coordinate and raise their prices. Another detrimental effect to competition may be a reduction of the companies' abilities and/or incentives to compete which may result in higher prices or a lack of innovation. Therefore the most important goal of merger policy is to avoid the creation of a market structure that would significantly facilitate coordination of market behaviour between different market players. Contrary to the *ex post* control of abusive market practices by dominant undertakings under Article 102 TFEU, EU merger control is designed to preclude undertakings from creating a dominant position which might in future enable them to abuse their market power to the detriment of consumers.

Effective merger control also helps to maintain competitive market structures leading to better welfare outcomes for consumers. Since merger control is of a preventive nature its implementation may be solely based on predicting the future effects on competition in the relevant market resulting from the intended concentration. This approach requires a comparison between the potential 'post-merger' situation and the market situation were the merger not to be consummated. For this reason economic simulation models need to be applied in most cases in order to assess whether the planned concentration is likely to have negative effects on competition.

Apart from goals related to competition policy, merger control may also pursue some public interest goals defined at the political level such as social policy or reasons of industrial policy. From this standpoint merger control may be implemented as a tool to block or support business projects that are not necessarily efficient from a competition point of view. Examples of such industrial policy driven implementation of merger control laws are attempts by national governments to create national champions or to block take-overs of the existing, often partially State-owned, national dominant undertakings by foreign competitors or other investors.[1]

1.2 Body of legislation

EU merger control is governed by the EU Merger Regulation 139/2004.[2] The EUMR is complemented by Implementing Regulation 804/2004[3] setting out procedural rules pertaining to time limits, the conduct of hearings etc.

The non-binding notices and guidelines issued by the Commission are also of great importance for the stakeholders:

- Guidelines on the assessment of horizontal mergers;[4]
- Guidelines on the assessment of non-horizontal mergers;[5]
- Jurisdictional Notice;[6]

---

[1] On the conflict between industrial policy and merger laws, see Galloway, 'The Pursuit of National Champions: The Intersection of Competition Law and Industrial Policy', *European Competition Law Review*, 28 (2007), 172.

[2] Council Regulation (EC) No. 139/2004 of 20 January 2004 on the control of concentrations between undertakings, OJ No. L 24 of 29 January 2004, p. 1 (hereinafter: EUMR).

[3] Commission Regulation (EC) No. 802/2004 of 21 April 2004 implementing Council Regulation (EC) No. 139/2004 on the control of concentrations between undertakings, OJ No. L 133 of 30 April 2004, p. 1 as amended by the Commission Regulation (EC) No. 1033/2008 of 20 October 2008, OJ No. L 279 of 22 October 2008, p. 3.

[4] Commission Guidelines on the assessment of horizontal mergers under the Council Regulation on the control of concentrations between undertakings, OJ No. C 31 of 5 February 2004, p. 5 (hereinafter: Horizontal Merger Guidelines).

[5] Commission Guidelines on the assessment of non-horizontal mergers under the Council Regulation on the control of concentrations between undertakings, OJ No. C 265 of 18 October 2008, p. 6 (hereinafter: Non-horizontal Guidelines).

[6] Commission Consolidated Jurisdictional Notice under Council Regulation (EC) No. 139/2004 on the control of concentrations between undertakings, OJ No. C 95 of 16 April 2008, p. 1 (hereinafter: Jurisdictional Notice).

- Notice on a simplified procedure for treatment of certain concentrations;[7]
- Notice on restrictions directly related and necessary to concentrations;[8]
- Best Practices on the conduct of EC merger control proceedings.[9]

Summary of Section 1

Merger control is the 'third pillar' of EU competition law. The purpose of merger control is to prevent the creation or strengthening of a market structure that is detrimental to effective competition. In this sense merger control is related to Article 102 TFEU: while Article 102 TFEU acts *ex post* against abuses of a market situation that is detrimental to effective competition, merger control aims at preventing such situations from arising *ex ante*. Accordingly, any analysis of the competitive forces in a merger control procedure is a prospective one that seeks to anticipate market developments within a foreseeable timeframe.

EU merger control is governed by the EU Merger Regulation. This regulation is accompanied by an implementing regulation and various Commission notices setting out the Commission's approach to individual aspects of EU merger control.

2. JURISDICTIONAL SCOPE

The EUMR applies to all concentrations with a Union dimension, i.e. transactions that fulfil the requirements laid down in Articles 1 and 3 EUMR.

2.1 Concept of concentration

As follows from the decisional practice of the EU courts and the Commission the concept of concentration shall be understood widely and encompasses all operations bringing about a lasting change in the control of undertakings concerned and therefore in the structure of the market.[10] It covers mergers, acquisitions of sole or joint control and the creation of autonomous full-function joint ventures.

The notion of concentration is defined in Article 3 EUMR. Article 3(1) EUMR distinguishes two general categories of concentrations: (a) mergers and (b) acquisitions of control. However, this distinction does not influence the substantial assessment of the proposed transaction in any way and is only helpful in determining the party obliged to notify the concentration to the Commission pursuant to Article 4(2) EUMR.

---

[7] Commission Notice on a simplified procedure for treatment of certain concentrations under Council Regulation 139/2004, OJ No. C 56 of 5 March 2005, p. 32.

[8] Commission Notice on restrictions directly related and necessary to concentrations, OJ No. C 56 of 5 March 2005, p. 24.

[9] Available at: http://ec.europa.eu/competition/mergers/legislation/proceedings.pdf (hereinafter: Best Practices).

[10] EUMR, recital 20.

2.1.1 Mergers

A merger within the meaning of Article 3(1)(a) EUMR occurs where two or more independent undertakings amalgamate into a new one and cease to exist as separate legal entities.[11] Such a course of action is often referred to as 'merger of equals', e.g. the merger of Glaxo Wellcome and SmithKline Beecham when the new company GlaxoSmithKline was created.[12] There can also be a legal merger where one undertaking is absorbed by another. In such case the former ceases to exist and the latter still operates as an independent legal entity.[13]

The EUMR also applies to de facto mergers, i.e. situations in the absence of a legal merger where two or more undertakings combine their activities so that a single economic unit is created. In particular this may be the case where a common management for two or more companies retaining their individual legal personalities is established.[14]

2.1.2 Acquisition of control

Pursuant to Article 3(1)(b) EUMR a concentration arises when change of control results from the acquisition of direct or indirect control of the whole or parts of one or more other undertakings. It is irrelevant whether the control is acquired by purchase of securities or assets, by contract or any other means.

The most common way to acquire control is the acquisition of shares. The acquisition of assets amounts to a concentration only if those assets constitute the whole or a part of an undertaking. According to the Commission's practice this should be the case where the assets are part of a separate business having its own market presence to which a market turnover may be assigned.[15] The same applies to intangible assets such as brands, patents or copyrights.[16]

An acquisition of control on a contractual basis falls within the scope of EUMR when control of the management and the resources of the acquired undertaking will

---

[11] Jurisdictional Notice, para. 9.

[12] Commission decision of 8 May 2000, Case COMP/M.1846 – *Glaxo Wellcome/SmithKline Beecham*, available at http://ec.europa.eu/competition/mergers/cases/decisions/m1846_fn.pdf.

[13] Commission decision of 26 July 2000, Case COMP/M.1806 – *AstraZeneca/Novartis*, OJ No. L 110 of 16 April 2004, p. 1; Commission decision of 26 January 2001, Case COMP/M.2208 – *Chevron/Texaco*, available at http://ec.europa.eu/competition/mergers/cases/decisions/m2208_fn.pdf.

[14] Commission decision of 12 June 2006, Case COMP/M.4048 – *Sonae Industria/Tarkett/JV*, available at http://ec.europa.eu/competition/mergers/cases/decisions/m4048_20060612_20310_fn.pdf; the same applies to cases where the structure of a dual listed company has been established: Commission decision of 24 July 2002, Case COMP/M.3071 – *Carnival Corporation/P&O Princess II*, available at http://ec.europa.eu/competition/mergers/cases/decisions/m3071_fn.pdf.

[15] E.g. rights to flight routes between the United States and Europe: Commission decision of 13 September 1991, Case IV/M.130 – *Delta Air Lines/PanAm*, available at http://ec.europa.eu/competition/mergers/cases/decisions/m130_fn.pdf; transfer of the client database: Commission decision of 23 December 2002, Case COMP/M.2857 – *ECS/IEH*, available in French at http://ec.europa.eu/competition/mergers/cases/decisions/m2857_fr.pdf.

[16] Jurisdictional Notice, para. 24.

be transferred. Examples of such contracts are company control contracts[17] and business leasing contracts[18]. Furthermore, control may also be established on a de facto basis. In particular this may be the case where a long-term supply agreement allows the supplier to exercise substantial influence on the activities of its customer.[19]

2.1.3 Interrelated transactions

The EUMR covers not only concentrations consisting of one particular transaction such as a share or asset deal but applies also to acquisitions comprising a number of different elements. According to the case law and the Commission's decisional practice two or more transactions amount to a single concentration if they are unitary in nature.[20] In order to determine the unitary nature of a transaction it is necessary, in each individual case, to establish whether those transactions are interdependent in such a way that one transaction would not have been carried out without the other.[21] This requirement is met when the transactions at issue are linked either de iure or de facto. In the first case the relevant acquisitions are mutually conditional, i.e. closing of one transaction is the triggering factor for the final acquisition. For a de facto conditionality to be demonstrated an assessment of the economic rationale behind the transactions has to be made. In particular, the Commission will examine whether from the economic point of view the conclusion of one agreement depends on the closing of the other transaction. This was the case in *LGI/Telenet* where the Commission found two transactions to be de facto conditional on the ground that they were carried out simultaneously and the companies involved were ready to go ahead with the acquisition only as long as both transactions could be closed.[22] The concept of a single concentration applies only when the same persons or undertakings acquire control of one or more undertakings.

Pursuant to Recital 20 EUMR a series of transactions in securities taking place within a reasonably short period of time can also be regarded as a single concentration. In such a scenario concentration does not encompass the acquisition of the

---

[17] Commission decision of 28 July 2006, Case COMP/M.4225 – *Celsa/Fundia*, available at http://ec.europa.eu/competition/mergers/cases/decisions/m4225_20060728_20310_fn.pdf.

[18] Commission decision of 12 January 2001, Case COMP/M.2060 – *Bosh/Rexroth*, OJ No. L 43 of 13 February 2004, p. 1.

[19] Commission decision of 23 August 1995, Case IV/M.625 – *Nordic Capital/Transpool*, available at http://ec.europa.eu/competition/mergers/cases/decisions/m625_fn.pdf.

[20] GC (23 February 2006), Case T-282/02 – *Cementbouw Handel & Industrie v Commission* [2006] ECR, II-319, paras. 102–109; Commission decision of 26 February 2007, Case COMP/M.4521 – *LGI/Telenet*, available at http://ec.europa.eu/competition/mergers/cases/decisions/m4521_20070226_20310_fn.pdf, para. 9.

[21] GC (23 February 2006), Case T-282/02 – *Cementbouw Handel & Industrie v Commission*, [2006] ECR, II-319, para. 107.

[22] Commission decision of 26 February 2007, Case COMP/M.4521 – *LGI/Telenet*, available at http://ec.europa.eu/competition/mergers/cases/decisions/m4521_20070226_20310_fn.pdf, paras. 11 et seq.

'sole and decisive' share but covers all securities transactions which take place in the relevant period of time.[23]

2.1.4 Concept of control

Article 3(2) EUMR defines the notion of control for the purpose of the Regulation. Accordingly, control shall be constituted by rights, contracts or any other means which confer the possibility of exercising decisive influence on an undertaking in particular by (i) ownership or the right to use all or parts of the assets of an undertaking or (ii) rights or contracts which confer decisive influence on the composition, voting or decisions of the organs of an undertaking.

From this definition it is apparent that both de iure as well as de facto control are covered. The acquiring undertaking has decisive influence when it can autonomously decide about the appointment of senior management, budget, business plan, significant investments or market-specific rights. In order to determine whether control has been acquired it is, however, not necessary to establish that decisive influence is exercised. The sole possibility of its exercise shall be sufficient.

Since the EUMR applies only to operations bringing about a lasting change in the structure of the market, control must be acquired on a lasting basis. Therefore the regulation does not cover transactions resulting in temporary change of control or concluded for a definite period of time.[24]

A distinction has to be made between sole and joint control.

a) Sole control

Sole control may be acquired on a legal or factual basis. In principle de iure sole control is transferred with acquisition of the majority of voting rights. It may also occur when a minority shareholder has some special rights allowing him to determine the strategic commercial behaviour of the company. The Commission acknowledged this possibility in *CCIE/GTE*[25] where it recognised that a company holding 19% of voting rights had acquired sole control as it was granted the right to appoint the chairman of the supervisory board as well as the CEO and had the right to block significant business decisions.

Acquisition of de facto sole control may occur in cases where neither of the shareholders has sole de iure control over the target company. Minority shareholders owning enough votes to block strategic decisions are given negative control and thus have the possibility of exercising decisive influence on the company. This can be the case when one of the shareholders has control by virtue of its sole veto right over a range of strategic decisions such as major financial commitments, approval of the

[23] Jurisdictional Notice, para. 48.   [24] See also Jurisdictional Notice, paras. 28–35.
[25] Commission decision of 25 September 1992, Case IV/M.258 – *CCIE/GTE*, available at http://ec.europa.eu/competition/mergers/cases/decisions/m258_fn.pdf.

budget and the business plan.[26] In companies where the ownership of shares is dispersed, even a substantial minority share may give control over the company when it is highly likely that the shareholder will achieve a stable majority at shareholders' meetings. Normally the attendance ratio at shareholders' meetings in the previous three years will serve as an indicator. The Commission will also analyse the possible changes in the voting pattern after execution of the notified operation and look at the position and role of other shareholders, i.e. their economic or family links with the majority shareholder. In *Société Générale/Générale de Banque* a share of 25% was recognised by the Commission as sufficient to confer decisive influence.[27] The Commission based its decision on the past voting pattern and shareholder turnout ratio during the last three shareholders' meetings prior to the acquisition, and anticipated that the share of 25% would give Société Générale a stable majority amounting to over 55% of the votes usually represented at the shareholders' meeting.

b) Joint control

Joint control occurs where two or more undertakings have the possibility of exercising decisive influence over another company. In most cases joint control is characterised by deadlock situations where one or some of the parent companies may influence operations of the undertaking by blocking other shareholders' strategic decisions. Therefore a common understanding between the shareholders as to the market behaviour and strategy is necessary for the controlled undertaking to operate on the market. Joint control can be exercised on both a de iure and de facto basis. In the first scenario two parent companies have equal rights with regard to the business conduct of the joint venture company, e.g. by appointing the same number of board members. The EUMR applies also in cases where minority shareholders have veto rights relating to strategic decisions of the joint venture on issues such as budget, business plan, major investments or appointment of senior management.[28] It is, however, not required that veto rights will confer on minority shareholders decisive influence in the day-to-day operations. Another example for de facto joint control is joint acting in exercising voting rights either as a result of a binding contractual agreement or because of 'strong common interests'.[29] Such commonality of interests may occur where parent companies provide controlling undertakings with know-how, services and financial resources that are vital for its operations.[30]

---

[26] Commission decision of 8 May 2002, Case COMP/M.2777 – *Cinven Limited/Angel Street Holding*, available at http://ec.europa.eu/competition/mergers/cases/decisions/m2777_20020508_310_fn.pdf.

[27] Commission decision of 3 August 1993, Case IV/M.343 – *Societé Générale/Générale de Banque*, available in French at http://ec.europa.eu/competition/mergers/cases/decisions/m343_fr.pdf.

[28] Jurisdictional Notice, paras. 67 et seq.; GC (23 February 2006), Case T-282/02 – *Cementenbouw Handel & Industrie v Commission* [2006] ECR II-319, para. 67.

[29] Jurisdictional Notice, paras. 76–80.

[30] Commission decision of 13 November 1997, Case IV/M.975 – *Albacom/BT/ENI/Mediaset*, available at http://ec.europa.eu/competition/mergers/cases/decisions/m975_fn.pdf, para. 12.

2.1.5 Changes in the quality of control

A transaction qualifies as a concentration covered by the EUMR when it leads to change between sole and joint control. Also, an increase in the number or change in the identity of the controlling shareholders may be considered as a concentration. Similarly the EUMR applies when one or more of the parent companies exit the controlled undertaking, resulting in a change from joint to sole control.[31]

2.1.6 Full-function joint venture undertaking

Pursuant to Article 3(4) EUMR:

The creation of a joint venture performing on a lasting basis all the functions of an autonomous economic entity shall constitute a concentration within the meaning of Article 3(1)(b) EUMR.

These so called full-function joint ventures fall within the scope of EUMR when the criteria of (i) full functionality and (ii) lasting basis are met. Joint ventures not covered by Article 3(4) EUMR do not have to be notified to the Commission, but may be subject to scrutiny under Article 101 TFEU.

The first requirement is met when the newly created entity is independent of its parent companies at the operational level. In particular a joint venture (JV) must have sufficient resources to operate independently on the market. The Commission will not find full functionality of a JV where its activities do not go beyond one specific function of its parent's activities such as for example R&D or production.[32] Parent companies are allowed to make strategic decisions, but their influence on a day-to-day business must be minimal. Another requirement is that the JV has a separate management capable of implementing its own and independent policy within the strategic framework designed by the JV agreement. The Commission considers it irrelevant whether the JV's personnel has been seconded by the parent companies or hired directly by the JV.[33] A full-function joint venture must also have independent access to the market place, i.e. it must not be dependent on sales and purchases to or from its parents. A JV shall be regarded as autonomous when it sells more than 50% of its products to the market and does not have an outstanding number of long-term purchase obligations with its parent companies. This threshold is only of indicative nature and a case-by-case analysis is required to establish whether the JV deals with its parents at arm's length and may deal with third parties on normal commercial conditions. For example in *SNPE/MBDA* the Commission recognised the autonomy of a JV despite the fact that the majority of its sales were made to its parents.[34]

---

[31] Jurisdictional Notice, paras. 83–90.   [32] Ibid., paras. 95–6.

[33] Commission decision of 20 December 2002, Case COMP/M. 2992 – *Brenntag/Biesterfeld/JV*, available in German at http://ec.europa.eu/competition/mergers/cases/decisions/m2992_de.pdf.

[34] Commission decision of 30 October 2002, Case COMP/M.2938 – *SNPE/MBDA/JV*, available at http://ec.europa.eu/competition/mergers/cases/decisions/m2938_fn.pdf.

A full-function joint venture must perform its functions on a lasting basis. The durability requirement is in principle fulfilled when the joint venture agreement has been concluded for an indefinite time or the parent companies have equipped the JV with necessary financial and other resources. JVs established for a short period of time or in order to complete a particular business project shall not be regarded as operating on a lasting basis. This was the case in *Teneo/Merrill Lynch/Bankers Trust* where a JV was established as an investment vehicle for temporary holding of shares with the intention to dissolve it after achievement of the JV's business objectives.[35] A joint venture will also not be regarded as full-function if the instigation of its business activities is conditional on some factors which parent companies may not influence, e.g. granting of a public tender or a private licence.

2.1.7 Exceptions

Article 3(5) EUMR provides a list of operations that fall outside the scope of the EUMR:

- Acquisition of securities by credit or other financial institutions on an investment basis as long as the voting rights are not exercised to determine the competitive behaviour of that undertaking (Article 3(5)(a)).

  The securities must be acquired on a temporary basis with a view to their resale. In principle the controlling interest should be disposed within one year of the date of acquisition. Lastly, the acquiring bank, insurance undertaking or other financial institution must not exercise its voting rights in order to determine the commercial behaviour of the target company.
- Acquisition of control according to the law of a Member State relating to a liquidation, insolvency or similar proceedings (Article 3(5)(b)).

  This exception applies only to liquidators or similar office-holders appointed according to the statutes of Member States. It pertains only to acquisition of control and not to its disposal.[36]
- Acquisitions by financial holding companies (Article 3(5)(c)).

  The notion of financial holding companies relates only to companies that manage their investments without being involved in the operational management on a day-to-day basis. The holding company must not be allowed to determine the competitive conduct of the target company. In *Charterhouse/Porterbrook* the Commission found the exception not applicable because the acquiring company

---

[35] Commission decision of 15 April 1996, Case IV/M.722 – *Teneo/Merrill Lynch/Bankers Trust*, available at http://ec.europa.eu/competition/mergers/cases/decisions/m722_fn.pdf.

[36] Commission decision of 11 April 1995, Case IV/M.573 – *ING/Barings*, available at http://ec.europa.eu/competition/mergers/cases/decisions/m573_fn.pdf.

was granted the right to appoint 'special directors' one of whose consent was necessary to permit the target company to undertake certain transactions.[37]

2.2 Union dimension

The EUMR applies only to concentrations having a Union dimension.[38] The nature and purpose of this test have been explained by the General Court with regard to the predecessor regulation of the EUMR in *Cementenbouw*:

It follows from Article 1 of Regulation No 4064/89 that the Community legislature intended that, in the context of its role in respect of concentrations, the Commission would become involved only where the proposed concentration – or the concentration already carried out – attains a certain economic size and geographic scope, that is to say, a 'Community dimension'.[39]

The concept of Union dimension as defined in Article 1 EUMR relies solely on the turnover of the undertakings concerned. It is their task to assess the relevant turnover and to determine the authority competent for the substantial assessment of the concentration to be notified.[40] For this purpose the market shares are irrelevant.

According to the Jurisdictional Notice the relevant date for establishing Union jurisdiction over a concentration is the date of:

- the conclusion of the binding legal agreement, or
- the announcement of a public bid, or
- the acquisition of the controlling interest, or
- the date of the first notification.[41]

Article 1 EUMR sets out two turnover tests.

2.2.1 Turnover test pursuant to Article 1(2) EUMR

According to Article 1(2) EUMR a concentration has a Union dimension when the following three criteria are fulfilled:

(i) the combined aggregate worldwide turnover of all undertakings concerned is more than EUR 5,000 million, and

---

[37] Commission decision of 11 December 1995, Case IV/M.669 – *Charterhouse/Porterbrook*, available at http://ec.europa.eu/competition/mergers/cases/decisions/m669_fn.pdf.

[38] Due to the entering into force of the Treaty of Lisbon the term 'Union Dimension' is to be understood as an equivalent to 'Community Dimension' as referred to in the EUMR, the Jurisdictional Notice and literature.

[39] GC (23 February 2006), Case T-282/02 – *Cementenbouw Handel & Industrie v Commission* [2006] ECR, II-319, para. 115.

[40] See GC (14 July 2006), Case T-417/05 – *Endesa v Commission* [2006] ECR, II-2533, para. 99.

[41] Jurisdictional Notice, para. 156

(ii)   the aggregate Union-wide turnover of each of at least two of the undertakings concerned is more than EUR 250 million, and

(iii)   neither of the undertakings involved achieves more than two-thirds of its aggregate Union-wide turnover within one and the same Member State.

These criteria have been designed in order for the EUMR to cover only concentrations between undertakings having some significant impact on the EU market. However, due to the fact that only two of the undertakings involved must generate a Union-wide turnover of no less than EUR 250 million, it occurs repeatedly that the Commission must deal with concentrations of large non-EU undertakings that intend to establish a JV operating outside the EU market. For example, the EUMR was applicable to a concentration where four big Japanese companies set up a JV to provide telecommunication services in Japan and which had virtually no effect in the EU.[42]

2.2.2 Turnover test according to Article 1(3) EUMR

Article 1(3) EUMR provides for an alternative set of turnover thresholds:

(i)   the combined aggregate worldwide turnover of all undertakings concerned exceeds EUR 2,500 million, and

(ii)   the aggregate Union-wide turnover of each of at least two of the undertakings concerned is more than EUR 100 million, and

(iii)   in each of at least three Member States, the combined aggregate turnover of all the undertakings concerned is more than EUR 100 million, and

(iv)   in each of at least three Member States taken into account under (iii) the aggregate turnover of each of at least two of the undertakings concerned is more than EUR 25 million, and

(v)   neither of the undertakings involved achieves more than two-thirds of its aggregate Union-wide turnover within one and the same Member State.

The set of thresholds provided in Article 1(3) EUMR aims mainly at tackling concentrations not covered by Article 1(2) EUMR which due to their significant impact on national markets would have to be notified in several Member States. This was the case in *Ryanair/Aer Lingus* where the Commission established its jurisdiction based on Article 1(3) in order to prohibit the take-over of Aer Lingus.[43]

---

[42] Commission decision of 30 June 1993, Case IV/M.346 – *JCSAT/SAJAC*, available at http://ec.europa.eu/competition/mergers/cases/decisions/m346_fn.pdf. In practice such concentrations are examined following the simplified procedure which does not require a lengthy and complex investigation.

[43] Commission decision of 27 June 2007, Case COMP/M.4439 – *Ryanair/Aer Lingus*, available at http://ec.europa.eu/competition/mergers/cases/decisions/m4439_20070627_20610_fn.pdf.

2.2.3 Turnover calculation

a) Undertaking concerned

The question whether a concentration has a Union dimension depends on the turnover of the undertakings involved. The methods of calculating turnover are set out in Article 5 EUMR and apply only to undertakings concerned. The Jurisdictional Notice gives guidance on how to determine the undertakings concerned.[44] It distinguishes the following scenarios:

- In case of mergers the undertakings concerned are all merging entities

  Where A and B merge and a new entity C is established, A and B are the undertakings concerned.
- Acquisition of sole control

  Both the acquiring undertaking and the target are undertakings concerned when sole control over a whole company is to be acquired.

  Where A takes over B from C, only A and B are the undertakings concerned.

  The acquirer and the acquired parts of the target company are undertakings concerned when the control over part of an enterprise is to be transferred.

  Where A takes over part of B from C, only A and the relevant part of B are the undertakings concerned.
- Acquisition of joint control

  Each of the companies involved in an acquisition of joint control over a newly created JV excluding the JV itself.

  Where A and B create a JV C, only A and B are the undertakings concerned.

  In cases where a company acquires joint control in an already existing undertaking solely controlled by another company the acquirer and the controlling undertaking are undertakings concerned.

  Where A acquires from B joint control over C that was previously solely controlled by B, only A and B are the undertakings concerned.
- Acquisition of control through a JV

  If the control is acquired through a full-function JV already active on the market only the JV and the target are the undertakings concerned.

  Where A and B have joint control over C being a full-function JV and C acquires control over D, only C and D are the undertakings concerned.

  However, if the control is acquired through a JV being only a transaction vehicle its parent companies and the target must be considered as undertakings concerned.

  Where A and B have joint control over C being a transaction vehicle and C acquires control over D, the companies A, B and D are the undertakings concerned.

---

[44] Jurisdictional Notice, paras. 129–53.

b) Turnover calculation

Article 5(1) EUMR provides for a general definition of turnover. For the purpose of EU merger control, turnover shall be understood as amounts derived by the undertakings from 'the sale of products and the provision of services falling within the undertakings' ordinary activities'. Normally the Commission takes into consideration the most accurate data and refers to the closest financial year to the date of transaction. Then only turnover corresponding to the ordinary activities of the undertakings concerned, i.e. sales in the normal course of their business, is included in the calculation. Additionally, any sales rebates, VAT and other taxes directly related to the turnover are deducted from the main turnover figure.

Some special and more detailed rules are provided for the calculation of turnover of capital groups/holdings (Article 5(4) EUMR), credit institutions (Article 5(3)(a) EUMR) and insurance undertakings (Article 5(3)(b) EUMR).[45]

c) Geographic allocation of turnover

The main purpose of the thresholds set out in Article 1(2) and (3) EUMR is to identify mergers being cross-border in nature and having a Union dimension. In this way the Commission's jurisdiction over certain transactions can be determined. For this reason the required turnover shall be allocated geographically to the Union and/or to Member States. The general rule is that the turnover shall comprise products sold and services provided to undertakings or consumers in the Union or in the particular Member State.[46] The decisive factor is the location of the customer. Some additional criteria have to be applied when the location of the customer at the time of purchase cannot be identified, e.g. services with cross-border aspects such as sale of flight tickets. For this reason in *Ryanair/Aer Lingus* the Commission applied a calculation method based on the place of departure and not the place of destination of the traveller or the location of the customer.[47]

A detailed guidance on methods applicable when allocating geographically the turnover of concerned undertakings can be found in the Jurisdictional Notice.[48]

Summary of Section 2

Two criteria must be fulfilled for a transaction to be subject to EU merger control: it has to qualify as a 'concentration' as defined in the EUMR and it has to be of 'Union dimension'.

---

[45] For an extensive guidance on the attribution of turnover under Article 5(4) EUMR see Jurisdictional Notice, paras. 175–94.

[46] Jurisdictional Notice, para. 196.

[47] Commission decision of 27 June 2007, Case COMP/M.4439 – *Ryanair/Aer Lingus*, available at http://ec.europa.eu/competition/mergers/cases/decisions/m4439_20070627_20610_fn.pdf, paras. 20–31.

[48] Jurisdictional Notice, paras. 195 et seq.

The concept of concentration is designed to identify transactions that bring about a lasting change of the market structure. This is the case with regard to mergers in the sense of the amalgamation of two previously independent undertakings. It is also the case where a transaction results in a lasting change of control.

Control describes a scenario in which decisive influence can be exercised on another undertaking. Such influence can arise from holding a majority of the voting rights in another undertaking. It may also arise from a right to appoint the majority of the members of the main decision-making body of an undertaking. Ownership of major assets of another undertaking may also confer control.

Both sole and joint control can amount to control in the sense of the EUMR. Sole control exists where an undertaking can exercise decisive influence on another undertaking alone. In a case of joint control two undertakings can only exercise such influence jointly. Such a situation may arise where two undertakings have equal shares in another undertaking or equal rights with regard to the composition of the main decision-making bodies.

A change in the quality of control may also constitute a concentration for the purposes of EU merger control.

The concept of concentration includes also the establishment of a full-function joint venture. A full-function joint venture is a jointly controlled undertaking that performs on a lasting basis all the functions of an autonomous economic entity. Accordingly, a joint venture despite its nature of being established by its parent companies has to enjoy a sufficient degree of independence in relation to its parent companies to qualify as a concentration for merger control purposes. The key point is that merger control applies only to lasting structural changes in the market. Such a change does not occur in case of a joint venture that does not determine its market conduct independently of its parent companies but rather has limited functions to support the market activities of its parent companies. Joint ventures that do not qualify as full-function joint ventures are not subject to EU merger control but will be reviewed as a horizontal cooperation under Article 101 TFEU.

Only lasting structural changes of the market qualify as a concentration under the EUMR. Under certain conditions the acquisition of shares by a financial institution for investment purposes may thus escape the concept of concentration. The acquisition of shares by certain office-holders such as liquidators etc. to perform their official duties is also not considered a concentration.

EU merger control applies only to concentrations of a Union dimension. These are concentrations the parties to which exceed the turnover thresholds stipulated in the EUMR. The turnover thresholds have a dual purpose: the resources of the Commission for the review of concentrations are limited. EU merger control law therefore has to single out the most significant concentrations that are likely to have an appreciable impact on competition. Moreover, the turnover thresholds have the purpose of identifying concentrations that are likely to have an effect on the internal market. For this reason, a certain minimum turnover in the EU or a certain turnover spread within the EU is required to assure that there is a nexus to the internal market.

3. RELATIONSHIP BETWEEN EU AND NATIONAL MERGER CONTROL

The central principle of EU merger control is the one-stop shop rule. According to this rule concentrations having a Union dimension are to be investigated only by the Commission. Article 21(2) EUMR confirms this by stating that, subject to review by EU courts, only the Commission may take decisions with regard to the application of the EUMR and the Member States shall not apply their national laws to such concentrations (Article 21(3) EUMR).

However, in certain cases the EUMR allows for the Commission to refer a concentration having a Union dimension to be investigated by a national competition authority. This mechanism works also in the reverse direction and enables the Member States to have certain concentrations assessed by the Commission. The referrals are possible both in the pre- and the post-notification phase. Such an approach is in line with the principle of subsidiarity[49] as it allows for the most appropriate authority to carry out the investigation. For this reason the jurisdiction should only be reattributed to a national competition authority where the latter is more appropriate for dealing with a merger. A detailed guidance on the case referral system under the EUMR has been provided by the Commission in its Notice on Case Referral in Respect of Concentrations.[50] The Merger Working Group consisting of national competition authorities and the Commission has issued Best Practices on cooperation of national competition authorities in merger cases.[51] The Best Practices enhance the already existing mechanisms on exchange of information between national competition authorities in multi-jurisdictional cases and are addressed to both national competition authorities and the notifying parties. The Best Practices apply to all mergers notified within the EU at a national level in more than one Member State. Accordingly each national competition authority being notified of a multi-jurisdictional case will inform other competition authorities

---

[49] Pursuant to Article 5 TEU the Union is to take action only if and insofar as the objectives of the action cannot be achieved by the Member States.

[50] Commission Notice on Case Referral in respect of concentrations, OJ No. C 56 of 5 March 2005, p. 2 (hereinafter: Referral Notice).

[51] EU Merger Working Group, Best Practices on Cooperation between EU National Competition Authorities in Merger Review, 8 November 2011, accessible at: http://ec.europa.eu/competition/ecn/ nca_best_practices_merger_review_fn.pdf. For further information see Bardong, 'Cooperation between National Competition Authorities in the EU in Multijurisdictional Merger Cases. The Best Practices of the EU Merger Working Group', *Journal of European Competition Law and Practice*, 3 (2012), 126.

including the Commission about the relevant case details and notify its counterparts on all procedural steps undertaken including the initiation of a Phase II investigation.

3.1 Pre-notification reallocation of jurisdiction

3.1.1 Article 4(4) EUMR

Pursuant to Article 4(4) EUMR undertakings involved in a concentration with Union dimension may apply to the Commission to have the case referred in whole or in part to a national competition authority. A pre-notification referral is at the Commission's discretion and is possible when the following two criteria are fulfilled: (i) there are some indications that the proposed concentration may significantly affect competition in a market within a Member State, and (ii) the market concerned presents all the characteristics of a distinct market. Where these requirements are met and the Commission agrees to reallocate the case to a national competition authority the parties to the concentration are obliged to notify it according to national rules. The concentration will be reviewed under national merger rules.

This was the case in *Deutsche Bank/Postbank* where the case was referred to the German competition authority due to the national scope of the relevant market for financial services in Germany.[52] By June 2012 the Commission had referred seventy-one cases to national authorities and did not decline to do so in any case.[53]

3.1.2 Article 4(5) EUMR

Under Article 4(5) EUMR the parties to a proposed concentration are entitled to apply for review of a concentration not having a Union dimension by the Commission. The main requirement is that the concentration at issue is capable of being reviewed under the national merger laws of at least three Member States. If none of the Member States concerned exercises its right of veto the concentration is deemed to have a Union dimension.[54] No prior approval by the Commission is required. As of 30 June 2012 only six referral requests have been vetoed by a Member State.[55] In *Reuters/Telerate*[56] the Commission assessed a referral made by two producers of market data products.

---

[52] Commission decision of 6 February 2009, Case COMP/M.5446 – *Deutsche Bank/Postbank*, available in German at http://ec.europa.eu/competition/mergers/cases/decisions/ m5446_20090206_201220_1936638_DE.pdf.

[53] Commission, http://ec.europa.eu/competition/mergers/statistics.pdf (visited on 6 August 2012).

[54] More on the procedural issues in Connolly, Rab and McElwee, 'Pre-Notification Referral under the EC Merger Regulation: Simplifying the Route to the One-Stop Shop', *European Competition Law Review*, 28 (2007), 167.

[55] Commission, http://ec.europa.eu/competition/mergers/statistics.pdf. The last one being *Van Drie/Alpuro*, where the referral of concentration on the veal production market has been vetoed by the Dutch competition authority.

[56] Commission decision of 23 May 2005, Case COMP/M.3692 – *Reuters/Telerate*, available at http://ec.europa. eu/competition/mergers/cases/decisions/m3692_20050523_20212_fn.pdf.

Since the concentration did not meet the criteria set out in Article 1(2) and 1(3) EUMR it had to be reviewed under the merger laws of twelve Member States.

3.2 Post-notification referral

The EUMR contains provisions governing the referral of cases after their notification to the competent national competition authorities or to the Commission. Since the EU merger procedure is based on the principle of efficiency, the post-notification referral system sets out several deadlines that need to be observed by the Commission and national competition authorities.

3.2.1 Referrals to Member States – Article 9 EUMR

Article 9 EUMR entitles Member States to request that a concentration having a Union dimension will be referred to them. This may be the case in one of the following two scenarios. First, a concentration must threaten to affect significantly competition in a market within the applying Member State and the market concerned presents all the characteristics of a distinct market. The Commission has the discretion to refer the case or at least part of it when it considers that these conditions are met. In the second scenario a concentration must affect competition in a market within that Member State, which presents all the characteristics of a distinct market and which does not constitute a substantial part of the internal market, i.e. is generally narrower than national in scope. If the Member State demonstrates that a distinct market is affected then the Commission is obliged to refer the case. The concept of the distinct market has been clarified in Article 9(7) EUMR. The relevant geographical reference market must be an area in which the undertakings concerned are involved in the supply and demand of products and services, where the conditions of competition are sufficiently homogeneous, and which can be distinguished from neighbouring areas because of appreciably different conditions of competition.

In both scenarios Member States act on their own initiative and must lodge their request within fifteen working days after being informed by the Commission about the notification of the concentration. A referral is also possible after initiation of a Phase II investigation.

From the Commission's practice it is evident that Article 9 EUMR is most likely to apply in cases where the relevant market is smaller than the territory of a Member State and the proposed concentration has only a local or regional dimension. For example, in *REWE/Plus Discount* the relevant geographic market was defined as twenty local markets with a radius of 20–30 minutes' driving time for the retail sale of daily consumer goods and the Commission referred the concentration of two retailers to the Czech competition authority.[57] Article 9 EUMR may also apply when the relevant geographic market covers the territory of one Member State.[58]

3.2.2 Article 22 EUMR

Article 22 EUMR was originally drafted for Member States that did not have any merger control regime at the time as was the case for the Netherlands. It equipped the Member States with the right to an individual or joint request to the Commission to investigate a concentration that does not fall within the scope of the EUMR. For a referral request to be accepted two conditions must be fulfilled:

(i) the concentration has an effect on trade between Member States, i.e. it must be demonstrated that the pattern of trade between Member States may be affected, and

(ii) the concentration threatens significantly to affect competition within the territory of the Member State(s) making the request. The Member States are required to demonstrate that, based on a preliminary analysis, there is a serious risk that the transaction may have significant negative influence on competition.

In the Referral Notice the Commission has identified the following scenarios where Article 22 EUMR may be applicable:[59]

- Cases which give rise to serious competition concerns in one or more markets wider than national, or where some of the potentially affected markets are wider than national, and where the main economic impact of the concentration is connected to such markets.

  For example the Commission examined upon a referral by the UK Office of Fair Trading a concentration between producers of equipment for satellite communication as all markets concerned by the operation were at least EU-wide.[60]

- Cases which give rise to serious competition concerns in a series of national or narrower than national markets located in a number of Member States, when coherent treatment of the case is considered desirable and where the main economic impact of the concentration is connected to such markets.

---

[57] Commission decision of 3 July 2008, Case COMP/ M.5112 – *REWE/Plus Discount*, available at http://ec. europa.eu/competition/mergers/cases/decisions/m5112_20080703_20330_fn.pdf.

[58] See for example Commission decision of 8 January 2002, Case COMP/M.2621, *SEB/Moulinex*, available in French at http://ec.europa.eu/competition/mergers/cases/decisions/m2621_20020108_230_fr.pdf, confirmed by GC on appeal: Case T-119/02 – *Royal Philips Electronics v Commission* [2003] ECR II-1433.

[59] Referral Notice, para. 45.

[60] Commission decision of 11 December 2006, Case COMP/M.4465 – *Thrane&Thrane/Nera*, available at http:// ec.europa.eu/competition/mergers/cases/decisions/m4465_20061211_201310_1768676_fn.pdf.

In *Procter & Gamble/Sara Lee Air Care* the Commission found itself to be the best placed authority to assess a concentration among air freshener manufacturers that had been notified with ten national competition authorities.[61]

After receiving a referral request from a Member State the Commission transmits it to national competition authorities that may join the request within 15 working days. The final decision stays with the Commission which must decide whether or not to apply EUMR within ten working days. The Commission is not bound by the referral and may also review the aspects of concentration that were not covered by the referral request.[62] This was the case in *RTL/Veronica/Endemol* where the Commission extended its review to markets not mentioned by the Dutch government in its submission.[63]

3.3 Legitimate interest clause – Article 21(4) EUMR

Member States are in principle not entitled to apply national competition rules to concentrations having a Union dimension and which are thus covered by the EUMR. However, according to Article 21(4) EUMR, Member States may in exceptional circumstances apply their national laws in order to protect certain legitimate interests as long as those interests are compatible with the general principles and other provisions of EU law. As a result Member States have the competence to prohibit concentrations that would otherwise be approved by the Commission in specific cases. Article 21(4) EUMR lists three types of legitimate interests that may be pursued by Member States:

- **Public security and defence:** Member States are allowed to take measures aimed at protection of their public security interests. This exception encompasses the supply of services and goods that are essential for public health.
- **Plurality of the media:** this exception has been introduced to protect the Member States' legitimate interest in maintaining plurality of information and opinions by preserving the independence of different sources of information.
- **Prudential rules:** these are of great relevance in the financial sector. Member States are entitled to block concentrations in the financial services sector that would put at risk the financial system, or part of it, or threaten interests of consumers.

---

[61] Commission decision of 31 March 2010, Case COMP/M.5828 – *Procter & Gamble/Sara Lee Air Care*, available at http://ec.europa.eu/competition/mergers/cases/decisions/m5828_20100331_201310_1687604_fn.pdf.

[62] More on the Commission's decisional practice with regard to Art. 22 EUMR in Drauz, Mavroghenis and Ashall, 'Recent Developments in EU Merger Control', *Journal of European Competition Law and Practice*, 3 (2012), 52, 63 et seq.

[63] Commission decision of 20 September 1995, Case IV/M.553 – *RTL/Veronica/Endemol*, OJ No. L 134 of 5 June 1996, p. 32; confirmed on appeal by the GC (28 April 1999), Case T-221/95 – *Endemol v Commission* [1999] ECR II-1299.

Member States may also invoke other legitimate interests than those explicitly listed in Article 21(4) EUMR.[64] In such cases the legitimate interest that could serve as ground for application of national competition rules must be communicated to the Commission.[65] After the assessment of the compatibility of the demonstrated public interest with the general principles and other provisions of EU law the Commission informs the Member State about its approval of the referral within 25 working days. Should a Member State fail to comply with the material or formal requirements set out in Article 21(4) EUMR, the Commission is entitled to instigate the infringement procedure pursuant to Article 258 TFEU.[66]

Summary of Section 3

EU merger control enjoys priority over national merger control of the Member States. Only transactions that do not have a Union dimension as defined in the EUMR or that do not qualify as a concentration in the sense of EU merger control law can be subject to national merger control.

There are various possibilities for a referral of merger cases from national competition authorities to the Commission and vice versa. The purpose is to allocate a merger case to the authority that is best placed to review it. For example, a merger case that is notifiable in at least three Member States can be referred to the Commission upon request to ensure a consistent review. If a merger is likely to have effects mainly in one national market even though it has a Union dimension it may be referred from the Commission to the respective national authority.

In some cases legitimate interests of a Member State may justify the application of national law to cases which otherwise are subject to review by the Commission. Such legitimate interests include the safeguarding of the plurality of media that may require the review of a transaction not only under merger control law but also sector-specific national law.

4. SUBSTANTIVE APPRAISAL

Once the Commission's jurisdiction in relation to a particular concentration has been established the investigation will focus on its compatibility with the internal

---

[64] For a review of the relevant case-law see Whish and Bailey, *Competition Law* (Oxford University Press, 7th edn, 2012), pp. 852–4.

[65] In *BSCH/A.Champalimaud* (decision of 3 August 1999, Case IV/M.1616, available at http://ec.europa.eu/competition/mergers/cases/decisions/m1724_19990720_1290_fn.pdf) the Commission decided that cases where one of the interests named in Article 21(4) EUMR is to be invoked must also be notified.

[66] ECJ (3 June 2008), Case C-196/07 – *Commission v Spain* [2008] ECR I-41. See also Busa and Zaera Cuadrado, 'Application of Article 21 of the Merger Regulation in the E.ON/Endesa Case', *Competition Policy Newsletter* (No. 2, 2008), 1.

market. Because there is no general presumption as to the compatibility or incompatibility of the concentration the Commission bears the burden of proof and is obliged to demonstrate that the notified transaction is not compatible with the internal market.[67] The main material assessment criterion is set out in Article 2(3) EUMR:

A concentration which would significantly impede effective competition in the common market or in a substantial part of it, in particular as a result of the creation or strengthening of a dominant position, shall be declared incompatible with the common market.

This substantive test is known as the 'SIEC test' (significant impediment to effective competition) and has replaced the 'dominance test' existing under the previous merger regulation.

In appraising the possible anticompetitive effects resulting from a concentration the Commission must take a prospective view and estimate the post-merger market developments in a mid-term perspective. In a second step the result of this prognosis has to be compared with a counterfactual situation that would arise in the absence of the notified concentration.[68] Normally the Commission draws on the pre-transaction status quo, i.e. the situation prevailing at the time of the review. However in recent decisions it also took into account future changes to the relevant market and compared the most likely post-merger situation with some alternative scenarios.[69] Since the EUMR has been designed to prevent concentrations harmful to customers the conditions outlined in Article 2(3) EUMR will in principle apply to mergers which lead to increased market power thus enabling the undertakings involved to increase prices or reduce output, choice or quality of goods and services or diminish innovation or otherwise influence the parameters of competition to the detriment of consumers. When appraising the compatibility of a merger with the internal market the Commission and national competition authorities should therefore estimate the most likely negative effects of concentration on a relevant market and weigh them against countervailing factors such as buyer power, the extent of barriers to entry or existence of efficiencies demonstrated by the undertakings involved.

---

[67] ECJ (10 July 2008), Case C-413/06 – *Bertelsmann AG and Sony Corporation of America v Impala* [2008] ECR I-4951, para. 48. For a comment from the Commission's point of view see Luebking and Ohrlander, 'The Joint Venture SonyBMG: Final Ruling by the European Court of Justice', *Competition Policy Newsletter* (No. 2, 2009), 68.

[68] For an example of such counterfactuals see Partsch and Wellens, 'The Delta Airlines and Northwest Airlines Merger: Potentially Anticompetitive Co-operation as a Counterfactual to Assess a Significant Impediment to Effective Competition under the EC Merger Regulation?', *European Competition Law Review*, 30 (2009), 491.

[69] Commission decision of 28 August 2009, Case COMP/M.5440 – *Lufthansa/Austrian Airlines*, available at http://ec.europa.eu/competition/mergers/cases/decisions/m5440_20090828_20600_fn.pdf, para. 60.

According to the EUMR the following steps shall be taken when assessing the compatibility of a concentration with the internal market and EU competition rules:

- definition of the relevant product, geographic and temporal markets;
- determination of competitive effects caused by the concentration, i.e. horizontal, vertical or conglomerate effects;
- application of the SIEC test;
- assessment of additional countervailing factors such as efficiencies.

4.1 Market definition

Starting point for the substantive assessment of concentrations under the EUMR is the identification of the relevant market. Its importance for merger review has been stressed in *Kali & Salz* where the ECJ observed that 'a proper definition of the relevant market is a necessary precondition for any assessment of the effect of a concentration on competition'.[70] A guidance on the market definition has been provided in the Notice on Market Definition issued by the Commission.[71] It explains the concept of the relevant market as follows:

The objective of defining a market in both its product and geographic dimension is to identify those actual competitors of the undertaking involved that are capable of constraining those undertakings' behaviour and of preventing them from behaving independently of effective competitive pressure.[72]

Another objective of proper market delineation is to identify in a systematic way the immediate competitive constraints facing the merged entity.[73] A correct definition of the relevant market is essential for the proper assessment of competitive effects brought about by any concentration. In case of an overly broad market definition the market share of each concentrating party will be small and the anticompetitive effects may be unnoticed. On the other side a too narrow market definition may result in prohibiting a concentration which has pro-competitive effects or is neutral.

Since the enactment of the first Merger Regulation in 1990 the Commission has adopted market definitions with regard to many products and product groups. Despite this fact the Commission is nevertheless obliged to define the relevant market in each case and is not allowed to base its decision on findings made in previous

---

[70] ECJ (31 March 1998), Joined Cases C-68/94 and C-30/95 – *France and Others v Commission ('Kali & Salz')* [1998] ECR I-1375, para. 143.

[71] Commission Notice on the definition of relevant market for the purposes of Community competition law, OJ No. C 372 of 9 December 1997, p. 5 (hereinafter: Notice on market definition).

[72] Ibid., para. 2.   [73] Merger Horizontal Guidelines, para. 10.

cases.[74] Although prior decisions are not legally binding, in practice they usually serve as a point of departure for later cases.

4.1.1 Relevant product market

The definition of the relevant product market recurs primarily on the concept of interchangeability of products and services offered by the undertakings involved in a merger. Goods and services are presumed to constitute a relevant product market if they can be substituted by each other. This approach has been adopted by the ECJ in the *Continental Can* case according to which the delineation of the product market should be based upon the analysis of:

[those] characteristics of the products in question by virtue of which they are particularly apt to satisfy an inelastic need and are only to a limited extent interchangeable with other products.[75]

In the case it was disputed whether Continental Can abused its dominant position on the market for light metal containers for canned food and seafood products and the market for metal closures for the food packaging industry. The ECJ annulled the Commission's decision holding that the Commission had failed to demonstrate to the requisite standard that these three markets were in fact separate from the general market for light metal containers for juices, vegetables, fruits, olive oil, condensed milk and chemico-technical products.

The case law on definition of the product market has been summarised by the General Court in the *Ladbroke* judgment where it found that transmissions from France of sound and pictures of French horse races are from the perspective of those who bet substitutable with transmissions of the same horse races from other EU countries:

the relevant product or service market includes products or services which are substitutable or sufficiently interchangeable with the product or service in question, not only in terms of their objective characteristics, by virtue of which they are particularly suitable for satisfying the constant needs of consumers, but also in terms of the conditions of competition and/or the structure of supply and demand on the market in question.[76]

A similar approach has been adopted by the Commission in the Notice on Market Definition. The starting point for market definition is the consideration that undertakings are subject to three main competitive restraints being demand side substitutability, supply side substitutability and potential competition.[77] Of those three factors the concept of demand side substitutability plays the central role as its application

---

[74] GC (22 March 2000), Joined Cases T-125/97 and T-127/97 – *Coca-Cola v Commission* [2000] ECR II-1733, para. 82.

[75] ECJ (21 February 1973), Case 6/72 – *Europemballage Corporation and Continental Can Company v Commission* [1973] ECR 215, para. 32.

[76] GC (12 June 1997), Case T-504/93 – *Tiercé Ladbroke v Commission* [1997] ECR II-923, para. 81.

[77] Notice on market definition, para. 13.

gives concrete evidence whether the market power of merging entities may be balanced by the buyer power held by their customers. Supply side substitutability is of relevance in concentrations which give rise to competitive concerns on the purchasing markets. This was the case in *Friesland Foods/Campina* where the Commission examined whether the notified concentration would strengthen the buyer power of the parties in the market for procurement of raw milk.[78] A transaction can have anticompetitive effects on both the supply and the purchasing markets. This pertains in particular to concentrations of consumer goods retailers. For example in *Rewe/ Meinl* the Commission analysed the following two relevant markets:

The distribution market, in which food retailers act as suppliers to final consumers;

The procurement market ('demand market'), in which retailers act as buyers vis-à-vis producers of products forming part of the food-retailing trade's range.[79]

Therefore it is important to note that demand and supply substitutability tests should not be regarded as alternatives and may be applied at the same time. Each relevant product market test should focus on a current situation. As the Commission suggests in its notice on market definition, potential competition is usually not taken into consideration because it requires analysis of factors that may be observed only at a later stage of the cooperation between parties to the concentration once their position on the relevant market has been ascertained.[80]

a) Demand side substitutability

Demand side substitution is the most important factor in delineating the relevant product market. Two or more products are substitutable when a sufficient number of consumers of one product considers another product as an alternative and would purchase it in case the price of the first product increases. The starting point for the market analysis are the product characteristics and their functional interchangeability. Hence it is required to establish whether from the perspective of consumers two or more products have similar characteristics and serve the same functions. This test was applied by the ECJ in *United Brands* where it had to ascertain whether bananas formed a separate product market or were merely part of a broader market for fresh fruits. The ECJ analysed the characteristics of bananas and consumers' preferences:

The banana has certain characteristics, appearance, taste, softness, seedlessness, easy handling, a constant level of production which enable it to satisfy the constant needs of an important section of the population consisting of the very young, old and the sick.[. . .]

---

[78] Commission decision of 17 December 2008, Case COMP/M.5046 – *Friesland Foods/Campina*, available at http://ec.europa.eu/competition/mergers/cases/decisions/m5046_20081217_20600_fn.pdf.

[79] Commission decision of 3 February 1999, Case IV/M.1221 – *Rewe/Meinl*, OJ No. L 274 of 23 October 1999, p. 1, para. 9.

[80] Notice on market definition, para. 24.

A very large number of consumers having a constant need for bananas are not noticeably or even appreciably enticed away from the consumption of this product by the arrival of other fresh products on the market.[81]

The court came to the conclusion that the banana market is distinct from other fruit markets.

In order to determine products that could form the relevant market the Commission usually follows the approach taken by the ECJ. However, a review of the decisional practice demonstrates the Commission's tendency to define the product markets rather narrowly:

- bottled mineral water and soft drinks are separate markets since they have different characteristics (taste, composition), intended use (spring water is drunk to quench thirst whereas soft drinks are drunk more in a social context) and price;[82]
- oceanic cruises form a distinct market from other land-based holidays due to their unique features such as 'the experience of the sea', customers' expectations and prices;[83]
- pop music and classical music form distinct markets and within the pop music category a large number of different categories or 'genres' (e.g. jazz, soul, gospel, heavy metal, rap and techno) are readily identifiable and these categories may also form separate markets;[84]
- in mergers of air carriers each single pair point-of-origin/point-of-destination is deemed to constitute a relevant product market;[85]
- manual and electric toothbrushes are distinct markets because of substantial price differences.[86]

According to the Commission's decisional practice, one product market does not necessarily have to encompass only similar products that are interchangeable. In the past the Commission included in its market description the so called 'aftermarkets' consisting of complementing products such as computers and software updates or spare parts.[87] Consequently, similar products with similar functionalities do not

[81] ECJ (14 February 1978), Case 27/76 – *United Brands v Commission* [1978] ECR 207, paras. 31 and 34.

[82] Commission decision of 22 July 1992, Case IV/M.190 – *Nestlé/Perrier*, OJ No. L 356 of 5 December 1992, p. 1, paras. 10 et seq.

[83] Commission decision of 24 July 2002, Case COMP/M.3071 – *Carnival Corporation/P&O Princess II*, available at http://ec.europa.eu/competition/mergers/cases/decisions/m3071_fn.pdf, paras. 32 et seq.

[84] Commission decision of 27 April 1992, Case IV/M.202 – *Thorn EMI/Virgin Music*, available at http://ec. europa.eu/competition/mergers/cases/decisions/m202_fn.pdf; Commission decision of 2 September 2002, Case COMP/M.2883 – *Bertelsmann/Zomba*, available at http://ec.europa.eu/competition/mergers/cases/ decisions/m2883_fn.pdf, para. 11.

[85] Commission decision of 28 August 2009, Case COMP/M.5440 – *Lufthansa/Austrian Airlines*, available at http://ec.europa.eu/competition/mergers/cases/decisions/m5440_20090828_20600_fn.pdf, para. 11.

[86] Commission decision of 15 July 2005, Case COMP/M.3732 – *Procter & Gamble/Gillette*, available at http://ec. europa.eu/competition/mergers/cases/decisions/m3732_20050715_20212_fn.pdf, paras. 8 et seq.

[87] More on this aspect in Veljanovski, 'Markets without Substitutes: Substitution versus Constraints as the Key to Market Definition', *European Competition Law Review*, 31 (2010), 122.

always form one relevant product market. For example, luxury and standard versions of the same product do not always belong to the same relevant market.

In its Notice on Market Definition the Commission proposes to apply the so-called SSNIP test (the acronym stands for 'Small but Significant Non-transitory Increase in Price') as the most appropriate quantitative method for analysing the customers' preferences. Accordingly it has to be established whether a small but significant non-transitory increase in price would cause the purchasers of a certain product to switch to its credible alternatives after a price increase. The basic question behind this test is whether the producer may raise prices of its products without losing market share.[88] The Commission describes the SSNIP test in the following way:

The question to be answered is whether the parties' customers would switch to readily available substitutes or to suppliers located elsewhere in response to a hypothetical small (in the range 5% to 10%) but permanent relative price increase in the products and areas being considered. If substitution were enough to make the price increase unprofitable because of the resulting loss of sales, additional substitutes and areas are included in the relevant market.[89]

In practice the application of the SSNIP test begins with the narrowest possible product definition based on functional interchangeability. Then the question has to be answered whether a hypothetical monopolist supplier on the identified product market could profitably increase price for the relevant product or service. This would be the case when the customers were not able to switch to other products or services in reaction to price increase. If the price increase turns out to be unprofitable then the next closest substitutes of the product or service must be included in the market examination and the process is to be repeated. The test is completed when a set of products or services is identified where the SSNIP would be profitable for the hypo-thetical monopolist. An example for practical application of the SSNIP test gives the *Pernod Ricard/V&S* decision where the test was implemented to clarify whether flavoured and non-flavoured vodkas are parts of the same product market.[90]

When applying the SSNIP test the Commission routinely uses two types of empirical tests based on market data collected during the investigation: critical loss analysis and pricing analysis.[91] However, not every result of the SSNIP test may be deemed reliable and meaningful for the competitive assessment of a concentration. In particular this may be the case if the starting price used in the SSNIP test was not

---

[88] For this reason the SSNIP test is sometimes referred to as the 'hypothetical monopolist test'. More on operation of the test in context of merger control in Crocioni, 'The Hypothetical Monopolist Test: What It Can and Cannot Tell You', *European Competition Law Review*, 23 (2002), 354; Kokkoris, 'The Concept of Market Definition and the SSNIP Test in the Merger Appraisal', *European Competition Law Review*, 26 (2005), 207.

[89] Notice on market definition, para. 17.

[90] Commission decision of 17 July 2008, Case COMP/M.5114 – *Pernod Ricard/V&S*, available at http://ec. europa.eu/competition/mergers/cases/decisions/m5114_20080717_20212_fn.pdf, para. 29. For further examples see Rosenthal and Thomas, *European Merger Control* (C.H. Beck, 2010), p. 96.

[91] Their application in Commission practice has been discussed by Amelio and Donath, 'Market Definition in Recent EC Merger Investigations: The Role of Empirical Analysis', *Concurrences*, No. 3 (2009), p. 1.

reached under competitive conditions, e.g. it has already been set at a monopoly level.[92] Another unresolved issue with regard to the SSNIP test is the extent of price increase that is to be implemented: for example, a smaller hypothetical price increase may result in a definition of a narrower market. Thus the Commission suggests testing an increase between 5% and 10%, while the US Federal Trade Commission sets out the benchmark of 5% that can be adjusted as required by the facts of the case.[93] Lastly, the results of SSNIP tests may be only of an approximate nature due to insufficient or imprecise empirical data or market information collected by the Commission. For these reasons the test is not best suited to serve as the only instrument to properly define the relevant product market. Therefore the Commission resorts to additional quantitative methods that may help verify results of the SSNIP test. These include the following tests:

- Own-price elasticity shows the changes in demand for a product in case of its price increase/reduction. If a price change does not affect demand, i.e. the demand is inelastic, a conclusion may be drawn that there are no close competitors to the product in question and that it forms a separate market. For example, in *Gencor/ Lonrho* the Commission concluded that due to low price elasticity platinum jewellery products formed a separate market from golden jewellery.[94]
- Cross-price elasticity shows changes in demand for one product in case of price increase/reduction of another product. This test helps to establish the existence of a competitive relationship between two products and whether they are part of the same product market.
- Price correlation analysis measures whether prices of two products moved according to one pattern in the past. A high degree of correlation over time suggests that the products concerned belong to the same market.[95]

Although the SSNIP test and other quantitative methods are the most credible method of determining the relevant product market the Commission relies often on other empirical evidence depending on the characteristics of the product, industry or customers' preferences. There is no formal hierarchy of different sources or types of evidence.[96] Therefore in determining the product market the Commission may base its consideration on the following evidence:[97]

- Evidence of substitution in the recent past, 'shock analysis' – the Commission will consider recent events or shocks in the market such as entry of a new market player

---

[92] However, the risk of this so called 'cellophane fallacy' is rather small in the EU merger control as the Commission tries to apply the prevailing price on the given market as the starting point for its examination.

[93] Notice on market definition, para. 17; DoJ and FTC, Horizontal Merger Guidelines, August 2010, p. 10.

[94] Commission decision of 24 April 1996, Case IV/M.619 – *Gencor/Lonrho*, OJ No. L 11 of 14 January 1997, p. 30, para. 42.

[95] Commission decision of 27 June 2007, Case COMP/M.4439 – *Ryanair/Aer Lingus*, http://ec.europa.eu/competition/mergers/cases/decisions/m4439_20070627_20610_fn.pdf, para. 166.

[96] Notice on market definition, para. 25.   [97] Ibid., paras. 38–43.

or launching a new product that resulted in substitution between two products or services. In *Piaggio/Aprilia* the Commission examined which scooters were bought as substitutes when Aprilia reduced its sales due to financial problems.[98]

- Customer preferences and perceptions – the Commission usually has recourse to diverse studies, surveys and reports that reflect customer preferences. The Commission may also carry out its own market surveys by contacting customers and competitors during the market investigation process. In the *Carnival Corporation/P&O Princess* case which concerned a concentration between two of the world's four largest cruise lines the Commission conducted a market investigation into the reasons why consumers book a cruise. The goal of this investigation was to ascertain whether oceanic cruises might be regarded as a separate market from land-based holidays.[99] Another source of information on the current market situation and its past developments may also be internal documents submitted by the merging parties.

- Switching costs – high costs for customers for switching to alternative products may affect the results of the SSNIP test. The Commission also investigates the existence of other legal or technological barriers that may prevent customers from switching to other products. When examining a merger of two manufacturers of metal packaging the Commission differentiated between the market for tinplate and the market for aluminium aerosol cans. One of the reasons for such demarcation was the high costs of switching production from tinplate to aluminium.[100]

- Different categories of customers and price discrimination – a distinct group of customers on a relevant market may belong to a narrower market when the merging entities will be able to impose on that group different conditions from those for other customers.[101]

b) Supply-side substitutability

Although in most cases the interchangeability is analysed in the light of the demand-side substitutability, in certain cases the supply-side substitutability also has to be considered. For example, in *Continental Can* the ECJ rejected the Commission's finding that there were separate markets for different types of light metal containers. Its main argument was that the Commission failed to examine whether producers of types of light metal containers other than containers for fish and meat might be able to switch to supply the relevant products without incurring significant additional

---

[98] Commission decision of 22 November 2004, Case COMP/M.3570 – *Piaggio/Aprilia*, available in Italian at http://ec.europa.eu/competition/mergers/cases/decisions/m3570_20041122_20212_it.pdf.

[99] Commission decision of 24 July 2002, Case COMP/M.3071 – *Carnival Corporation/P&O Princess II*, available at http://ec.europa.eu/competition/mergers/cases/decisions/m3071_fn.pdf.

[100] Commission decision of 14 November 1995, Case IV/M.603 – *Crown Cork & Seal/Carnaud Metalbox*, OJ No. L 75 of 23 March 1996, p. 38, para. 19.

[101] Notice on market definition, para. 43.

costs.[102] Firstly, the SSNIP test must be applied. It involves examining whether in response to a small increase in price undertakings operating outside the candidate relevant market could easily divert their manufacturing resources in order to enter or compete more intensively on the examined market. Secondly, two additional requirements set out by the Commission in its notice on market definition must be fulfilled for the supply-side substitution to be taken into account.[103] Firstly, the suppliers must be able to switch to supply the product in a short term. In the *TomTom/Tele Atlas* case concerning a vertical merger between a manufacturer of portable navigation devices and its main supplier of digital maps, the Commission evaluated the supply-side substitution to assess whether the relevant product market covered both high-quality digital databases for navigation purposes and basic databases for non-navigation purposes. According to the Commission's findings both products belong to separate markets due to substantial costs and the time required to upgrade a basic database to navigable quality, as a producer of a basic database would have to employ substantial field forces that could drive down every single road and catalogue all relevant features.[104] Moreover, a switch in production must be possible without incurring any significant additional cost or risks. At this point all other barriers to switching production such as statutory restrictions or technological barriers need to be taken into consideration. For example, in the *Microsoft* case the Commission highlighted the importance of IP rights when assessing supply-side substitutability on the market for media players.[105]

If both of these criteria are fulfilled the relevant product market will in principle consist of all products produced by the respective suppliers.[106] The Commission's notice on market definition gives a practical example of paper producers. Although paper is usually supplied in a range of different qualities that are not substitutable (standard writing paper, high-quality publishing paper, paper for newspapers etc.) there is one market for different types of papers because paper plants are prepared to produce different types of paper and may adjust their production within a short period of time without incurring any significant additional costs.[107]

---

[102] ECJ (21 February 1973), Case 6/72 – *Europemballage Corporation and Continental Can Company v Commission* [1973] ECR 215.

[103] Notice on market definition, para. 20.

[104] Commission decision of 14 May 2008, Case COMP/M.4854 – *TomTom/Tele Atlas*, available at http://ec.europa.eu/competition/mergers/cases/decisions/m4854_20080514_20682_fn.pdf, paras. 23–7.

[105] Commission decision of 24 March 2004, Case COMP/C-3/37.792 – *Microsoft*, available at http://ec.europa.eu/competition/antitrust/cases/dec_docs/37792/37792_4177_1.pdf, para. 418.

[106] A distinction may have to be made between wholesale and retail markets though, see Inderst and Valletti, 'A Tale of Two Constraints: Assessing Market Power in Wholesale Markets', *European Competition Law Review*, 28 (2007), 84.

[107] Notice on market definition, para. 22.

4.1.2 Relevant geographic market

Definition of the relevant market is not limited to analysis of the product inter-changeability but also covers geographic aspects. Proper delineation of the relevant geographic market helps to establish the real market power of the undertakings involved in the concentration and thereby to assess the effects of the proposed merger on the market and the competitors. The ECJ construes the concept of relevant geographic market as a:

clearly defined geographic area in which [the product] is marketed and where the conditions are sufficiently homogenous for the effect of economic power of the undertaking concerned to be able to be evaluated.[108]

The above definition has been developed further by the General Court in *Deutsche Bahn/Commission*:

the definition of the geographical market does not require the objective conditions of competition between traders to be perfectly homogeneous. It is sufficient if they are 'similar' or 'sufficiently homogeneous' and, accordingly, only areas in which the objective conditions of competition are 'heterogenous' may not be considered to constitute a uniform market.[109]

The General Court confirmed then the Commission's findings that carriage routes from Germany to Belgian and Dutch ports and carriage routes between Germany and German ports are part of the same geographic market.

When delineating the relevant geographic market the Commission usually starts with a working hypothesis based on preliminary analysis of data and information delivered by the notifying parties. Then both the demand- and supply-side aspects are taken into consideration and the SSNIP test is applied. At this point the Commission usually analyses the customers' readiness to switch to suppliers located further away after a price increase by their actual supplier and the willingness of suppliers in other areas to enter new markets.[110]

From the demand-side perspective the following factors are of relevance:

- **Transportation costs** – high transport costs in relation to the value of the supplied goods decrease the customers' willingness to pay additional costs and look for new suppliers located in more distant areas. In such case the geographic market is more likely to be defined narrowly.[111] On the other side mass products which are easily

---

[108] ECJ (14 February 1978), Case 27/76 – *United Brands v Commission* [1978] ECR 207, paras. 10–11.

[109] GC (21 October 1997), Case T-229/94 – *Deutsche Bahn v Commission* [1997] ECR II-1689, para. 92.

[110] Commission's analytical approach to geographic market definition has been discussed by Bonova and Corriveau et al., 'Ineos/Kerling: Raising the Standard for Geographic Market Definition?', *Competition Policy Newsletter*, 1 (2008), 61.

[111] Commission decision of 13 July 2005, Case COMP/M. 3625 – *Blackstone/Acetex*, OJ No. L 312 of 29 November 2005, p. 60.

transported and have low transport cost tend to belong to larger regional geographic markets.[112]

- **Product pricing** – continuous substantial price differences in several Member States may suggest the existence of national markets. This was the case in *GE/ Instrumentarium* where the Commission investigated prices for medical equipment in different national markets.[113]
- **National and local preferences** – according to the *Notice on Market Definition* 'national preferences or preferences for national brand, language, culture and life style, and the need for local presence have a strong potential to limit the geographic scope of competition'.[114] These criteria were decisive in *RTL/Veronica/Endemol* where the Commission decided on the limitation of the market for TV broadcasting and came to the conclusion that due to differences in 'verbal expressions, in national taste, and in preferences for certain TV personalities' the TV markets in the Netherlands and the Flanders region of Belgium are two distinct geographic markets.[115]
- **Legal barriers** – different administrative policies, national technical standards or procurement policies are factors that need to be considered when defining the relevant geographical market. In *News Corp/Premiere*, a case which concerned the acquisition of a German pay per view TV station, the Commission argued that the Austrian and the German markets have to be regarded as separate markets due, *inter alia*, to regulatory differences on parental guidance film ratings applied more strictly in Germany than in Austria.[116]

The jurisprudence of the Union courts shows that the following types of geographic markets are most often examined:

- **Worldwide** – for example, the worldwide market for platinum and palladium[117] or computer processors.[118]
- **Union-wide** – for example, the market for industrial gases[119] or hydroelectric power station equipment.[120]

---

[112] Commission decision of 3 May 2000, Case COMP/M.1671 – *Dow Chemical/Union Carbide*, OJ No. L 245 of 14 September 2001, p. 1.

[113] Commission decision of 2 September 2003, Case COMP/M.3083 – *GE/Instrumentarium*, OJ No. L 109 of 16 April 2004, p. 1, para. 82.

[114] Notice on market definition, para. 46.

[115] Commission decision of 20 September 1995, Case IV/M.553 – *RTL/Veronica/Endemol*, OJ No. L 134 of 5 June 1996, p. 32, paras. 25 and 26; confirmed on appeal by the GC (28 April 1999), Case T-221/95 – *Endemol v Commission* [1999] ECR II-1299.

[116] Commission decision of 25 June 2008, Case COMP/M.5121 – *News Corp/Premiere*, available at http://ec. europa.eu/competition/mergers/cases/decisions/m5121_20080625_20212_fn.pdf, para. 25.

[117] Commission decision of 24 April 1996, Case IV/M.619 – *Gencor/Lonrho*, OJ No. L 11 of 14 January 1997, p. 30, para. 72.

[118] Commission decision of 26 January 2011, Case COMP/M.5984 – *Intel/McAfee*, available at http://ec.europa. eu/competition/mergers/cases/decisions/m5984_20110126_20212_1685278_fn.pdf, para. 33.

[119] Commission decision of 13 March 2004, Case COMP/M.3314 – *Air Liquide/Messer Targets*, available at http://ec.europa.eu/competition/mergers/cases/decisions/m3314_fn.pdf.

[120] Commission decision of 13 July 2005, Case COMP/M.3653 – *Siemens/VA Tech*, summary of the decision in OJ No. L 353 of 13 December 2006, p. 19.

- **Intra-EU regional markets** – the Commission tends to define regional markets when there are different competition conditions in parts of the EU and limited possibilities to import goods or services from one part to another: for example, the German-speaking market for installation of high pressure pipes due to specific legal implementation standards and language[121] or the French-speaking area of the EU for book publications.[122]

- **National** – for products sold under distinct national brands or distributed solely on a national basis: for example, pay-per-view TV,[123] insurances[124] or meat production.[125]

- **Local** – especially in cases where competition from other areas is limited by transportation issues: for example, cement distribution[126] or mergers of retailers where the relevant geographic market was defined as 20 local markets within a radius of 20–30 minutes' driving time for the retail sale of daily consumer goods.[127] In *Exxon/Mobil* the Commission considered even London's Gatwick airport as a relevant geographic market for the supply of aviation fuel.[128] In cases where the relevant geographic market is defined narrowly the Commission, depending on the facts of the case, may also adopt a radial distance in order to determine the area where the merging companies are competitors. In case of consumer goods retailers this radius usually covers the driving distance of 20–30 minutes. However, with regard to purchase of pigs for slaughter the Commission applied a radius of 150 km,[129] and the relevant range for production of private label tissues amounted to 1,000 km.[130]

---

[121] Commission decision of 18 December 2009, Case COMP/M.5664 – *Bilfinger Berger/MCE*, available at http://ec.europa.eu/competition/mergers/cases/decisions/M5664_20091218_20212_252329_fn.pdf, paras. 16 et seq.

[122] Commission decision of 7 January 2004, Case COMP/M.2978 – *Lagardère/Natexis/VUP*, available at http://ec.europa.eu/competition/mergers/cases/decisions/m2978_20040107_600_fn.pdf, para. 296.

[123] Commission decision of 25 June 2008, Case COMP/M.5121 – *News Corp/Premiere*, available at http://ec.europa.eu/competition/mergers/cases/decisions/m5121_20080625_20212_fn.pdf, paras. 24–7.

[124] Commission decision of 28 June 2004, Case COMP/M.3446 – *UNIQA/Mannheimer*, available in German at http://ec.europa.eu/competition/mergers/cases/decisions/m3446_de.pdf, para. 13.

[125] Commission decision of 9 March 1999, Case IV/M.1313 – *Danish Crown/Vestjyske Slagterier*, OJ No. L 20 of 25 January 2000, p.1, paras. 50 et seq.

[126] Commission decision of 28 May 2004, Case COMP/M.3415 – *CRH/Semapa/Secil JV*, available at http://ec.europa.eu/competition/mergers/cases/decisions/m3415_20040528_310_fn.pdf, paras. 16 et seq.

[127] Commission decision of 3 July 2008, Case COMP/M.5112 – *REWE/Plus Discount*, available at http://ec.europa.eu/competition/mergers/cases/decisions/m5112_20080703_20330_fn.pdf.

[128] Commission decision of 29 September 1999, Case IV/M.1383 – *Exxon/Mobil*, OJ No. L 103 of 7 April 2004, p. 1, para. 812.

[129] Commission decision of 21 December 2005, Case COMP/M. 3968 – *Sovion/Südfleisch*, http://ec.europa.eu/competition/mergers/cases/decisions/m3968_20051221_20310_fn.pdf, paras. 16 et seq.

[130] Commission decision of 5 September 2007, Case COMP/M.4533 – *SCA/P&G (European tissue business)*, available at http://ec.europa.eu/competition/mergers/cases/decisions/m4533_20070905_20212_fn.pdf, paras. 38–41.

4.1.3 Temporal market

Because competitive conditions may vary over certain periods of time it may be necessary to examine the temporal dimension of a market. This pertains in particular to markets experiencing significant fluctuations of demand and supply depending on the time of day or year.[131] The proper definition of the relevant temporal market was discussed in the *United Brands* case[132] where the ECJ had to decide whether there were two seasonal markets for bananas: one for the period of time when also other fruits such as apples, pears etc. were accessible and the other one for winter time where the consumer of bananas could not switch to other fruits in case of price increase.

4.2 The SIEC test

The main criteria for assessment of compatibility of a concentration with the internal market are set out in Article 2 EUMR. According to Article 2(3) EUMR a concentration shall be prohibited if it would significantly impede effective competition in the internal market or in a substantial part of it, in particular as a result of the creation or strengthening of a dominant position.

Closing the so-called non-collusive oligopoly gap was one of the main objectives of the modernisation of EU merger control.[133] The previous Merger Regulation was based on a substantive test which did not allow for prohibition of concentrations not leading to creation of market dominance but still being harmful to competition. The adoption of the SIEC test made it possible to prohibit these types of mergers as well:[134]

SIEC should be extended beyond the concept of dominance only to the anticompetitive effects resulting from the non-coordinated behaviour of undertakings which would not have a dominant position.[135]

---

[131] Bellamy and Child, *European Community Law of Competition* (Oxford University Press, 6th edn, 2008), p. 293.

[132] ECJ (14 February 1978), Case 27/76 – *United Brands v Commission* [1978] ECR 207.

[133] For a detailed review of the reasons for the amendment of the substantive test see Röller and de la Mano, 'The Impact of the New Substantive Test in European Merger Control', *European Competition Journal*, 6 (2006), 9. For an overview of the debate concerning the introduction of the new test see Kokkoris, 'The Reform of the European Merger Regulation in the Aftermath of the *Airtours* Case – the Eagerly Expected Debate: SLC vs. Dominance Test', *European Competition Law Review*, 26 (2005), 37.

[134] For an economic appraisal of the case law since the adoption of the new substantive test, see Maier-Rigaud and Parplies, 'EU Merger Control Five Years after the Introduction of the SIEC Test: What Explains the Drop in Enforcement Activity?,' *European Competition Law Review*, 30 (2009), 565.

[135] EUMR, Recital 25.

One of the few cases where the Commission considered challenging a merger which could not be prohibited under the old dominance test was *T-Mobile Austria/Tele. ring*.[136] Austrian network operator T-Mobile acquired control over one of its smaller rivals Tele.ring. Following the concentration a market structure with two major operators and two smaller operators would have emerged and could have given rise to non-coordinated effects on the relevant market leading to price increases despite the fact that T-Mobile would not have had the largest market share post-merger. The transaction was conditionally cleared after T-Mobile submitted some commitments.[137]

Under the new substantive test, dominance is no longer a prerequisite for a concentration to be prohibited. Creation or strengthening of a dominant position remains, however, a central consideration as most cases of mergers prohibited under Article 2(3) EUMR are still based upon a finding of dominance.

For Article 2(2) EUMR to apply, a causal link between the concentration and the infringement of competition on the relevant market needs to be established. In *Kali & Salz* the ECJ noted, for example, that such a link does not exist where a reduction of competition has also to be expected in the absence of the concentration at issue.[138]

4.3 Horizontal mergers

For the assessment of concentrations between undertakings that are actual or potential competitors the Commission issued the Horizontal Merger Guidelines. In this document it discusses the aspects that need to be taken into consideration when applying the SIEC test: market shares and concentration thresholds, likelihood of anticompetitive effects, existence of countervailing buyer power and efficiencies. These factors should not be regarded as an official checklist to be implemented mechanically. On the contrary, the competitive analysis in each particular case should be based on an overall assessment of the economic impact of the merger on the relevant market.[139]

---

[136] Commission decision of 26 April 2006, Case COMP/M.3916 – *T-Mobile Austria/Tele.ring*, summary of the decision in OJ No. L 88 of 29 March 2007, p. 44. For a comment on the case from the Commission's perspective, see Luebking, 'T-Mobile Austria/tele.ring: Remedying the Loss of Maverick', *Competition Policy Newsletter*, No. 2 (2006), 46.

[137] For a discussion of the case law on mergers which facilitate exclusionary conduct see Käseberg, 'Are Merger Control and Article 82 EC in the Same Market? The Assessment of Mergers which Facilitate Exclusionary Conduct under EC Merger Control', *European Competition Law Review*, 27 (2006), 409.

[138] ECJ (31 March 1998), Joined Cases C-68/94 and C-30/95 – *France and Others v Commission ('Kali & Salz')* [1998] ECR I-1375, paras. 90 et seq.

[139] Horizontal Merger Guidelines, para. 13.

4.3.1 Market shares and concentration levels

According to the Guidelines market shares of the merged entity and concentration levels post-merger provide only for useful first indications as to the structure of the market and the competitive strength of the undertakings concerned. Therefore they should never be regarded as decisive for the substantial appraisal of a concentration.

a) Market shares

For the purpose of the merger assessment the market share of the merged entity is taken into consideration. It is calculated by combining the market shares of parties to concentration.

The importance of the market share for the competitive assessment of any case has been stressed by the General Court in *Cementbouw* where the General Court found the 60% market share of the merged entity and the fact that it was at least fourteen times higher than the market share of its closest competitor to be strong evidence of its dominant position:

The existence of very large market shares is highly important and the relationship between the market shares of the undertakings involved in the concentration and their competitors, especially those of the next largest, is relevant evidence of the existence of a dominant position. That factor enables the competitive strength of the competitors of the undertaking in question to be assessed. Furthermore, a particularly high market share may in itself be evidence of the existence of a dominant position, in particular where the other operators on the market hold only much smaller shares.[140]

The following market share thresholds are deemed to be relevant for the application of the EUMR:

- **Combined market share of more than 50%** – shall be regarded as evidence of the existence of a dominant position.

  According to settled case law a particularly high market share may in itself be evidence of a dominant position, especially in cases where the other competitors hold only smaller market shares.[141] On the other hand, a high market share post-merger does not necessarily indicate the existence of a dominant position. In *Rhône Poulenc Rorer/Fisons* the Commission approved a concentration of drug producers leading to a combined market share of 65–70% arguing that it would not lead to the creation of a dominant position since both undertakings had

---

[140] GC (23 February 2006), Case T-282/02 – *Cementenbouw Handel & Industrie v Commission* [2006] ECR II-319, para. 201.

[141] GC (28 April 1999), Case T-221/95 – *Endemol v Commission* [1999] ECR II-1299, para. 134; ECJ (13 February 1979), Case 85/76 – *Hoffmann-La Roche v Commission* [1979] ECR 461, paras. 40–1.

lost almost 10% of their market share in the last two years as a result of increased competition.[142]

- **40–50%** – high likelihood of dominance, though some additional risk factors must be apparent.

  The lack of any sizeable competitors in the Spanish market for dry cat food was found by the Commission to be such a risk factor in *Nestlé/Ralston Purina*.[143] Since the post-merger market share would be 40–50% the Commission decided that commitments by merging companies were necessary to clear the transaction.

- **Below 40%** – in some cases even a combined market share below 40% may lead to the creation of a dominant position when in the light of other factors such as strength and number of competitors, presence of capacity constraints etc. some serious competition concerns may be raised.

  For example in a case concerning a merger on the Austrian market for retail sales outlets the Commission found that the market share increase from 30% to at least 37% would lead to a dominant position.[144] The Commission took into consideration the fact that the closest competitor of the merging parties had a market share of only 26%. Furthermore, one of the merging companies Rewe/Billa already had specific strengths as compared to its competitors. These were market leadership in eastern Austria, the best-developed chain of highly productive large outlets, a strong position in urban centres and the advantage of a centralised structure.

- **Below 25%** – safe harbour; there is a rebuttable presumption that such concentrations are compatible with the internal market.

In practice the estimation of the combined post-merger market share is only a starting point for an in-depth assessment of competitive effects resulting from the notified concentration. Mostly the market share serves as a reliable parameter on the competitive position of the merged entity. However, in some cases its relevance may be diminished. For example, market shares are less indicative in innovative markets and fast-growing industries such as computer games publishing.[145]

b) Concentration levels

Another factor that in the Commission's view may be of importance is the level of concentration. The degree of concentration is calculated on the basis of the

---

[142] Commission decision of 21 September 1995, Case IV/M.632 – *Rhône Poulenc Rorer/Fisons*, available at http://ec.europa.eu/competition/mergers/cases/decisions/m632_fn.pdf, para. 51. For another example see Karlsson, 'Clearance of Near-Duopoly', *European Competition Law Review*, 27 (2006), 514.

[143] Commission decision of 27 July 2001, Case COMP/M.2337 – *Nestlé/Ralston Purina*, available at http://ec.europa.eu/competition/mergers/cases/decisions/m2337_fn.pdf, paras. 48 et seq.

[144] Commission decision of 3 February 1999, Case IV/M.1221 – *Rewe/Meinl*, OJ No. L 274 of 23 October 1999, p. 1.

[145] Commission decision of 16 April 2008, Case COMP/M.5008 – *Vivendi/Activision*, available at http://ec.europa.eu/competition/mergers/cases/decisions/m5008_20080416_20310_fn.pdf.

Herfindahl–Hirschman Index (HHI). This sums up the squares of the market shares of the undertakings involved. In principle, the higher the total the more concentrated the market and the higher the risk of an oligopoly with reduced competitive pressure being created post-merger.[146] The Horizontal Merger Guidelines outline the following thresholds of market concentration which may be helpful when assessing the competitive post-merger situation:

- HHI < 1000 – safe harbour; horizontal anticompetitive effects are unlikely to appear;
- 1000 < HHI < 2000 and *delta*[147] < 250 – competition concerns unlikely;
- HHI > 2000 and *delta* < 150 – competition concerns unlikely unless:
  - a merger involves a potential entrant or a recent entrant with a small market share;
  - one or more of the merging parties are important innovators;
  - there are significant cross-shareholdings among the undertakings involved;
  - one of the merging firms is a maverick firm with a high likelihood of disrupting coordinated conduct;
  - indications of past or ongoing coordination are present;
  - one of the undertakings has a pre-merger share of 50% or more.

    For example in *ACE/CICA* the Commission cleared the merger of insurance companies despite the fact that the post-merger HHI would be 3500–4500. It was a small delta of less than 150 that the Commission found decisive for the clearance.[148]
  - HHI < 2000 – competition concerns are possible and further investigation of other relevant factors is required. In such case the particular circumstances listed above need to be given further consideration.

According to the Horizontal Merger Guidelines there is no general presumption that HHI levels exceeding certain thresholds may give rise to the existence of competitive concerns.[149] However, in *Sun Chemical Group/Commission* the General Court pointed out that 'the greater the margin by which those thresholds are exceeded, the more the HHI values will be indicative of competition concerns'.[150]

---

[146] For more information on the calculation of HHI and respective examples, see Whish and Bailey, *Competition Law*, pp. 43–4.

[147] *Delta* is the degree of variation in the HHI pre- and post-merger.

[148] Commission decision of 11 March 2008, Case COMP/M.5031 – *ACE/CICA*, available at http://ec.europa.eu/competition/mergers/cases/decisions/m5031_20080311_20310_fn.pdf, para. 24.

[149] Merger Horizontal Guidelines, para. 21.

[150] GC (9 July 2007), Case T-282/06 – *Sun Chemical Group and Others v Commission* [2007] ECR II-2149, para. 138.

4.3.2 Non-coordinated effects

In the Horizontal Merger Guidelines the Commission makes a distinction between non-coordinated and coordinated effects arising from a concentration.[151] This distinction reflects two ways in which a merger may impede effective competition.

The main feature of non-coordinated effects (often referred to as unilateral effects) is that horizontal mergers may eliminate competitive constraints on one or more of the merging undertakings and result in a reduction of competition. Consequently this may lead to increase of their market power and ultimately to price increases. Generally such risk is particularly high if a dominant position will be created as the result of a horizontal concentration. Following the introduction of the SIEC test, Article 2(3) EUMR also covers the creation of non-collusive oligopoly and prohibits mergers in markets without any company being dominant (oligopolistic markets) which would lead to an elimination of competitive restraints previously exerted by one of the merging parties on the remaining competitors.[152]

In addition to market share and the level of concentration the Commission uses further factors to assess horizontal mergers.

Anticompetitive effects of a merger are more likely if the merging parties are close competitors and their products are particularly close substitutes. A merger between manufacturers of two very similar products could enable the merged entity to increase prices for one of the products without risking a substantial decrease in its sales volume as consumers would switch to the substitute offered by the same producer. This risk may be eliminated if the competitors of the undertakings concerned also offer close substitutes to the products offered by the merging parties. The degree of closeness between the merging parties and their products was decisive for clearance in *GE/Instrumentarium* where the Commission conducted a win/loss analysis.[153] The Commission did not raise any competitive concerns although the merging parties enjoyed high market shares (in some markets significantly higher than 50%) in several national markets for medical equipment. The win/loss analysis showed that third parties such as Siemens and Philips and not Instrumentarium were the runner-ups in tenders won by GE. This led the Commission to the conclusion that market shares overstated the impact of GE's and Instrumentarium's combined market power.

---

[151] Merger Horizontal Guidelines, para. 22.

[152] On the relationship of the concept of collective dominance and the concept of unilateral effects see Baxter and Dethmers, 'Collective Dominance under EC Merger Control: After Airtours and the Introduction of Unilateral Effects is there Still a Future for Collective Dominance?', *European Competition Law Review*, 27 (2006), 148.

[153] Commission decision of 2 September 2003, Case COMP/M.3083, OJ No. L 109 of 16 April 2004, p. 1, paras. 244 et seq. See also comment on this decision by Bishop and Lofaro, 'Assessing Unilateral Effects in Practice. Lessons from GE/Instrumentarium', *European Competition Law Review*, 26 (2005), 205.

Another factor to be considered is whether the customers will have limited possibilities to switch to other products post-merger. An impediment to competition is more likely when the customers have difficulties in switching to alternative sources of supply, for example because of high switching costs or a lack of other suppliers. This was the case in *Ryanair/Aer Lingus* where the Commission blocked the acquisition of the Irish air carrier because it would have significantly reduced customers' ability to switch between different suppliers by reducing the number of alternative airlines or even removing the possibility to switch to an alternative airline on some routes.[154]

Mergers on markets where barriers to entry or expansion are high may enable the undertakings involved to reduce their output and increase the prices since there is a relatively low risk that competitors will be able to enter the market or expand their output. Economic risks and high costs of market entry or expansion as well as regulatory restrictions, the need for access to technical facilities or a distribution network as well as consumer brand loyalty are regarded as such barriers. The Commission also regards excess production capacity as a relevant factor. For example in *UCB/Solutia* it approved a merger between chemical manufacturers that led to a combined market share of 50%, arguing that any attempt to increase prices or restrict output by the merged entity would benefit the parties' competitors due to excess production capacity on the market.[155]

There may also be a serious risk of anticompetitive effects in cases where a merged entity will be able to hinder the expansion of smaller or potential competitors through control of the required inputs, a distribution network or intellectual property rights. This risk was identified by the Commission in *CVC/Lenzing* where it found that the merging parties would be able to effectively block market entries through their patent rights.[156]

The Commission will further consider whether the merger may result in an elimination of an important competitive force. Mergers where one or both of the parties are particularly vigorous and innovative undertakings (so called 'mavericks') may change the competitive dynamics of the market and produce some anticompetitive effects. This pertains in particular to highly concentrated markets if a smaller but more innovative competitor is expected to exercise competitive pressure on the bigger players in the future or has already changed the dynamics of the relevant market. The competitive effects of a maverick being acquired by a major market

---

[154] Commission decision of 27 June 2007, Case COMP/M.4439 – *Ryanair/Aer Lingus*, available at http://ec.europa.eu/competition/mergers/cases/decisions/m4439_20070627_20610_fn.pdf, para. 542.

[155] Commission decision of 31 January 2003, Case COMP/M.3060 – *UCB/Solutia*, available at http://ec.europa.eu/competition/mergers/cases/decisions/m3060_fn.pdf, paras. 41 et seq.

[156] Commission decision of 17 October 2001, Case COMP/M.2187 – *CVC/Lenzing*, OJ No. L 82 of 19 March 2004, p. 20, paras. 247 et seq. The concentration was cleared after the parties offered appropriate remedies.

player were investigated by the Commission in *Oracle/Sun Microsystems*.[157] Oracle, the largest and strongest database vendor, notified its acquisition of Sun Microsystems, the provider of the largest open source database MySQL. In the Commission's opinion the transaction eliminated an important competitive constraint exercised by open source-based MySQL on Oracle. The merger was cleared in Phase II after Oracle made a public pledge that it would not undertake any measures to degrade or eliminate MySQL post-merger.

4.3.3 Coordinated effects

Coordinated effects are likely to occur in oligopolistic markets since the actual market players may consider it possible, economically rational and preferable to reach an understanding on how to coordinate their actions in order to reduce or eliminate the competitive pressure exerted on each other, for example by adopting a common course of action aiming at a price increase.[158] Therefore it has to be examined whether the merger under scrutiny will facilitate existing or create new tacit collusion situations between members of an oligopoly. In collective dominance cases the ECJ requires the Commission to establish a link between coordination and anticompetitive effects:

In the case of an alleged creation or strengthening of a collective dominant position, the Commission is obliged to assess, using a prospective analysis of the reference market, whether the concentration which has been referred to it will lead to a situation in which effective competition in the relevant market is significantly impeded by the undertakings which are parties to the concentration and one or more other undertakings which together, in particular because of correlative factors which exist between them, are able to adopt a common policy on the market in order to profit from a situation of collective economic strength, without actual or potential competitors, let alone customers or consumers, being able to react effectively.[159]

In practice tacit coordination can only rarely be proven by hard evidence and must be inferred from a detailed analysis of current market conduct of the parties in the light of market conditions. As stated in the Horizontal Merger Guidelines, collective dominance is more likely to occur where it is relatively easy for the undertakings involved to find a common understanding on the coordination because of market

---

[157] Commission decision of 21 January 2010, Case COMP/M.5529 – *Oracle/Sun Microsystems*, available at http://ec.europa.eu/competition/mergers/cases/decisions/m5529_20100121_20682_fn.pdf, For a comment on the case from the Commission's perspective, see Buhr and Crome et al., 'Oracle/Sun Microsystems: The Challenge of Reviewing a Merger Involving Open Source Software, *Competition Policy Newsletter*, No. 2 (2010), 20. On the role of open-source software in merger analysis in general, see Sher, Biggio, Shehadeh and Lutinski, 'The Emerging Role of Open-source Software in Merger Analysis', *European Competition Law Review*, 32 (2011), 323.

[158] Merger Horizontal Guidelines, para. 39.

[159] ECJ (10 July 2008), Case C-413/06 – *Bertelsmann AG & Sony Corporation of America v Impala* [2008] ECR I-4951, para. 120.

transparency. In order to determine whether a concentration may result in coordinated effects the criteria set out by the General Court in the *Airtours* and confirmed by the ECJ in the *Impala* judgment[160] have to be applied. Additionally, it should be noted that not only a reduction of the number of companies in the market may facilitate the coordination but also the removal of a 'maverick' may lead to anti-competitive effects. Coordinated effects are likely to occur when the following criteria are met:

(i) **Reaching terms of coordination.** Coordination is more likely to emerge if competitors can easily arrive at a common perception as to how coordination should occur.[161] In principle the coordinating companies should have similar views on the scope of their cooperation. In this regard several structural market characteristics, such as stability and complexity of the economic environment, number of market players, product substitutability, degree of innovation etc., may need to be considered. These criteria were applied by the Commission in the *ABF/GBI* case concerning a merger of yeast manufacturers. Following an in-depth market investigation the Commission found the small number of active competitors (reduced post-merger to only two), the high frequency of repeated interaction between them and the fact that there were only few bulky orders to be indicators that the market may be 'coordination-friendly'.[162]

(ii) **Transparency.** Since the coordination is only possible when the coordinating undertakings are able to monitor each other, a high degree of market transparency is required. The Commission found in *Travelport/Wordspan* that the market for global distribution services is not transparent enough as there are significant differences in pricing structures and product offerings and this makes coordination impracticable.[163]

(iii) **Deterrence mechanisms.** Coordination will only work if there is a threat of retaliation against undertakings that decide to deviate from the cooperation scheme. The deterrence mechanism must be sufficiently credible, i.e. the coordinating firms must have economic incentives to retaliate and the retaliation must be prompt and adequate from the economic point of view. However, the sanctions imposed by members of the oligopoly need not necessarily take effect on the same market as the coordination.

---

[160] GC (6 June 2002), Case T-342/99 – *Airtours v Commission* [2002] ECR II-2585, para. 62; ECJ (10 July 2008), Case C-413/06 – *Bertelsmann AG & Sony Corporation of America v Impala* [2008] ECR I-4951, paras. 123 and 124.

[161] Merger Horizontal Guidelines, para. 44.

[162] Commission decision of 23 September 2008, Case COMP/M.4980 – *ABF/GBI Business*, available at http://ec.europa.eu/competition/mergers/cases/decisions/m4980_20080923_20600_fn.pdf. See also Amelio and Asbo et al., 'ABF/GBI Business: Coordinated Effects Baked Again', *Competition Policy Newsletter*, No. 1 (2009), 91.

[163] Commission decision of 21 August 2007, Case COMP/M.4523 – *Travelport/Wordspan*, summary of the decision in OJ No. L 314 of 1 December 2007, p. 21.

(iv) **No reactions of outsiders.** Coordination will only be successful if there is no risk that non-coordinating firms such as actual or potential competitors will jeopardise the operation of the oligopoly. In particular the post-merger removal of a 'maverick' that prevented tacit collusion may cause competitive concerns. This approach was adopted by the Commission in *Linde/BOC*:

> The removal of Linde as a maverick and the combination of Linde's and BOC's sources after the merger would therefore be likely to result in coordinated effects by eliminating Linde as a maverick being ready to enter aggressively and to increase total supply by its newly available quantities.[164]

In the *Impala* judgment the ECJ underlined that these criteria must not be applied mechanically and that an approach involving separate verification of each of those criteria taken in isolation must be avoided. Moreover, account of the overall economic mechanism of a hypothetical tacit coordination should be taken when ascertaining potential anticompetitive effects of the concentration at issue.[165] On this basis the Commission has to assess whether, given current market conditions, each oligopoly member considers it possible, economically rational, and hence preferable, to adopt on a lasting basis a common policy on the market with the aim of selling at above competitive prices, without having to enter into an agreement or resort to a concerted practice within the meaning of Article 101 TFEU and without any actual or potential competitors, let alone customers or consumers, being able to react effectively.[166]

4.3.4 Merger with a potential competitor

Anticompetitive effects similar to effects of horizontal mergers may also result from concentrations with potential competitors. Such mergers may lead to an elimination of future competition on the relevant market and may generate coordinated or non-coordinated anticompetitive effects in the future. The Commission applies a two-prong test to assess whether a concentration with a potential competitor may cause a significant impediment to effective competition.[167] First, the potential competitor must already exert a significant constraining influence or there must be a significant likelihood that it would grow into an effective competitive force. As regards the second requirement there has to be a lack of other potential competitors, which could maintain sufficient competitive pressure post-merger. Both conditions were fulfilled in *Omya/Huber* where the Commission found that the acquisition of Huber's calcium

---

[164] Commission decision of 6 June 2006, Case COMP/M.4141 – *Linde/BOC*, available at http://ec.europa.eu/competition/mergers/cases/decisions/m4141_20060606_20212_fn.pdf, para. 192.

[165] ECJ (10 July 2008), Case C-413/06 – *Bertelsmann AG & Sony Corporation of America v Impala* [2008] ECR I-4951, para. 125.

[166] Ibid., para. 122.   [167] Merger Horizontal Guidelines, para. 60.

carbonate business by Omya would result in the elimination of a potential competitor that otherwise would very likely grow into an effective competitive force.[168]

4.3.5 Strengthening buyer power in upstream markets

Horizontal concentrations may strengthen or create market power not only on supply markets but also on procurement markets. Accordingly a merged entity would be able to reduce its purchase of inputs thus reducing its output in the final product and increasing its price. This risk was identified by the Commission in *Rewe/Meinl* where the concentration would lead to a strengthening of the merged entity's dominant position in the procurement market in eastern Austria.[169] The transaction was cleared after the notifying party offered to divest most of the food-retailing outlets in eastern Austria to third parties.

4.3.6 Failing firm defence

A merger that normally could be found incompatible with the internal market may be approved by the Commission if in the absence of the merger one of the parties would disappear from the market. This defence was first applied in *Kali & Salz* where the German potash market would have been narrowed from duopoly to monopoly if the transaction had not been approved.[170] The Commission recognised that in the absence of the concentration the market position of the target would have been taken over by the already dominant Kali & Salz as well and cleared the transaction to prevent this scenario. The failing firm defence is another example of a situation where the Commission does not apply the pre-merger status quo as a counterfactual but examines an alternative scenario in which the merging company exits the market. For the failing firm defence to apply, the following three conditions have to be met:

(i) The allegedly failing firm would in the near future be forced out of the market because of financial difficulties if not taken over by another firm.
(ii) There is no less anticompetitive alternative than the proposed concentration.
(iii) The assets of the failing firm would inevitably exit the market in the absence of the merger.

---

[168] Commission decision of 19 July 2006, Case M.3796 – *Omya/J.M. Huber PCC*, summary of the decision in OJ No. L 72 of 13 March 2007, p. 24. The concentration has been cleared after Omya submitted commitments to divest one of Huber's production plants.
[169] Commission decision of 3 February 1999, Case IV/M.1221 – *Rewe/Meinl*, OJ No. L 274 of 23 October 1999, p. 1.
[170] Commission decision of 9 July 1998, Case IV/M.308 – *Kali & Salz/MdK/Treuhand*, available in German at http://eur-lex.europa.eu/LexUriServ/LexUriServ.do?uri=CELEX:31998M0308:DE:HTML. The applicability of failing firm defence was confirmed by ECJ on appeal, ECJ (31 March 1998), Joined Cases C-68/94 and C-30/95 – *France and Others v Commission ('Kali & Salz')* [1998] ECR I-1375.

4.3.7 Countervailing factors

The anticompetitive effects of a concentration may be outweighed by a number of factors. In the Horizontal Merger Guidelines the Commission discusses three counter-vailing factors that it will usually consider: buyer power, market entry and efficiencies.

a) Countervailing buyer power

Harmful effects arising from a concentration may be counteracted by the bargaining strength that buyers have vis-à-vis the merged entity due to their size or commercial significance to the seller.[171] According to the Horizontal Merger Guidelines this is the case if the buyer could immediately switch to other suppliers or refuse to purchase products in reaction to a price increase by the merged entity.[172] The Commission will usually consider the buyer's characteristics, i.e. its size and commercial significance for the merged company. It will also analyse current market conditions as counter-vailing buyer power is less likely to occur in fragmented markets.

b) New market entry

Anticompetitive concerns arising from a concentration may be reduced or even fully eliminated when the market power of the merged entity will be restrained by a new market entrance. By offering new products or lowering prices a new market player may influence the competitive situation on the relevant market and thus outbalance the anticompetitive risk involved in the concentration. According to the Horizontal Merger Guidelines, for an entry to be considered a serious competitive constraint on the merging parties it must be shown to be likely, timely and sufficient to deter or defeat any potential anticompetitive effects of the merger.[173] The Commission will in particular examine whether there are any potential barriers to entry which might hinder the competitor from breaking into a new market. In *Cementenbouw* the General Court defined barriers to entry as follows:

such barriers may consist in elements of various natures, in particular economic, commercial or financial elements, which are likely to expose potential competitors of the established undertakings to risks and costs sufficiently high to deter them from entering the market within a reasonable time or to make it particularly difficult for them to enter the market, thus depriving them of the capacity to exercise a competitive constraint on the conduct of the established undertakings.[174]

---

[171] For a comparative appraisal of bidding markets under EU and UK competition law from an economic point of view, see Szilagyi, 'Bidding Markets and Competition Law in the European Union and the United Kingdom', *European Competition Law Review*, 29 (2008), 16, 89.

[172] Merger Horizontal Guidelines, para. 64.   [173] Ibid., para. 69.

[174] GC (23 February 2006), Case T-282/02 – *Cementenbouw Handel & Industrie v Commission* [2006] ECR II-319, para. 219.

c) Efficiencies

Recital 29 of the EUMR states that:

In order to determine the impact of a concentration on competition in the common market, it is appropriate to take account of any substantiated and likely efficiencies put forward by the undertakings concerned. It is possible that the efficiencies brought about by the concentration counteract the effects on competition, and in particular the potential harm to consumers, that it might otherwise have and that, as a consequence, the concentration would not significantly impede effective competition, in the common market or in a substantial part of it, in particular as a result of the creation or strengthening of a dominant position.

The Commission is therefore obliged to take all relevant factors into account, including technical development and economic progress as laid down in Article 2(1) EUMR. The burden of proof for the existence of efficiencies rests however on the notifying parties that are obliged to provide all relevant information demonstrating the likelihood of claimed efficiencies. In the Horizontal Merger Guidelines the Commission discusses three conditions that must be met for an efficiency to be taken into account.[175] Efficiencies should benefit consumers in the relevant markets and should be both substantial and timely. Furthermore, the undertakings involved must have incentives to pass the efficiencies on to consumers. Possible efficiency gains may be lower prices, new products and/or services and technical improvements. Secondly, efficiencies claimed must be a direct consequence of the notified concentration. It is also required that they cannot be achieved to a similar extent by less restrictive alternatives. Finally, the Commission must be able to establish that the efficiencies are likely to materialise and that they are substantial enough to counteract the harm caused by the merger under scrutiny.

So far efficiencies have played only a limited role in the Commission's merger control practice as no concentrations were cleared solely on the basis of efficiency gains demonstrated by the parties. The main practical hurdle for the undertakings is the fact that proving an efficiency requires extensive analysis of economic data which must be provided by the notifying parties. The Commission rejected the efficiency claim in *Inco/Falconbridge*, a merger between two Canadian mining companies arguing that the horizontal integration of both businesses would increase the production of nickel, lower the overall costs of production, purchases of equipment and services as well as eliminate unnecessary duplicate cost, resulting in savings that could be passed on to consumers.[176] The Commission considered that these efficiencies were unlikely to be passed on to consumers. It also took the view that

---

[175] Merger Horizontal Guidelines, paras. 79–88.
[176] Commission decision of 4 July 2006, Case M.4000 – *Inco/Falconbridge*, available at http://ec.europa.eu/competition/mergers/cases/decisions/m4000_20060704_20600_fn.pdf, paras. 529 et seq.

similar efficiencies could have been achieved through means less restrictive of competition than a full merger, such as a joint venture.[177]

4.4 Non-horizontal mergers

The EUMR applies also to non-horizontal concentrations, i.e. mergers between undertakings active on different relevant markets and operating at different levels in the chain of production and distribution. Depending on the relationship between the merging companies a distinction has to be made between vertical and conglomerate mergers. Vertical and conglomerate mergers may harm competition by causing foreclosure effects or facilitating tacit collusion. Generally, such mergers are less likely to impede effective competition because they do not eliminate competition between undertakings acting on the same relevant market and provide for a wide range of efficiencies.[178]

The Commission issued Guidelines on the assessment of non-horizontal mergers which provide for instructions on the substantive appraisal of vertical and conglomerate mergers.[179]

4.4.1 Market shares and concentration levels

The Non-horizontal Guidelines stipulate that a merger is unlikely to raise any competitive concerns when the market share of the new entity would be below 30% or the post-merger HHI would be below 2000. In both cases a closer examination may, however, be required under 'special circumstances', especially if one of the parties is a company that is likely to expand in the near future or the merger would result in removing a maverick from the market.[180]

---

[177] For a detailed discussion of the efficiency defence in merger cases, see Iversen, 'The Efficiency Defence in EC Merger Control', *European Competition Law Review*, 31 (2010), 370. On the use of econometrics in the review of merger cases in general, see Lofaro and van der Veer, 'Fuelling the Debate? The Role of Econometrics in Statoil/JET', *European Competition Law Review*, 31 (2010), 222.

[178] Non-horizontal Guidelines, paras. 11 et seq.

[179] For comments on the content of the Guidelines see Petrasincu, 'The European Commission's New Guidelines on the Assessment of Non-Horizontal Mergers: Great Expectations Disappointed', *European Competition Law Review*, 29 (2008), 221; Weck and Scheidtmann, 'Non-horizontal Mergers in the Common Market: Assessment under the Commission's Guidelines and Beyond', *European Competition Law Review*, 29 (2008), 480; Bishop, '(Fore)closing the Gap: The Commission's Draft Non-Horizontal Merger Guidelines', *European Competition Law Review*, 29 (2008), 1; Weck and Scheidtmann, 'Non-horizontal Mergers in the Common Market: Assessment under the Commission's Guidelines and Beyond', *European Competition Law Review*, 29 (2008), 480; Schwaderer, 'Conglomerate Merger Analysis – the Legal Context: How the European Court's Standard of Proof Put an End to the Ex Ante Assessment of Leveraging', *Zeitschrift für Wettsewerbsrecht*, (2007), 482.

[180] For a non-exhaustive list of such circumstances, see Non-horizontal Guidelines, para. 26.

4.4.2 Vertical effects

Similar to horizontal mergers the Commission distinguishes between unilateral and coordinated effects of vertical mergers. Foreclosure effects belong to the first category and may arise if the merged entity limits its competitors' access to upstream supply markets or downstream distribution networks and thereby increases their costs.

Generally, two types of foreclosure effects can be distinguished. Input foreclosure may occur where a vertically integrated supplier is able to limit the competitors' access to products or services on a downstream market and raise their costs. In such case the Commission is required to demonstrate (i) that the merged entity would have the ability to foreclose access to inputs, (ii) that it would have an incentive to do so and (iii) that the foreclosure would have a negative effect on competition on the downstream market.[181] These criteria have been recently applied by the Commission in *Blackstone/Mivisa*.[182] Blackstone, an international investment management firm, acquired sole control over Mivisa, a metal food cans manufacturer. Since Blackstone had already controlled the food can machine producer Stolle, the Commission investigated whether the envisaged merger might lead to input foreclosure. It examined whether the merged entity could increase prices for new can machines causing Mivisa's competitors to increase their prices for food cans and lose market share as a consequence. The Commission approved the transaction and concluded that the foreclosure strategy would be highly unlikely because Stolle had only a very small market share and that there were several alternative machine producers that could provide machines with similar characteristics.

Customer foreclosure is likely to arise where a vertically integrated supplier limits access of competitors on an upstream market to the customer base on the downstream market. In such a case the Commission will apply a three-step test similar to the one implemented when examining input foreclosure. The risk of customer foreclosure was considered in the Premiere acquisition by News Corp.[183] The Commission found it highly unlikely that Premiere would, after the merger, exclusively purchase TV channel content from News Corp thereby foreclosing other rival media content producers. The attractiveness of a pay-TV operator's offers depends mainly on the bundle of channels broadcasted through a platform and it would not

---

[181] Non-horizontal Guidelines, para. 36. On the operation of these criteria in practice see Majumdar and Mullan, 'Nokia/NAVTEQ – Navigating the Non-horizontal Merger Guidelines', *European Competition Law Review*, 30 (2009), 487; Brockhoff Jehanno et al., 'Google/DoubleClick: The First Test for the Commission's Non-horizontal Merger Guidelines', *Competition Policy Newsletter*, No. 2 (2008), 53.

[182] Commisison decision of 25 March 2011, Case COMP/M.6128 – *Blackstone/Mivisa*, available at http://ec.europa.eu/competition/mergers/cases/decisions/m6128_20110325_20310_1717114_fn.pdf.

[183] Commission decision of 25 June 2008, Case COMP/M.5121 – *News Corp/Premiere*, available at http://ec.europa.eu/competition/mergers/cases/decisions/m5121_20080625_20212_fn.pdf, paras. 64 et seq.

be profitable for Premiere to reduce its offer to only the three programmes produced by News Corp.[184]

A non-horizontal merger may also lead to coordinated effects. In such a case the Commission will base its substantive appraisal on the application of the *Airtours* criteria taking into consideration the specifics of potential vertical cooperation.[185]

4.4.3 Conglomerate effects

Conglomerate effects may occur in mergers between undertakings that are in a relationship which is neither purely horizontal nor vertical.[186] Mostly conglomerate mergers do not have any anticompetitive effects and no in-depth investigation is required. Some significant competition concerns may however arise when the merging companies are active in closely related or neighbouring markets, offer complementary products or when a party to a concentration has substantial market power in one of the related or neighbouring markets.

The most common conglomerate concern is the threat of foreclosure. For this reason the Commission will usually examine whether 'the combination of products in related markets may confer on the merged entity the ability and incentive to leverage a strong market position from one market to another by means of tying or bundling or other exclusionary practices'.[187] Analysis of possible foreclosure effects comprises a three-step test similar to the one applied in the context of vertical mergers. Accordingly, the Commission will evaluate whether the merged entity would have the ability to foreclose, its possible incentives to do so and, finally, the overall competitive effects of the concentration.[188] Foreclosure effects resulting from tying were investigated by the Commission in *GE/Honeywell*.[189] During its investigation the Commission found GE to hold a dominant position in the market for large commercial jet-aircraft engines and that Honeywell was the market leader for avionics equipment. The Commission observed also that jet-aircraft engines and avionics were complementary products that were often sold together to the same customers. In the Commission's opinion the merger would have strengthened GE's dominant positions held in the markets for large civil and regional aircrafts and would have created a dominant position in the market for jet engines for business aircrafts and avionics products. The merger was prohibited based on the argument that GE/Honeywell would be able to bundle its products in diverse packages

---

[184] For an example of a merger decision under EU and UK competition law involving vertical effects, see Federico and Jackson, 'Draining Liquidity: A Novel Vertical Effect in Electricity Mergers?', *European Competition Law Review*, 31 (2010), 187.

[185] Non-horizontal Guidelines, paras. 79–90.   [186] Ibid., para. 91.   [187] Ibid., para. 93.

[188] For more details on the practical application of the test, see Rosenthal and Thomas, *European Merger Control*, p. 96.

[189] Commission decision of 3 July 2001, Case COMP/M.2220 – *General Electric/Honeywell*, OJ No. L 48 of 18 February 2004, p. 1.

foreclosing its smaller rivals that were not able to offer similar packages. The merged entity would also be in the position to offer lower prices for the packages, causing its competitors to exit the market. On appeal the General Court confirmed the Commission's decision but only with regard to horizontal effects stemming from the concentration.[190] The General Court rejected, however, the view that the merger would enable GE/Honeywell to implement bundling practices as the Commission did not demonstrate sufficient evidence to support the likelihood of such anticompetitive effects arising.

Another common conglomerate concern is portfolio or range effects, where the strength of the merged entity may be based partly (or wholly) on its strong position across a wide range of related product markets and/or countries, which competitors cannot match. Conglomerate effects may also arise due to a strengthening of financial resources of the company to be acquired. Following the acquisition the target company may obtain access to new or cheaper resources or capital and be able to offer lower prices or engage in costly price wars.

In practice the Commission may have significant difficulties in establishing that a concentration would bring about conglomerate harm because the requirements imposed by the EU courts with regard to standard of proof are very challenging. In the *Tetra Laval* judgment the ECJ stated that the Commission must in any case demonstrate that the conglomerate effects are likely to occur and will lead to significant impediments to competition:

The analysis of a 'conglomerate-type' concentration is a prospective analysis in which, first, the consideration of a lengthy period of time in the future and, secondly, the leveraging necessary to give rise to a significant impediment to effective competition mean that the chains of cause and effect are dimly discernible, uncertain and difficult to establish. That being so, the quality of the evidence produced by the Commission in order to establish that it is necessary to adopt a decision declaring the concentration incompatible with the common market is particularly important, since that evidence must support the Commission's conclusion that, if such a decision were not adopted, the economic development envisaged by it would be plausible.[191]

4.4.4 Countervailing factors

The Commission recognises that anticompetitive effects of non-horizontal concentrations may be outweighed by countervailing factors such as the presence of significant buyer power or the likelihood of new market entry. Vertical and

---

[190] GC (14 December 2005), Case T-210/01 – *General Electric v Commission* [2005] ECR II-5575. For a detailed review of the judgment see Baxter, Dethmers and Dodoo, 'The GE/Honeywell Judgment and the Assessment of Conglomerate Effects: What's New in the EC Practice?', *European Competition Law Review*, 6 (2006), 141; Pflanz, 'Economic Analysis and Judicial Review: The CFI on GE/Honeywell', *Zeitschrift für Wettbewerbsrecht* (2006), 139.

[191] ECJ (15 February 2005), Case C-12/03 P – *Commission v Tetra Laval*, [2005] ECR I-987, para. 44.

conglomerate mergers also provide substantial scope for efficiencies that may be demonstrated by the notifying parties. The efficiencies may for example result from an elimination of double marginalisation or better cost-coordination between the merged companies.[192]

4.4.5 Assessment of full-function joint ventures

Full-function joint ventures give rise to concentrations within the meaning of EUMR and are therefore subject to material assessment in the light of Article 2(3) EUMR and the SIEC test laid down therein. The creation of a full-function joint venture may also give rise to anticompetitive coordination that is not covered by Article 2(3) EUMR. In particular, the creation of a joint venture may enable the parent companies to coordinate their market activities in a way that is detrimental to undisturbed competition (so called 'spill-over effects'). The EUMR introduced a separate test in Article 2(4) EUMR that is designed to limit the risk of coordination between parent companies.

Article 2(4) EUMR comprises a two-prong test.[193] Firstly, it needs to be assessed whether the creation of the joint venture has as its object or effect the coordination of the competitive behaviour of the parent companies. The Commission will examine whether the parent companies retain activities in a downstream, upstream or the same market as the joint venture. Secondly, their ability to eliminate competition on the relevant market as a consequence of the cooperation will be considered as well.

Summary of Section 4

The substantive test to be applied under the EUMR is whether the proposed transaction will create a significant impediment to effective competition. In particular the creation or strengthening of a dominant position may give rise to such an impediment.

Before a substantive test can be applied to a proposed transaction the relevant market needs to be defined. Market definition comprises three aspects: the relevant product market, the relevant geographical market and the relevant temporal market.

As a general rule products that are regarded as substitutes by customers belong to the same product market. Demand-side substitutability looks at the function and price of the product as well as other properties considered relevant by

---

[192] Non-horizontal Guidelines, paras. 13–14, 54–7 and 114–18. See also Svetlicinii, 'Assessment of the Non-Horizontal Mergers: Is there a Chance for the Efficiency Defence in EC Merger Control?', *European Competition Law Review*, 28 (2007), 529.

[193] For an example of its application in practice see Commission decision of 6 October 2004, case COMP/M.3099 – *Areva/Urenco/JV*, summary of the decision in OJ No. L 61 of 2 March 2006, p. 11.

customers. Supply-side substitutability may also be relevant for market definition. If suppliers can easily shift production from one product to another this may indicate a single market.

Territories with homogeneous competitive conditions usually constitute a relevant geographic market. Prices, transportation costs, regulatory requirements and customer preferences belong to the factors that need to be considered for geographic market definition.

In some cases there is even a relevant temporal market since the respective products will be available only for a limited period, for example tickets for sports events.

Once the relevant market has been defined the Commission in a horizontal merger case will review market shares and concentration levels, the likelihood of coordinated or non-coordinated effects, the existence of countervailing buyer power and potential efficiencies resulting from the proposed transaction.

A combined market share exceeding 40% may be seen as an indicator of a dominant position being created or strengthened by the proposed transaction. The concentration level is measured by the Herfindahl–Hirschman Index which recurs on the sum of the squares of the market shares of all market participants pre- and post-merger. A certain absolute value in combination with a certain delta between the index pre- and post-merger indicates a degree of concentration caused by the proposed transaction that is assumed to be detrimental to competition.

Apart from market shares and the level of concentration the Commission will also assess whether a proposed transaction is likely to generate any non-coordinated effects. Such effects may occur in a market where a specific undertaking exercises competitive pressure on the other undertaking. If this undertaking is acquired by a competitor and ceases to exercise such pressure, competition on the market may be reduced.

A concentration may also restrict competition through coordinated effects. Those are likely to arise in an oligopolistic market with a high degree of transparency and a structure that facilitates coordination. Another factor contributing to coordinated effects is the possibility of deterrence or retaliation in case a competitor does not comply with the market conduct adopted by the others.

Countervailing factors may outbalance the market power of a merged entity. For example, a high degree of buyer power will not give the merged entity an opportunity to raise prices above competitive level. Moreover, new market entrants may dilute the market share of the merged entity and reduce its market power. Efficiencies may also be taken into account. If a proposed transaction can be expected to lead to lower prices or the introduction of new products and those efficiencies otherwise could not be generated, the efficiencies may compensate for the restrictions of competition resulting from the merger.

Under the failing firm defence a horizontal merger can be declared compatible with the internal market if the target is in financial difficulties and would have to leave the market in absence of the merger.

The main concern with regard to vertical mergers is potential foreclosure effects. Input foreclosure can arise where an undertaking acquires a supplier of an important input for its products. Rivals of the undertaking may find it difficult to source that input if the market share of the target is substantial and if it stops supplying those rivals. Customer foreclosure occurs where an undertaking acquires an important player on a downstream market. In this case rivals may find it difficult to sell their products if the market share of the downstream undertaking is substantial and if it stops sourcing from those rivals.

Conglomerate mergers may result in foreclosure or portfolio effects. The merged entity may be able to offer packages of products that smaller rivals are unable to offer. Furthermore, customers may find it more attractive to purchase an entire portfolio of products they need from a single source.

5. ANCILLARY RESTRAINTS

The Commission's decisions clearing notified mergers also cover contractual restrictions directly related to and necessary for the implementation of the merger. The Notice on ancillary restraints identifies three main types of restrictions that are most common to concentrations: non-compete clauses, licence agreements and purchase and supply agreements.[194] A clearance decision covers only ancillary restrictions that are directly related and necessary to the transaction. Both requirements are objective in nature. In general terms the Commission regards restrictions benefiting the acquirer of an undertaking as necessary since it is the purchaser who needs to be assured that he will acquire the full value of the purchased business.[195]

Summary of Section 5

Parties to a transaction may agree on certain ancillary contractual obligations to ensure that the purchaser obtains the full value of the respective undertaking. For example, the purchaser may impose a non-compete obligation on the seller. Restrictions that are necessary to reasonably implement a transaction are referred to as ancillary restraints and are covered by the clearance decision for the respective transaction.

---

[194] Commission Notice on restrictions directly related and necessary to concentrations, OJ No. C 56 of 5 March 2005, p. 24, paras. 18 et seq.
[195] Ibid., para. 17.

6. PROCEDURAL ASPECTS

EU merger procedure is governed by the EUMR and the Implementing Regulation 802/2004. EU merger procedure is based on the following principles:

- **Efficiency principle** – the Commission is obliged to issue its decisions in a way that is bearable for the undertakings involved. For this reason time limits for each phase of investigation have been introduced.
- **Preventive control** – all concentrations with a Union dimension must be notified to the Commission prior to their implementation and must not be carried out without authorisation.
- **Commission's exclusive decision-making power** – the Commission has the exclusive jurisdiction to decide whether a concentration falling within the ambit of the EUMR can be cleared and implemented.

6.1 Notification

Each concentration falling into the Commission's jurisdiction has to be notified to the Commission. The EUMR defines both the point in time at which this obligation arises as well as the party which has the obligation to notify the proposed transaction.

Under certain circumstances the notification date may be of significance for the material assessment of the proposed concentration. In particular the Commission will apply the priority rule in so called 'parallel mergers', i.e. mergers within the same industry being reviewed at the same time. This was the case in *Seagate/Samsung* and *Western Digital/Viviti Technologies* where the producers of hard disk drives notified the concentrations on two following days.[196] In accordance with the priority rule the Commission cleared the earlier notified merger without any conditions and imposed some conditions on the later one. This was due to the fact that while reviewing the concentration that was notified one day later, the Commission took into consideration the market developments resulting from unconditional clearance of the other transaction.

Article 4(2) EUMR specifies who is obliged to submit the notification to the Commission. In case of a merger within the meaning of Article 3(1)(a) EUMR or the acquisition of joint control the concentration must be notified by all parties. In all other cases only the undertaking or undertakings acquiring control are obliged to submit the notification.

---

[196] Commission decision of 19 October 2011, Case COMP/M.6214 – *Seagate/HDD Business of Samsung*, available at http://ec.europa.eu/competition/mergers/cases/decisions/
m6214_20111019_20682_2390485_fn.pdf; Commission decision of 23 November 2011, Case COMP/M.6203 – *Western Digital/Viviti Technologies*, nyp, see press release at http://europa.eu/rapid/pressReleasesAction.do?reference=IP/11/1395.

6.2 Standstill period

Pursuant to Article 7(1) EUMR a notified concentration must not be completed before the Commission has granted clearance or the respective review period has expired triggering the presumption of clearance under Article 10(6) EUMR. The suspension obligation covers not only all transactions fulfilling the requirements of a 'concentration' within the meaning of EUMR but may also apply to the acquisition of minority shareholdings. In *Aer Lingus* the General Court held that 'the acquisition of a shareholding that does not, as such, confer control for the purposes of Article 3 of the merger regulation may fall within the scope of Article 7'.[197] As a general rule the parties must abstain from taking any actions that would enable the merging undertakings to coordinate their market activities before the closing of the transaction. However, during the waiting period the parties involved are allowed to engage in some transaction-related activities such as completion of the due diligence or integration planning.

An exception to this rule is public bids which may be implemented prior to the Commission's decision. The only restriction on the acquirer is that it must not exercise the voting rights attached to the securities in question or may do so only in order to maintain the full value of the investment. A derogation rule applies also to security transactions. Under Article 7(3) EUMR the Commission, acting on a reasoned request, may grant a conditional or unconditional derogation from the suspension period. The notifying party has to demonstrate that the derogation is necessary for the operation of the undertaking(s) involved and the concentration will not pose any threat to competition. The Commission relied on this provision and granted a derogation from the suspension obligation during the financial crisis in 2008 when target companies were facing serious financial difficulties and the full and immediate implementation of the notified transaction was the only possibility to avoid insolvency.[198]

The suspension obligation does not apply to so-called 'warehousing' cases. Parties to a concentration may arrange for an interim buyer, mostly a bank, to temporarily acquire a business from the seller on behalf of an ultimate purchaser and to hold it until the final acquirer is granted all the necessary regulatory clearances including an approval decision under the EUMR.[199] Such a transaction structure was implemented by the French undertaking Lagardère which intended to buy some assets from

---

[197] GC (6 July 2010), Case T-411/07 – *Aer Lingus Group v Commission* [2010] ECR II-3691, para. 83. On the assessment of minority shareholdings under EU merger control law see Hatton and Cardwell, 'Treatment of Minority Acquisitions under EU and International Merger Control', *European Competition Law Review*, 31 (2010), 436.

[198] In 2008 and 2009 the Commission approved derogation requests in eleven transactions whereas in 2007 such derogation was granted only in three cases and in 2010 only in one case.

[199] On two-step transactions and the suspension obligation in general, see Anttilainen-Mochnacz, 'Two-step Transaction Structures in the Context of the EC Merger Regulation: To Have or to Hold?', *European Competition Law Review*, 29 (2008), 238.

Vivendi Universal and asked a French bank NBP to acquire the assets on a temporary basis and to sell them to Lagardère once the Commission's approval was obtained. The Commission cleared the transaction under the EUMR but its decision was appealed by a third party claiming, *inter alia*, that the 'warehousing' structure adopted by the parties was subject to notification. The General Court rejected this argument and held that the final purchaser did not acquire control over the target company during the 'warehousing' period hence there was no concentration to be notified.[200] This judgment clearly contrasts with the Commission's Jurisdictional Notice stating that 'warehousing' arrangements are not covered by the exception under Article 3(5)(a) EUMR but have to be notified.[201]

In cases where a concentration has been implemented without the Commission's authorisation (so called 'gun-jumping') the validity of the transaction depends solely on the decision by the Commission. Moreover, the Commission may impose a fine of up to 10% of the aggregate turnover or take appropriate interim measures in order to restore or maintain effective competition. For example, the Commission imposed on Electrabel, a Belgian energy company, a fine of EUR 20 million for breach of the suspension obligation.[202]

6.3 Phase I investigation

After receiving a merger notification the Commission initiates a Phase I investigation and publishes a notice in the Official Journal setting out the main features of the proposed transaction. A Phase I investigation is only preliminary and must be completed by the Commission within twenty-five working days. This period may be extended for another ten working days if a request for a referral from a Member State or commitments from the merging parties have been submitted.

Article 6 EUMR lists types of decisions which may be issued by the Commission following a Phase I investigation:

- **no jurisdiction decision** – after finding that the Commission has no jurisdiction to assess the concentration, for example there is no concentration or because the concentration does not have a Union dimension (Article 6(1)(a) EUMR);
- **clearance decision** – is issued if the Commission holds that the concentration does not give serious doubts about the compatibility with the internal market (Article 6 (1)(b) EUMR);

---

[200] GC (13 September 2010), Case T-279/04 – *Éditions Odile Jacob v Commission* [2010] ECR II-185, paras. 133–4; currently on appeal to ECJ as case C-551/10.

[201] Jurisdictional Notice, para. 35.

[202] Commission decision of 10 June 2009, Case COMP/M.4994 – *Electrabel/Compagnie Nationale du Rhône*, available at http://ec.europa.eu/competition/mergers/cases/decisions/m4994_20090610_1465_fn.pdf; currently under appeal to GC, case T-332/09.

- **conditional clearance decision** – following modification of the concentration by commitments declared by the parties (Article 6(1)(b) and 6(2) EUMR);
- **launch of Phase II investigation** – if the concentration gives rise to serious doubts as to its compatibility with the internal market an in-depth investigation is initiated (Article 6(1)(c) EUMR).

Additionally the Commission may refer the case to a national competition authority pursuant to Article 9(3) EUMR.

According to Article 10(6) EUMR, in cases where the Commission has not taken any formal decision within the Phase I timeframe the notified concentration shall be deemed compatible with the internal market.

In a Phase I investigation the procedural rights of the notifying parties are rather limited. They are entitled to be heard only before one of the decisions listed in Article 18(1) EUMR is to be taken. The Commission may also offer the parties involved a state of play meeting in case some anticompetitive concerns have been identified during the market test. Such meetings are however 'entirely voluntary in nature'.[203] Pursuant to Article 18(4) EUMR third parties have to demonstrate sufficient interest in the result of the proceeding to be heard by the Commission.

In 2011 the Commission approved 299 of 309 notified transactions in Phase I.

6.4 Phase II investigation

In cases where the Commission decides that there are serious doubts as to the compatibility of the proposed merger with the internal market an in-depth Phase II investigation is initiated. The Commission's examination must generally be completed within 90 working days. This period may be extended for up to a maximum of 110 days when the parties have submitted commitments or the case has been declared to be a complex one.

6.4.1 Formal elements of the investigation

A Phase II investigation is initiated only in complex cases where an extended market investigation is required. Therefore it is necessary to involve both undertakings concerned and third parties such as competitors, suppliers or customers in the investigation. The Commission usually gets support from the Chief Competition Economist's office as well. The EUMR provides that Phase II investigations involve several formal elements that aim at safeguarding a due process and effective fact finding. In

---

[203] Best Practices, para. 30.

particular the following steps have to be completed after initiation of a Phase II investigation:

- **Written Statement of Objections (SO)** – the SO is a document in which the Commission outlines in detail reasons for which it has serious doubts as to the compatibility of the concentration with the internal market. It is addressed in writing to the notifying parties and gives them an opportunity to be heard before a final decision is adopted. The SO may be amended after receipt of the parties' observations.[204] However, pursuant to Article 18(3) EUMR the Commission can base its final decision only on objections on which the parties have been able to submit their observations. Otherwise the decision may be annulled by the General Court since it violates the right to be heard.[205]
- **Access to the Commission's file** – after receiving the SO, parties to the concentration have a formal right to access the Commission's file to prepare their response to the SO. The right of access to the file does not apply to documents containing business secrets of third parties, other confidential and commercially sensitive information and internal documents of the Commission.
- **Reply to SO** – undertakings involved in the merger have to be granted the opportunity to present their views on the compatibility of the merger with the internal market and to rebut the Commission's competition concerns. The reply submitted by them may contain additional documents or further information or proposals to hear persons who may support the facts pleaded in their response. The parties have ten working days to submit their comments or to request a formal oral hearing.
- **Formal oral hearing** – notifying parties have the right to request the Commission to arrange an oral hearing. The right to be heard may be also granted to third parties if they present a sufficient interest in the outcome of the proceedings. The hearing is conducted by the Hearing Officer.
- **State of play meetings** – during these informal and voluntary meetings the parties and the Commission discuss the material issues resulting from the concentration at different stages of the proceedings. According to the Best Practices, at least four such meetings should take place during a Phase II investigation: within two weeks after the decision to open Phase II, before the SO being issued by the Commission, following the response to the SO, and before the meeting of the Advisory Committee.[206]

---

[204] ECJ (10 June 2008), Case C-413/06 – *Bertelsmann AG & Sony Corporation of America v Impala* [2008] ECR I-4951, paras. 63–66.

[205] GC (22 October 2002), Case T-310/01 – *Schneider Electric v Commission* [2002] ECR II-4071, paras. 437 et seq.

[206] Best Practices, para. 33.

6.4.2 Possible outcomes of the Phase II investigation

Following a Phase II investigation the Commission may issue the following decisions:

- **unconditional clearance decision** – if the concentration is compatible with the internal market (Article 8(1) EUMR);
- **conditional clearance decision** – a clearance decision may contain conditions and obligations that have to be fulfilled by the parties in order to ensure that their commitments accepted by the Commission are complied with. The conditions and obligations may require structural changes or oblige the undertakings to adopt a certain market conduct (Article 8(2) EUMR);
- **prohibition decision** – if the concentration is not compatible with the internal market. In case of already implemented mergers the Commission may order divestitures or other structural remedies (Article 8(3) EUMR);
- **referral** to a Member State at its request (Article 9(3)(b) EUMR).

All Phase II decisions have to be notified to the parties and national competition authorities. Final decisions are also published in the Official Journal pursuant to Article 20 EUMR.

In 2011 the Commission initiated eight Phase II investigations of which only one ended with a prohibition of the notified transaction.[207]

Summary of Section 6

Under the EUMR proposed transactions have to be notified before their implementation. The suspension obligation requests parties not to close a transaction before merger clearance has been obtained. The review of merger notifications by the Commission is subject to certain time limits. If the time limit expires without the Commission having taken any decision, clearance is deemed to have been granted.

Most merger cases are cleared in the summary Phase I review. If the Commission identifies competitive concerns in Phase I that require an in-depth investigation it may commence a Phase II review that entails an extended review period. Before a proposed transaction is prohibited the Commission has to give the parties the opportunity to be heard. To this end a statement of objections will be issued in which the Commssion sets out its findings and conclusions. The parties may present their observations before a final decision is adopted.

---

[207] Commission decision of 26 January 2011, Case M.5830 – *Olympic/Aegean Airlines*, summary of the decision in OJ No. C 195 of 3 July 2012, p. 11.

7. COMMITMENTS

Both within Phase I and Phase II investigations the undertakings concerned may offer the Commission commitments if the proposed concentration gives rise to serious competition concerns or is unlikely to be cleared.[208] If the Commission accepts the proposed commitments a conditional decision is issued and the commitments shall be attached to it as conditions and obligations. A detailed guidance on all procedural and material issues relating to commitments can be found in the Commission's Notice on remedies.[209]

In order for the commitments to be accepted they must be proportionate to the competition concerns identified by the Commission and entirely eliminate them.[210] The burden of proof rests on the notifying parties. Furthermore, the commitments have to be comprehensive and effective from all points of view and must be capable of being implemented effectively within a short period of time.[211]

Generally the Commission accepts three types of commitments.

Firstly, divestitures are the best way to eliminate competition concerns resulting from horizontal overlaps. The divested assets must consist of viable business units that, if operated by a suitable purchaser, can compete effectively with the merged entity on a lasting basis. Normally only businesses operating on a stand-alone basis can be divested but the Commission may also accept divestiture of certain assets such as particular brands or licences. For example, in *Kraft Foods/Cadbury* the Commission identified some horizontal competition concerns within chocolate confectionery in Poland, and to remedy these concerns Kraft committed to divest Cadbury's Polish confectionery business to a third party.[212] In general, divestitures are preferred structural remedies by the Commission as they bring an immediate and clear-cut change in market structure and their fulfilment can be monitored at relatively low cost.

Secondly, the Commission may also accept other structural remedies such as granting access to key infrastructure or technology including licensing intellectual property rights on a non-discriminatory and transparent basis.[213] Although their main objective is to facilitate market entry by new undertakings, they may also be granted in order to ensure that the already existing competition will not be

---

[208] For an overview of the remedies accepted by the Commission, see Papandropoulos and Tajana, 'The Merger Remedies Study: In Divestiture We Trust?', *European Competition Law Review*, 27 (2006), 443.

[209] Commission Notice on remedies acceptable under Council Regulation (EC) No 139/2004 and under Commission Regulation (EC) No 802/2004, OJ No. C 267 of 22 October 2008, p. 1 (hereinafter: Notice on remedies). For a comment on this notice see Berg and Lipstein, 'The Revised Merger Remedies Notice: Some Comments', *European Competition Law Review*, 30 (2009), 281.

[210] EUMR, Recital 30.   [211] Notice on remedies, para. 9.

[212] Commission decision of 6 January 2010, Case COMP/M.5644 – *Kraft Foods/Cadbury*, available at http://ec.europa.eu/competition/mergers/cases/decisions/m5644_20100106_20212_fn.pdf.

[213] For example, transfer of landing and starting slots at airports is a typical structural remedy accepted by the Commission in airline merger cases: decision of 28 August 2009, Case M.5440 – *Lufthansa/Austrian Airlines*, summary of the decision in OJ No. C 16 of 22 January 2010, p. 11.

significantly impeded. Such structural remedies may be adopted only if they are equally effective as divestitures. Their primary benefit to both the Commission and the undertakings involved is that they are flexible and can be narrowly tailored to remedy the identified competition concerns.

Thirdly, the merging companies may offer behavioural commitments[214] such as an undertaking to abstain from a particular market conduct. Since such commitments are less likely to eliminate the competition constraints stemming from the notified concentration and the monitoring of their implementation may require significant resources,[215] the Commission will accept behavioural remedies only under exceptional circumstances, for example with respect to vertical or conglomerate mergers.[216]

Commitments are part of the Commission's decision and the parties to the transaction are obliged to act in line with them, i.e. by complying with obligations and fulfilling conditions imposed by the regulator. In case an obligation is not complied with it is at the Commission's discretion to revoke merger clearance. If one or all of the undertakings concerned do not fulfil a condition the clearance decision is deemed to have not been granted. In both cases the Commission has the power to proceed with its Phase I or Phase II investigation without being bound by any time limits. Furthermore, the Commission may order interim measures to restore or maintain effective competition without consulting the parties. Additionally fines of up to 10% of the aggregate turnover may be imposed on undertakings not complying with the obligations/conditions resulting from the decision.

Summary of Section 7

Parties may address competitive concerns identified in a merger review procedure by offering commitments to the Commission. Those commitments typically aim at limiting the market position of the merged entity through structural remedies such as divestitures or at improving the chances of rivals by behavioural remedies, for example an obligation not to adopt a certain market conduct.

Commitments will become a part of the clearance decision and will take the form of conditions or obligations.

---

[214] For an appraisal of the cases involving behavioural remedies, see Paas, 'Non-structural Remedies in EU Merger Control', *European Competition Law Review*, 27 (2006), 209.

[215] The Commission may request to include arbitration clauses in behavioural commitments: see Blanke, 'The Use of Arbitration in EC Merger Control: Latest Developments', *European Competition Law Review*, 28 (2007), 673.

[216] Notice on remedies, para. 69. For example in *Deutsche Bahn/EWS*, decision of 16 November 2007, Case COMP/M.4746, available at http://ec.europa.eu/competition/mergers/cases/decisions/ m4746_20071106_20212_fn.pdf, the Commission accepted behavioural commitments by the parties to ensure that an already existing dominant position of a third party, the French SNCF, would not be strengthened. For a discussion of structural and behavioural remedies, see Papon, 'Structural versus Behavioural Remedies in Merger Control: A Case-by-Case Analysis', *European Competition Law Review*, 30 (2009), 36.

8. INVESTIGATIVE POWERS

Under the EUMR the Commission is given wide investigative powers in order to carry out its regulatory functions. Article 11 EUMR gives the Commission the power to issue requests for information. A simple information request is a typical instrument applied by the Commission in both Phases I and II. It may be addressed to both the notifying companies and third parties. Although there is no legal duty to respond, providing the Commission with an incorrect or misleading reply may be fined. In contrast to information requests, information decisions must be responded to by the addressees and are issued very rarely, mostly in cases where a simple information request remained unanswered. The Commission is also authorised to carry out on-the-spot inspections at the premises of undertakings if it is necessary to complete an investigation. In practice such 'dawn raids' are an exception as the Commission tends to gather all the relevant information by issuing informal requests. For breach of obligations under the EUMR the Commission is authorised to impose fines and periodical penalty payments on the notifying undertakings and third parties. According to Article 14 EUMR, fines imposed for providing incorrect or misleading information may amount to 1% of the group worldwide turnover in the preceding fiscal year whereas fines for implementing a concentration without prior notification to the Commission or in breach of conditions attached to a decision can be up to 10% of the group worldwide turnover. The Commission imposed a fine of EUR 20 million on Electrabel, a Belgian energy company, for breach of the suspension obligation.[217] Periodical payments are imposed in order to compel undertakings to provide the relevant information or submit to a Commission inspection and may not exceed 5% of the average daily aggregate turnover.

Summary of Section 8

In the course of a merger review procedure the Commission in many cases carries out an extensive market investigation to establish all facts relevant for the assessment of the proposed transaction. The Commission usually sends out simple information requests but is empowered under the EUMR also to adopt formal decisions requesting information and to carry out inspections. In case of non-compliance with investigative measures fines may be imposed.

---

[217] Commission decision of 10 June 2009, Case COMP/M.4994 – *Electrabel/Compagnie Nationale du Rhône*, available at http://ec.europa.eu/competition/mergers/cases/decisions/m4994_20090610_1465_fn.pdf; currently under appeal to GC, case T-332/09.

9. JUDICIAL REVIEW

The jurisdiction of the EU courts to review merger control decisions is primarily based on Article 263 TFEU as most appeals brought against the Commission decisions are actions for annulment. However, an action for failure to act under the EUMR regime may also be admissible pursuant to Article 265 TFEU.[218] The parties to a notified concentration also have standing to bring an action against the Commission in order to recover damages following an erroneous decision under the EUMR.

Until more recent times the seeking of legal protection from the EU courts by undertakings was rather exceptional. This was mainly due to the fact that most transactions were envisaged in a certain business context and reflected parties' interests at a particular time. Under such circumstances there was strong business pressure on the merging parties to obtain clearance as soon as possible, even at the cost of far-reaching commitments, and any delay resulting either from initiation of a Phase II investigation or a prohibition decision caused the parties to lose their original interest in completing the notified transaction. From this perspective, lodging a court appeal that has no suspensive effect on the Commission's decision would usually cause significant further delay without bringing the appealing party any substantial benefits. An annulment judgment by the General Court would in principle only 'reset' the review process with the Commission initiating the Phase I (and possibly Phase II) investigation and examining the latest market developments as a consequence.

However, in 2002 the General Court annulled three prohibition decisions because of manifest errors of assessment of the Commission.[219]

9.1 Action for annulment

An action for annulment can primarily be brought by the parties to the notified transaction. However, under Article 263(4) TFEU third parties that are directly and individually concerned by the decision may also be granted *locus standi*. In the merger context the General Court has recognised standing of actual or even potential competitors,[220] customers and suppliers under the condition that their market situation is affected by the concentration.[221] It has also recognised standing of potential

---

[218] ECJ (25 September 2003), Case C-170/02 – *Schlüsselverlag J.S. Moser and Others v Commission* [2003] ECR I-9889.

[219] GC (6 June 2002), Case T-342/99 – *Airtours v Commission* [2002] ECR II-2585; GC (22 October 2002), Case T-310/01 – *Schneider Electric v Commission* [2002] ECR II-4071; GC (25 October 2002), Case T-5/02 – *Tetra Laval v Commission* [2002] ECR II-4381.

[220] GC (30 September 2003), Case T-158/00 – *ARD v Commission* [2003] ECR II-3825, paras. 61 et seq.

[221] GC (8 July 2003), Case T-374/00 – *Verband der freien Röhrenwerke and Others v Commission* [2003] ECR II-2275, para. 51.

acquirers of assets and businesses that were offered to be divested following a conditional clearance decision.[222] The General Court applies the admissibility test in a rather strict manner and it has rejected annulment actions brought by shareholders of the merging company,[223] employees' representatives[224] and a consumer rights group.[225]

Although the case law under Article 263 TFEU provides for a broad catalogue of admissible grounds for annulment, only two have turned out to be of major significance in the merger context: error in law and infringement of an essential procedural requirement. With regard to the former the EU courts apply the manifest error standard in the following way:

> while the Court of First Instance must not substitute its own economic assessment for that of the Commission for the purposes of applying the substantive rules of the Regulation, that does not mean that the Community judicature must refrain from reviewing the Commission's interpretation of information of an economic nature. Not only must the Community judicature establish, among other things, whether the evidence relied on is factually accurate, reliable and consistent but also whether that evidence contains all the information which must be taken into account in order to assess a complex situation and whether it is capable of substantiating the conclusions drawn from it.[226]

In *Impala* the ECJ also held that there is no general presumption in favour of approving concentrations and that this standard of proof applies in the same manner in cases where the merger has been cleared or blocked.[227]

Generally, this standard of review pertains to all types of final decisions in merger cases that may be subject to an annulment action. However, the General Court ruled that some of the procedural decisions adopted by the Commission in the course of its investigation may be challenged as well. Those are mainly decisions imposing fines and penalties[228] and referral decisions based on Articles 4, 9 or 22 EUMR.[229] On the other hand the General Court denied the reviewability of a decision to open a Phase II investigation which constitutes merely an 'intermediate step' leading to a final decision.[230] For similar reasons the General Court declared an action against a

---

[222] GC (3 April 2003), Case T-342/00 – *Petrolessence and SG2R v Commission* [2003] ECR II-1161, para. 41.

[223] GC (28 October 1993), Case T-83/92 – *Zunis Holding and Others v Commission* [1993] ECR II-1169. For a more nuanced approach see ECJ (31 March 1998), Case 68/94 – *France and Others v Commission* [1998] ECR I-1375, paras. 48 et seq.

[224] GC (27 April 1995), Case T-12/93 – *Comité central d'entreprise de la société anonyme Vittel v Commission* [1995] ECR II-1247, para. 50.

[225] GC (12 October 2011), Case T-224/10 – *Association Belge des Consommateurs Tests-Achats v Commission*, nyr, paras. 27 et seq.

[226] ECJ (10 July 2008), Case C-413/06 – *Bertelsmann AG & Sony Corporation of America v Impala* [2008] ECR I-4951, para. 145. For a comment on this case see Golding, 'The Impala Case: A Quiet Conclusion but a Lasting Legacy', *European Competition Law Review*, 31 (2010), 261.

[227] Ibid., para. 48.   [228] See wording of Article 16 EUMR.

[229] GC (3 April 2003), Case T-119/02 – *Royal Philips Electronics v Commission* [2003] ECR II-1433, paras. 285 and 343.

[230] GC (11 July 2007), Case T-351/03 – *Schneider Electric v Commission*, [2007] ECR II-2231, para. 240.

decision not to refer a case under Article 9 EUMR inadmissible, holding that such a decision does not in any way jeopardise the procedural rights and judicial protection enjoyed by the claimants.[231]

9.2 Action for damages

The strengthening of judicial control over merger control decisions which led to the annulment of several Commission decisions gave rise to subsequent claims for non-contractual liability. Following two judgments by the General Court in *MyTravel* and *Schneider Electric*, where the court annulled the prohibition decisions, the EU courts were called to decide whether the conduct by the Commission in both cases could constitute a breach of law within the meaning of Article 340 TFEU and to establish the Commission's liability for damages resulting from the unlawful prohibition of the mergers.[232]

In 2007 the General Court delivered its judgment in the *Schneider* case and ordered the Commission to compensate Schneider for its expenses caused by the participation in the renewed merger review before the Commission as well as for two-thirds of the loss sustained from the purchase of the target company Legrand following the prohibition decision.[233] One year later, in a similar case brought by MyTours, the General Court decided however that the Commission had not committed any serious error in assessing the alleged collective dominance and the remedies proposed by the parties in order to obtain clearance.[234] The court held that the Commission's decision to prohibit the notified transaction did not amount to a sufficient and serious infringement of its decisional competence. With regard to the 'sufficiently serious breach' test the General Court set a rather high standard of proof and this approach was subsequently confirmed by the ECJ that partially annulled the General Court's judgment awarding damages to Schneider.[235] The ECJ also summed up the criteria for application of Article 340 TFEU in EUMR-related cases:

- **An unlawful act by the Commission**: the decision at issue must constitute a sufficiently serious breach of a rule of law intended to confer rights on individuals. The decisive criterion in that regard is whether the disputed conduct of the

---

[231] GC (12 October 2011), Case T-224/10 – *Association Belge des Consommateurs Tests-Achats/Commission*, nyr, para. 80.

[232] On the action for damages under Article 340 TFEU in general, see Gutman, 'The Evolution of the Action for Damages against the European Union and Its Place in the System of Judicial Protection', *Common Market Law Review*, 48 (2011), 695.

[233] GC (11 July 2007), Case T-351/03 – *Schneider Electric v Commission* [2003] ECR II-2237. For a comment see Dawes and Peci, 'Sorry, But There's Nothing We Can Do to Help: Schneider II and the Extra-contractual Liability of the European Commission in Merger Cases', *European Competition Law Review*, 29 (2008), 151.

[234] GC (9 September 2008), Case T-212/03 – *MyTravel v Commission* [2008] ECR II-1967.

[235] ECJ (16 July 2009), Case C-440/07 P – *Commission v Schneider Electric* [2009] ECR I-6413.

Commission 'takes the form of action manifestly contrary to the rule of law and seriously detrimental to the interests of persons outside the institution and cannot be justified or accounted for by the particular constraints to which the staff of the institution, operating normally, is objectively subject'.[236] According to the General Court a mere 'documentary or logical inadequacy' in the Commission's reasoning or a shortcoming in its economic assessment does not meet this requirement. At the same time the General Court recognised – and the ECJ upheld this finding – that an infringement of a procedural right, here the right to be heard, may also constitute a sufficiently serious breach.[237]

- **Actual damage** suffered by the applicant: in *Schneider Electric* the General Court recognised that damage may be derived from financial loss caused by a forced sale of assets in the target company at a lower price than the acquisition price.[238] The ECJ rejected this claim on the ground of missing causality but upheld the judgment of the General Court ordering the Commission to pay the costs of legal and economic advisors in the repeated review procedure before the Commission.[239]

- **Causal link between the unlawful act and the damage**: under Article 340 TFEU the applicant must also demonstrate that the damage suffered was caused by the unlawful conduct of the Commission. In the merger context this requirement may be a rather difficult hurdle for the claimant to overcome. The ECJ has recently stated that the notifying parties have no vested right to recognition of the compatibility of the transaction and that they bear the financial risk of a prohibition decision adopted by the Commission.[240] On this ground the ECJ recognised that the sale of assets by Schneider at a reduced price was a direct consequence of Schneider's business decision and was not in any way caused by the Commission's prohibition decision.

In the *Schneider* judgment the ECJ struck a balance between the individual right to compensation and the effectiveness of the merger control regime. The ECJ construed the requirements of sufficient breach and causal link in a narrow way and therefore put potential claimants in a rather difficult position. In particular, the finding that shortcomings in the economic examination of a notified concentration may only exceptionally trigger the Commission's liability limits the prospect of success in a damages action significantly.[241]

---

[236] Ibid., para. 124.   [237] Ibid., paras. 110 et seq.

[238] GC (11 July 2007), Case T-351/03 – *Schneider Electric v Commission* [2003] ECR II-2237, para. 322.

[239] ECJ (16 July 2009), Case C-440/07 P – *Commission v Schneider Electric* [2009] ECR I-6413, paras. 212 et seq.

[240] Ibid., para. 204; see also Grzeszick, 'Case Comment, C-440/07 P Schneider Electric SA v. Commission', *Common Market Law Review*, 49 (2011), 907, 916 et seq.

[241] For an in-depth analysis of damages actions in merger cases see Bailey, 'Damages Actions under the EC Merger Regulation, *Common Market Law Review*, 45 (2007), 101.

Summary of Section 9

Final decisions of the Commission in merger cases are subject to judicial review. They can be challenged by the parties in a nullity action. Actual and potential competitors also have standing to bring such an action, as well as other market participants with a sufficient degree of exposure to the effects of the decision. Parties may also seek damages from the Commission if the merger decision amounts to an unlawful act of the Commission, there is actual damage and there is a causal link between these elements.

QUESTIONS ON CHAPTER 5

1. What is the purpose of merger control? (1.1)
2. How is the jurisdictional scope of EU merger control determined? (2)
3. Please explain which types of transaction qualify as a concentration under EU merger control law. (2.1)
4. What are the distinctive elements of joint control? (2.1.4)
5. Are joint ventures subject to EU merger control? (2.1.6)
6. What is the role of the concept of Union dimension? (2.2)
7. What is the relationship of EU and national merger control? (3)
8. What is the substantive test applied under EU merger control law? (4)
9. How is the relevant product market defined? (4.1.1)
10. How should one define the relevant geographic market? (4.1.2)
11. What is the role of market shares in the substantive appraisal of a concentration? (4.3.1)
12. Please give an example of a non-coordinated effect of a concentration. (4.3.2)
13. Please describe the foreclosure effects that may arise from a vertical concentration. (4.4.2)
14. What are the potential restrictive effects of conglomerate mergers? (4.4.3)
15. Please explain the notion of suspension obligation under EU merger control law. (6.2)
16. Please describe the categories of remedies that may be offered in a merger control procedure. (7)

SUGGESTED ESSAY TOPICS

1. The assessment of joint ventures under EU merger control law
2. The impact of non-coordinated effects on the substantive appraisal of concentrations under the EUMR
3. The efficiency defence in EU merger control law

6 Cartels

1. INTRODUCTION

Article 101(1) TFEU prohibits all agreements and concerted practices between undertakings which have as their object the prevention, distortion or restriction of competition within the internal market. The cartel prohibition is a central point of EU competition law which aims at protecting the internal market from any form of collusion between independent undertakings.

1.1 Profits from collusion

Although the significance of antitrust law both in the EU and in other jurisdictions around the world has significantly increased in recent years, it is assumed that national and cross-border cartels are still attractive. The main reason for the undertakings to enter into prohibited agreements with their competitors is higher profits that may be gained from the implemented collusion practices.[1] The coordination of market conduct may bring higher profits than competition. Collusive practices allow the undertakings concerned to exercise market power that they would not otherwise have. For example, through coordinated behaviour market and/or customer allocation may become possible which enables the firms participating in the cartel to request from their purchasers and final consumers prices above the market level, thereby increasing their own profits. Another potential benefit from cartel participation is lower costs. Cartels help to preserve the market status quo and to avoid investments in innovative assets and R&D that would be required in the presence of competition pressure.

---

[1] For a discussion of the economics of cartels see Trier et al., 'The Economics of Cartels: Incentives, Sanctions, Stability, and Effects', *Journal of European Competition Law and Practice*, 2 (2011), 405.

1.2 Factors facilitating collusion

In principle, undertakings decide to enter collusive practices only when the expected gains outweigh the probable costs. In assessing whether collusive practice may be profitable, companies take into account a number of factors that may facilitate collusion and thus reduce its costs:

- Level of market concentration – collusion is more likely the smaller the number of players in the market is. High concentration facilitates the coordination of market behaviour and makes the enforcement of the collusion easier and more effective. It is also easier to track and punish undertakings that decide to deviate from the agreement.
- Barriers to entry – the easier the entry into the market the more difficult to sustain the collusive prices. Low barriers to entry enable potential competitors to exercise pressure on the colluding undertakings and therefore reduce the risk of welfare losses.
- Cross-ownership and other links between competitors – participation in the competitor's shares or presence in its board enhances the scope for the collusion as it makes the coordination of pricing and/or marketing policies much easier. The exchange of sensitive information may also be facilitated.
- Product homogeneity – with regard to similar products collusion is easier to execute because of the similarities in the cost structure and similar price expectations.
- Demand inelasticity – the more inelastic the demand the higher the price the cartel can set and the greater the profits it will generate.
- Demand stability – increases the transparency in the market and enables the colluding undertakings to observe the market behaviour of other firms involved in the cartel.

1.3 Stability of cartels

In the short term cartels do not represent the optimal solution. Collusion requires the firms concerned to cut their production in order to limit output and raise prices. Hence each of them could increase their profits in the short term by cheating the other undertakings involved and raising its output. This is the main reason why most cartels are unstable. The companies involved in a cartel have a strong incentive to cheat by raising production and undercutting the cartel price. In this way they may increase their profits.

The following factors are considered to contribute to cartel stability:

- Low benefits of cheating – deviation from collusion may only be profitable when the extra profits earned by selling more units for the price below cartel level outweigh the increased production costs and lost profit on the units that would be sold anyway. Such benefits are unlikely to occur in industries with high fixed costs.

- High likelihood of cheating being detected – the more difficult and costly the detection of potential deviations the less sustainable cartel agreements become. In principle, cheating will become apparent immediately in the markets with a high degree of price transparency. A small number of colluding undertakings also allows for easy and prompt identification of cheaters.
- Existence of credible punishment mechanisms – this effectively discourages potential cheaters from deviating from the collusion agreements. The most effective punishment mechanisms are either lowering the cartel price to a more competitive level and reduction of the cheater's profit or entering the geographical market originally allocated to the cheater.

1.4 Approach in the EU

In its *Cement* judgment the ECJ summarised the approach to cartels under EU competition law in the following way:

Participation by an undertaking in anticompetitive practices and agreements constitutes an economic infringement designed to maximise its profits, generally by an intentional limitation of supply, an artificial division of the market and an artificial increase in prices. The effect of such agreements or of such practices is to restrict free competition and to prevent the attainment of the common market, in particular by hindering intra-Community trade. Such harmful effects are passed directly on to consumers in terms of increased prices and reduced diversity of supply. Where an anticompetitive practice or agreement is adopted in the cement sector, the entire construction and housing sector, and the real-estate market, suffer such effects.[2]

A similar view has been taken by the Commission which insisted on strengthening its investigative powers within the framework of Regulation 1/2003. One of the main aims of this piece of legislation was to furnish the Commission and national competition authorities enforcing EU competition law with effective instruments that would enable them to tackle the major cartels.

In 2010 the Commission adopted decisions to fine 69 undertakings in cartel cases a total of EUR 3,057 million. The highest fine to date in a cartel case was EUR 1,383 million and was imposed in the *Carglass* case.[3]

An examination of 18 cartels which were the subject of Commission decisions in the years 2005–2007 showed that the overall consumer harm suffered due to these

---

[2] ECJ (7 January 2004), Joined Cases C-204/00 P, C-205/00 P, C-211/00 P, C-213/00 P, C-217/00 P and C-219/00 P – *Aalborg Portland AS and Others v Commission* [2004] ECR I-123, para. 53.

[3] See Commission's press release of 12 November 2008, IP/08/1685.

cartels ranged from around EUR 4 billion to EUR 11 billion. An average overcharge for each by these cartels has been estimated as between 5% and 15%.[4]

Summary of Section 1

Cartels are the most severe restrictions of competition. Through a cartel, competitors replace competitive restraints exercised on each other by collusion. Thus they collectively achieve a higher degree of market power which they can exploit to the detriment of consumers. Cartels usually seek to raise prices above competitive level and to increase the profits of their participants.

Cartels are likely to occur in markets that show a high degree of concentration, which allows competitors to monitor each other's market conduct. High entry barriers also contribute to the existence of cartels since they ensure that potential competitors cannot easily enter the market and offer lower prices jeopardising the functioning of the cartel. Often there are links between the cartel members, for example employees that previously worked for another undertaking in the business. Stable demand also facilitates the operation of a cartel since it increases market transparency.

Cartel members have a strong incentive to cheat on each other, for example by selling at lower prices than those agreed in the cartel. This will raise their short-term profits. Cartels will try to prevent such cheating by punishment mechanisms. Still, cartels tend to be unstable.

The Commission has made the investigation of cartels an enforcement priority. The Commission has stressed the strong detrimental impact of cartels on consumer welfare.

2. CARTEL PROHIBITION UNDER ARTICLE 101 TFEU

Article 101(1) TFEU provides for a list of agreement types that are deemed as particularly harmful and therefore having as their object the restriction of competition. The agreements listed therein are presumed to have negative effects on the markets and do not have to be examined with regard to their effects on competition. The likelihood of individual exemption under Article 101(3) TFEU is relatively low in such cases.

2.1 Horizontal price fixing

Article 101(1)(a) TFEU states that agreements which directly or indirectly fix purchase or selling prices or any other trading condition constitute restrictions to competition and are therefore prohibited. Price-fixing agreements are a widespread type of cartel

---

[4] Commission, Report on Competition Policy 2008, COM(2009) 374 final, para. 13.

that can be found in many industries. An illustrative example is the *Fine Art Auction Houses* case that involved Sotheby's and Christie's.[5] These two auction houses are considered to cover 90% of the worldwide market for auctions of fine art objects, antiques, furniture, collectibles and memorabilia. A high degree of concentration, as set out above, is a prerequisite for a cartel to work since it will not be possible to control and monitor the market behaviour of a larger number of market participants.

At the beginning of the 1990s, the international art market was in a period of recession that affected both Christie's and Sotheby's. The companies were not achieving the desired revenue levels. In this sense too the case is typical since many cartels are set up in a situation of economic recession which puts an industry under competitive pressure.

In this situation officers of Sotheby's and Christie's met to discuss the market situation and to consider how profits could be increased.

Auction houses generate income by charging the consigner of the arts object a 'vendor's commission' which is usually calculated on the price at which the merchandise is knocked down to the final bidder. In addition, persons buying at auctions are charged a 'buyer's premium'.

After a series of meetings, the respective officers agreed to adopt sliding scales for the vendor's commission. Depending on the lot value, the commission would amount to 10%–20%. The scales were almost identical and were introduced simultaneously, taking effect in the auction season beginning in September 1995. It was also agreed not to grant any rebates on the commission as set out in the scale. Apparently, the senior executives of the auction houses considered the risk of detection by competition authorities but concluded, according to the notes of an officer of Christie's, that they were worried not about the risk but about top management time that would be tied up in investigation.[6]

In the press releases accompanying the introduction of the new commission scale it was made clear that property already consigned for future planned sales would not be affected by the new scales.

This obvious exception, however, opened the door to 'cheating' by the two auction houses. They could not trust each other not to offer attractive terms in getting a particular high-profile sale, on the basis that this followed from past obligations. In order to ensure that neither took on new business at the old rates or at no commission, the auction houses exchanged lists of 'grandfathered' clients. These lists identified the customers with whom conditions had been agreed, prior to the announcement of the new scale.

Another measure taken to exclude any cheating by one of the cartelists was an instruction given by senior management of Sotheby's to personnel across its offices

---

[5] Commission decision of 30 October 2002, Case COMP/E-2/37.784 – *Fine Art Auction Houses*, available at http://ec.europa.eu/competition/antitrust/cases/dec_docs/37784/37784_8_4.pdf.

[6] Ibid., para. 124.

to monitor and report any discounts offered by Christie's in contravention of its published rates.

Following the introduction of the new vendor's commission scale, sales of Sotheby's and Christie's increased strongly.

The cartel was later detected in the US, resulting in fines and a jail term for one of the senior executives of Sotheby's. In Europe, the Commission imposed a fine on Sotheby's while Christie's benefited from the leniency notice (which will be discussed below).

2.1.1 Triangular cartels

Article 101(1) TFEU may be infringed not only by an explicit agreement to fix prices but also by an informal concertation between suppliers. This may for example occur when information on the dates and amounts of price increases is circulated among competitors through a third party. This type of cartel is also referred to as a 'hub and spoke cartel'. Typically a supplier acts as a 'hub' by collating and distributing sensitive information from its distributors (the 'spokes') on pricing intentions. When the supplier obtains information from one distributor about an intended price increase, the supplier will pass on this information to other distributors. This will reduce uncertainty over the pricing intentions of rival distributors.[7] This type of behaviour may be challenged by competition authorities both as resale price maintenance (i.e. a vertical hardcore infringement) and an indirect concerted practice between competitors (i.e. a horizontal price-fixing cartel). Still, it is debatable whether a distributor who receives 'unsolicited' information about the pricing intentions of his competitors through a supplier engages in a concerted practice. It will be difficult to distance oneself from having taken into account this information given the far-reaching concept of 'concerted practice' discussed in Chapter 2 above.

Triangular cartels may also function as a way to indirectly exchange information between suppliers through a common distributor. A distributor may receive information from a supplier on (wholesale) pricing intentions and pass on this information to competing suppliers. This will reduce uncertainty over the pricing intentions of competing suppliers and may be seen as a horizontal price-fixing cartel. Again, it is uncertain whether such an indirect and possibly unsolicited information exchange can amount to a concerted practice.

So far there is no case law at EU level dealing with triangular cartels of the nature described in this section.[8] However, there is some enforcement activity by national

---

[7] For an economic appraisal of triangular cartels, see Overd, 'Effects Analysis in Hub-and-spoke Cartels', *European Competition Law Review*, 32 (2011), 248.

[8] There are some cases that come close to a hub and spoke scenario though. For an appraisal of such cases and the conclusions for the concept of agreement under Article 101 TFEU, see Lianos, 'Collusion in Vertical Relations under Article 81 EC', *Common Market Law Review*, 46 (2011), 1027, 1056.

competition authorities. The solution this enforcement acitivity can provide to issues involving the concept of concerted practice remains to be seen.[9]

2.1.2 Scope of price fixing

The prohibition of Article 101 TFEU covers not only direct fixing of prices but also any type of agreement relating to the regulation of pricing mechanisms between competitors. One of the most common types of horizontal price fixing is setting a target price to be reached at a certain point in time without agreeing on the specific stepwise price increases towards the target price. Such conduct is prohibited even if there is no evidence on the influence of the target price on the pricing policy of the colluding undertakings. Such an approach was adopted by the General Court in the *Amino Acids Cartel* case:

Specifically, the fixing of a price, even one which merely constitutes a target, affects competition because it enables all the participants in a cartel to predict with a reasonable degree of certainty what the pricing policy pursued by their competitors will be. More generally, such cartels involve direct interference with the essential parameters of competition on the market in question. By expressing a common intention to apply a given price level for their products, the producers concerned cease independently determining their policy in the market and thus undermine the concept inherent in the provisions of the Treaty relating to competition.[10]

Apparently, the General Court takes the view that agreeing on a price increase without even quantifying the price increase may constitute a price-fixing cartel since competitors align their pricing policy in the sense that none of them will lower prices. However, this is problematic since a mere agreement on raising prices by an undefined amount and without setting a minimum price leaves room for competition between the participants in the agreement. The undertaking which has the lowest prices after the increase is likely to attract the most business.

As already mentioned, price fixing does not necessarily have to pertain to the price itself. Article 101 TFEU also covers agreements that determine some elements of the price or market measures having only indirect influence on the pricing mechanisms:

- **Measures having only indirect effect on prices** – tying the cartel price to the market price of other products; price recommendations by associations and industry groups as long as they enable the undertakings involved to determine their competitor's pricing policies; exchange information that facilitates the pursuit of a collaborative strategy; restrictions on advertising and promotions. An example of

---

[9] For a detailed discussion of the legal issues raised by triangular cartels, see Weck, 'Antitrust Infringements in the Distribution Chain: When is Leniency Available to Suppliers?', *European Competition Law Review*, 31 (2010), 394.

[10] GC (9 July 2003), Case T-224/00 – *Archer Daniels Midland and Archer Daniels Midland Ingredients v Commission* [2003] ECR II-2597, para. 120.

a measure having an indirect effect on prices by restricting advertising is provided by a decision by the Commission on some rules of the Code of professional conduct of the European patent agents. The Code was issued by the Institute of Professional Representatives before the European Patent Office, an organisation comprising all European patent agents. It was challenged by the Commission as a decision of an association of undertakings under Article 101(1) TFEU.[11] The Commission took the view that the prohibition of comparative advertising contributes to an intransparent market environment and thus reduces price competition. The Code also contained a prohibition on offering services to clients who have already been clients of another patent agent. The Commission considered this clause to restrict the ability of more efficient representatives to develop their services to the detriment of less efficient representatives and therefore to ultimately reduce competition over prices.[12]

- **Agreements relating to different elements of the price**
  Price-fixing agreements may not only relate to the total price of a given product but also to individual elements of the price. If competitors agree on maximum discounts, margins, credit terms, commission rates, common tariff structures or surcharges this is considered to restrict competition between them although they still could compete on other elements of the price or criteria unrelated to the price, such as the quality of after-sales services.

  Coming back to the *Fine Art Auction Houses* case discussed above, it has to be added that Sotheby's and Christie's not only reached an agreement on their vendor's commission rates but also on other terms. One of them was not to grant any discounts from the commission scales. Another concerned further conditions for vendors. The two auction houses agreed to no longer grant any interest-free advances to vendors but to charge a minimum interest rate based upon LIBOR (London inter-bank interest offer rate).[13]

  The *Alloy surcharge* case[14] is also a good example of the restraint of competition caused by an agreement on individual price elements.[15] The six companies accounting for 80% of European output of finished stainless steel products found themselves in a situation where the prices for stainless steel fell sharply and nickel prices

---

[11] Commission decision of 7 April 1999, Case IV/36.147 – *EPI Code of Conduct*, OJ No. L 106 of 23 April 1999, p. 14.

[12] Ibid., paras. 39–45.

[13] Commission decision of 30 October 2002, Case COMP/E-2/37.784 – *Fine Art Auction Houses*, available at http://ec.europa.eu/competition/antitrust/cases/dec_docs/37784/37784_8_4.pdf, paras. 86 and 90.

[14] Commission decision of 21 January 1998, Case IV/35.814 – *Alloy surcharge*, OJ No. L 100 of 1 April 1998, p. 55. The decision was upheld upon appeal by the General Court (14 July 2005), Joined Cases C-65/02 P and C-73/02 P – *ThyssenKrupp v Commission* [2005] ECR I-6778.

[15] Since stainless steel fell into the ambit of the Treaty Establishing the European Coal and Steel Community (ESCS Treaty) the Commission had to assess the case under Article 65 of the ESCS Treaty. The assessment, as far as it is relevant here, follows the same criteria as the assessment under Article 101 TFEU and is therefore instructive also for EU competition law.

rose. Nickel is an alloy used in the production of stainless steel that forms a very large proportion of the total production costs. The price of alloys is added as an alloy surcharge to the basic price for stainless steel. Since prices for alloys are extremely volatile, producers of stainless steel have a desire to offset the price fluctuations without recourse to frequent alterations in the basic price. To explore the possibilities of increasing profitability the stainless steel producers arranged a meeting in Madrid. At the meeting, the different methods of calculating the alloy surcharge were discussed. Following the meeting, all the participants took identical action. Within a certain timeframe they applied to their sales in a number of European countries an alloy surcharge based upon the same method and the same reference values. The prices for stainless steel virtually doubled within roughly a year, which the Commission partly attributed to the higher alloy surcharge.[16]

2.1.3 Purchasers' cartels

Article 101 TFEU applies also to collusive agreements between competing buyers. In the tobacco cases the Commission found that several Italian and Spanish tobacco processors infringed Article 101 TFEU by fixing maximum delivery prices offered to producers of raw tobacco.[17] In both countries, there was only a small number of processors active, which facilitated collusion. Interestingly, not only the tobacco processors colluded in this case but also the tobacco producers. The latter were organised in three agricultural unions that together conducted negotiations with the processors about the terms of the tobacco cultivation contracts the processors would conclude with the producers. In particular, they agreed on price brackets for each tobacco variety to be negotiated with the processors. On both sides of the market any competition was excluded. The Commission found competition was restricted by object. According to the Commission the fact that lower prices paid to the tobacco growers could be passed on to the consumers should not be regarded as a potential justification because the agreements on purchases that were investigated eliminated autonomy in determining the market conduct and reduced the degree of competition on the merits:

In this case, it is clear that the agreements and/or concerted practices [. . .] have by their very nature the object to restrict competition within the meaning of Article 81(1) [Article 101(1) TFEU] as they shelter processors and producers of raw tobacco in Italy from full exposure to market forces. By eliminating the autonomy of strategic decision-making and competitive

---

[16] Commission decision of 21 January 1998, Case IV/35.814 – *Alloy surcharge*, OJ No. L 100 of 1 April 1998, p. 55, para. 49.

[17] Commission decision of 20 October 2004, Case COMP/C.38.238/B.2 – *Raw Tobacco Spain*, available at http://ec.europa.eu/competition/antitrust/cases/dec_docs/38238/38238_249_1.pdf. The appeal to the General Court was largely rejected (8 September 2010), Case T-29/05 – *Deltafina v Commission* [2010] ECR II – 4077; Commission decision of 20 October 2005, Case COMP/C. 38.281/B.2 – *Raw Tobacco Italy*, available at http://ec.europa.eu/competition/antitrust/cases/dec_docs/38281/38281_508_1.pdf. (also as COMP/38.281). The appeal to the General Court was rejected (9 September 2011), Case T-25/06, nyr.

conduct, they prevent such undertakings from competing on the merits and enhancing their position on the market vis-à-vis the less efficient firms. The result could be reduced pressure to control costs, to improve quality and to innovate, thereby limiting productive and dynamic efficiencies.[18]

This confirms the important role EU competition law attributes to price competition not only with regard to selling but also with regard to purchase prices.

2.2 Horizontal market sharing

Another way for undertakings to restrict competition is market allocation between themselves. The firms involved may either apportion particular geographic markets to themselves (market sharing) or agree which products each of them will supply (product sharing). The parties to a collusion agreement may also determine who will supply each customer (customer sharing). From the producers' point of view geographical market sharing is even more effective than price fixing. Whereas in the latter case some competition on the merits other than price is still possible, the geographical market delineation eliminates competition, giving the undertakings concerned market positions close to that of a monopolist. Furthermore, consumers are deprived of the possibility to choose between alternative products. Market allocation facilitates the isolation of geographical markets and slows down the process of market integration which is one of the main objectives of the EU Treaty. For all these reasons market partitioning is regarded as a very serious breach of competition:

Apart from the serious distortion of competition which they entail, such agreements, by obliging the parties to respect distinct markets, often delimited by national frontiers, cause the isolation of those markets, thereby counteracting the EC Treaty's main objective of integrating the Community market. Also, infringements of this type, especially where horizontal cartels are concerned, are classified by the case-law as 'particularly serious' or 'obvious infringements'.[19]

2.2.1 Geographical market sharing

Market-sharing agreements that allocate to the parties the territories to which they can supply their products are prohibited by Article 101(1)(c) TFEU. An instructive example is the *Choline Chloride* cartel.[20] Choline Chloride, also known as vitamin B4,

---

[18] Commission decision of 20 October 2005, Case COMP/C.38.281/B.2 – *Raw Tobacco Italy*, available at http://ec.europa.eu/competition/antitrust/cases/dec_docs/38281/38281_508_1.pdf (also as COMP/ 38.281), para. 285.

[19] GC (18 July 2005), Case T-241/01 – *Scandinavian Airline Systems v Commission* [2005] ECR II-2917, para. 85.

[20] Commission decision of 9 December 2004, Case COMP/E-2/37.533 – *Choline Chloride*, available at http://ec.europa.eu/competition/antitrust/cases/dec_docs/37533/37533_43_1.pdf.

is mainly used in the animal feed industry as a feed additive, especially for poultry and swine. A higher purity food grade is used for nutrient supplements and infant formulae. In a situation of decreasing profitability of the choline chloride business because of excess capacities, six manufacturers which accounted for 80% of world-wide choline chloride production met 'to bring discipline to the worldwide pricing' of the product.[21] One of the measures eventually agreed upon was that the North American producers would withdraw from the European market in exchange for the European producers' withdrawal from the North American market.[22] Follow-up meetings were held to monitor implementation of the agreement. To disguise the meetings, the cartel members sought to combine them with industry conferences such as the Southeastern Poultry Convention. The Commission held that the allocation of territories potentially reduced or eliminated sales from other areas into the allocated territories and therefore restricted competition.[23] Fines were imposed.

The prohibition applies also in cases where the market segmentation is confined to the territory of one Member State provided that the agreement between suppliers affects the pattern of potential imports and/or exports to or from the territory at issue. Geographical markets may be shared by virtue of multipartite horizontal exclusive dealing agreements. Such an agreement was found to infringe Article 101 TFEU in the *Sugar* cartel where sugar producers from different Member States obliged themselves to send all cross-border deliveries through each other on a 'producer-to-producer' basis.[24] Sugar producers in Belgium had engaged in a concerted practice with sugar producers in the Netherlands to 'protect' the Netherlands market from competition from Belgium. To this end, sugar was not delivered to other customers in the Netherlands but to sugar producers and to the milk products and chemical industries.[25] This mechanism gave sugar producers in the Netherlands the possibility to control the prices of imported sugar. Enquiries of other customers in the Netherlands were rejected.[26] At the same time, sugar producers prevented trading companies in Belgium and the Netherlands from selling sugar to non-approved customers in the Netherlands. The Belgian sugar producer involved in the cartel occupied a dominant position on the Belgo-Luxembourg sugar market. They exercised pressure on trading companies by refusing to sell sugar to them if this sugar was resold for purposes which the producer had not authorised.[27]

One of the messages of a Belgian sugar producer to a trading company in Belgium reads:

In the case of the Netherlands import requirements of sugar for consumption in the Netherlands, you cease to deal with any transactions other than the requests made by the Netherlands sugar

---

[21] Ibid., para. 68.   [22] Ibid., para. 69.   [23] Ibid., para. 161.
[24] ECJ (16 December 1975), Joined Cases 40/73 to 48/73, 50/73, 54/73 to 56/73, 111/73, 113/73 and 114/73 – *Suiker Unie* [1975] ECR 1663.
[25] Ibid., paras. 131 et seq.   [26] Ibid., paras. 138 et seq.   [27] Ibid., para. 367.

industry which intends to keep control of this market. The Netherlands sugar industry, as you moreover have confirmed to us, told us that at present the situation in the Netherlands does not justify import operations. Since we do not intend to do anything at all in connexion with consumption in the Netherlands which is not approved by our Netherlands colleagues, there is no need to examine at the moment transactions in Belgian sugar for these outlets. [...] Supplying the milk products industry is another matter.[28]

In return, the Netherlands sugar producers refrained from exports to Belgium without the approval of the Belgian sugar producers:

So far as the Netherlands are concerned we do not want to do anything which might upset SU or CSM [the major Netherlands sugar producers], just as they do not want to do anything which would disturb us.[29]

In a similar way, the western part of Germany was protected from imports of Belgian sugar.[30]

The effect of market partitioning may also result from agreements between holders of particular intellectual property rights such as patents and trade marks and prohibiting the parties to grant licences to third parties. In *Bronbemaling* the Commission had to assess a scenario in which a Dutch company lodged two patent applications which were opposed by three other companies which claimed that the process to be patented was no longer patentable.[31] The patents related to a process for horizontal drainage. An agreement was reached under which the opponents would withdraw their oppositions. In return, the patent applicant would grant them licences for the patent once it was granted. The agreement further stipulated that the licences would contain a clause prohibiting the licensor from granting any identical or similar licences to other firms in the Netherlands without the consent of a majority of the parties to the agreement. The Commission considered that the agreement and the decisions taken jointly violated Article 101(1) TFEU since they prevented the patent holder from freely granting licences under the patent to other firms in the Netherlands. The Commission found that the agreement and the decisions restricted competition on the market for horizontal drainage as there was little alternative to the patented process.

Similar rules apply to market-sharing agreements determining which particular products may be supplied by the undertakings involved. In this way the parties to such agreement are granted exclusivity rights to produce and supply certain categories of goods. For instance, in the *Needles* cartel[32] two firms involved entered into an agreement whereby one of them would restrict its manufacturing and distribution activities in the haberdashery sector to hand-sewing needles and special

---

[28] Ibid., para. 151.   [29] Ibid., para. 152.   [30] Ibid., paras. 227 et seq.

[31] Commission decision of 25 July 1975, Case IV. 28.967 – *Bronbemaling*, OJ No. L 249 of 25 September 1975, p. 27.

[32] Commission decision of 26 October 2004, Case COMP/F-1/38.338 – *PO/Needles*, available at http://ec.europa.eu/competition/antitrust/cases/dec_docs/38338/38338_332_1.pdf.

needles only. This left other types of needles and the wider haberdashery market to the other party.[33]

2.2.2 Customer allocation

Pursuant to Article 101(1) TFEU, undertakings are not allowed to enter into agreements determining to which customers the collaborating parties may supply their products. This type of cartel has the same effect as market allocation. It is just a more detailed kind of agreement that occurs typically in markets with a relatively concentrated demand side. The *Carglass* cartel may serve as an example.[34] In this case the Commission imposed fines on four undertakings totalling EUR 1.4 billion. The car glass market is very concentrated on both the supply and the demand side. There are only three glass groups with global automotive glazing capability and presence. They account for more than 90% of all deliveries of glass parts for new passenger vehicles in Europe.[35] At the same time, the six largest vehicle manufacturers account for more than 80% of the production of light vehicles in Europe. The procurement by those car manufacturers of glass parts for a specific car model is carried out through a bidding process. The car manufacturers invite car glass suppliers to quote for the development, production and supply of glass parts for a new model or a new body type of an existing model. Car glass producers then submit their quotations to the car manufacturer who will send out a nomination letter to the producer that will be retained as the supplier for the part in question. From a certain point in time the suppliers regularly coordinated their replies to the car manufacturers for contracts coming onto the market and discussed who should win these contracts or which glass parts should be won by whom. Each supplier was interested in securing the supply contracts it wanted most and would compromise over contracts it wanted less. Sometimes certain glass parts were better for one supplier based, for instance, on how much free production capacity it had or on low transport costs. The suppliers had basically two means to 'pre-select' the winner. The first mechanism required not participating in a bidding process for a supply contract by claiming that no capacity was available. The second mechanism consisted in letting the 'pre-selected' winner set a price, with the other competitors agreeing to quote higher prices.[36] Through these mechanisms the cartelists intended to keep their market shares stable. They coordinated their market conduct in meetings and phone calls. A customer informed the Commission about suspected cartel conduct on the part of the manufacturers.[37]

---

[33] Ibid., para. 245.
[34] Commission decision of 12 November 2008, Case COMP/39125 – *Carglass*, available at http://ec. europa.eu/competition/antitrust/cases/dec_docs/39125/39125_1865_4.pdf.
[35] Ibid., para. 34.   [36] Ibid., paras. 102 and 103.   [37] Ibid., paras. 38 and 39.

2.3 Quotas and restrictions on production

Agreements between competing undertakings which limit and/or control production or markets are covered by Article 101(1)(b) TFEU. EU competition law prohibits any kind of bi- or multilateral agreements the objective of which is to adopt production quotas or reduce output as they lead to price increases in the concerned markets. A quota cartel may be difficult to distinguish from a customer allocation cartel. Cartels in many cases have a number of goals that typically comprise price and market share stabilisation. Market share stabilisation can be reached by customer allocation as well as by a quota cartel in which supply quotas are agreed between competitors. The difference is possibly just the primary mechanism on which the cartel is based. In a customer allocation cartel, supplies to individual customers are coordinated with a view to stabilising market shares. In a quota cartel, market shares are agreed without allocating individual customers.

The *French Breweries* case[38] is usually referred to as a quota cartel. In this case the two main French breweries entered into an 'armistice' agreement relating to the acquisition of beverage distribution companies and the establishment of equilibrium in the parties' integrated distribution networks.[39] The two breweries had earlier fought an 'acquisition war' during which both of them acquired a number of beverage wholesalers selling major quantities of beer brands produced by their rivals. Through these acquisitions each of them tried to cut off the rival brewery from its external distribution network. The prices for beverage wholesalers reached a level that was no longer justified by their profits but that was driven by the race between the two breweries. In this situation, the following 'armistice' was concluded:

Armistice

Yesterday we have reached agreement with [the other brewery] to put an end to the stupid and costly acquisition war. We share the objective that between our two groups, equilibrium must exist according to a general rule that none of the two is dominant in the [French] market with regard to three main aspects:

1. Volume integrated through each of the distribution networks must be equal. [. . .]
2. Volume of the other party's brands, controlled by integrated network of the competitor, must be equal.
3. Wholesalers to be integrated in the future must be identified as 'naturally' belonging to one of the two groups, conditional to the long term equilibrium according to items 1 and 2.[40]

The document was accompanied by two lists showing the wholesalers acquired by each group. The Commission challenged the 'armistice' as an agreement limiting or controlling investment or sharing markets.[41]

---

[38] Commission decision of 29 September 2004, Case COMP/C.37.750/B2 – *Brasseries Kronenbourg, Brasseries Heineken*, available at http://ec.europa.eu/competition/antitrust/cases/dec_docs/37750/37750_87_1.pdf.
[39] Ibid., para. 1.   [40] Ibid., para. 41.   [41] Ibid., para. 66.

A relatively rare type of cartel involves capacity reductions in order to raise the price level. This type of cartel falls into the ambit of Article 101(1)(b) TFEU as an agreement limiting production. An instructive example is the *EATA* case.[42] EATA stands for Europe Asia Trades Agreement, an agreement between major European and Asian shipping lines concerning scheduled maritime transport services for the carriage of containerised cargo from Northern Europe to the Far East. The member shipping lines claimed that a structural problem of overcapacity existed on the Northern Europe/Far East trades. Based on this assertion they agreed to reduce capacity by allocating to each of the parties a 'maximum allowed capacity', i.e. the maximum amount of capacity that each party was allowed to offer to the market for the carriage of goods. The maximum permitted capacity of each party was to be calculated according to the eastbound slots available per vessel declared by each party. In practice, this was done by calculating the total which would be available in the absence of the EATA and reducing it by a certain percentage.[43]

However, agreements on the reduction of production capacities may under special circumstances fall outside the scope of Article 101(1) TFEU. This pertains in particular to crisis cartels which aim at reduction of structural overcapacities.[44] Their implementation can result in the economic recovery of the industry concerned and can enable its profitable operation. In such cases the individual exemption under Article 101(3) TFEU applies when the following two conditions are met:

(i)   there is a long-lasting overcapacity of the industry concerned, and
(ii) the main goal of the arrangement is a production cutback secured by contractual penalties.

In the *Synthetic Fibres* case[45] the Commission accepted a coordinated capacity reduction of major players in the industry in a structural crisis. At the time, the European synthetic fibres industry was experiencing difficulties due to an imbalance between supply and demand. The imbalance stemmed partly from adverse market trends characterised by weak demand and increased import penetration and partly from the existence of increasing surplus capacity in the industry. To bring the market back into balance nine major European manufacturers of synthetic fibres collectively defined a maximum production capacity for each type of fibre that should not be exceeded by the industry. The participating companies committed themselves to

---

[42] Commission decision of 30 April 1999, Case IV/34.250 – *Europe Asia Trade Agreement*, OJ No. L 193 of 26 July 1999, p. 23.
[43] Ibid., paras. 10 and 11.
[44] Commission decision of 4 July 1984, Case IV/30.810 – *Synthetic Fibres*, OJ No. L 207 of 2 August 1984, p. 17; Commission decision of 19 July 1984, Case IV/30.863 – *BPCL/ICI*, OJ No. L 212 of 8 August 1984, p. 1.
[45] Commission decision of 4 July 1984, Case IV/30.810 – *Synthetic Fibres*, OJ No. L 207 of 2 August 1984, p. 17.

lodging details of the capacities they intended to cut and of the implementation of the cuts with an independent trustee body.

In its discussion of the conditions set out in Article 101(3) TFEU the Commission acknowledged that in a market economy it ought to be principally a matter for the individual undertaking to judge the point at which overcapacity becomes economically unsustainable and to take the necessary steps to reduce it.[46] In the present case, however, market forces had failed to achieve the capacity reductions necessary to re-establish and maintain in the longer term an effective competitive structure within the internal market.[47] The Commission found that the agreement created the following efficiencies justifying an exemption under Article 101(3) TFEU:

- The industry will shed the financial burden of keeping underutilised excess capacity open without incurring any loss of output, since the remaining capacity can be operated more intensively.
- The capacity reductions will also provide the undertakings with an opportunity to develop their particular strengths, since each has selected for closure those of its plants which are less profitable or competitive because of their obsolescence or small size.
- The elimination of the capital and labour costs of unprofitable activities will make resources available for the capacity that remains in production.
- The coordination of plant closures will also make it easier to cushion the social effects of the restructuring by making suitable arrangements for the retraining and redeployment of workers made redundant.

The fair share of consumers in the resulting benefit was seen in the healthier industry that would be able to offer them better products.[48]

It has to be noted that the Commission decision discussed above was taken at a point in time when the Commission was already aware of the continuous structural crisis in the synthetic fibres industry and had taken measures to stabilise capacity. The Commission had already restricted State aid to be granted for the production of synthetic fibres, a measure that is still in force.[49] In this sense, the agreement of the synthetic fibres manufacturers was in line with the Commission's industrial policy goals which may have facilitated approval by the Commission.[50]

---

[46] Ibid., para. 30.   [47] Ibid., para. 31.   [48] Ibid., para. 39.

[49] See Commission Regulation (EC) No. 800/2008 of 6 August 2008 declaring certain categories of aid compatible with the common market in application of Articles 87 and 88 of the Treaty (General Block Exemption Regulation), OJ No. L 214 of 9 August 2008, p. 3, para. 14.

[50] In the steel industry the Commission even allocated production quotas to individual steel producers and thus restricted competition itself in response to a structural crisis. Commission, decision no. 1831/81/ECSC of 24 June 1981 establishing for undertakings in the iron and steel industry a monitoring system and a new system of production quotas in respect of certain products, OJ No. L 180 of 1 July 1981, p. 1.

2.4 Other types of prohibited agreements

The list of prohibited agreements provided in Article 101(1) TFEU is not exhaustive. Therefore a number of other market conducts also fall within the scope of the cartel prohibition.

2.4.1 Collusive tendering

Collusive tendering (also referred to as bid rigging) is a market practice whereby the undertakings involved collaborate over their responses submitted to invitations to tender. This type of coordination is most likely to occur in the engineering and construction industries where large projects are tendered. A typical example is the *Pre-Insulated Pipe* cartel.[51] Pre-insulated pipes are principally used in district heating systems and consist essentially of steel pipes enclosed with pipes, with a layer of foam insulation in between. During the material period, eight major producers supplied the West European market, four of them located in Denmark. Customers are primarily municipally owned energy or district heating supply companies which procure pre-insulated pipes in tender procedures. The Danish manufacturers initially agreed on quotas for their home market but later expanded the cartel to other European countries and included the major suppliers active in those countries. To implement the quotas, the bidding procedure for individual projects was manipulated so as to ensure that the contract in question was awarded to the producer designated in advance by the cartel. The designated producer would calculate a price he would quote in the tender procedure and communicate it to the other cartel members. The other producers had to either decline to bid or give a higher 'protect' quote.[52] The cartel ended when an outsider complained to the Commission about efforts of the cartel members to drive it out of the market. The Commission imposed a fine for price fixing and market sharing.

2.4.2 Information exchange agreements

Exchange of information between collaborating parties is an inevitable element of most agreements caught by Article 101 TFEU. A bid-rigging cartel will only work if the members notify each other of upcoming projects and if the preselected winner of the contract communicates the price he will quote to the other cartel members.

---

[51] Commission decision of 21 October 1998, Case IV/35.691/E-4 – *Pre-Insulated Pipe Cartel*, OJ No. L 24 of 30 January 1999, p. 1. Confirmed by ECJ (28 June 2005), Joined Cases C-189/02 P, C-202/02 P, C-205/02 P to C-208/02 P and C-213/02 P – *Dansk Rørindustri A/S and Others v Commission* [2005] ECR I-5425.

[52] Commission decision of 21 October 1998, Case IV/35.691/E-4 – *Pre-Insulated Pipe Cartel*, OJ No. L 24 of 30 January 1999, p. 1, para. 68.

Information exchange is also necessary to make sure that the cartel members are not deviating from the agreed rules. In such cases the exchange of information is ancillary to the unlawful agreements and *per se* prohibited.

Under certain conditions an exchange of information between competitors which is not part of a control mechanism implemented within a framework of an illegal agreement may also be covered by Article 101(1) TFEU. This may in particular be the case where, as a result of the exchange of information, a platform is created that enables the competing undertakings to coordinate their market conduct without entering into an agreement or a concerted practice. An example can be seen in the *Asnef-Equifax* judgment of the ECJ.[53] A group of Spanish credit institutions had set up a register with the purpose of providing solvency and credit information relating in particular to the identity and economic activity of debtors as well as to special situations such as credit default. In the proceedings there was discussion about whether the exchange of such information restricted competition by eliminating risk factors and facilitating a homogeneous reaction by credit institutions towards an applicant for credit.[54] The court held in this regard:

> According to the case law on agreements on the exchange of information, such agreements are incompatible with the rules on the competition if they reduce or remove the degree of uncertainty as to the operation of the market in question with the result that competition between undertakings is restricted.[55]

However, the court did not exclude that such an information exchange agreement in a particular case might not restrict competition and thus not violate Article 101(1) TFEU. According to the court, this cannot be assessed in the abstract and depends on the economic conditions on the relevant market, the specific characteristics of the system concerned and the type of information exchanged.[56] Interestingly, the court held that the exchange of credit information disclosing the identity of the lender is restrictive of competition.[57] One would rather have expected such a statement with regard to information on the terms of individual contracts that clearly would facilitate a coordination of the interest rates and other terms offered by the banks.

An information exchange agreement such as the Spanish credit database may qualify for an exemption under Article 101(3) TFEU. It was recognised by the court that such a database might lead to a greater overall availability of credit and thus benefit consumers.[58] Indeed, the exchange of information about the solvency of debtors may lower the overall risk in the industry and ultimately lead to lower interest rates. Similar registers are maintained in many other Member States.

---

[53] ECJ (23 November 2006), Case C-238/05 – *Asnef-Equifax – Ausbanc*, [2006] ECR I-11125.
[54] Ibid., para. 27.   [55] Ibid., para. 51.   [56] Ibid., para. 54.   [57] Ibid.   [58] Ibid., para. 71.

2.4.3 Collective exclusive dealing agreements

Collective exclusive dealing agreements are agreements whereby a group of producers agree to deal exclusively through designated distribution channels. The same applies to exclusive agreements entered into by suppliers and wholesalers.[59] In general such agreements prohibit their parties from dealing with particular market players or certain categories of purchasers and/or suppliers. In a case involving the Dutch electrotechnical fittings industry[60] an association of wholesalers had entered into an agreement with suppliers of such fittings under which the suppliers would only sell their products to members of the association. The members of the association were not allowed to sell the products to any wholesalers that were not a member of the association.[61] The exclusive dealing agreement was supplemented by practices that affected the prices and discounts offered by the members of the wholesale association.[62] The purpose of these arrangements was to keep margins for wholesalers above competitive levels. The Commission regarded these arrangements as a decision of an association of undertakings, since the association had adopted binding decisions for its members to the effect that they were obliged not to buy from or sell to any non-members. Since agreements were reached with all major suppliers a significant part of the industry was affected and there were foreclosure effects for outsiders. Independent wholesalers would find it difficult to obtain any supplies from manufacturers or wholesalers. The Commission did not find that the agreements created any efficiencies and rejected any possibility of an exemption under Article 101(1) TFEU.[63]

The main anticompetitive risk resulting from this type of agreement is market segmentation and creation of market foreclosure effects. In principle such agreements tend to restrict the parties' freedom to determine their business partners, and place the non-member wholesalers at a disadvantage. A collective exclusive dealing agreement may however fall outside the scope of Article 101(1) TFEU if it is based on purely objective qualitative criteria such as technical qualifications of the reseller or the suitability of its business premises. In a judgment of the ECJ concerned with the Italian press distribution system[64] the operator of a newspaper outlet had requested to be supplied by publishing companies. However, the orders were rejected because the operator was not authorised by the respective body of the newspaper publishing companies.[65] The ECJ held that an agreement between publishing companies and

---

[59] Bellamy and Child, *European Community Law of Competition* (Oxford University Press, 6th edn, 2008), para. 5.098.

[60] Commission decision of 26 October 1999, Case IV/33.884 – *FEG and TU*, OJ No. L 39 of 14 February 2000, p. 1, confirmed by GC (16 December 2003), Joined Cases T-5/00 and T-6/00 – *DEP Nederlandse Federatieve Vereniging voor de Groothandel op Elektrotechnisch Gebied v Commission* [2003] ECR II-5768.

[61] Commission decision of 26 October 1999, Case IV/33.884 – *FEG and TU*, OJ No. L 39 of 14 February 2000, p. 1, para. 39.

[62] Ibid., para. 111.   [63] Ibid., para. 127.

[64] ECJ (16 June 1981), Case 126/80 – *Salonia v Poidomani and Giglio* [1981] ECR 1563, paras. 23 to 27.

[65] Ibid., p. 1567.

an association of retailers does not infringe Article 101(1) TFEU if the authorised retailers are selected on the basis of objective criteria relating to the capacity of the retailer and his staff and the suitability of his trading premises if such criteria are laid down uniformly for all potential retailers and are not applied in a discriminatory fashion.[66] It is noteworthy that such agreements already do not constitute an infringement of Article 101(1) TFEU and are not just justifiable under Article 101(3) TFEU as an improvement in distribution.

The most common means of enforcing a collective exclusive dealing agreement is a collective boycott or a concerted refusal to deal. Where an agreement is concluded under the auspices of a business association the restrictions on admission of newcomers to the agreement may be deemed as contrary to Article 101(1) TFEU. The Commission has fined Visa for refusing to admit the American bank Morgan Stanley to the Visa credit card system without objective justification.[67] Visa is a private commercial corporation which is owned by the financial institutions that are its members. Visa is responsible for the management and coordination of the international payment card network of the same name which includes, in particular, laying down the rules of the network and providing authorisation and clearing services to its member institutions. A UK subsidiary of Morgan Stanley applied for membership but was informed by Visa that it was not eligible for membership in the EU region. Under the membership rules of Visa, applicants would not be accepted if they were competitors of Visa. Morgan Stanley owned a payment card system in the US. It lodged a complaint with the Commission claiming that the denial of membership violated both Articles 101 and 102 TFEU.[68] The Commission considered that it was not realistic to think that Morgan Stanley was in a position to extend its payment card system in the EU and to compete with Visa. The Commission held that the denial of membership either was an agreement or a decision of an association that restricted competition on the market for services provided to merchants, enabling them to accept cards.[69] A fine was imposed against Visa.

2.4.4 Collective selling of goods

Agreements on joint sale of products and services normally infringe Article 101(1) TFEU as they eliminate price competition between the parties. They may also restrict the volume of products offered on the markets and thus result in price increases. A similar approach has been taken by the Commission with regard to the exploitation

---

[66] Ibid., para. 27.
[67] Commission decision of 3 October 2007, Case COMP/37.860 – *Morgan Stanley/Visa*, summary of the decision published in OJ No. C 183 of 5 August 2009, p. 6, confirmed by GC (14 April 2011) T-461/07 – *Visa Europe and Visa International Service v Commission*, nyr.
[68] GC (14 April 2011), Case T-461/07 – *Visa Europe and Visa International Service v Commission*, nyr, para. 5.
[69] Ibid., para. 25.

of intellectual property and media rights. In a series of decisions the Commission has made clear that joint selling agreements in this sector infringe competition law so long as they are not justified by an efficiency gain, for example by giving the potential licensees the possibility to obtain a 'one-stop' licence for the whole EU.[70] With regard to joint selling of sports broadcasting rights the Commission's policy is to prohibit market foreclosure effects resulting from joint selling arrangements concluded for a long period of time and covering all matches. For this reason, the Commission promotes joint selling schemes ensuring that the TV rights are offered to the market on a regular basis so that all interested parties have a chance to acquire relevant broadcasting and content rights. Furthermore, the rights being subject to the transaction shall be sold in relatively small packages so as to permit several purchasers to purchase different types of rights. In a decision concerning the broadcasting rights for the UEFA Champions League[71] the Commission held that a single point of sale for broadcasting rights covering a large number of football matches creates efficiencies that compensate the restrictions of competition caused by joint selling. Originally, UEFA had concluded joint selling agreements with the football clubs participating in the UEFA Champions League which allowed UEFA to sell all TV rights on an exclusive basis in a single bundle to a single TV broadcaster per territory (typically an EU Member State) for several years in a row. Since the broadcasting rights agreements covered all TV rights of the UEFA Champions League, it made it possible for a single large broadcaster per territory to acquire all TV rights to the exclusion of all other broadcasters.[72] The Commission argued that joint selling not only restricted competition between the football clubs in selling their media rights but could also enhance concentration on the broadcasting markets. In many countries football is an essential programme item for TV broadcasters. The exclusive exploitation of the football TV rights by one broadcaster per Member State would make it very difficult for competing broadcasters to establish themselves successfully in that market.[73]

In the course of the Commission's procedure UEFA proposed a new joint selling agreement to the Commission. The new arrangement would allow the football clubs to sell on a non-exclusive basis in parallel with UEFA certain media rights relating to action where they are participating. Other media rights continued to be exclusively exploited by UEFA. UEFA's proposal also implied an unbundling of the media rights by splitting them up into several different packages that would be offered for sale in separate packages to different third parties.[74] The media rights contracts were limited

---

[70] E.g. Commission Notice published pursuant to Article 27(4) Regulation 1/2003 in Cases COMP/C2/39152 – *BUMA* and COMP/C2/39151 – *SABAM* (COMP/C2/38126 – *Santiago Agreement*), OJ No. C 200 of 17 August 2005, p. 11.
[71] See the Commission's landmark decision of 23 July 2003, Case COMP/C.2–37.398 – *UEFA Champions League*, OJ No. L 291 of 8 November 2003, p. 25.
[72] Ibid., para 19.   [73] Ibid., para. 20.   [74] Ibid., para. 22.

to three UEFA Champions League seasons. The Commission found that the exclusive exploitation of certain media rights relating to important matches in the league by UEFA restricted competition since it prevented the individual football clubs from individually marketing such rights.[75] However, the Commission accepted the argument that a single point of sale created an improvement of distribution within the meaning of Article 101(3) TFEU that justifies an exemption from Article 101(1) TFEU. The tournament involved a great number of football clubs from many different countries and that had different ownership structures. This could lead to multiple co-ownership of the media rights to each match. Furthermore, there was dispersed demand from broadcasters who were likewise of different nationalities and operating in many different national markets.[76] The Commission also held that no individual club knew before the start of the season how far it would get in the tournament. Accordingly, it could not sign an agreement with a broadcaster giving the broadcaster any certainty that the football clubs would make it to the very end of the UEFA Champions League season. This provided an element of uncertainty for broadcasters that was removed by joint selling.[77]

Summary of Section 2

Cartels may take very diverse forms. A common type of cartel is the price-fixing cartel. The participants either agree on the total prices or certain elements of the price such as a surcharge for specific raw materials. Competitors may also indirectly harmonise prices, for example by agreeing on the scope of guarantees. Price-fixing cartels may be arranged directly between competitors or indirectly through a common customer or a common supplier. This type of cartel is referred to as a triangular or hub and spoke cartel. Purchasers may collude with regard to the purchase price they pay to their suppliers and thus engage in price fixing in the form of a purchasers' cartel.

Market sharing is another frequent type of cartel. In such cases competitors allocate markets to each other geographically or by product. Customer allocation is also a type of market-sharing cartel.

In a quota cartel the manufacturers of a given product agree on production quotas or fix a maximum quantity for production. This is an indirect way of raising prices above competitive levels by limiting supply.

Collusive tendering refers to a type of collusion in which competitors allocate orders that are awarded by customers in a tender procedure. The cartel members will determine who is to win the tender and the other cartel members will quote higher prices to ensure the pre-agreed outcome.

In some industries information exchange systems operate. Such systems may be compatible with the competition rules if only aggregate information is exchanged that

[75] Ibid., para. 114.   [76] Ibid., para. 139.   [77] Ibid., para. 140.

does not give any indication of the future strategic intentions of the cartel members. However, if information of strategic relevance is exchanged, such as information on future price increases, the information exchange is presumed to result in a concerted practice in the sense of Article 101(1) TFEU.

3. SANCTIONS

Corporate fines are the primary instrument in the prevention of antitrust violations. Although they may be combined with fines on individuals, imprisonment or even private damages, under most competition laws including the EU competition rules fines constitute the main pillar of competition law enforcement. The imposition of fines on undertakings found to be in breach of competition laws contributes to prevention of potential infringements in three ways:[78]

- Fines create a credible threat of being prosecuted and sanctioned. This influences the balance of potential gains and costs of participation in a cartel. However, a threat of penalties may only then be regarded as credible when from the undertaking's perspective the expected fine exceeds the expected profit from the infringement.[79]
- Fines have a moral effect as they reinforce the moral commitment of law-abiding undertakings to the provisions of the competition law.
- The introduction of additional mechanisms enables the competition authorities to modify the amount of fines such as, for example, leniency programmes that increase the costs of setting up and running cartels.

3.1 General principles of fining policy

A deterrence approach has been applied in EU competition law. Pursuant to Article 103(2)(a) TFEU regulations and directives enforcing Article 101 and 102 TFEU shall be designed 'to ensure compliance with the prohibition laid down in Article 81(1) and in Article 82 [Articles 101(1) and 102 TFEU] by making provision for fines'. According to the ECJ the main objective of the fines imposed for breach of EU competition law 'is to suppress illegal activities and to prevent any reference'.[80] The Commission formulates the catalogue of objectives pursued by its fining policy in the following way:

---

[78] Wils, *Efficiency and Justice in European Antitrust Enforcement* (Hart Publishing, 2008), p. 181.
[79] For an economic appraisal of the Commission's fining policy, see Motta, 'On Cartel Deterrence and Fines in the European Union', *European Competition Law Review*, 29 (2008), 209.
[80] ECJ (15 July 1970), Case 41/69 – *Chemiefarma NV v Commission* [1970] ECR 661, para. 173.

the purpose of the fines is twofold: to impose a pecuniary sanction on the undertaking for the infringement and prevent a repetition of the offence, and to make the prohibition in the Treaty more effective.[81]

The fining policy of the Commission is based upon Article 23 Regulation 1/2003 and the Fining Guidelines.[82] National competition authorities applying EU competition law are obliged to use the respective national laws pertaining to fines for infringement of competition law. The legal basis for fines imposed on undertakings found to have infringed Article 101 TFEU is Article 23(2) Regulation 1/2003. According to this provision, the fine shall not exceed 10% of the total turnover[83] generated by the concerned undertaking in the preceding business year. When fixing the amount of fine the Commission shall take into account both the gravity and the duration of the infringement – Article 23(3) Regulation 1/2003. A fine may be imposed only in cases of negligent or intentional violation of EU competition law.

With regard to the degree of discretion the Commission enjoys the ECJ has stated on many occasions that the Commission is left

a particularly wide discretion as regards the choice of factors to be taken into account for the purposes of determining the amount of the fines, [. . .] without the need to refer to a binding or exhaustive list of criteria which must be taken into account.[84]

The Commission's discretion is, however, limited in two ways: by the general principles of equal treatment and proportionality and its Fining Guidelines.[85]

The principle of equal treatment is infringed when comparable situations are treated differently and different situations are treated in the same way, unless such difference in treatment is objectively justified. Therefore 'a "considerable" disparity between the sizes of the undertakings committing infringements of the same type is, in particular, capable of justifying differentiation in assessing the gravity of the infringement.'[86] The principle of proportionality requires the Commission to impose

---

[81] Commission, Thirteenth Report on Competition Policy (1983), para. 62.

[82] Commission Guidelines on the method of setting fines imposed pursuant to Article 23(2)(a) of Regulation No. 1/2003, OJ No. C 210 of 1 September 2006, p. 2 (Fining Guidelines). For the reasons to adopt new Fining Guidelines, see Völcker, 'Rough Justice? An Analysis of the European Commission's New Fining Guidelines', Common Market Law Review, 45 (2007), 1285.

[83] The calculation of fines by reference to the turnover has been criticised as not reflecting the actual gravity of the infringement. Commentators hold that fines should be calculated rather in proportion to the effect of a cartel on the market. However, that effect will be difficult to quantify. See Riley, 'The Modernisation of EU Anti-cartel Enforcement: Will the Commission Grasp the Opportunity?', European Competition Law Review, 31 (2010), 191, 202.

[84] ECJ (8 February 2007), Case C-3/06 – Groupe Danone v Commission [2007] ECR I-1331, para. 37.

[85] For a detailed analysis of the developments of fining policy under the Fining Guidelines of 2006, see Connor, 'Has the European Commission Become More Severe in Punishing Cartels? Effects of the 2006 Guidelines', European Competition Law Review, 32 (2011), 27. For an overview of the fining policy since the enactment of the first procedural Regulation No. 17/62, see Forrester, 'A Challenge for Europe's Judges: The Review of Fines in Competition Cases', European Law Review, 36 (2011), 185.

[86] GC (29 November 2005), Case T-62/02 – Union Pigments v Commission [2005] ECR II-5057, para. 155.

fines that are proportionate in relation to the duration of the infringement and to the other factors capable of entering into the assessment of the seriousness of the infringement.[87]

Another limitation of the Commission's discretion is the Fining Guidelines issued in 2006. Although not legally binding, the Fining Guidelines form rules of practice from which the Commission is not allowed to depart in an individual case without giving reasons. Those reasons must be compatible with the principle of equal treatment. The main goal of the Guidelines is to ensure the transparency and impartiality of the decisions taken by the Commission:

> The principles outlined here should ensure the transparency and impartiality of the Commission's decisions, in the eyes of the undertakings and of the Court of Justice alike, while upholding the discretion which the Commission is granted under the relevant legislation to set fines within the limit of 10% of overall turnover. This discretion must, however, follow a coherent and non-discriminatory policy which is consistent with the objectives pursued in penalizing infringements of the competition rules.[88]

All fining decisions by the Commission are subject to the judicial review exercised by the General Court and the ECJ.[89] Although Article 23(5) of Regulation 1/2003 states that the fining decisions shall not be of criminal law nature, their legal nature has not been clearly defined. Some commentators find them to be closely linked to criminal or penal sanctions that would allow for application of the ECHR[90] to the respective proceedings before the Commission.[91]

3.2 Calculation of fines

The Fining Guidelines provide for a two-step test according to which the Commission shall calculate the amount of the fine to be imposed.[92] First, the basic amount shall be determined for each concerned undertaking. The second step is to take into account all aggravating and mitigating circumstances.

---

[87] On the proportionality requirement and the review of proportionality by the General Court, see Forrester, 'A Challenge for Europe's Judges', 185.

[88] Commission Guidelines on the method of setting fines imposed pursuant to Article 15(2) of Regulation No. 17 and Article 65(5) of the ECSC Treaty (Fining Guidelines 1998), OJ No. C 9 of 14 January 1998, p. 3; see also Fining Guidelines 2006, para. 3.

[89] For an overview of the legal issues regarding fines imposed under the Fining Guidelines in 2010, see Barbier de La Serre and Winckler, 'A Survey of Legal Issues Regarding Fines Imposed in EU Competition Proceedings (2010)', *Journal of European Competition Law and Practice*, 2 (2011), 356.

[90] Möschel, 'Fines in European Competition Law', *European Competition Law Review*, 32 (2011), 369; Forrester, 'A Challenge for Europe's Judges', 185, 201.

[91] In general on the application of the ECHR to EU competition law, see Bellamy and Child, *European Community Law of Competition*, pp. 1194 et seq.

[92] On the interpretation of the Fining Guidelines in detail, see Völcker, 'Rough Justice? An Analysis of the European Commission's New Fining Guidelines', 1285.

3.2.1 Basic amount

The starting point for the calculation of the fine is to determine the basic amount. It is set by reference to the value of the undertaking's sales of goods and services to which the infringement directly or indirectly relates in the relevant geographic area. Normally sales made during the last full business year will be taken into consideration. The basic amount will be related to a proportion of the value of sales, depending on the gravity of the infringement, multiplied by the number of years of infringement.[93] In principle, the proportion of the value of sales shall not exceed the level of 30%. The exact proportion shall be calculated after assessment of the gravity of the infringement on a case-by-case basis. In particular the Commission shall have regard to the following factors:

- the nature of the infringement;
- the combined market share of the undertakings concerned;
- the geographic scope of the infringement; and
- implementation of the infringement.

Hardcore infringements such as price-fixing, market-sharing and output-limitation agreements shall be fined heavily. In those cases the proportion of the value of sales shall be set at the end of the 30% scale. Additionally, under paragraph 25 of the Fining Guidelines the Commission may include in the basic amount a sum of between 15% and 25% of the value of sales in order to strengthen the deterrence effects of its fines (the so-called 'entry fee').

In the *Carglass* decision[94] the Commission set the basic amount of the fine at 16%. The decision relates to a market-sharing and price-fixing cartel of several flatglass producers. The Commission took into consideration the nature of the cartel ('most harmful'), the average relevant combined market share (close to 100%), the geographic scope (the entire EEA) and the implementation.[95] Some of the cartel members had argued that the cartel had 'almost never resulted in any actual agreements or understandings between the parties'.[96] The Commission rejected this argument since it had been established that the infringement was at times implemented. By stating that the cartel 'almost never' resulted in any actual agreements the parties had implicitly accepted that the discussions had, at least sometimes, resulted in the conclusion of actual agreements.[97] Article 101(1) TFEU does not require an anticompetitive agreement to have any effect; it is sufficient for a violation of the competition rules that it has as its object a restriction of competition. In case of a market-sharing and price-fixing cartel this object is evident. Nonetheless, the Commission did not take into

---

[93] Fining Guidelines, para. 19.
[94] Commission decision of 12 November 2008, Case COMP/39125 – *Carglass*, available at http://ec.europa.eu/competition/antitrust/cases/dec_docs/39125/39125_1865_4.pdf.
[95] Ibid., paras. 670–3.   [96] Ibid., para. 674.   [97] Ibid., para. 676.

account the implementation of the agreement for the calculation of the basic amount of the fine.

The Commission then multiplied the basic amounts set for the individual cartel members by the factors corresponding to their involvement in the cartel. The cartel leader, Saint-Gobain, was involved for five years which resulted in a multiplying factor of five.[98]

An additional amount was imposed under paragraph 25 of the Fining Guidelines to increase the deterrent effect of the fines. The additional amount was set at 16% of the sales of the parties.[99]

3.2.2 Adjustment of the basic amount

The second step in calculating the final amount of the fine is to take into account all additional aggravating or mitigating circumstances. In that regard, it is clear from the case law that, where an infringement has been committed by several undertakings, the relative gravity of the participation of each of them must be examined in order to determine whether aggravating or mitigating circumstances exist in relation to them.[100] That conclusion follows from the principle that penalties must be specific to the offender and the offence, according to which an undertaking may be penalised only for acts imputed to it individually. That principle applies in any administrative procedure that may lead to the imposition of sanctions under EU competition law.[101]

a) Aggravating circumstances

The Fining Guidelines give three examples of circumstances which may give reason to increase the fine. This list is however non-exhaustive.[102]

(i) *Repeated infringement.* The basic amount will be increased by up to 100% for each repeated infringement where an undertaking continues or repeats the same or similar infringement after the Commission or national competition authority has made a finding of an infringement of Article 101 TFEU. The increased fine shall have deterrent effect on potential offenders:

'it must be recalled to mind that, for the purpose of determining the amount of the fine, the Commission must ensure that its action has the necessary deterrent effect [. . .]. Recidivism is a circumstance which justifies a significant increase in the basic amount of the fine. Recidivism constitutes proof that the sanction previously imposed was not sufficiently deterrent.'[103]

---

[98] Ibid., para. 680.   [99] Ibid., para. 682.
[100] GC (9 July 2003), Case T-220/00 – *Cheil Jedang Corporation v Commission* [2003] ECR II-2473, para. 165.
[101] Ibid., para. 185; see, as regards imputing fines, GC (13 December 2001), Joined Cases T-45/98 and T-47/98 – *Krupp Thyssen Stainless v Commission* [2001] ECR II-3757, para. 63.
[102] Fining Guidelines, para. 28.
[103] GC (30 September 2003), Case T-203/01 – *Michelin v Commission* [2003] ECR II-4071, para. 293.

There are no strict rules on maximum time periods between the date of first infringement and the starting date of new infringement. The Commission may take into consideration all relevant circumstances when assessing the time lapse.[104]

In the *Carglass* case,[105] the basic amount for Saint-Gobain was increased by 60% since the company had already been the addressee of two previous Commission decisions concerning cartel activities.[106] For Saint-Gobain, a total fine of EUR 896 million was imposed. The Commission verified whether this amount was still within the 10% limit set by Article 23(2) of Regulation 1/2003 which it found to be the case.[107] This limit refers to the total turnover of the respective company, not just the turnover generated with the products affected by the cartel.

(ii) *Refusal to cooperate with the Commission and obstruction of Commission's investigations.* The conduct of the undertaking during the Commission's investigations is one of the factors that may influence the amount of the fine. The undertaking concerned cannot, however, be fined for exercising its rights of defence.

(iii) *Role of leader, instigator or coercer in the cartel.* Differentiation of fines pursuant to roles played by the different cartelists is one of the instruments the implementation of which raises the costs of setting up and running the cartel. Therefore it is necessary to establish the role of each conspirator throughout the duration of the cartel, in particular who had the role of the ringleader.

In cases (ii) and (iii) the Fining Guidelines do not provide any instructions on the maximum or minimum increase of the basic amount. The Commission shall base its decision on the facts of a particular case and their overall assessment.

b) Mitigating circumstances

The fine may be reduced when the Commission finds a mitigating circumstance applicable to the case. A non-exhaustive list of such mitigating circumstances is provided by the Fining Guidelines:[108]

(i) *Termination of the infringement after the Commission's first intervention.*

(ii) *Negligence.* In principle higher sanctions should be imposed for intentional violations than for negligent ones. For the purposes of the EU competition law negligence is defined as follows:

---

[104] The provision on recidivism has drawn criticism by commentators as overly broad. It is argued that there should at least be a certain connection between the first and the second infringement. See Riley, 'The Modernisation of EU Anti-cartel Enforcement', 203.

[105] Commission decision of 12 November 2008, Case COMP/39125 – *Carglass*, available at http://ec. europa.eu/competition/antitrust/cases/dec_docs/39125/39125_1865_4.pdf.

[106] Ibid., para. 686.   [107] Ibid., para. 711.

[108] Fining Guidelines, para. 29. The Fining Guidelines are criticised for not encouraging compliance with the competition rules through compliance programmes. In fact, the Fining Guidelines are not addressing compliance programmes at all. See Riley, 'The Modernisation of EU Anti-cartel Enforcement', 204.

'it is not necessary for an undertaking to have been aware that it was infringing Article 85 [Article 101 TFEU] for an infringement to be regarded as having been committed intentionally; it is sufficient that it could not have been unaware that the contested conduct had as its object the restriction of competition.'[109]

(iii) *Substantially limited involvement in the infringement.* The undertaking concerned may have its fine reduced if it demonstrates that during the cartel it avoided implementing the anticompetitive conduct in the market. Undertakings are granted a reduction for cheating other members of the cartel because it in principle undermines the efficiency of the cartel agreements and thus raises their costs.

(iv) *Effective cooperation with the Commission outside the scope of the Leniency Notice.*[110]

(v) *Anticompetitive conduct has been encouraged or authorised by public authorities or by legislation.*[111]

c) Specific circumstances

According to the Fining Guidelines the Commission may additionally increase the fine in order to ensure a sufficiently deterrent effect of the fine.

In particular, an increased fine may be imposed on an undertaking which has a large turnover beyond the sales of goods and/or services to which the infringement relates. In this way the size of the undertaking concerned may become one of the decisive factors when calculating the fine by the Commission. The general rule behind this solution has been explained by AG Geelhoed:

in the event of a collective infringement like a cartel as opposed to an infringement by a single offender, the Commission must also consider the subsequent effects of the fines and take into account the size of a given company. [...]The example given by the Commission is a cartel consisting of one big player and several small players. The big player cooperated with the Commission and receives immunity under the Leniency Notice. In such a case very high fines could have put the smaller players out of business, in which case the Commission's intervention would have resulted in a monopoly.[112]

The Commission may also increase the fine when the amount of profits made as a result of the infringement does not exceed the original amount of the fine. The main requirement is, however, that the Commission has sufficient economic data to estimate the amount of improperly made profit.

---

[109] ECJ (11 June 1989), Case 246/86 – *Belasco and Others v Commission* [1989] ECR 2191, para. 41.
[110] Examples of such cooperation can be found at Völcker, 'Rough Justice? An Analysis of the European Commission's New Fining Guidelines', 1313.
[111] Ibid., for examples of anticompetitive conduct encouraged by the State.
[112] AG Geelhoed, opinion of 19 January 2006 in case C-289/04 P – *Showa Denko v Commission* [2006] ECR I-5859, para. 61 and footnote 16.

Finally, in cases where the imposition of fines calculated in line with the Fining Guidelines could 'irretrievably jeopardize the economic viability of the undertaking concerned and cause its assets to lose all their value', the Commission may reduce the amount of fine.[113] Such a reduction may be granted only upon request and must be based on objective evidence.[114]

3.3 Fines on parents and subsidiaries

It is settled case law that an anticompetitive conduct of a subsidiary may by imputed to the parent company.[115] The requirement is, however, that the subsidiary does not decide independently upon its own conduct on the market but carries out, in all material respects, the instructions given to it by the parent company. Having regard to the economic, organisational and legal links between the parent company and subsidiary, the Commission must demonstrate that they form a single economic unit and that the parent company has exercised its decisive influence in the particular case. There is a rebuttable presumption[116] of the existence of a single economic unit in cases where the parent company owns 100% of the shares in the subsidiary:

In the specific case where a parent company has a 100% shareholding in a subsidiary which has infringed the Community competition rules, first, the parent company can exercise a decisive influence over the conduct of the subsidiary and, second, there is a rebuttable presumption that the parent company does in fact exercise a decisive influence over the conduct of its subsidiary.

In those circumstances, it is sufficient for the Commission to prove that the subsidiary is wholly owned by the parent company in order to presume that the parent exercises a decisive influence over the commercial policy of the subsidiary. The Commission will be able to regard the parent company as jointly and severally liable for the payment of the fine imposed on its subsidiary, unless the parent company, which has the burden of rebutting that presumption, adduces sufficient evidence to show that its subsidiary acts independently on the market.[117]

---

[113] Cases where the Commission accepted a claim for inability to pay are discussed in Kienapfel and Wils, 'Inability to Pay: First Cases and Practical Experiences', *Competition Policy Newsletter*, No. 3 (2010), p. 3.

[114] The provision on inability to pay is challenged by commentators as too deterrent and as potentially leading to an insolvency of otherwise viable firms thus increasing concentration and undermining competition. See Riley, 'The Modernisation of EU Anti-cartel Enforcement', 191, 204.

[115] There are slight differences in the case law though. For a detailed discussion of recent judgments, see La Rocca, 'The Controversial Issue of the Parent-company Liability for the Violation of EC Competition Rules by the Subsidiary', *European Competition Law Review*, 32 (2011), 68; Riesenkampff and Krauthausen, 'Liability of Parent Companies for Antitrust Violations of their Subsidiaries', *European Competition Law Review*, 31 (2010), 38; Svetlicinii, 'Who is to Blame? Liability of "Economic Units" for Infringements of EU Competition Law', *European Law Review*, 36 (2011), 52.

[116] For a discussion of the evidence required to rebut the presumption, see Svetlicinii, 'Parental Liability for the Antitrust Infringements of Subsidiaries: A Rebuttable Presumption or Probatio Diabolica?', *European Law Review*, 36 (2011), 288.

[117] ECJ (10 September 2009), Case C-97/08 P – *AKZO Nobel and Others v Commission* [2009] ECR I-8237, paras. 60 and 61.

The imputation of cartel conduct of a subsidiary may have a very substantial effect on the amount of the fine imposed under the Fining Guidelines. The Commission will base the calculation of the fine not only on the turnover of the subsidiary but will also take into account the turnover of the parent company to which the cartel conduct can be imputed.

With regard to the attribution of market conduct of a 100% subsidiary to the parent company, the case law of the Union courts is in line with their case law on the question whether two legal entities can restrict competition between them or whether this can be excluded since they have to be regarded as a single economic unit. In this context there is also a presumption that the parent company will control the market conduct of its 100% subsidiary.[118]

However, there is a certain friction in the jurisprudence on the relationship of joint ventures to their parent companies.

The parent companies of a joint venture may be jointly and severally liable for cartel behaviour of the subsidiary if they exercise decisive influence over the joint venture. In the *Chloroprene Rubber* cartel case,[119] the General Court considered the facts in detail and noted in particular that the parent companies jointly supervised and set the strategy for the joint venture. In addition, both parent companies had the possibility to block strategic decisions of the joint venture.

Interestingly, the court held that it is irrelevant for the attribution of liability to a parent company whether or not a joint venture qualifies as a full function joint venture for merger control purposes. Although the definition of a full function joint venture encompasses that the entity performs on a lasting basis all the functions of an autonomous economic entity, that autonomy does not mean that an infringement of the joint venture cannot be attributed to its parent companies. The autonomy for merger control purposes does not imply that the joint venture enjoys autonomy as regards the adoption of its strategic decisions and that it is not therefore under the decisive influence exercised by its parent companies for the purposes of Article 101(1) TFEU.[120] Accordingly, there appear to be different concepts of autonomy under different lines of jurisprudence of the Union's courts in competition matters.

3.4 Liability of successor undertaking

There are several constellations that may occur during the existence of a cartel or the subsequent investigation of the Commission. An undertaking participating in a cartel may be sold to a new owner and continue to participate in the cartel. The new

---

[118] See Chapter 2.
[119] GC (2 February 2012), Case T-76/08 – *EI Du Pont de Nemours and Others v Commission*, nyr.
[120] Ibid., para. 78.

owner may also terminate the engagement in the cartel activity. The undertaking will perhaps be sold only after the Commission began its investigation and after it has discontinued its cartel activity. In these cases the question will arise whether the new owner of the undertaking is liable for cartel conduct that was committed prior to the acquisition of the entity.

The legal principle that is relevant in such situations is the principle of personal liability,[121] under which a person can be held liable only for his own acts. In general it falls to the person managing the undertaking when the infringement was committed to answer for that infringement, even if, at the date of the decision finding the infringement, that undertaking is the responsibility or under the management of a different person.[122]

Legal entities within an undertaking having participated in their own right in an infringement and which have subsequently been acquired by another undertaking continue to bear responsibility themselves for their unlawful behaviour prior to their acquisition, when they have not been absorbed by the acquirer, but continued their activities as subsidiaries (that is to say they retain their legal personality).[123] In such a case, the acquirer may only be liable for the conduct of the subsidiary from the moment of its acquisition, if the latter persists in the infringement and liability of the new parent company can be established.[124] If the undertaking which has acquired the assets infringes Article 101 TFEU, liability for the infringement is apportioned between the seller and the acquirer of the infringing assets.[125]

The *GIS* cartel case[126] illustrates the application of the principle of personal liability to some of these constellations. Two wholly owned subsidiaries of Alstom had been involved in a price-fixing and market-sharing cartel for a certain type of electrical equipment, so-called 'gas insulated switchgear'. While the cartel conduct was ongoing, Alstom sold the two subsidiaries to Areva. A couple of months after the transfer to Areva, the Commission carried out inspections at the subsidiaries and the cartel activity ceased. The Commission held Alstom and the two subsidiaries jointly and severally liable for their involvement in the infringement for the period before

---

[121] ECJ (14 July 1972), Case 48/69 – *ICI v Commission* [1972] ECR 619, paras. 131–141; ECJ (8 July 1999), Case C-49/92 P – *Commission v Anic Partecipazioni* [1999] ECR I-4125, para. 78; ECJ (11 December 2007), Case C-280/06 – *ETI and Others* [2007] ECR I-10893, para. 39; see also AG Kokott, opinion of 3 July 2007 in case C-280/06 – *ETI and Others* [2007] ECR I-10892, paras. 71 et seq.

[122] ECJ (16 November 2000), Case C-297/98 P – *SCA Holding v Commission* [2000] ECR I-10101, para. 27, and ECJ (16 November 2000), Case C-286/98 P – *Stora Kopparbergs Bergslags v Commission* [2000] ECR I-9925, para. 37; see also, to that effect, ECJ (16 November 2000), Case C-279/98 P – *Cascades v Commission* [2000] ECR I-9693, para. 79.

[123] ECJ (16 November 2000), Case 279/98 P – *Cascades v Commission* [2000] ECR I-9693, paras. 78–80.

[124] ECJ (16 November 2000), Case T-354/94 – *Stora Kopparbergs Bergslags AB v Commission* [1998] ECR II-2111, para. 80.

[125] GC (5 June 2012), Case T-214/06 – *Imperial Chemical Industries v Commission*, nyr, para. 107.

[126] Commission decision of 24 January 2007, Case COMP/F/38.899 – *Gas Insulated Switchgear*, available at http://ec.europa.eu/competition/antitrust/cases/dec_docs/38899/38899_1030_7.pdf.

the sale of the subsidiaries.[127] Areva was held jointly and severally liable with the two subsidiaries for their involvement in the infringement after the acquisition of the subsidiaries by Areva.[128]

The apportioning of liability for an infringement of the competition rules affects the amount of the fine imposed by the Commission only insofar as it reflects the duration of the infringement. Under the Fining Guidelines, the basic amount of the fine is multiplied by a factor that depends on the duration of the cartel. This factor will be reduced by the apportioning of liability but not the basic amount as such. The basic amount is also calculated in light of the gravity of the infringement. The gravity of the infringement is not affected if an undertaking involved in a cartel is sold while the cartel is still active. The Commission treats this as two infringements, the gravity for each of which is assessed individually. Both the previous and the current owner of the undertaking have to pay a fine that is based on the full basic amount under the Fining Guidelines. In total, the fines imposed on the previous and the current owner will exceed the amount that would have been imposed if the undertaking had not been sold. The General Court has confirmed this practice to be in line with the principles of equal treatment and proportionality.[129]

A change in the ownership of an undertaking participating in a cartel may also have an effect on the amount of the fine in another respect. In the *Acrylic Glass* cartel case,[130] Total had acquired two subsidiaries that had been involved in cartel conduct. In calculating the fine, the Commission imposed an increase of 200%, in order to ensure that the pecuniary penalty would have a sufficient deterrent effect, in the light of the undertaking's size and economic strength. That increase was based on Total's worldwide turnover. However, two weeks before the Commission adopted the fining decision, Arkema had been floated on the stock exchange. Since then, the former subsidiaries were no longer controlled by Total. The General Court observed that the need to ensure a sufficient deterrent effect for a fine requires, *inter alia*, that its amount be adapted to take account of the impact sought on the undertaking on which it is imposed, so that the fine is not made negligible nor, on the contrary, excessive, in the light of, *inter alia*, its financial capacity. Consequently, the objective of deterrence can be legitimately attained only by reference to the situation of the undertaking on the day when it is imposed. In the case at hand, the General Court considered that the 200% increase could be justified only in the light of Total's sizeable turnover figures on the day when the fine was imposed. Since the economic unit which linked the subsidiaries to Total ceased to exist before the date on which the decision was adopted, the latter company's resources could not be taken into account in determining the increase in the fine imposed on the subsidiaries. The

---

[127] Ibid., para. 358.   [128] Ibid., para. 371.
[129] GC (5 June 2012), Case T-214/06 – *Imperial Chemical Industries v Commission*, nyr, paras. 112 et seq.
[130] GC (7 June 2011), Case T-217/06 – *Arkema France and Others v Commission*, nyr; GC (7 June 2011), Case T-206/06 – *Total and Elf Aquitaine v Commission*, nyr.

General Court accordingly held that the 200% increase was excessive in respect of them and that a 25% increase was adequate to ensure a sufficiently deterrent effect of the fine imposed on them. On that ground, the General Court reduced the amount of the fine on the subsidiaries.[131] As regards Total, the General Court upheld the amount of the fines imposed.[132]

In certain exceptional circumstances, the case law accepts that it is possible to derogate from the principle of personal liability under the so-called 'economic continuity' criterion, under which an infringement of the rules on competition may be imputed to the economic successor of the legal person which committed it, even where the latter has not ceased to exist on the date of adoption of the decision finding the infringement, in order that the effectiveness of those rules will not be compromised owing to the changes to, *inter alia*, the legal form of the undertakings concerned.[133]

According to the case law, a change in the legal form or name of the undertaking to be fined does not allow the newly created entity to escape its liability for the anti-competitive behaviour so long as the new company and its predecessor are identical from an economic point of view. This was the case in *Suiker Unie* where the ECJ acknowledged the liability of Suiker Unie which had been formed by four undertakings found to have infringed Article 101 TFEU. The Court's main argument was that the new entity had been assigned all rights and obligations of the four companies and its business had been carried out by the same persons from the same office.[134]

A legal entity originally not involved in the anticompetitive conduct may be found liable for the infringement of EU competition law where the legal person responsible for the violation has ceased to exist by the time the fine was imposed. The liability for fines is then assigned to the entity which took over material and human resources responsible for the infringement:

However, where between the commission of the infringement and the time when the undertaking in question must answer for it the person responsible for the operation of that undertaking has ceased to exist in law, it is necessary, first, to find the combination of physical and human elements which contributed to the commission of the infringement and then to identify the person who has become responsible for their operation, so as to avoid the result that because of the disappearance of the person responsible for its operation when the infringement was committed the undertaking may fail to answer for it.[135]

These principles were applied by the Commission in the *GIS* cartel case discussed above. Another participant in the cartel was a wholly owned subsidiary of VA Tech.

---

[131] GC (7 June 2011), Case T-217/06 – *Arkema France and Others v Commission*, nyr, paras. 272 et seq.
[132] GC (7 June 2011), Case T-206/06 – *Total and Elf Aquitaine v Commission*, nyr.
[133] GC (20 March 2002), Case T-9/99 – *HFB and Others v Commission* [2002] ECR II-1487, paras. 105 and 106.
[134] ECJ (16 December 1975), Joined Cases 40 to 48, 50, 54 to 56, 111, 113 and 114–73 – *Suiker Unie v Commission* [1975] ECR 1663, para. 85.
[135] GC (17 December 1991), Case T-6/89 – *Enichem Anic v Commission* [1991] ECR II-1623, para. 237.

Siemens acquired VA Tech while the Commission's investigation was pending. VA Tech merged into an entity of Siemens and ceased to exist as a legal entity. The Commission held the entity of Siemens jointly and severally liable with the subsidiary that was involved in the cartel conduct.[136]

3.5 Criminal sanctions against individuals

Although the administrative fines for a violation of competition law are the most common instrument for combating cartels in most EU Member States and at the EU level, there is a current debate as to whether the administrative enforcement should be supplemented by the introduction of criminal sanctions against individuals. The main argument for criminalisation of the EU competition law enforcement is that the deterrent effect of administrative fines could be significantly intensified. According to some commentators the actual maximum level of fines to be imposed by the Commission is not sufficient to deter price cartels and other antitrust offences.[137] Pursuant to economic analysis one of the options would be to significantly increase the maximum level of fines, even up to ten times the existing maximum fines. Such a solution would, however, not be proportionate and might have detrimental effects on the economy as more than 50% of the fined companies would have to be liquidated if required to pay the increased fines. For this reason the introduction of additional criminal sanctions against individuals involved in anticompetitive practices should be regarded as a proportionate solution to the underdeterrence problem.[138]

The current legal framework does not allow the Commission to impose criminal sanctions against individuals. First, such competence has not been granted to the Commission by virtue of Regulation 1/2003 which provides only for administrative fines. Second, it is widely accepted that under the EU Treaty there is a lack of legal competence to introduce criminal sanctions at the EU level. The Treaty of Lisbon does not furnish the EU with such competences either.[139]

On the other hand, there is a tendency among Member States to include criminal sanctions in their competition laws as a means to increase the deterrent effect of

---

[136] Commission decision of 24 January 2007, Case COMP/F/38.899 – *Gas Insulated Switchgear*, available at http://ec.europa.eu/competition/antitrust/cases/dec_docs/38899/38899_1030_7.pdf, para. 468.

[137] For more information and further references, see Wils, *Efficiency and Justice in European Antitrust Enforcement*, paras. 547 et seq.

[138] More on this line of argumentation in the document presented by the UK Department of Trade and Industry to the Parliament and setting out the case for introduction of criminal cartel offence: A World Class Competition Regime, July 2001, para. 7, available at www.archive.official-documents.co.uk/document/cm52/5233/523310.htm.

[139] Nonetheless, it is suggested by commentators that EU competition law should provide for individual sanctions such as director disqualification or expulsion of aliens from the EU. See Riley, 'The Modernisation of EU Anti-cartel Enforcement', 205.

competition law enforcement.[140] Resting mainly on the line of arguments presented above, some of them have decided to provide for criminal enforcement of their national competition laws. It has to be noted that the criminalisation of competition law at national level also has some implications for the enforcement of Article 101 TFEU. Pursuant to the principle of equivalence, penalties imposed by Member States for infringements of Article 101 TFEU must at least be equivalent in effectiveness and dissuasiveness to the sanctions imposed for violation of national competition laws. Therefore criminal cartel sanctions for violations of national laws must be imposed when enforcing EU competition law. This is in line with Article 5 Regulation 1/2003, according to which Member States may empower the national competition authorities to impose penalties others than fines on undertakings violating Article 101 TFEU and which also covers criminal sanctions.

The tendency to criminalise enforcement of competition law is inspired by the example of the United States where violations of sections 1 and 2 of the Sherman Act are punishable by criminal law fines for both companies and individuals. The sanction of imprisonment may also be imposed. Currently individual violators can be fined up to US$1 million and sentenced to up to ten years in federal prison, and corporations can be fined up to US$100 million. In 2010/2011 defendants prosecuted in the US for violations of competition law were sentenced to serve 18,295 jail days with an average of 24 months. Criminal fines imposed in 2011 amounted to more than US$ 524 million.[141]

In the EU, the United Kingdom and Ireland are the two most significant examples of the criminalisation of antitrust enforcement. In Ireland violations of national and EU competition laws are criminal offences punishable with fines for companies and imprisonment and/or fines for individuals. In the UK the criminal penalties have been introduced by enactment of the Enterprise Act 2002. The UK was the first Member State to extradite an individual to the US to face criminal charges. An extradition requires 'dual criminality' in the sense that the conduct which is the subject of the extradition request must amount to a criminal act in both the country issuing the request and the country in which the relevant individual resides. Accordingly, extradition is possible only from Member States which have enacted criminal sanctions for competition law infringements.[142]

Imprisonment for individuals is also provided for by other Member States such as Estonia, France, Cyprus, Sweden and the Slovak Republic. In some other jurisdictions

---

[140] This is criticised by others as intimidating potential leniency applicants, see Billiet, 'How Lenient is the EC Leniency Policy? A Matter of Certainty and Predictability', *European Competition Law Review*, 30 (2009), 14, 18.

[141] www.justice.gov/atr/public/criminal/264101.html.

[142] For a detailed discussion of UK/US extradition cases in the cartel context, see Girardet, '"What if Uncle Sam wants you": Principles and Recent Practice Concerning US Extradition Requests in Cartel Cases', *Journal of European Competition Law and Practice*, 1 (2010), 286.

other criminal penalties such as criminal fines or director disqualifications may be imposed. In Germany only bid rigging is punishable with imprisonment.[143]

Summary of Section 3

The Commission can impose fines on cartel members amounting to a maximum of 10% of their total turnover in the last preceding business year. The amount of the fine within this range depends on a number of factors such as the duration and the severity of the infringement. The role of the individual undertaking in the cartel is also taken into consideration. Instigators and repeat offenders are likely to have to pay a higher fine than other cartel members.

Parent companies are liable for infringements of their subsidiaries if they are able to determine the market conduct of such subsidiaries. This is presumed in the case of a 100% subsidiary. In the case of a sale of an undertaking involved in cartel activity the principle of personal liability applies. If an undertaking retains its legal personality it will remain responsible for its cartel conduct. If such conduct continues and it can be established that the new owner is able to determine its market conduct, the acquirer can be held liable for cartel conduct after the acquisition as well. If the legal personality ceases to exist it will have to be assessed whether the material and human resources which were essential to the cartel member can still be located. If this is the case, the new owner of such resources may be held liable.

There are no criminal sanctions for cartel infringements under EU competition law. However, national law in a number of Member States provides for such sanctions.

4. JUDICIAL REVIEW

Decisions of the Commission imposing fines for cartel conduct in many cases are challenged in court. The addressees of such a decision typically claim that the Commission's findings are not sufficiently supported by the facts established by the Commission or that the Commission committed errors of law or of fact when calculating the fine under the Fining Guidelines.

4.1 General considerations regarding evidence

A question that arises in connection with pleas challenging the Commission's factual findings is the level of evidence the Commission has to adduce to prove an infringement. In general terms the Union courts have held that the Commission must prove

---

[143] Overview at Wils, *Efficiency and Justice in European Antitrust Enforcement*, para. 521.

the infringements which it has found and adduce evidence capable of demonstrating to the requisite legal standard the existence of circumstances constituting an infringement.[144] The legal standard to be met by the Commission has been defined as 'sufficiently precise and consistent evidence to support the firm conviction that the alleged infringement took place'.[145]

This legal standard does not apply to every individual item of evidence. It is rather required that the body of evidence in its entirety meets the standard defined by the Union courts.[146]

Documentary evidence is a typical type of evidence relied on by the Commission. It is usually attributed a high probative value, but the Union courts will nevertheless assess its credibility on an individual basis. According to the general rules relating to evidence developed by the Union courts, the credibility and thus the probative value of a document depends on the person from whom it originates, the circumstances in which it came into being, the person to whom it was addressed and whether it appears sound and reliable.[147]

However, the Commission does not have to adduce documentary evidence to prove an infringement. The Commission may rely on indicia and coincidences which taken together support the finding of an infringement. The prevailing principle of EU law is the unfettered evaluation of evidence.[148] In the words of the General Court in *Sodium Chlorate*:

Moreover, as anticompetitive agreements are known to be prohibited, the Commission cannot be required to produce documents expressly attesting to contacts between the traders concerned. The fragmentary and sporadic items of evidence which may be available to the Commission should, in any event, be capable of being supplemented by inferences which allow the relevant circumstances to be reconstituted. The existence of an anticompetitive practice or agreement may thus be inferred from a number of coincidences and indicia which,

---

[144] ECJ (17 December 1998), Case C-185/95 P – *Baustahlgewebe v Commission* [1998] ECR I-8417, para. 58, and ECJ (8 July 1999), Case C-49/92 P – *Commission v Anic Partecipazioni* [1999] ECR I-4125, para. 86; GC (25 October 2011), Case T-348/08 – *Aragonesas Industrias y Energía v Commission*, nyr, para. 90.

[145] ECJ (28 March 1984), Joined Cases 29/83 and 30/83 – *Compagnie Royale asturienne des mines and Rheinzink v Commission* [1984] ECR 1679, para. 20; ECJ (31 March 1993), Joined Cases C-89/85, C-104/85, C-114/85, C-116/85, C-117/85, C-125/85 to C-129/85 – *Ahlström Osakeyhtiö and Others v Commission (Woodpulp II)* [1993] ECR I-1307, para. 127; GC (10 March 1992), Joined Cases T-68/89, T-77/89 and T-78/89 – *SIV and Others v Commission* [1992] ECR II-1403, paras. 193–195, 198–202, 205–210, 220–232, 249, 250 and 322–328; and GC (6 July 2000), Case T-62/98 – *Volkswagen v Commission* [2000] ECR II-2707, paras. 43 and 72; GC (25 October 2011), Case T-348/08 – *Aragonesas Industrias y Energía v Commission*, nyr, para. 95.

[146] GC (25 October 2011), Case T-348/08 – *Aragonesas Industrias y Energía v Commission*, nyr, para. 96.

[147] GC (15 March 2000), Joined Cases T-25/95, T-26/95, T-30/95 to T-32/95, T-34/95 to T-39/95, T-42/95 to T-46/95, T-48/95, T-50/95 to T-65/95, T-68/95 to T-71/95, T-87/95, T-88/95, T-103/95 and T-104/95 – *Cimenteries CBR and Others v Commission* [2000] ECR II-491, paras. 1053 and 1838; GC (25 October 2011), Case T-348/08 – *Aragonesas Industrias y Energía v Commission*, nyr, para. 103.

[148] GC (25 October 2011), Case T-348/08 – *Aragonesas Industrias y Energía v Commission*, nyr, para. 98.

taken together, may, in the absence of another plausible explanation, constitute evidence of an infringement of the competition rules.[149]

Consequently, an absence of documentary evidence is relevant only in the overall assessment of the body of evidence relied on by the Commission. It does not, in itself, enable the undertaking concerned to call the Commission's claims into question by submitting a different version of the facts. The applicant may do so only where the evidence submitted by the Commission does not enable the existence of the infringement to be established unequivocally and without the need for interpretation.[150]

In the absence of documentary evidence, the Commission may also rely on statements made by other undertakings. The General Court held that

if that were not the case, the burden of proving conduct contrary to Article 101 TFEU, which is borne by the Commission, would be unsustainable and incompatible with its task of supervising the proper application of those provisions.[151]

However, an admission by one undertaking accused of having participated in a cartel, the accuracy of which is contested by several other undertakings similarly accused, cannot be regarded as constituting adequate proof of an infringement committed by the latter undertakings unless it is supported by other evidence, given that the degree of corroboration required may be lower in view of the reliability of the statements at issue.[152]

As regards the probative value of the various items of evidence, the sole criterion relevant in that evaluation is the reliability of the evidence.[153]

The General Court had to apply these principles in a case where the Commission relied on references in the notes of an employee (Mr S) of one cartel member to telephone conversations with another alleged cartel member (EIA). Mr S had mentioned in the minutes of telephone conversations with a third cartel member that he had previously spoken with EIA. This was the only evidence adduced by the Commission to prove the involvement of EIA in the cartel in a certain period of time. EIA claimed not to have engaged in any cartel activity during that period and that the references in the notes of the employee of another cartel member were not sufficiently reliable evidence to prove an infringement.[154] The General Court found that Mr S had not mentioned, and thus had not confirmed, the telephone conversations with EIA when he was interviewed by the Commission in a hearing. Moreover, he had not kept any minutes of the telephone conversations with EIA even though he had a clear tendency to note down contacts he had with other cartel members. The Commission had not confronted him with this deviation from his usual practice in the hearing. The

---

[149] Ibid., para. 97.
[150] GC (12 September 2007), Case T-36/05 – *Coats Holdings and Coats v Commission* [2007] ECR II – 110, para. 74; GC (25 October 2011), Case T-348/08 – *Aragonesas Industrias y Energía v Commission*, nyr, para. 99.
[151] GC (25 October 2011), Case T-348/08 – *Aragonesas Industrias y Energía v Commission*, nyr, para. 100.
[152] Ibid., para. 101.   [153] Ibid., para. 102.   [154] Ibid., para. 21.

General Court concluded that in the absence of any evidence to confirm the content of the notes of Mr S the reference to EIA in those notes did not constitute evidence which was sufficiently reliable to prove that it participated in the infringement.[155] The General Court therefore held that the Commission had not adduced sufficient evidence to prove EIA's involvement in the cartel at certain periods of time. EIA had admitted its participation in the cartel for a particular period but the Commission had taken the view that EIA had participated for a longer period. This was rejected by the General Court.

The shorter duration of EIA's participation in the cartel as assumed by the General Court also led to a reduction of the fine imposed by the Commission. The General Court held that the Commission's calculation of the basic amount of the fine was erroneous.[156]

EIA had also claimed that the Commission failed to take account of mitigating circumstances in EIA's favour. According to EIA, the company had adopted a passive role in the cartel and had not actively participated in the creation of any anticompetitive agreements. In addition, EIA had not adhered to any agreements of the cartel members. Both parts of this plea were rejected. The General Court found that EIA had participated in the cartel (in the relevant period) as actively as the other cartel members. Further, it is settled case law that the fact that an undertaking proved to have participated in collusion on prices did not behave in the manner agreed with the other cartel members does not necessarily have to be taken into account as a mitigating circumstance.[157]

4.2 Presumption of innocence

If there is doubt remaining after consideration of all items of evidence, the benefit of that doubt must be given to the undertakings accused of the infringement.[158] In proceedings for the annulment of a Commission decision imposing a fine the General Court cannot conclude that the Commission has established the existence of the infringement at issue to the requisite legal standard if it still entertains doubts on that point.[159]

In the latter situation, the principle of the presumption of innocence applies. It results in particular from Article 6(2) ECHR and is one of the fundamental rights which, according to the case law of the Union courts and as reaffirmed by Article 47

---

[155] Ibid., para. 196.   [156] Ibid., para. 302.   [157] Ibid., paras. 294–7.

[158] ECJ (14 February 1978), Case 27/76 – *United Brands v Commission* [1978] ECR 207, para. 265; GC (25 October 2011), Case T-348/08 – *Aragonesas Industrias y Energía v Commission*, nyr, para. 93.

[159] GC (8 July 2004), Joined Cases T-67/00, T-68/00, T-71/00 and T-78/00 – *JFE Engineering v Commission* [2004] ECR II-2501, para. 177; GC (25 October 2011), Case T-348/08 – *Aragonesas Industrias y Energía v Commission*, nyr, para. 93.

of the Charter,[160] are protected in the legal order of the EU. Given the degree of severity of the penalties in cartel cases, the principle of the presumption of innocence applies in particular to the procedures relating to infringements of the competition rules applicable to undertakings that may result in the imposition of fines or periodic penalty payments.[161]

4.3 Scope of judicial review

Fining decisions of the Commission are subject to full judicial review by the Union courts. This was confirmed by the ECJ in the *Copper Tubes* case.[162]

The appellants challenged both the manner in which the General Court stated in its first instance judgment that it was obliged to take account of the Commission's broad margin of discretion and the manner in which it actually reviewed the decision at issue. They relied on Article 6(1) ECHR and on the Charter.[163]

The ECJ first confirmed the principle of effective judicial protection as a general principle of EU law to which expression is given by Article 47 of the Charter. According to the ECJ, the judicial review of the decisions of the institutions was arranged by the founding Treaties. In addition to the review of legality, now provided for under Article 263 TFEU, a review with unlimited jurisdiction was envisaged in regard to the penalties laid down by regulations.[164]

The ECJ referred to earlier cases in which it has held that whilst, in areas giving rise to complex economic assessments, the Commission has a margin of discretion with regard to economic matters, that does not mean that the Union courts must refrain from reviewing the Commission's interpretation of information of an economic nature.[165] Those courts have not only to establish whether the evidence relied on is factually accurate, reliable and consistent but also whether that evidence contains all the information which must be taken into account in order to assess a complex situation and whether it is capable of substantiating the conclusions drawn from it.[166]

Furthermore, the Union courts must carry out the review of legality incumbent upon them on the basis of the evidence adduced by the applicant in support of the

---

[160] Charter of Fundamental Rights of the European Union, OJ No. C 364 of 18 December 2000, p. 1.
[161] ECtHR (21 February 1984), Application No. 8544/79 – *Öztürk v Germany*, Series A No. 73, and ECtHR (25 August 1987), Application No. 9912/82 – *Lutz v Germany*, Series A No 123-A, and ECJ (8 July 1999), Case C-199/92 P – *Hüls v Commission*, [1999] ECR I-4287, paras. 149 and 150, and ECJ (8 July 1999), Case C-235/92 P – *Montecatini v Commission* [1999] ECR I-4539, paras. 175 and 176; GC (25 October 2011), Case T-348/08 – *Aragonesas Industrias y Energia v Commission*, nyr, para. 94.
[162] ECJ (8 December 2011), Case C-272/09 P – *KME Germany and Others v Commission*, nyr.
[163] Ibid., para. 88.   [164] Ibid., para. 93.
[165] For a critical appraisal of this light standard of review, see Jaeger, 'The Standard of Review in Competition Cases Involving Complex Economic Assessments: Towards the Marginalisation of the Marginal Review?', *Journal of European Competition Law and Practice*, 2 (2011), 295.
[166] ECJ (8 December 2011), Case C-272/09 P – *KME Germany and Others v Commission*, nyr, para. 94.

pleas in law that are put forward. In carrying out such a review, the courts cannot use the Commission's margin of discretion[167] – either as regards the choice of factors taken into account in the application of the criteria mentioned in the Fining Guidelines or as regards the assessment of those factors – as a basis for dispensing with the conduct of an in-depth review of the law and of the facts.[168]

The review of legality is supplemented by the unlimited jurisdiction which the Union courts are afforded by Article 31 of Regulation 1/2003, in accordance with Article 261 TFEU. That jurisdiction empowers the Union courts, in addition to carrying out a mere review of the lawfulness of the penalty, to substitute their own appraisal for the Commission's and, consequently, to cancel, reduce or increase the fine or penalty payment imposed.[169] This is a statement that goes far beyond the previous case law by the Union courts in which they had rather limited themselves to reviewing whether the Commission had properly applied its Fining Guidelines.[170]

The review provided for by the Treaties thus involves review by the Union courts of both the law and the facts, and means that they have the power to assess the evidence, annul the contested decision and alter the amount of a fine.[171]

The judgment of the ECJ reflects the decision of the ECtHR in the *Menarini* case.[172] The *Menarini* judgment addresses the question whether the combination of the investigatory, prosecutorial and adjudicatory powers of the Commission leads to a bias when imposing fines under the competition rules that is contrary to the require-ments of Article 6(1) ECHR. Article 6(1) ECHR provides that 'everyone is entitled to a fair and public hearing within a reasonable time by an independent and impartial tribunal established by law' when a 'criminal charge' is determined against him. It has been argued that the very substantial fines in cartel cases amount to a criminal charge and that the Commission is not entitled to impose such a criminal charge since it is not an 'independent and impartial tribunal' due to its investigatory and prose-cutorial functions.[173]

---

[167] On the concept of discretion of EU institutions in general, in competition cases and judicial review, see Fritzsche, 'Discretion, Scope of Judicial Review and Institutional Balance in European Law', *Common Market Law Review*, 48 (2010), 361.

[168] ECJ (8 December 2011), Case C-272/09 P – *KME Germany and Others v Commission*, nyr, para. 102. On the line of jurisprudence referring to the Commission's discretion see Forrester, 'A Challenge for Europe's Judges', 194.

[169] ECJ (8 December 2011), Case C-272/09 P – *KME Germany and Others v Commission*, nyr, para. 103.

[170] Such unlimited jurisdiction has long been called for by commentators. Previously, the General Court had been seen as not allowing fair dialectic exchanges about the substance of cases on an equal footing with the Commission. See Gerard, 'Breaking the EU Antitrust Enforcement Deadlock: Re-empowering the Courts?', *European Law Review*, 36 (2011), 457; Forrester, 'A Challenge for Europe's Judges', 185.

[171] ECJ (8 December 2011), Case C-272/09 P – *KME Germany and Others v Commission*, nyr, para. 104.

[172] ECtHR (27 September 2011), Application No. 43509/08 – *Menarini*, nyr.

[173] On this debate see Nazzini, 'Administrative Enforcement, Judicial Review and Fundamental Rights in EU Competition Law: A Comparative Contextual-Functionalist Perspective', *Common Market Law Review*, 50 (2012), 971.

The first question arising with regard to this debate[174] is whether competition law fines are 'criminal charges' under Article 6(1) ECHR. Article 23(5) Regulation 1/2003 provides that fining decisions 'shall not be of a criminal law nature'. However, this categorisation by the EU legislator is not binding for the categorisation of competition law fines under Article 6(1) ECHR. There is a separate notion of 'criminal charge' under this body of law which distinguishes between 'traditional categories of criminal law' and 'cases not strictly belonging to the traditional categories of criminal law'.[175] Competition law fines do not belong to the first category of 'hardcore' criminal law but to the second category of criminal law in the wider sense.[176] Criminal sanctions of this category can be imposed by an administrative or non-judicial body that combines the investigative and decision-making powers, provided there is a possibility to appeal before a judicial body that has full jurisdiction, including the power to set aside the decision in all respects, on questions of fact and of law. Administrative procedures resulting in penal sanctions can deviate from a strict criminal procedure as long as the rights stipulated in Article 6(1) ECHR are respected. In *Menarini* the ECtHR quoted this line of case law and held that a fining decision of the Italian competition authority does not violate Article 6(1) ECHR since it is subject to unlimited review by an adminstrative court the judgment of which can be appealed to a second instance tribunal.[177]

The *Menarini* judgment has several implications for the compatibility of fining decisions of the Commission based on a violation of the competition rules. It suggests that the lawfulness of competition law fines depends on the way in which decisions are reviewed by the Union courts. Only if the Union courts exercise full jurisdiction in the sense of the *Menarini* judgment will fining decisions of the Commission be compatible with Article 6(1) ECHR. The ECJ appears to address this suggestion in the *Copper Tubes* judgment discussed above by emphasising the unlimited jurisdiction of the General Court regarding fining decisions under Article 261 TFEU and Article 31 Regulation 1/2003 in an effort to justify the pre-existing EU system of competition law sanctions. At the same time, the ECJ raised the bar with regard to what is expected of the General Court's review in future cases. A deferential review of competition law fines will not satisfy the requirement of effective judicial protection. The General Court will rather have to perform an in-depth review of law and of facts. It is also questionable whether the General Court can continue to be allowed to concede to the Commission a certain margin of discretion with regard to complex

---

[174] Commentators challenged the compatibility of the Commission's contentious procedure with Article 6(1) ECHR due to a lack of separation of powers. It has been argued that fines imposed by the Commission are in fact criminal penalties that require due process under Article 6(1) ECHR before an independent tribunal. See Riley, 'The Modernisation of EU Anti-cartel Enforcement', 197; Forrester, 'Due Process in EC Competition Cases: A Distinguished Institution with Flawed Procedures', *European Law Review*, 34 (2009), 817, 823 et seq.; Forrester, 'A Challenge for Europe's Judges', 201.

[175] ECtHR (23 November 2006), Application No. 73053/01 – *Jussila v Finland*, nyr, para. 43.   [176] Ibid.

[177] Ibid., para. 59.

economic[178] or technical[179] appraisals. So far, the General Court has limited its review of such an appraisal to

verifying whether the relevant procedural rules have been complied with, whether the statement of the reasons for the decision is adequate, whether the facts have been accurately stated and whether there has been any manifest error of appraisal or a misuse of powers.[180]

In light of the *Menarini* judgment the General Court will have to increase the thoroughness of its review and to intensify its control over the Commission.

Summary of Section 4

Final decisions of the Commission in cartel cases can be challenged in the EU courts.

To prove a cartel infringement, the Commission has to adduce sufficiently precise and consistent evidence to support the firm conviction that the alleged infringement took place. Such evidence does not necessarily have to consist of documentary evidence. Any other type of evidence may be used as well so long as it is sufficiently reliable. If doubts remain after consideration of all available evidence the presumption of innocence applies.

The principle of effective judicial protection requires that the General Court does not limit its review of Commission decisions in cartel cases to a legality review in the sense that it will assess only whether the Commission committed any errors of law. The EU courts enjoy full jurisdiction which empowers them, in addition to carrying out a mere review of the lawfulness of the penalty, to substitute their own appraisal of the evidence for the Commission's and, consequently, to cancel, reduce or increase the fine or penalty payment imposed.

5. LENIENCY NOTICE

Participation in leniency schemes implemented by the competition authorities provides for undertakings involved in illegal cartel practices a very important way to escape fines for violations of competition law. The main idea in leniency schemes is that parties to cartel agreements are granted full or partial immunity from fines in exchange for disclosure of information regarding the operation of the cartel to the competent competition authority.

Competition authorities may generally obtain information about possible violations of competition law from three main sources. The first and the most expensive one in terms of workload and costs is to monitor the actual developments on the relevant markets by the competition authority itself. The second source of

---

[178] ECJ (11 July 1985), Case 42/84 – *Remia v Commission* [1985] ECR 2566, para. 34.
[179] GC (17 September 2007), Case T-201/04 – *Microsoft v Commission* [2007] ECR II-3619, para. 87.
[180] ECJ (11 July 1985), Case 42/84 – *Remia v Commission* [1985] ECR 2566, para. 34.

information comes from third parties acting on the markets affected by anticompetitive practices. They may provide public authorities with some insider information in order to facilitate the punishment of their competitors involved in cartels and to enhance their market position. Customers of undertakings involved in anticompetitive practices may also have an interest in bringing the infringement to an end since they may be overcharged as a result of the restriction of competition. Finally, competition authorities may use information possessed by the undertakings involved in alleged anticompetitive market practices either by conducting unannounced inspections (so-called 'dawn raids'), forcing the undertakings to provide all relevant evidence under threat of financial sanctions or by granting certain privileges in exchange for evidence. In recent years the last method has turned out to be the most efficient tool of competition authorities around the globe. In the EU more than half of fining decisions adopted by the Commission originated from a whistleblower's application for leniency. In comparison to other instruments implemented by competition authorities the main advantages of leniency schemes are:

- Relatively low costs of obtaining relevant intelligence and evidence with regard to hardcore cartels the operation of which is kept secret from the public.
- Higher costs of sustaining cartels in operation. Granting immunity to individual cartel members increases the uncertainty and diminishes trust between parties to an illegal agreement thus elevating the costs of monitoring.
- Costs savings by the competition authorities since the main requirement for granting immunity is the recognition of the violation and acceptance of the penalty.

It is, however, important to note that leniency schemes can only be effectively implemented when they are complemented by other mechanisms and instruments. In other words there must be a credible threat for the undertaking involved in illegal activities that the existence of a cartel will also be detected without implementation of a leniency policy ('carrot and stick' approach).

In EU competition law[181] the Leniency Notice issued in 2006[182] stipulates conditions under which an undertaking may apply for full or partial immunity.

5.1 Requirements for full immunity

According to the Leniency Notice full immunity will be granted to the first undertaking[183] in a cartel to submit information and evidence which enables the Commission to:

---

[181] On the Commission's earlier leniency notices and the development of leniency programmes in the US, see Riley, 'The Modernisation of EU Anti-cartel Enforcement', 191; Sandhu, 'The European Commission's Leniency Policy: A Success?', *European Competition Law Review*, 28 (2007), 148.

[182] Commission Notice on Immunity from fines and reduction of fines in cartel cases, OJ No. C 298 of 8 December 2006, p.17.

[183] The Leniency Notice falls short of providing a solution in case several cartel participants approach the Commission together with a joint immunity application. See Billiet, 'How Lenient is the EC Leniency Policy? A Matter of Certainty and Predictability', *European Competition Law Review*, 30 (2009), 14, 20.

(i)   carry out a targeted investigation (so-called 'Paragraph 8(a) leniency'), or
(ii) find an infringement of Article 101 TFEU (so-called 'Paragraph 8(b) leniency').

For a Paragraph 8(a) immunity to be granted the applicant must provide the Commission with a corporate statement containing the following information:

- detailed description of the alleged arrangement, including aims, activities and functioning of the cartel; product or service concerned; geographical scope as well as specific dates, locations, content of and participants in alleged cartel contacts;
- names and addresses of all undertakings participating in the cartel agreement;
- names, positions, office locations and home addresses of all individuals involved in the alleged cartel;
- information on other competition authorities that have been approached or are intended to be approached in relation to the alleged cartel; and
- all other relevant evidence in the possession of the applicant including in particular any evidence contemporaneous to the infringement.

The Commission will not grant full immunity if, at the time of submission it had already sufficient evidence to adopt the decision to carry out an inspection.

Paragraph 8(b) immunity may be granted under the condition that no Paragraph 8(a) immunity has already been granted. Furthermore, the applicant must submit contemporaneous, incriminating evidence of the alleged cartel and a corporate statement containing information mentioned above. Immunity is not possible if, at the time of submission the Commission had sufficient evidence to find a violation of Article 101 TFEU.

Additionally, an undertaking applying for immunity on the basis of either Paragraph 8(a) or 8(b) must fulfil the following conditions:[184]

- genuine and full cooperation with the Commission on a continuous basis which includes providing the Commission with all relevant information and evidence, remaining at the Commission's disposal to respond promptly to any request, not destroying, falsifying or concealing relevant information and/or evidence and not disclosing the fact or the content of application before the Commission issues its statement of objections;
- termination of the applicant's involvement in the cartel following the submission of the leniency application;
- not destroying, falsifying or concealing any kind of relevant information and/or evidence prior to submission of the leniency application to the Commission.

Immunity from fines is not eligible to undertakings that coerced other undertakings to join the cartel or remain in it.[185]

---

[184] Leniency Notice, para. 12.
[185] Some authors hold that the threshold for immunity is very high and that there is a lack of certainty in the process and an unpredictable outcome, see Billiet, 'How Lenient is the EC Leniency Policy?', 16.

There is little case law of the Union courts on the interpretation of the individual elements of the Leniency Notice. The ECJ only held in very general terms that

a reduction under the Leniency Notice can be justified only where the information provided and, more generally, the conduct of the undertaking concerned might be considered to demonstrate a genuine spirit of cooperation on its part.[186]

These criteria are not met where an undertaking pretends to cooperate with the Commission but in fact supplies misleading or incomplete information.[187]

5.2 Requirements for fine reduction

Undertakings that do not qualify for full immunity may still be granted a reduction of their fine. The main requirement is that the applicant provides the Commission with evidence that represents significant added value with respect to the evidence already possessed by the Commission. Moreover, the three conditions listed above have to be fulfilled.[188]

Evidence is deemed to represent significant added value when it strengthens, by its nature and level of detail, the Commission's ability to prove the alleged cartel. The Leniency Notice gives some further guidance on the quality of information required for reduction of a fine. The Commission has, however, a wide margin of discretion in the assessment of particular pieces of evidence.[189]

The level of reduction depends on the time of submission of the leniency application. The first undertaking to provide significant evidence will be granted a reduction of 30–50% and the second one a reduction of 20–30%. All subsequent applicants may be granted a reduction of up to 20%.

5.3 Procedure

A leniency application must be submitted to the Commission before the statement of objections is issued. Each of the undertakings involved may either make a formal application for immunity from fines or apply for a marker. In the latter case the applicant's place in the queue for full immunity will be protected and he will be given additional time to gather information and evidence necessary for a complete

---

[186] ECJ (28 June 2005), Joined Cases C-189/02 P, C-202/02 P, C-205/02 P to C-208/02 P and C-213/02 P – *Dansk Rørindustri and Others v Commission* [2005] ECR I-5425, paras. 388–403, particularly para. 395.

[187] ECJ (29 June 2006), Case C-301/04 P – *Commission v SGL Carbon AG* [2006] ECR I-5915, paras. 66–80.

[188] Leniency Notice, para. 24.

[189] The standard of evidence for fine reduction is criticised by commentators as unclear and therefore to act as a deterrent to file a leniency application. See Riley, The Modernisation of EU Anti-cartel Enforcement', 195; Sandhu, 'The European Commission's Leniency Policy', 148, 152.

application. If the applicant complements the marker within the time limit set by the Commission, the information and evidence provided will be deemed to have been submitted on the date when the marker was granted. A formal application must contain either all information or evidence pertaining to the alleged infringement or may present this information and evidence in hypothetical terms. In such case the complete version of the application must be submitted on a later agreed date.[190] The Commission grants conditional immunity when the information and evidence submitted by the undertaking concerned fulfils all formal and material requirements laid down in the Leniency Notice. Where the information provided is not sufficient to grant full immunity the applicant may withdraw all evidence submitted or apply for a reduction of the fine.

With regard to the reduction of fines the Commission does not grant conditional consent. It will also not take any position on an application for reduction of a fine before it has taken a position on any existing applications for conditional immunity in relation to the same infringement. Information from the Commission as to whether all formal and material conditions for reduction of a fine have been fulfilled shall be released no later than the date when the statement of objections is notified. The final decision will be taken at the end of the administrative procedure and will be announced in the final infringement decision.

The main element of each leniency application is the corporate statement. It is a voluntary presentation by or on behalf of an undertaking to the Commission of the undertaking's knowledge of the cartel and its role therein and is prepared specifically to be submitted under the Leniency Notice.[191] In order to protect the information contained in the statement from being disclosed to third parties (for example, plaintiffs in civil damages proceedings), the corporate statement may be provided orally.[192] It will be recorded at the Commission's premises and transcribed as an internal Commission document.[193] Access to the corporate statement is granted only to the addressees of the statement of objections in the matter and subject to

---

[190] The marker system is criticised by commentators as overly discretionary and requiring excessively detailed information. See Riley, 'The Modernisation of EU Anti-cartel Enforcement', 195; Billiet, 'How Lenient is the EC Leniency Policy?', 14; Sandhu, 'The European Commission's Leniency Policy', 149.

[191] Leniency Notice, para. 31.

[192] Corporate statements may be discoverable under the civil procedure rules of other jurisdictions, in particular in the US. For a detailed discussion of this aspect, see Billiet, 'How Lenient is the EC Leniency Policy?', 16; Sandhu, 'The European Commission's Leniency Policy', 148, 155.

[193] There is a certain tension between leniency programmes and private enforcement. If an undertaking 'confesses' to having participated in a cartel within the framework of a leniency application this increases the risk of private damages claims. The Commission's leniency system is currently not addressing this issue which has drawn criticism, in particular with a view to the US where a certain degree of protection from full civil damages is offered to leniency applicants under the Antitrust Criminal Penalty Enhancement and Reform Act. See Riley, 'The Modernisation of EU Anti-cartel Enforcement', 195. The contradictions between the Commission's leniency programme and its efforts to facilitate private enforcement are described in detail by Walsh, 'Carrots and Sticks: Leniency and Fines in EC Cartel Cases', *European Competition Law Review*, 30 (2009), 30.

certain restrictions set out in paragraph 33 of the Leniency Notice. They are not allowed to make any copy of the statement in order not to create any documents that may have to be disclosed in civil litigation.

In general, access to file in pending cartel cases is granted only to the addressees of a statement of objections and is governed by the Commission's notice on access to file in competition cases[194] which specifies in greater detail the general statement in Article 27(2) Regulation 1/2003 linking access to file in competition cases to the rights of defence of the addressees of a statement of objections.[195] The limitation of access to file to the addressees of the statement of objections is in line with the general rules for access to documents of EU institutions under the Transparency Regulation.[196] Article 4(2) third indent of the Transparency Regulation provides for an exception to the general right to access to Commission documents where the disclosure of the document would undermine the purpose of 'inspections, investigations and audits'. Until the Commission has adopted a final decision in a cartel case this exception can be invoked.

Once the Commission has concluded its investigation of a cartel case and has adopted a final decision, it can no longer reject applications for access to documents in its file on this basis. The General Court on several occasions held that Article 4(2) third indent of the Transparency Regulation does not apply to applications for access to a document if the Commission has adopted a final decision in the relevant case many months ago.[197] Article 4(2) third indent of the Transparency Regulation cannot be interpreted as protecting the leniency programme as such by providing leniency applicants with a certain degree of shelter from private damages claims, as the General Court has stressed that nothing in the Transparency Regulation 'leads to the supposition that EU competition policy should enjoy, in the application of that regulation, treatment different from other EU policies'.[198] With regard to the relationship of the leniency programme and private damages claims, the General Court noted that 'the

---

[194] Commission Notice on the rules for access to the Commission file in cases pursuant to Articles 81 and 82 of the EC Treaty, Articles 53, 54 and 57 of the EEA Agreement and Council Regulation (EC) No. 139/2004, OJ No. C 325 of 22 December 2005, p. 7.

[195] The relevance of confidentiality for leniency programmes in the EU and in the US is assessed in detail in Caruso, 'Leniency Programmes and Protection of Confidentiality: The Experience of the European Commission', *Journal of European Competition Law and Practice*, 1 (2010), 453. Recent judgments of the EU courts on access to documents in competition cases are analysed in Goddin, 'Recent Judgments Regarding Transparency and Access to Documents in the Field of Competition Law: Where does the Court of Justice of the EU Strike the Balance?', *Journal of European Competition Law and Practice*, 2 (2011) 10.

[196] Regulation (EC) No. 1049/2001 of the European Parliament and of the Council of 30 May 2001 regarding public access to European Parliament, Council and Commission documents. OJ No. L 145 of 31 May 2001, p. 43. An analysis of recent case law under this regulation is provided in Leino, 'Just a Little Sunshine in the Rain: The 2010 Case Law of the European Court of Justice on Access to Documents', *Common Market Law Review*, 49 (2011), 1215.

[197] GC (15 December 2011), Case T-437/08 – *CDC Hydrogene Peroxide v Commission*, nyr, para. 60; GC (22 May 2012), Case T-344/08 – *EnBW Energie Baden-Württemberg v Commission*, nyr, para. 117.

[198] GC (15 December 2011), Case T-437/08 – *CDC Hydrogene Peroxide v Commission*, nyr, para. 72; GC (22 May 2012), Case T-344/08 – *EnBW Energie Baden-Württemberg v Commission*, nyr, para. 127.

leniency and co-operation programmes whose effectiveness the Commission is seeking to protect are not the only means of ensuring compliance with EU competition law. Actions for damages before the national courts can make a significant contribution to the maintenance of effective competition in the EU.'[199]

The position of the General Court which appears to aim at fostering private enforcement does not, however, prejudice national rules for access to documents in the file of a national competition authority relating to a procedure under the national leniency programme. The ECJ in the *Pfleiderer* case held that EU competition law requires national courts and tribunals only to weigh the interest of the national competition authority in an effective leniency programme as an element of public competition law enforcement against the interest of persons wishing to bring an action for damages as an element of private competition law enforcement, but does not determine the outcome of this weighing exercise.[200] This may lead to diverging standards for access to a leniency file in the Member States. While the English High Court ordered the disclosure of leniency documents[201] following the ECJ's judgment, German courts are refusing access to such documents.[202]

In the EU there is no one-stop shop in applying for leniency.[203] Undertakings involved in an alleged cartel have to consider submitting separate applications to national competition authorities that have the competence to hear the case. The application made to the Commission does not serve as a leniency application in other jurisdictions.[204]

5.4 Settlement procedure

The fines imposed on undertakings may be further reduced by 10%[205] if the parties to an infringement choose to acknowledge their involvement in the cartel and their liability for it. Such a decision may be made by the undertaking after examination of the evidence collected by the Commission. The settlement can be reached with regard

---

[199] GC (15 December 2011), Case T-437/08 – *CDC Hydrogene Peroxide v Commission*, nyr, para. 77; GC (22 May 2012), Case T-344/08 – *EnBW Energie Baden-Württemberg v Commission*, nyr, para. 128.

[200] ECJ (14 June 2011), Case C-360/09 – *Pfleiderer*, nyr, para. 30. See also Müller, 'Access to the File of a National Competition Authority', *European Law Review*, 36 (2011), 56.

[201] EWHC (4 April 2012), Claim no. HC08C03243 – *National Grid v ABB & Others* [2012] EWHC 869 (Ch).

[202] AG Bonn (18 January 2012), Case no. 51 Gs 53/09 – *Pfleiderer v Bundeskartellamt*.

[203] There is an ECN Model Leniency Programme though, see Gauer and Jaspers, 'Designing a European Solution for a "one-stop leniency shop"', *European Competition Law Review*, 27 (2006), 685.

[204] For a more detailed discussion of this aspect, see Sandhu, 'The European Commission's Leniency Policy', 154; Reynolds and Anderson, 'Immunity and Leniency in EU Cartel Cases: Current Issues', *European Competition Law Review*, 27 (2006), 82, 86.

[205] The reduction offered in settlement procedures has been criticised as not sufficiently generous to make a settlement attractive. The small number of settlements reached so far may confirm this. See Brankin, 'The First Cases under the Commission's Cartel-settlement Procedure: Problems Solved?', *European Competition Law Review*, 32 (2011), 165, 167.

to the scope and duration of the cartel as well as the individual liability of each of the parties involved.[206] The settlement procedure,[207] which was introduced in 2008 and is laid down in the Settlement Notice,[208] may be applied cumulatively with the EU leniency scheme.

Typically, the Commission will explore the parties' interest to engage in settlement discussions taking account of factors such as the number of parties involved, foreseeable conflicting positions on the attribution of liability and the extent of the contestation of facts by the parties. If the Commission concludes that a settlement may be possible it will request all parties in writing to express their interest in a settlement. With those parties who agree to enter into settlement discussions, the Commission will engage in bilateral negotiations. During those meetings, the Commission will inform the parties of the objections it envisaged raising against them and will disclose the evidence relied on to establish these objections. The parties have the possibility to access the Commission's file and to review further documents.[209] The Commission will also provide the parties with an estimation of the range of fines likely to be imposed by it.

Following these meetings, the parties will consider whether to submit a formal request to settle. A formal request to settle has to contain an acknowledgement in clear and unequivocal terms of the party's liability for the infringement as well as a description of the infringement. In addition, the party has to indicate the maximum amount of the fine the party would accept in the framework of a settlement procedure. The Commission will send out a brief statement of objections endorsing the settlement submissions if it considers them appropriate. If the company confirms that the statement of objections properly reflects its settlement submission, the Commission will adopt a final decision that is considerably shorter than a normal decision in a cartel case.[210]

It is not a prerequisite of a settlement procedure that all parties to an infringement engage in negotiations with the Commission. The Commission may also enter into a

---

[206] These aspects may have a very substantial impact on the fine to be imposed and may go far beyond the formal 10% reduction offered by the Settlement Notice. For a detailed analysis see Ortega Gonzalez, 'The Cartel Settlement Procedure in Practice', *European Competition Law Review*, 32 (2011), 170, 173.

[207] For a comparison of settlements in cartel cases in the EU and in the US see Macchi di Cellere and Mezzapesa, 'The Commission's Settlement Package: EU–US Comparison', *European Competition Law Review*, 30 (2009), 604.

[208] Commission Notice on the conduct of settlement procedures in view of the adoption of Decisions pursuant to Article 7 and 23 of Council Regulation (EC) No. 1/2003 in cartel cases, OJ No. C 167 of 2 July 2008, p. 1.

[209] Access to file is, however, limited in comparison to a normal procedure, which has led to concerns that procedural rights might be infringed. Other commentators hold that the right of defence is fully protected through the possibility to request additional documents. See Ortega Gonzalez, 'The Cartel Settlement Procedure in Practice', 174.

[210] A recent example is Commission decision of 7 December 2011, Case COMP/39600 – *Refrigeration compressors*, available at http://ec.europa.eu/competition/antitrust/cases/dec_docs/39600/39600_2147_3.pdf.

settlement with individual members of a cartel while others prefer to contest the Commission's allegations (so-called 'hybrid' cartel settlement cases). In such cases the Commission will in parallel conduct a settlement procedure and an ordinary procedure. It will adopt a short decision against the parties willing to settle and a comprehensive decision against the other parties.[211] In such hybrid cases the settlement procedure will not lead to the full scale of efficiencies it generates where all parties to an infringement agree to settle.[212] The Commission will have to conduct an ordinary procedure against some of the parties including a comprehensive statement of objections and a detailed final decision. Still there is some benefit in hybrid cases since the Commission has to establish in an ordinary procedure the individual involvement of each cartel member. In a hybrid case this burden is reduced at least with regard to some parties since the Commission can adopt a short statement of objection and final decision in relation to them.[213]

Summary of Section 5

The Commission's Leniency Notice seeks to give cartel members an incentive to disclose the existence of the cartel and to come forward with evidence that enables the Commission to initiate or continue the investigation of a cartel. If a cartel member is the first to cooperate with the Commission it may obtain immunity from fines subject to certain conditions. Cartel members that come in later may still obtain a substantial reduction of the fine if they provide the Commission with additional information and fulfil a number of additional requirements. Leniency is not available to the instigator of a cartel.

It may be necessary to submit leniency applications to the Commission and a number of national competition authorities. There is no 'centralised' system for leniency. The Commission will review all information obtained on the alleged cartel and issue a statement of objections to the cartel members setting out its preliminary findings. The addressees may access the Commission's file and submit their observations on the statement of objections before a final decision is adopted by the Commission.

To abbreviate this process the Commission may invite cartel members to enter into a settlement agreement. This will reduce the Commission's procedural obligations by allowing for a swift termination of the procedure. Cartel members can get a fine reduction of an additional 10% as an incentive for entering into a settlement.

---

[211] An example of a hybrid cartel settlement case is Commission decision of 20 July 2010, Case COMP/ 38866 – *Animal feed phosphates*, available at http://ec.europa.eu/competition/antitrust/cases/dec_docs/ 38866/38866_1655_6.pdf.

[212] This is also criticised by Riley, 'The Modernisation of EU Anti-cartel Enforcement', 201.

[213] A different view is taken by Ortega Gonzalez, 'The Cartel Settlement Procedure in Practice', 176.

6. PRIVATE ENFORCEMENT

Competition law may be enforced not only by means of administrative or criminal sanctions but also through civil law actions brought before national courts by companies and individuals which have suffered harm as a result of anticompetitive behaviour.

6.1 Concept

Private enforcement is, contrary to public enforcement, independent of public policy considerations as it enables individual market players to protect their rights whenever they find them infringed by private conduct.[214] The most obvious case of private enforcement is damages claims where the victims of cartels may claim compensation for harm caused by prohibited market conduct. Civil actions may also be used to enforce cease and desist orders or to be granted interim protection against allegedly prohibited practices. In all these cases civil law is used as a 'sword' against prohibited activities. Additionally, cartel prohibitions may also be invoked as a 'shield' when they are used as a defence against a contractual claim for performance or damages for non-performance. The use of Article 101 TFEU as a shield has its direct foundation in the TFEU. Pursuant to Article 101(2) TFEU all agreements covered by Article 101(1) TFEU shall be automatically void.

Depending on policy considerations, private enforcement may pursue one or two goals. The first and basic one is compensation. Damages actions for infringement of competition law serve this objective as they are designed to compensate those who have suffered a loss as a consequence of anticompetitive behaviour. In order to achieve this goal by means of private enforcement, national laws may provide for presumptions to facilitate the calculation of damages or to establish the existence of an infringement. The second goal of private enforcement is deterrence.[215] Damages actions present an incentive for private claimants to exercise their rights before national courts thus creating a credible threat of sanctions and discouraging anticompetitive behaviour of other market players.[216] This goal is in particular pursued

---

[214] On the risks and benefits of a dissemination of competition law enforcement to private claimants, see Hodges, 'Competition Enforcement, Regulation and Civil Justice: What is the Case?', *Common Market Law Review*, 44 (2006), 1381, 1386 et seq.

[215] On the compensation/deterrence dichotomy under the EU competition rules in detail, see Nebbia, 'Damages Actions for the Infringement of EC Competition Law: Compensation or Deterrence?', *European Law Review*, 33 (2010), 23.

[216] An argument to limit private damage actions to the compensation goal is made by Aresu, 'Optimal Contract Reformation as a New Approach to Private Antitrust Damages in Cartel Cases', *European Law Review*, 33 (2010), 349.

by US antitrust law where treble-damages for infringement of antitrust law may be obtained under section 4 of the Clayton Act.[217]

Private and public enforcement may of course be combined in order to enhance the effectiveness of the competition rules. The structure of the enforcement system is however a policy decision and is subject to economic, cultural and political considerations.[218] Generally there are two models of antitrust enforcement. The first one is based on strong public enforcement with competition authorities furnished with far-reaching investigative powers and a wide margin of discretion regarding the fining policy. The most important cases are handled in an administrative procedure, and private enforcement has only a complementing function. Such a model seems to be pursued by the Commission which declared in its White Paper on private enforcement of the EU competition rules:

> Another important guiding principle of the Commission's policy is to preserve strong public enforcement of Articles 81 and 82 [Articles 101 and 102 TFEU] by the Commission and the competition authorities of the Member States. Accordingly, the measures put forward in this White Paper are designed to create an effective system of private enforcement by means of damages actions that complements, but does not replace or jeopardise, public enforcement.[219]

A different approach has been taken in the United States where about 90% of antitrust cases are private actions handled by civil courts.[220] Public enforcement by the Department of Justice, the Federal Trade Commission or State authorities exists too, but is rather limited in its scope and focuses only on the most blatant cases.

6.2 Reasons for underdevelopment of private enforcement in EU law

As already mentioned, the enforcement system of the EU competition rules is based on public enforcement by the Commission and national competition authorities acting within the framework of Regulation 1/2003. No legislation on private

---

[217] 'Except as provided in subsection (b) of this section, any person who shall be injured in his business or property by reason of anything forbidden in the antitrust laws may sue therefore in any district court of the United States [. . .] and shall recover threefold the damages by him sustained, and the cost of suit, including a reasonable attorney's fee.'

[218] For an economic appraisal of public and private enforcement of competition law see Segal and Whinston, 'Public vs. Private Enforcement of Antitrust Law: A Survey', *European Competition Law Review*, 28 (2007), 306.

[219] Commission, White Paper on Damages actions for breach of the EC antitrust rules, COM(2008) 165 final, p. 2.

[220] The differences between private antitrust litigation in the US and in the EU/UK, taking the vitamins cartel as an example, are described in Krause and Mullette, 'How Vitamins Stimulated the Debate on Private Antitrust Litigation', *Zeitschrift für Wettbewerbsrecht* (2007), 466. For a discussion of the US private litigation system from an EU competition law point of view, see Martin, 'Private Antitrust Litigation in Europe: What Fence is High Enough to Keep out the US Litigation Cowboy?', *European Competition Law Review*, 28 (2007), 2.

enforcement has been released at EU level yet. Moreover, according to the study on the condition for claims for damages in the Member States the overall picture is one of 'astonishing diversity and total underdevelopment' of private enforcement.[221] There are many reasons for this status quo of which the most important ones will be briefly discussed below.

Private enforcement of EU competition law can be pursued by way of individual court actions. However, potential claimants are often reluctant to initiate private court actions against unlawful practices, in particular if the individual damage is small in comparison to the costs of litigation.[222]

Up to the enactment of Regulation 1/2003 the Commission's monopoly to apply Article 101(3) TFEU was considered the major obstacle for private enforcement of EU competition law. Although national courts were free to apply Article 101(1) TFEU they could not decide whether the requirements for an individual exemption pursuant to Article 101(3) TFEU were fulfilled. In such cases a decision by the Commission was required that, due to its limited resources, led to significant delays.

Another issue that needs clarification is access to evidence for potential plaintiffs. As hardcore cartels are always operated in secret it is in principle virtually impossible for private plaintiffs to get access to information pertaining to the operation of the cartel and its effects on the relevant market. Without this intelligence it is very difficult to establish the identity of all collaborating undertakings and to calculate the exact amount of damages to be claimed.

Another problem to be resolved is the scope of damages. Since there are no clear guidelines as to the definition of damages, several solutions are possible ranging from pure compensation theory to the concept of recovery of illegal gain by the participants in the cartel. Quantification of damages is also a key issue. Several economic models have been developed in economic theory to calculate damages but a clear-cut instruction on their compatibility with Article 101 TFEU is still not available. In principle such calculation should imply a comparison with the economic situation of the victim in the hypothetical scenario of a competitive market. This is often a very cumbersome exercise which can become excessively difficult or even practically impossible for a plaintiff to complete.[223] The Commission is currently preparing a Guidance Paper on the quantification of harm in antitrust damages cases. The Guidance Paper is the result of legal and economic considerations and has been circulated for public consultation. The Commission also held a round of workshops with economists on the paper.

---

[221] Ashurst, 'Study on the Conditions of Claims for Damages in Case of Infringement of EC Competition Rules', August 2004, available at http://ec.europa.eu/competition/antitrust/actionsdamages/comparative_report_clean_en.pdf.

[222] See Eilmannsberger, 'The Green Paper on Damages Actions for Breach of the EC Antitrust Rules and Beyond: Reflections on the Utility and Feasibility of Stimulating Private Enforcement through Legislative Action', *Common Market Law Review*, 45 (2007), 431, 446.

[223] Commission, White Paper on Damages actions for breach of the EC antitrust rules, COM(2008) 165 final, p. 7.

The legal basis for damages claims at EU level has also not been defined as yet. There is an ongoing discussion as to whether damages actions for violations of Article 101 TFEU are rooted directly in EU law or whether they are based on national provisions pertaining to compensation read in light of the principles of effectiveness and equivalence. This creates a great degree of legal uncertainty as the potential claimants do not possess sufficient information on the substantive requirements they have to fulfil in order to be awarded damages. The most important issue in this regard is the admissibility of the passing-on defence for defendants so that they can claim the passing-on of overcharges by claimants to their purchasers and/or consumers. It is also not clear whether indirect purchasers may invoke the passing-on of cartel overcharges as a basis to demonstrate the harm suffered, i.e. to be granted sufficient standing.[224]

6.3 Current legal status

The current discussion on the introduction of private enforcement of competition law at EU level has been accelerated by two events. Firstly, the Commission's monopoly to apply Article 101(3) TFEU has been abolished through the enactment of Regulation 1/2003. Article 101(3) TFEU became a legal exception that may be applied by national competition authorities and courts. Moreover, the ECJ has given a green light to the enhancement of private enforcement of EU competition law. In the landmark judgment *Courage v Crehan* the Court acknowledged the general admissibility of damages actions as an instrument designed to strengthen the practical effect of the cartel prohibition:[225]

The full effectiveness of Article 85 of the Treaty [Article 101 TFEU] and, in particular, the practical effect of the prohibition laid down in Article 85(1) [Article 101(1) TFEU] would be put at risk if it were not open to any individual to claim damages for loss caused to him by a contract or by conduct liable to restrict or distort competition.

Indeed, the existence of such a right strengthens the working of the Community competition rules and discourages agreements or practices, which are frequently covert, which are liable to restrict or distort competition. From that point of view, actions for damages before the national courts can make a significant contribution to the maintenance of effective competition in the Community.

---

[224] For a detailed assessment of the passing-on defence and the standing of indirect purchasers under the Commission's legislative initiatives and US law, see Petrucci, 'The Issues of the Passing-on Defence and Indirect Purchaser's Standing in European Competition Law', *European Competition Law Review*, 29 (2009), 33.

[225] For a detailed analysis of the judgment in light of the principle of effective judicial protection, see Drake, 'Scope of Courage and the Principle of "Individual Liability" for Damages: Further Development of the Principle of Effective Judicial Protection by the Court of Justice', *European Law Review*, 31 (2006), 841. See also Nebbia, 'Damages Actions for the Infringement of EC Competition Law', 28 et seq.

There should not therefore be any absolute bar to such an action being brought by a party to a contract which would be held to violate the competition rules.[226]

Shortly thereafter the Commission initiated a discussion among the stakeholders as to the possibilities and options for enhancement of private enforcement at EU level. A study on damages actions for breach of competition law was presented in 2004, and one year later a Green Paper[227] identifying the main obstacles to a more efficient system of damages claims was published.[228] After a period of consultations a White Paper has been released that outlines proposals for policy choices and specific measures aimed at improving private enforcement.[229]

The underlying principle applied by the Commission in the White Paper is to abandon deterrence as the primary objective of private enforcement and focus on compensation for the harm suffered as a result of anticompetitive behaviour.[230] The central issue of the passing-on defence has been resolved in the way favouring indirect purchasers as a means to ensure the attainment of the compensation objective. Defendants should therefore be allowed to rely on the passing-on defence,[231] and indirect purchasers including consumers should be granted the right to claim loss suffered due to illegal cartel activities. In order to facilitate the damages actions by consumers the Commission suggested the introduction of mechanisms of collective redress:

- representative actions brought by qualified entities such as consumer associations, State bodies or trade associations acting on behalf of identified or identifiable victims;[232]

---

[226] ECJ (20 September 2001), Case C-453/99 – *Courage and Crehan* [2001] ECR I-6297, paras. 26–28; confirmed by ECJ (13 July 2006), Joined Cases C-295/04–298/04 – *Vincenzo Manfredi v Lloyd Adriatico* [2006] ECR I-6619.

[227] Commission, Green Paper, Damages actions for breach of the EC antitrust rules, COM(2005) 672 final.

[228] For a detailed discussion of the Green Paper, see Eilmannsberger, 'The Green Paper on Damages Actions for Breach of the EC Antitrust Rules and Beyond', 431; Pheasant, 'Damages Actions for Breach of the EC Antitrust Rules: The European Commission's Green Paper', *European Competition Law Review*, 27 (2006), 365; Diemer, 'The Green Paper on Damages Actions for Breach of the EC Antitrust Rules', *European Competition Law Review*, 27 (2006), 309. For an analysis of the paper from a socio-legal point of view, see Hodges, 'Competition Enforcement, Regulation and Civil Justice', 1381.

[229] For an analysis of the White Paper also in comparison to the Green Paper see Kortmann and Swaak, 'The EC White Paper on Antitrust Damage Actions: Why the Member States are (Right to be) Less Than Enthusiastic', *European Competition Law Review*, 30 (2009), 340.

[230] The concept of damage is not defined in the White Paper. This is a significant shortcoming since there are different concepts of damage in the Member States. In some Member States exemplary or punitive competition damages are available, in others not. This leads to choice of law problems assessed in detail in Danov, 'Awarding Exemplary (or Punitive) Damages in EC Competition Cases with an International Element: The Rome II Regulation and the Commission's White Paper on Damages', *European Competition Law Review*, 29 (2008), 430.

[231] For a discussion of the passing on defence under the compensation and deterrence goals of private enforcement, see Nebbia, 'Damages Actions for the Infringement of EC Competition Law', 36 et seq.

[232] Collective redress leads to jurisdictional questions due to their cross-border character. For a detailed discussion of jurisdictional issues, see Tzakas, 'Effective Collective Redress in Antitrust and Consumer Protection Matters: A Panacea or a Chimera?' *Common Market Law Review*, 49 (2011), 1125, 1153.

- opt-in collective actions[233] brought by victims who decide to combine their claims into a single action.[234]

The White Paper also proposes some further measures regarding access to evidence, the binding effect of administrative decisions,[235] limitation periods, the relationship between leniency programmes and damages actions and, finally, the requirement of fault.[236]

Following the White Paper the Commission had prepared a proposal for a draft Council Directive on rules governing actions for damages for infringements of Articles 101 and 102 TFEU[237] in March 2009. A revised proposal was circulated in June 2009. However, in October 2009 the Commission abandoned this legislative initiative following a controversy regarding potential negative consequences for businesses.[238] In October 2010 a new initiative was launched that has not yet resulted in a legislative proposal.[239]

Summary of Section 6

Private enforcement refers to actions by private litigants for cartel damages. While private enforcement enjoys a quite prominent role in the US it is perceived by the Commission as being underdeveloped in the EU. There are no EU provisions on private enforcement. The applicable laws of the Member States are very diverse. Major hurdles for private litigants to overcome include quantification of the damage caused by the cartel which presupposes that the hypothetical price level in the absence of the cartel can be established. Moreover, individual litigants may have suffered only relatively small damages which creates a disincentive for costly litigation. The procedural laws of many Member States currently do not provide for collective actions similar to class actions in the US.

The Commission has been preparing legislative initiatives to address these issues following a judgment of the ECJ interpreted as encouraging private enforcement.

---

[233] Ibid., 1135 et seq., for an in-depth exploration of the legal issues raised by an opt-out model.

[234] The opt-in mechanism is characterised by commentators as being in conformity with the principle of party disposition which underlies the procedural rules in most civil law jurisdictions. However, it requests action from the victims of a cartel, which is seen as hampering its effectiveness. See Tzakas, 'Effective Collective Redress in Antitrust and Consumer Protection Matters', 1136.

[235] The proposal to afford administrative decisions finding an infringement binding effect for private damages claims has drawn criticism. See Komninos, 'Effect of Commission Decisions on Private Antitrust Litigation: Setting the Story Straight', *Common Market Law Review*, 45 (2007), 1387, 1422.

[236] For a detailed analysis of the concepts underlying the Commission's initiatives, see Tzakas, 'Effective Collective Redress in Antitrust and Consumer Protection Matters', 1125.

[237] Internal document of the Commission, not publicly available.

[238] Some commentators have raised the question whether a facilitation of damages claims through Union legislation is appropriate and legally possible. See Eilmannsberger, 'The Green Paper on Damages Actions for Breach of the EC Antitrust Rules and Beyond', 438.

[239] For a detailed discussion of recent developments, see Pinotti and Stepina, 'Antitrust Class Actions in the European Union: Latest Developments and the Need for a Uniform Regime', *Journal of European Competition Law and Practice*, 2 (2011), 24.

7. PROCEDURAL ASPECTS

Regulation 1/2003 reshaped and reorganised the public enforcement regime of EU competition law. As already mentioned the basic change is that national competition authorities and courts have been given the power to apply Articles 101 and 102 TFEU without any consent by the Commission. A decentralised enforcement system has been created in which the Commission retains the leading role.

The procedure before the Commission is governed by Regulation 1/2003 and is designed as an administrative one.[240] For investigations initiated by national competition authorities the national procedural rules apply. In certain cases they may, however, be limited by the provisions of Regulation 1/2003 or general principles of EU law. The procedure before the Commission consists of two successive stages. In the first stage the facts are investigated. In the second stage the undertakings concerned are informed by the Commission of its objections (the so-called 'statement of objections') and are given the opportunity to present their view and legal arguments. An oral hearing will be held by the Hearing Officer.[241] The Hearing Officer is a person independent of the Commission's Directorate General for Competition. The role of the Hearing Officer is to safeguard the observance of the procedural rights of the parties to an infringement procedure.[242] The oral hearing is a forum where all of the companies accused of an infringement of the competition rules are given the opportunity to present their views to a wider audience, including the team of Commission officials in charge of the investigation, the Legal Service and other associated Commission services, as well as representatives of the competition authorities of the Member States. After the hearing a final decision is adopted.[243] Decisions taken by the Commission in antitrust cases are subject to judicial review under Article 263 TFEU.

---

[240] Commentators hold that there should be a separate procedure for cartel cases that takes account of their criminal law nature and which provides for an independent tribunal presided over by a judicial panel which imposes the fining decision. This would not only ensure compliance of the Commission's contentious procedures but also reduce the backlog of cartel cases. See Riley, 'The Modernisation of EU Anti-cartel Enforcement', 201.

[241] The role of the Hearing Officer is defined in the Decision of the President of the European Commission of 13 October 2011 on the function and terms of reference of the hearing officer in certain competition proceedings, OJ No. L 275 of 20 October 2011, p. 29. It is described in detail in Albers and Jourdan, 'The Role of Hearing Officers in EU Competition Proceedings: A Historical and Practical Perspective', *Journal of European Competition Law and Practice*, 2 (2011), 185. For a discussion of decisions of the Hearing Officer see Kellerbauer and Repa, 'The Court of First Instance Upholds Two Decisions of the Hearing Officer Clarifying Important Procedural Questions in Antitrust Investigations', *European Competition Law Review*, 28 (2007), 297.

[242] Commentators hold that the institution of the Hearing Officer cannot safeguard a due process in contentious procedures conducted by the Commission since he is not the decision maker and thus the decision is not taken by an impartial body. See Forrester, 'Due Process in EC Competition Cases', 835.

[243] The decision making by the Commissioners has been criticised as being contrary to Article 6(1) ECHR, not only because the Commission is not an independent tribunal in the sense of that provision but also with regard to the fact that the Commissioners usually have not participated in the hearing of the case and form a political, not a judicial body. See Forrester, 'Due Process in EC Competition Cases', 832.

7.1 Case allocation

Prior to the opening of a formal investigation a decision regarding the allocation of the case to either the Commission or one of the national competition authorities has to be made. Regulation 1/2003 does not contain any provision on division of labour between the Commission and national authorities. They are however obliged to apply EU competition law in close cooperation. The institutional framework for this cooperation is the ECN formed by the Commission and all national competition authorities. The principles governing operation of the ECN have been laid down in the Network Notice.[244]

In general, the authority which starts the procedure will remain in charge unless another national competition authority is declared to be well placed to handle the case. According to the Network Notice a national competition authority is well placed if:

(i)   the alleged infringement has substantial direct effects on competition in its territory or originates in its territory;
(ii) it is able to bring the infringement to an end and sanction it adequately; and
(iii) it can gather the evidence required to prove the violation.

It has to be noted that pursuant to Article 11(6) Regulation 1/2003 the Commission has the power to relieve the national competition authority of its competence to apply EU competition law in a particular case even if the procedure has already been started by the national authority.

7.2 Complaints

The Commission may launch a procedure on its own motion or following a complaint lodged by a third party, most often a victim of the alleged cartel or a competitor of an undertaking involved in illegal cooperation. The Commission is not obliged to follow each of the complaints lodged and is entitled to give different degrees of priority to complaints made to it.[245] A formal complaint within the meaning of Article 7(2) Regulation 1/2003 may only be lodged by legal or natural persons who can demonstrate legitimate interest, i.e. where they are operating in the relevant market or where the conduct complained of is capable of directly and adversely affecting their interests. Complainants are granted certain procedural rights such as access to the

---

[244] Commission Notice on cooperation within the Network of Competition Authorities, OJ No. C 101 of 27 April 2004, p. 43.
[245] Commission Notice on the handling of complaints by the Commission under Articles 81 and 82 of the EC Treaty, OJ No. C 101 of 27 April 2004. p. 65, para. 28.

non-confidential version of the statement of objections or the right to participate in the oral hearing.

7.3 The Commission's powers of investigation

Under Regulation 1/2003 the Commission has wide powers to obtain information from undertakings allegedly involved in prohibited agreements. It may require information and conduct inspections. In all cases the investigative competences of the Commission are limited by fundamental rights acknowledged as general principles of EU law.

7.3.1 Power to obtain information

In order to carry out its duties the Commission may, pursuant to Article 18 Regulation 1/2003, by simple request or by decision require undertakings to provide all necessary information. In case of a simple request the Commission must state the legal basis and the purpose of the request as well as specify what kind of information is requested. Similar requirements apply to information requests adopted as decisions. The addressee of a simple request is not obliged to provide the required information. Where the request for information has been issued as a decision there is an obligation to comply within a time limit fixed by the Commission. Such a decision may, however, be subject to judicial review by the General Court.

Information may be requested by the Commission only where it is necessary. This criterion is fulfilled when there is a link between the information requested and the infringement being investigated. This relationship must be such that 'the Commission could reasonably suppose, at the time of the request, that the document would help it to determine whether the alleged infringement had taken place'.[246] The Commission has a wide margin of discretion when assessing this requirement.

As already mentioned, the addressee of a simple request is not obliged to provide the Commission with the information requested. Supply of incorrect or misleading information may, however, be sanctioned with a fine of up to 1% of the undertaking's total turnover in the preceding business year. Similar sanctions are applicable where incorrect or misleading information has been provided in response to a formal information request by Commission decision. Where such a decision is disobeyed a periodic penalty payment of up to 5% of the average daily turnover in the preceding business year calculated for each day of disobedience may be imposed.

---

[246] AG Jacobs, opinion of 15 December 1993 in case C-36/92 P – *SEP v Commission* [1994] ECR I-1911, para. 21.

Apart from requesting the necessary information from the concerned undertaking the Commission may also interview natural or legal persons. According to Article 19 Regulation 1/2003 the purpose of such interview must be to collect information relating to the subject-matter of an investigation. The interviews are voluntary and the interviewees may refuse to grant their consent without any legal consequences. Providing incorrect and misleading information may not be sanctioned either. Before beginning the interview the Commission must state the legal basis and purpose of the interview and inform the interviewee of its intent to record the interview.[247]

7.3.2 Powers of inspection

Article 20 Regulation 1/2003 gives the Commission the power to conduct all necessary inspections of undertakings. An inspection may be carried out under a written authorisation by Commission or pursuant to a formal decision. A prior notice to the undertaking involved is not required.[248] An inspection may take place either in the business premises or at any other premises, land and means of transport of undertakings, including the homes of directors and managers. In the latter case a reasonable suspicion must exist that books or other records related to the business are kept outside an undertaking's business premises.[249] The subject-matter of the inspection has to be determined in the authorisation or in the decision. It is up to the Commission's official to determine the documents that should be examined. During an inspection of business premises the Commission's officials and other authorised persons are empowered:

- to enter any premises, land and means of transport of undertakings;
- to examine the books and other business records related to the business irrespective of the medium on which they are stored;
- to take or obtain in any form copies of or extracts from such books or records;
- to seal any business premises and books or records for the period and extent necessary for the inspection; and
- to ask any representative or member of staff of the undertaking for explanations on facts or documents relating to the subject-matter and purpose of the inspection.

Inspections are carried out in cooperation with the national competition authority in whose territory the inspection is to be conducted. The national authorities are to be notified about the inspection and may request the Commission to admit their officials to assist actively during the inspection. Member States are required to afford the

---

[247] Commission Regulation (EC) No 773/2004 of 7 April 2004 relating to the conduct of proceedings by the Commission pursuant to Articles 81 and 82 of the EC Treaty, OJ No L 123 of 27 April 2004, Article 3.

[248] In such case the inspections are often referred to as 'dawn raids'.

[249] For a detailed analysis of the prerequisites of an inspection of business premises and the homes of directors and managers see Berghe and Dawes, '"Little Pig, Little Pig, Let Me Come In": An Evaluation of the European Commission's Powers of Inspection in Competition Cases', *European Competition Law Review*, 30 (2009), 407, 408 et seq.

Commission's officials the necessary assistance including, if necessary, the assistance of police or an equivalent enforcement authority in cases where the undertaking opposes the inspection. If required by national law an inspection at business premises must be authorised by national courts. Inspections of private premises must always be authorised by a national court. In both cases the national courts examine only whether the envisaged measures are neither arbitrary nor excessive in relationship to the subject-matter of the inspection. The national courts have no competence to declare the inspection unlawful.[250]

A fine of up to 1% of the total turnover in the preceding business year may be imposed by the Commission under Article 23(1) Regulation 1/2003 where the undertaking refuses to submit to inspections ordered by a formal decision, produces the ordered books and records in an incomplete form, gives a misleading or incorrect answer in response to a question posed by a Commission's official or breaks the seal affixed by the Commission in the course of inspection.[251] The Commission may also impose a periodic penalty payment of up to 5% of the average daily turnover in the preceding business year under Article 24(1) Regulation 1/2003 when the undertaking refuses to submit to an inspection ordered by a formal decision.

Opposing an inspection may be qualified by the Commission as an obstruction that may be sanctioned in two different ways: the Commission may either increase the fine since non-cooperation in an investigation is an aggravating circumstance under paragraph 28 of the Fining Guidelines or the Commission may commence a separate procedure and impose a fine under Article 23(1)(c) or Article 24(1)(e) Regulation 1/2003.[252]

During an investigation at the premises of E.ON the Commission's inspection team had gathered the items it intended to further review the following day in a room and sealed the doors to prevent any documents from being taken out of the room overnight. When the inspection team returned in the morning the seal showed the letters 'OPEN VOID' indicating that it had been detached. The seals used by the Commission are made of plastic film. When they are removed, they do not tear, but show irreversible 'OPEN VOID' signs on their surface. The Commission imposed a fine of EUR 38 million against E.ON under Article 23(1)(e) Regulation 1/2003 for seal breaking.[253] The decision was upheld by the General Court and was confirmed upon appeal.[254]

---

[250] Ibid., 410 et seq., for a detailed analysis of the role of national courts in the authorisation of inspections by the Commission.

[251] Council Regulation (EC) No 1/2003 of 16 December 2002 on the implementation of the rules on competition laid down in Articles 81 and 82 of the Treaty, OJ No. L 1 of 4 January 2003, p. 1, Article 20(2)(d) gives the Commission the right to 'seal any business premises and books or records for the period and the extent necessary for the inspection'.

[252] These powers of the Commission are discussed in detail in Berghe and Dawes, '"Little Pig, Little Pig, Let Me Come In"', 412 et seq.

[253] Commission decision of 30 January 2008, Case COMP/B-1/39.326 – E.ON Energie AG, OJ No. C 240 of 19 September 2008, p. 6.

[254] GC (15 December 2010), Case T-141/08 – E.ON Energie AG v Commission, nyr; ECJ (22 November 2012), Case C-89/11P, nyr.

A similar incident occurred during an inspection at the premises of water management companies in France, including Lyonnaise des Eaux. Coming back the morning of the second day, the Commission officials found that a seal had been broken. The company admitted that an employee breached the seal, arguing an unintentional act. Nonetheless, the Commission imposed a fine of EUR 8 million.[255]

7.3.3 Privilege

The Commission's power of investigation is limited by two exceptions: legal professional privilege and privilege against self-incrimination.

a) Legal professional privilege

Communications between independent lawyers and their client are protected. The scope of the exception also encompasses preparatory documents provided that it has been drafted with the sole aim of seeking legal advice from a lawyer. The privilege does not cover correspondence with in-house lawyers.

When examining business records the Commission has to observe potential legal professional privilege of the documents it intends to review. The rights of defence of any person under investigation by the Commission include the right that an undertaking may freely correspond with a lawyer to defend itself. However, under the case law of the ECJ, written communications between lawyers and their clients are protected at Union level subject to two cumulative conditions: (i) the exchange with the lawyer must be connected to the client's right of defence; and (ii) the exchange must emanate from independent lawyers who are not bound to the client by a relationship of employment.[256]

In the *Akzo* case[257] it was debated whether an in-house lawyer who is a member of the bar qualifies as an 'independent lawyer' in the sense of the ECJ's case law. During an investigation, the Commission had taken copies of two emails exchanged between a general manager and the company's coordinator for competition law, a member of the legal department enrolled in the Netherlands bar. The company claimed that those

---

[255] Commission decision of 24 May 2011, Case COMP/39.796 – *Suez Environnement*, available at http://ec.europa.eu/competition/antitrust/cases/dec_docs/39796/39796_554_6.pdf. On the practical implications of these decisions, see Riley, 'Seal Breaking: Practical Compliance Lessons from Recent Cases', *Journal of European Competition Law and Practice*, 3 (2012), 141.

[256] ECJ (18 May 1982), Case 155/79 – *AM&S Europe v Commission* [1982] ECR 1575, para. 21.

[257] ECJ (14 September 2010), Case C-550/07 P – *Akzo Nobel Chemicals and Akcros Chemicals v Commission* [2010] ECR I-8301. For a discussion of the first instance judgment as well as legal privilege in the UK and other Member States, see Murphy, 'Is it Time to Rebrand Legal Professional Privilege in EC Competition Law?', *European Competition Law Review*, 30 (2009), 125.

emails were protected by legal professional privilege and were excluded from review by the Commission. The ECJ held that the requirement of independence means the absence of any employment relationship between the lawyer and his client, so that legal professional privilege does not cover exchanges within a company or group with in-house lawyers.[258] The requirement as to the position and status as an independent lawyer is based on a conception of the lawyer's role as collaborating in the administration of justice and as being required to provide, with complete independence and having regard to the overriding interests of justice, such legal assistance as the client needs.[259] The ECJ found these criteria not to be met by an in-house lawyer:

Notwithstanding the professional regime applicable in the present case in accordance with the specific provisions of Dutch law, an in-house lawyer cannot, whatever guarantees he has in the exercise of his profession, be treated in the same way as an external lawyer, because he occupies the position of an employee which, by its very nature, does not allow him to ignore the commercial strategies pursued by his employer, and thereby affects his ability to exercise professional independence.[260]

It has to be noted that the judgment affects only legal professional privilege in relation to inspections by the Commission. Different rules on privilege may apply under national law for inspections carried out by national competition authorities.

b) Privilege against self-incrimination

The laws of the Member States in general grant the right to a natural person not to give evidence against himself/herself when charged with an offence in criminal proceedings. It is a delicate balancing act to determine to what extent this common principle applies in the type of proceedings conducted by the Commission in pursuit of competition law violations. In an effort to evade the procedural guarantees afforded to persons subject to criminal proceedings it is expressly stated in Article 23(5) Regulation 1/2003 that decisions imposing a fine for a competition law infringement 'shall not be of a criminal law nature'. Accordingly, Regulation 1/2003 does not provide for any right to remain silent in an investigation by the Commission.

Under Article 18(1) Regulation 1/2003 the Commission is entitled to request undertakings to provide 'all necessary information' to investigate an alleged infringement of the competition rules. If the Commission requests information by formal decision, such decision may be enforced through fines or periodic penalty payments under Article 23(1)(a) and Article 24(1)(d) Regulation 1/2003. However, under the case law of the ECJ, undertakings have the right to refuse to answer questions by the Commission to the extent that they 'would be compelled to provide answers which

---

[258] ECJ (14 September 2010), Case C-550/07 P – *Akzo Nobel Chemicals and Akcros Chemicals v Commission* [2010] ECR I-8301, para. 44.

[259] Ibid., para. 42.   [260] Ibid., para. 47.

might involve an admission on its part of the existence of an infringement which it is incumbent upon the Commission to prove'.[261]

In the facts underlying this judgment an alleged participant in a cartel had refused to comply with a formal information request by the Commission referring to his right not to incriminate himself. The ECJ made a distinction between two different types of question contained in the information request.

The first type of question was intended only to secure factual information on the circumstances in which cartel meetings were held and the capacity in which the participants attended them. The Commission also requested the disclosure of documents relating to those circumstances.[262]

The second type of question requested not only factual information but also statements on the purpose of the actions taken and the objective pursued by the measures under investigation. To respond to those questions, the undertaking under investigation would have had to acknowledge its participation in an agreement whose object was to fix selling prices and which was capable of preventing or restricting competition, or to state that it intended to achieve that objective.[263]

While the ECJ found the first type of question not to be open to criticism, the information request of the Commission was annulled with regard to the second type of question. The ECJ referred to the right of defence as a fundamental principle of the Union's legal order and the necessity to limit the Commission's powers of investigation to safeguard this principle.[264]

This line of jurisprudence is reflected in Recital 23 of Regulation 1/2003:

When complying with a decision of the Commission, undertakings cannot be forced to admit that they have committed an infringement, but they are in any event obliged to answer factual questions and to provide documents, even if this information may be used to establish against them or against another undertaking the existence of an infringement.

7.4 *Ne bis in idem* principle

The principle *ne bis in idem*, which is also enshrined in Article 4 of Protocol No. 7 to the ECHR, is a fundamental principle of Union law. The principle precludes a penalty being imposed on the same person more than once for the same unlawful conduct for the purpose of protecting the same legal interest. For the enforcement of the EU competition rules, this principle has relevance in particular with regard to two aspects: (i) whether fines can be imposed for participation in a worldwide cartel by several competition authorities; and (ii) whether fines increased because of a repeated infringement constitute a second fine for the first infringement and thus violate the principle.

---

[261] ECJ (18 October 1989), Case 374/87 – *Orkem v Commission* [1989] ECR 3283, para. 35.
[262] Ibid., para. 37.   [263] Ibid., para. 38.   [264] Ibid., para. 32.

The application of the principle *ne bis in idem* is subject to a threefold condition of (i) identity of the facts, (ii) unity of the offender and (iii) unity of the protected legal interest.[265] Undertakings on which fines were imposed, both by the Commission and other competition authorities in the world, for participation in a cartel involving a worldwide market have argued that those fines have to be deducted from the fine imposed by the Commission to comply with the principle. The General Court rejected this argument and held that in situations in which the legal orders and the competition authorities of non-member States intervene in the exercise of their own powers there is no unity of the protected legal interest. The legal interest protected by the EU competition rules is to safeguard free competition within the internal market while the competition laws of other jurisdictions outside the EU aim at protecting competition within that particular territory.[266] Accordingly, sanctions can be imposed for the same set of facts in several jurisdictions.

In the case of cartel recidivism it has been debated whether a fine on an undertaking involved in a cartel for the third time can be increased taking into account the two previous infringements or only the last preceding infringement. Parties have argued that under the principles of criminal law a sanction for a repeat infringement is final in the sense that it conclusively covers the first infringement and that any further infringement should be regarded as unrelated to the first infringement. This would bar the Commission from increasing a fine imposed on a repeat infringer taking into account two earlier infringements. Instead, the Commission could increase a fine only to reflect the last preceding infringement.[267]

The General Court did not follow this line of argument but held that an increase of a fine considering several previous infringements does not violate the principle of *ne bis in idem* due to a lack of identity of the facts. Each infringement is considered a separate set of facts in relation to which sanctions are imposed independently. A repeat infringement is a more serious infringement of the competition rules than a first-time infringement since it shows a tendency of the undertaking not to draw any consequences out of the previous sanctions.[268] It remains to be seen whether this reasoning will be confirmed by the ECJ since cartel recidivism indeed comprises an element of revising the sanction imposed on earlier infringements in the case of a repeat infringement.

7.5 Limitation period

Competition law infringements are subject to a limitation period of five years. The limitation period begins to run either on the day on which the infringement is

---

[265] GC (18 June 2008), Case T-410/03 – *Hoechst v Commission* [2008] ECR II-881, para. 600.
[266] Ibid., para. 602.
[267] GC (7 June 2011), Case T-217/06 – *Arkema France and Others v Commission*, nyr, para. 286.
[268] Ibid., para. 296.

committed or, in the case of continuing or repeated infringements, on the day on which the infringement ceases. Article 25(3) Regulation 1/2003 stipulates that any action taken by the Commission or a national competition authority of a Member State to investigate an infringement interrupts the limitation period. Each interruption starts time running afresh. However, Article 25(5) Regulation 1/2003 provides for an absolute limitation period: the limitation period expires at the latest on the day on which 'a period equal to twice the limitation period' has elapsed without the Commission having imposed any sanctions.

The absolute limitation period reflects the principle that a procedure must take place within reasonable time. This principle forms part of the general principles of Union law and has its origin in Article 6(1) ECHR. The General Court has held with regard to a predecessor regulation to Regulation 1/2003 that an absolute limitation period of ten years does not leave any 'room for consideration of the Commission's duty to exercise its power to impose fines within a reasonable period'.[269]

Summary of Section 7

The Commission enjoys far-reaching investigative powers to enforce the competition rules. The Commission may request information and conduct unannounced inspections of business premises and homes to search for evidence of a cartel infringement.

The scope of legal professional privilege is very limited under EU law. During an inspection, only documents created by an external lawyer escape review by Commission officials. Under the privilege against self-incrimination, parties have to provide to the Commission any factual information it has requested but are under no obligation to explain the purpose of certain acts or to otherwise qualify their behaviour. European courts hold that the *ne bis in idem* principle is not violated by the Commission's fining policy in cases of cartel recidivism. In the view of the EU courts each infringement constitutes a new set of facts even if a higher fine is imposed due to previous infringements.

The general limitation period for cartel infringements is five years. An investigation by the Commission or a national competition authority interrupts the limitation period. However, an absolute limitation period of ten years applies.

QUESTIONS ON CHAPTER 6

1. Please describe a market situation in which cartel activity is facilitated. (1.1, 1.2)
2. Why do cartels tend to be unstable? (1.3)

---

[269] GC (18 June 2008), Case T-410/03 – *Hoechst v Commission* [2008] ECR II-881, para. 224.

3. How does a triangular cartel function? (2.1.1)
4. Please describe the scenario of a purchaser's price-fixing cartel. (2.1.3)
5. What are the restrictive effects of a quota cartel? (2.3)
6. How does a collusive tendering cartel operate? (2.4.1)
7. What is the maximum fine that can be imposed under EU competition law? (3.1)
8. Are undertakings responsible for the cartel activity of their subsidiaries? (3.3)
9. What is the scope of judicial review with regard to fining decisions of the Commission? (4.3)
10. Please describe the Commission's leniency policy in general terms. (5)
11. What are the beneficial effects of a settlement in a cartel case? (5.4)
12. What are the main obstacles to private enforcement in the EU? (6.2)
13. Please describe the Commission's powers of investigation in a cartel case. (7.3)

SUGGESTED ESSAY TOPICS

1. The influence of the Charter and the ECHR on judicial review in EU cartel cases
2. The Commission's legislative initiatives in the area of private enforcement
3. The relationship between leniency policy and private enforcement

INDEX

absolute cost advantages, 201

abuse of dominant position, 188–239; assessment of dominance, 194–211; barriers to entry and expansion and, 199–204; collective dominance, 208–211, 281; countervailing buyer power, 204–205; defences, 216–221; defining abuse, 213–215; elements of violation involving, 188–190; exploitative abuses, 221–223; general economic interest, undertakings entrusted with performance of, 191; inter-state trade and, 192–193; market power, concepts of, 90, 194–195; market share thresholds and, 195, 197–199; monopolies, revenue-producing, 191; by small undertakings, 207; 'substantial part of the internal market' rule, 212–213; super-dominance, 205–207; undertaking defined for purposes of, 190-191, 207; *questions*, 241; *suggested essay topics*, 241. *See also* exclusionary abuses

active sales, 173–174, 182

Advisory Committee on Restrictive Agreements and Dominant Position, 46–47, 47n

agency agreements, 174–175

agreements, 75, 76–83; burden of proof regarding, 88–89; networks of, 99, 368; nullity of the agreement, 63, 114–117; single, overall agreement, concept of, 77–80; state measures not regarded as, 82–83; tying or bundling, 110; unilateral conduct as, 80–82; *questions*, 126. *See also* horizontal agreements; vertical agreements

agricultural products excluded from EU competition law, 37

Almunia, Joaquín, 64

ancillary restraints: commercial, 99–100; mergers, 292; regulatory, 100–102

annulment actions and merger control, 303–305

Antitrust Safety Zones, 135

appreciability, concept of, 112–113

association of undertakings, decision by, 75, 83–85

asymmetric information, 24–25

attorney–client privilege, 372–373

automatic nullity, 63, 114–117

barriers to entry and expansion, 199–204, 285, 310

Bertrand competition, 14, 17–19

bid rigging, 325

black clauses, 117

block exemptions, 31, 128; collusion, 63, 117, 120; horizontal agreements, 131; purchase agreements, 149–150; R&D agreements, 138–139, 143, 144; specialisation agreements, 146–149; technology transfer agreements, 178–184; vertical agreements, 160–176; withdrawals of, 175–176, 184

boycotts, collective, 328

bundling and tying, 110, 225–226

burden of proof: on agreements, decisions and concerted actions, 88–89; evidentiary standards, 345–348; on exemptions, 119; presumption of innocence, 348–349

buyers and sellers, 3–5

capacity constraints, 200

cartels, 309–376; collective exclusive dealing agreements, 327–328; collective sale of goods, 328–330; collusive tendering, 325; conditions encouraging, 310; EU institutions on, 311–312; fixing of prices or conditions by, 105–106; goods, restrictions on free movement of, 107–108; horizontal market sharing, 318–321; horizontal price-fixing, 312–318; information exchanges, 325–326; oligopolistic competition versus, 19–20; production quotas and restrictions, 322–324; profits from, 309–376; prohibitions under Article 101 TFEU 309, 312–330; purchasers' cartels, 317–318; recidivism by, 375; settlement procedure, 358–360; stability of, 310–311; triangular (hub-and-spoke), 314–315; *questions*, 376; *suggested essay topics*, 377. *See also* collusion, Article 101 TFEU prohibiting; enforcement; investigation of cartels; Leniency Notice; sanctions on cartels

Charter of Fundamental Rights of the European Union, as source of EU competition law, 34–36

civil actions privately brought. *See* private enforcement